Recasting German Identity

Studies in German Literature, Linguistics, and Culture

Edited by James Hardin
(*South Carolina*)

RECASTING GERMAN IDENTITY

Culture, Politics, and Literature in the Berlin Republic

Edited by
Stuart Taberner
and
Frank Finlay

CAMDEN HOUSE

First published 2002
by Camden House

Camden House is an imprint of Boydell & Brewer Inc.
PO Box 41026, Rochester, NY 14604–4126 USA
and of Boydell & Brewer Limited
PO Box 9, Woodbridge, Suffolk IP12 3DF, UK

ISBN: 1–57113–244–9

Library of Congress Cataloging-in-Publication Data

Recasting German identity: culture, politics, and literature in the Berlin Republic / edited by Stuart Taberner and Frank Finlay.
      p. cm. — (Studies in German literature, linguistics, and culture)
   Includes bibliographical references and index.
   ISBN 1–57113–244–9 (alk. paper)
      1. Germany — Intellectual life — 20th century. 2. Germany — Eth-
   nic relations. 3. National characteristics, German. 4. Holocaust, Jewish
   (1939-1945) — Psychological aspects. 5. German literature — 20th
   century — History and criticism — 20th century.   I. Taberner, Stuart.
   II. Finlay, Frank.   III. Studies in German literature, linguistics, and
   culture (Unnumbered)

DD239 .R43 2002
305.8'00943—dc21

                                                                    2002019454

A catalogue record for this title is available from the British Library.

This publication is printed on acid-free paper.
Printed in the United States of America

Contents

Difference

Acknowledgements

WE WOULD LIKE to express our gratitude to a number of institutions and individuals associated with the various stages of this project: Clare Flanagan and Mark Allinson of the University of Bristol, Department of German; the British Academy, for its financial support of the *Germany 2000* conference, which provided this volume with its point of departure; and the Research Support Fund of the German Department of the University of Leeds.

We wish to point out that the opinions expressed in the various chapters are those of their respective authors and are not necessarily shared by the editors or by the institutions that have made the completion of this volume possible.

Stuart Taberner
Frank Finlay
Leeds
June 2002

Introduction

Stuart Taberner

IN HIS CONTROVERSIAL speech on receipt of the *Friedenspreis des deutschen Buchhandels* in 1998 in the *Paulskirche* in Frankfurt, writer and intellectual Martin Walser (1927–) complained bitterly that the institutionalisation and apparent instrumentalisation, that is, the exploitation for political ends, of the Holocaust in the Federal Republic had made it impossible for Germans to see themselves, and to be seen from outside, as "ein normales Volk, eine gewöhnliche Gesellschaft."[1] Almost ten years after unification — which repaired the most tangible consequence of German enthusiasm for Nazism, that is, the division of the country — the nation still could not truly grow together, he suggested, because it lacked the adhesive of patriotic feeling.

Walser's version of normality rests upon an emotional attachment to a sense of what it means to be German that, ultimately, may have its roots in ethnicity — although, for Walser, as for many of the thinkers associated with the "New Right,"[2] the Jewish contribution to German life is accorded special respect in a display of compensatory inclusiveness and political point-scoring.[3] In fact, the author embodies the positions taken by conservatives (and large parts of the population) throughout the 1990s on immigration, naturalisation of foreigners permanently resident in Germany, and debates in the late 1990s on the existence of a "German" dominant culture, or *Leitkultur,* and on multiculturalism. A "normal" Germany, accordingly, is to look to the better parts of its past to nourish a harmonious community on the basis of cultural and ethnic homogeneity.

Since the mid-1990s, however, normalisation has no longer been exclusively associated with the more vocal conservative politicians, "New Right" intellectuals or even revisionist historians attempting to refight the so-called *Historikerstreit* of the mid-1980s.[4] In fact, normalisation has become a much less controversial term. Thus, an increasingly conventional understanding of the word has been used to secure the forty years of "successful" West German history between 1949 and 1989 as the "norm" from which a united Germany might derive its identity and socio-political stability.[5] This provokes the antipathy of some thinkers on the right who see the "old" Federal Republic as the true aberration of German history, a "deviant path," or *Sonderweg,* initiated by defeat, an overly zealous programme of "coming to terms with the past," and obsequiousness towards the USA.[6]

The more recently dominant vision of a "normal" nation to which these conservatives react with such virulence is based less in a "German" tradition and culture than in (by-now) archetypal western and liberal values. The internalisation of principles of good governance, equality before the law, human rights and multiculturalism (increasingly) are now felt to define the new Germany. With regard to the Nazi past, the Hitler period is "built into" the self-understanding of what is now known as the Berlin Republic, following the move of the capital from Bonn to that city in 1998, as the antithesis of what Germany now stands for. The incorpo- ration of this past as an almost positive foundation of state ideology and national consciousness is now enacted on the individual level. This in- volves openness about the Holocaust, contrition combined with practical steps to realise its lessons, and sorrow for the past without self- debasement. Such sentiments are "enabled" within individuals on occa- sions, or at locations, that are initiated, or at least fostered, by the state or public institutions, such as the "Crimes of the *Wehrmacht*" exhibition or the Berlin Holocaust Memorial.[7]

Following the Federal elections of late 1998 and the formation of a Social Democrat (SPD) Government in coalition with the Green Party after sixteen years of rule by the conservative CDU (in coalition with other parties), an interpretation of German normality as an adherence to western values in a continuation of the Federal Republic's painful process of overcoming Nazism became the established paradigm in domestic and foreign policy. During the Kosovo conflict of 1999, German reservations about military action against a country its *Wehrmacht* troops had occu- pied during the Second World War (Serbia), and about military action *per se*, were thus less decisive than the need to express solidarity with NATO partners in what was framed as a campaign in defence of hu- manitarian ideals fought to prevent a new Auschwitz.[8] In fact, as foreign policy analyst Hanns Maull maintains, Germany under Chancellor Gerhard Schröder and his Foreign Minister, Joschka Fischer, *is* still a *Zivilmacht,*[9] operating within a "culture of restraint," but this has not stopped it from presenting itself in a more strident fashion, as confidently multilateralist whilst simultaneously proud of its unique contribution to EU and global affairs, or, in the words used by Social Democrat politi- cian Richard Schröder as early as 1995, as "nichts Besonderes, aber etwas Bestimmtes."[10]

Testing the New "Normality"

This, at least, is the version of normalisation that appears to have achieved the status of a semi-official *Gründungsmythos* in the course of the SPD-Green coalition's stewardship of the incipient Berlin Republic. The present volume investigates the reality of this new normality. Specifically, it analyses the extent to which the current rhetoric concerning the identity of the new Germany can encompass people, political movements or regions with histories quite different from the experiences of the generation of politicians and opinion-formers now in a position to propagate their idea of the self-understanding of the Berlin Republic. This is the "generation of 1968": a product of the student movement, *Vergangenheitsbewältigung*, the state's response to terrorism, the anti-nuclear campaign, environmentalism, the years of opposition to Helmut Kohl, the love-hate relationship with the United States, and the FRG's adoption of western, liberal values. In short, it is a *West* German experience, and one that is simultaneously delimited by age, intellectual and ideological affinity, political standpoint, social and geographical mobility, ethnicity, class, and gender.

This book thus addresses a number of concrete questions: how do people who grew up in a very different political system fit into this new Germany? To what extent do people socialised in the GDR feel they have "arrived" in a Federal Republic in which normality is defined mainly by reference to the success of the old FRG and thus, by implication, the failure of the GDR? What of political parties in opposition, whether the ex-communist party, the Partei des demokratischen Sozialismus (PDS), or, on the right, the conservative CDU: how do they utilise local histories and loyalties to define counter-identities to a liberal-democratic model inherited from the old West Germany, or to set the rights of a region or a *Land* against the Federal government? To what extent does the rhetoric of a newly confident national consciousness united physically and in shared (western) values match the self-understanding of individuals attempting to combine their different ethnicity and rootedness in non-western countries with the experience of growing up and living in Germany? And how far can women expect the state's proclamation of equality of the sexes to be translated into concrete political influence commensurate with their numbers and role in society? And finally, to what degree can a nation that defines its normality in part by its successful integration into the markets and political conventions of global capitalism also integrate those who see this commitment as necessarily leading to a diminution of national identity or regional distinctiveness and powers of self-determination?

In seeking to respond to these questions, this book brings together a selection of the almost fifty papers delivered at an international conference held at the University of Bristol in the year 2000, under the banner: *Germany 2000: Taking Stock*, with a number of specially commissioned pieces. The papers have been revised and expanded specifically for this publication. The scope of the resulting collection is deliberately interdisciplinary. Historical chapters are set alongside sociological studies, or juxtaposed with contributions focusing on politics or literature; investigations into architectural debates or the semiotics of "event management" in Berlin are juxtaposed with a study in the history of ideas dealing with the controversy initiated by the Walser speech mentioned above. In organising the book in this way, the editors have been conscious that specialists might occasionally miss the detailed analysis that may be found in a more narrowly focused volume. It was our intention, however, that this would be compensated for by the cross-fertilisation of ideas produced by an interdisciplinary approach. The editors also hope that by so doing the book will appeal to a wider audience: undergraduates and postgraduates in German and European studies seeking an overview of the post-1989 period in the Federal Republic, its history, politics and literature; scholars from politics, sociology, media studies, and area studies, and, last but not least, Germanists.

The collection is divided into three separate but closely interrelated sections: "Berlin," "Political Formation" and "Difference." In what follows, we set out the rationale for these sections and attempt to highlight some of the "narrative strands" and interconnections that we felt to be particularly interesting and fruitful. We hope that readers will discover many more.

Berlin

In the chapter that opens the volume, Frank Brunssen argues that the term "self-understanding" should be used in the place of "identity." In this introduction, in fact, we have often preferred the former to the latter since it "includes the notion of construction," as Brunssen writes, in contrast to the word "identity," which tends to assume "absolute or essential sameness." This conception of identity as a narrative consciously or unconsciously constructed from the intersections between different histories — military, national, local, class, ethnic, gender, biographical, etc. — and contemporary contingencies of state-building and social integration has been advanced by theorists such as Benedict Anderson, Stuart Hall, and Michael Billig, British and American cultural studies, French postmodern thinkers, especially Michel Foucault, German *Kulturwissenschaft* (particularly Jan and Aleida Assmann), theorists of gender and sexuality, and, recently, British historian Mary Fulbrook, as well as many others. It also underlies and links the present contributions in their explorations of the manner in which different groups and regions "understand themselves" in relation to the homogenising impulses of the dominant discourses in media, politics, culture and intellectual debate.

Brunssen traces the history of German "self-understanding" from the total defeat of 1945 through to the present day, including the manner in which the two German states drew legitimacy, in different ways, from their rejection of fascism. His focus, however, is on competing interpretations of the history of the "old" Federal Republic. On the one hand, conservatives — insofar as they identify at all with a state that many of them now dismiss as an "un-German" aberration — may frame the story of West Germany as a success story, or *Erfolgsgeschichte*, in an effort to relativise the Nazi stench that preceded it, and which was not entirely absent in the 1950s and 1960s, or to damn the failed communist system of the GDR. Alternatively, on the left, the "old" FRG, by virtue of its (albeit belated) confrontation with the crimes of the past and its own democratic deficits — an achievement claimed by the generation of 1968 — and its wholehearted adoption of liberal, western values, has come to be seen as a model for the Berlin Republic. Brunssen argues forcefully in favour of this interpretation. He refers to the public debates initiated by the *Wehrmacht* exhibition in 1996–98, Daniel Jonah Goldhagen's book *Hitler's Willing Executioners* (1996–97) and official and popular support for Holocaust Memorial to be built in the middle of Berlin, at the symbolic heart of the new German state, and concludes that "the Germans' self-understanding is not marked by the formation of an uncritical normality."

A positive assessment of the Berlin Republic is also implied in Ulrike Zitzlsperger's chapter entitled "Berlin as a Public Showcase." The concentration is on a number of open "events" staged in Berlin by the civic authorities with the intention of involving the public in the city's post-Wall transformation into a unified space, commercial centre and political focal point. The *Stadtforum*, *InfoBox* and *Schaustelle Berlin* thus combined with other events to make concrete the way in which Berlin, and, by extension, the new Germany, wants to see itself, and be seen from outside: as a liberal, democratic order which encourages openness, dialogue and interaction. For Zitzlsperger, the events mostly achieve this, but she notes that the plethora of such occasions in itself reflects the present "transitory culture." True "normality," she argues, will come about only when the partly genuine, partly manufactured, euphoria generated by displays of self-confidence is replaced by a "substantial metropolitan culture, which — as in other cities — is able to make do without 'events' and constant soul-searching."

Zitzlsperger's essay perhaps also contains a note of caution in her description of the rapid emergence of concoctions such as *Infotainment* and *Architainment* and her suggestion that Berlin "became more marketable — whether for the sake of more transparency and the establishment of a new identity, or simply to commercialise new trends." The second part of this sentence introduces a degree of scepticism about the true foundations of the normality enjoyed by the Berlin Republic: its integration into global capitalism and the manner in which identity, whether national, regional or metropolitan, is marketed as a brand. Normality may thus function simply as a passport to global markets, respectability and credibility. What, then, is the fate of those who resist incorporation and homogeneity?

Janet Stewart's study of the Kunsthaus Tacheles, a Berlin landmark with a chequered past, presents an analysis of the Berlin architecture debate of the 1990s in micro-historical context that offers some answers to this question. Beginning with the bold insight that the "architecture of the new capital has come to provide reassurance of Germany's national identity and its orientation to the West," Stewart examines the negative implications of Berlin's efforts to reshape itself aesthetically, spatially and architecturally to promote the normality of the new Federal Republic.[11] Two trends dominate the redesign of the capital: "the space of global capitalism seen in the steel and glass skyscrapers" and so-called "critical reconstruction." The first results in an "*Ent-ortung* of space" lacking cultural memory, Stewart claims, citing Italian philosopher Massimo Cacciari; the second all too easily spawns "restorative nostalgia" for styles which elide the city's — and the country's — difficult past.

The controversies surrounding the partial demolition, preservation, redesign and present use of the Kunsthaus Tacheles are examined in detail in a case study of the fate of so-called *off-Kultur*, that is, non-incorporated art and politics that aims to sustain "difference" and exploit the "continuing tension between construction and reconstruction, art and global capitalism, public and private space, intimacy and anonymity, which characterises the contemporary urban environment." Subculture thus undermines, as it surely always has done, "normality" in its efforts to impose homogeneity.

A challenge to the "normality" of the Berlin Republic is also the theme of the final chapter in this section, Kathrin Schödel's piece on "normalising cultural memory" and the controversies surrounding Walser's *Friedenspreisrede* and his novel *Ein springender Brunnen*. Walser too has difficulties with a Berlin Republic that he sees as denying cultural memory in the name of incorporation into global capitalism and the West. If the defenders of the Kunsthaus Tacheles are what we would now — following protests in recent years against the G8 meetings of the most industrialised nations and the drive towards globalising trade under the rubric of the WTO — call left-wing anti-globalisers, then Walser belongs to a tradition of *conservative* anti-capitalism that has deep roots in the German intellectual tradition.[12]

Schödel analyses different public responses to Walser's contention that the institutionalisation of Holocaust remembrance as part of the "normality" of post-*Wende* Germany is harmful to national identity. Walser's speech in fact, hints at the tension between Germany's desire to be part of the western community — achieved, in part, by the incorporation of contrition into the "normality" of the Berlin Republic — and the price that it may have to pay for this. He berates a focus on the Nazi past that crowds out other aspects of the country's history and inhibits any sense of national belonging or notion of an organic community.

Many of Walser's arguments, however, are dismissed by Schödel as reruns of pleas for the relativisation of National Socialism. Walser's vision of "normalisation" challenges the current rhetoric, yet he offers in its place nothing more than "a concept of German identity" that is "based in a one-sided, falsified version of history." Schödel concludes: "It is to be hoped that a 'normal' democratic society can exist without a national identity of this kind." The next section examines other attempts to construct identity within, or against, the now dominant discourse of "a 'normal' democratic society" with reference to political histories peculiar to particular groups, generations or regions. In each case, it is open to debate whether the form of identity-construction under investigation is viable or even desirable.

Political Formation

Karen Leeder's essay on "glücklose Engel: fictions of history and the end of the GDR" introduces a section on the centrality of political formations — whether those into which people are socialised or those they consciously construct — to the self-understanding of groups or individuals. Her sources are literary: she thus explores the metaphor of the angel, briefly outlining the history of the angels that have populated German writing to show that the process of their "secularisation" has continued, "with every age more or less producing the angels it needs." Her primary interest lies in the "Modernist angel: the only true new angel, a very

German angel, the angel of history." Accordingly she looks at Paul Klee's *Angelus Novus* and the ninth thesis of Walter Benjamin's famous "Theses on the Philosophy of History," inspired by Klee's painting. She then examines the reception of both in the GDR, firstly by Heiner Müller in 1958 and in 1991, and then by two younger writers, Andreas Koziol (born 1957) and Thomas Martin (born 1963).

In a series of detailed close readings of a number of poems, Leeder explores the impact of GDR history, its utopian promise and totalitarian reality, on different generations of artists socialised in that state and then confronted with incorporation into the Federal Republic in 1990 and post-unification marginalisation. Her argument draws parallels between intellectual and literary developments to reveal the manner in which the political disillusionment of Müller's generation, metaphorically rendered as disappointment with "the angel of history" for the non-realisation of the utopian aspirations of the GDR, is followed by a withdrawal from politics by the younger generation in the new Germany. This corresponds to a re-aestheticisation of the motif of the angel, itself reflecting a shift "from a concern with history to one with aesthetics in some modern literature" (Stuart Parkes makes a similar point in the final chapter of the book).

Critical intellectuals of Heiner Müller's generation in the GDR did not have a "1968": their focus was Prague not Paris, that is, despair at the Soviet suppression of "socialism with a human face" rather than the heady anarchy of "demos," "happenings," street theatre, communes and free love, anti-authoritarianism and protests against the Vietnam War. Yet the fact of different experiences of 1968 not only divides east Germans from west Germans. As our next two chapters show, west German conservatives unhappy with the claim to *kultureller Hegemonie* implicitly made by the former student rebels who have graduated from street protests to running the country find some common ground with the PDS, a party rooted in the GDR experience of socialism. For the PDS, the "western individualism" of 1968 has hence all too swiftly "matured" into a facile acceptance of the blinkered consumerism associated with globalisation. For west German conservatives resentful of the FRG's ever more passionate embrace of "western" (read: "American") culture, as for leftist east Germans socialised into the collective values of the former GDR, therefore, the "normality" of the Berlin Republic may well mean nothing more than the freedom to pursue selfish interests without regard to the good of the community.

Ingo Cornils examines the disintegration after 1998 of the uneasy consensus achieved between left and right on the student movement as a "successful failure." The coming-to-power of the generation of 1968 in the form of the SPD-Green coalition provoked a re-examination of its claim to have democratised the "old FRG," and, by implication, its belief that it best embodies the normality of the new Germany: liberal, tolerant, open, pluralist, and cosmopolitan. Many of the attacks came from conservatives, who, in echoes of Martin Walser, saw the "68ers" as "responsible for the loss of 'German virtues' such as diligence, order, honesty and punctuality, thus contributing to a general weakening of the national fibre." Other criticisms came from the younger generation, on left *and* right, no longer swayed by the myth of 1968 or impressed by the "staatstragenden Yesterday Heroes der 68er," to cite one of the new parliamentarians referred to by Cornils.

Cornils asks for a "historicisation" of 1968, that is, a less politicised assessment of its impact. His suggestion that 1968 has in fact become less controversial, its positive influence on the democratisation of the FRG now willingly acknowledged by the public, is supported by his postscript on the "Joschka Fischer affair" of Spring 2000 when right-wing efforts to turn the voters against the Foreign Minister for his involvement in political extremism in the 1960s faltered. The student movement is now a firm part of West German history, and by virtue of the fact that the new Republic's political leaders were formed by it — either in support or in opposition — a part of the normal sense of identity impressed upon the nation.

Where the students were unsuccessful in realising their ambitions, Cornils maintains, is in the disjuncture between their rhetoric and their recognition of the need for compromise with a capitalist "economic system they despised" for the sake of political influence. In our next essay, on "*Heimat* and the left," Peter Thompson in fact looks at the PDS's challenge to the way in which the Berlin Republic, now governed by former student radicals, seems to have traded opposition to capitalism for normality. Political formation once again plays a key role — Thompson explains why it is that generations raised in East Germany, or even post-1990 in the space of the former GDR, have fewer difficulties with the notion of *Heimat* than their western counterparts, especially those on the left for whom it smacks of *Blut und Boden* propaganda. Ideas of collectivism inherited from the GDR thus form the basis for the PDS's programme of "regional identity" as a form of resistance to the enforced homogeneity of the Berlin Republic and to the rampant individualism that many people see as part of globalisation.

The title of Thompson's article contains a quotation and a question mark: "The PDS: 'CSU des Ostens'?" This paralleling of the leftist PDS with the ultra-conservative CSU in Bavaria insinuates the manner in which local identities can be moulded by regionally based political parties as a means of advancing political interests within the Federal system. Chris Szejnmann explores a similar process at work in the eastern state of Saxony (like Bavaria, a *Freistaat*) — this time, however, notions of *Heimat* are employed by the conservative CDU (the sister party of the CSU), with Premier Kurt Biedenkopf at its head, in order to secure a political power base and assert a regional identity at odds with efforts at the centre to "harmonise" German identity. Biedenkopf's strategy, Szejnmann argues, is to invent a history of Saxon "peculiarism." This creates political capital and enables the CDU to profit from dissatisfaction with the policies of the Federal Government (its willingness to "sacrifice" German interests for the sake of European integration, for example) and the political embarrassment of parties associated with the GDR dictatorship — primarily the PDS.

If Kurt Biedenkopf looks to regional identity to counter the Federal Government's promotion of a "progressive" German normality within the European Union, then the groups discussed by Sabine Lang in her piece on "Women in Post-1989 Germany" see further Europeanisation as the only way of compelling the government to realise its commitment to equality of influence and status for women. Lang's chapter begins with an analysis of the prominent role played by women's groups during the transformation of the GDR in 1989 and 1990 and asks why this influence has not been translated into real political influence in subsequent years. A speech by Biedenkopf himself is cited as an example of the manner in which "male hegemonic discourses and androcentric practices" associated with the "old" FRG were consolidated in the new Germany in order to inhibit any transference of the more progressive situation for women in the former GDR. Yet what Lang describes as the "sedimentation and rationalisation of male power within political organisations," as well as in the media and other influential institutions, permeates the entire Berlin Republic, not just regional bastions of conservatism. The new Germany's striking indifference to one of the few areas in which the former GDR made substantial political gains — equality for women, albeit in a form that was by no means unproblematic — must surely cast a shadow over its proud claims to openness, transparency and equality.

Difference

The third and final section of the volume focuses on the various ways in which "difference" — including biographical, regional, ethnic and cultural diversity — may feed into various forms of self-understanding. "Difference" can thus be accented and exploited to shape an alternative power base, as Chris Szejnmann demonstrated in the previous section. Or, it may disqualify particular people and groups from "feeling at home" in the new Germany. Alternatively, "difference" can be styled as a kind of distinctiveness that enables a new perspective on the "norm." Finally, "difference" may be played off against, or combined with, "German" identities to create hybrid forms.

Simon Ward introduces a section that is almost entirely literary. He examines the metaphor of the train in writing by three established authors from the former GDR, Wolfgang Hilbig, Brigitte Struyzk, and Reinhard Jirgl, and describes how this common motif is exploited to indicate a feeling of "not having arrived" in the new Germany. At the same time, Ward argues, the conventional association of the railways with technology and progress engenders ironic or melancholic commentary on the failed utopia of the GDR as well as bitter reflection on the rail network in post-1990 Germany. Instead of reuniting the country physically and symbolically, therefore, railways simply spread globalised capitalism to all corners of the nation as trains carry "the traffic of commerce" via a chain of rail stations decked out with the homogenising slogans of advertising and exuding the anonymity of "a service industry whose economic structure is largely invisible."

In her chapter on "the function of the foreign" in novels by Grit Poppe and Kerstin Jentzsch, Roswitha Skare cites a comment by one of Jentzsch's characters on the pace of change in the ex-GDR: "Die Zeit rast dahin wie ein D-Zug." A train metaphor once more indicates alienation and disorientation, this time in the work of a younger ex-GDR writer (born 1964). In the place of despair at the dissolution of biographical experience and local identity within the "normality" of united Germany's embrace of globalisation, however, characters in Poppe and Jentzsch travel abroad — as they now can after the fall of the Wall — in order to achieve some measure of *Reflexion über Heimat*. The result in each case is a meditation, within the conventionally "popular" genre of *Unterhaltungsliteratur*, on heritage and identity and the advantages of hybridity as a means of incorporating the foreign into the individual's self-understanding, and, by extension, into German identity and culture in the postmodern age. These novels, examples of a new "Lust am Erzählen" and "Unbefangenheit"[13] (terms that resurface in Stuart Parkes's chapter), thus attempt to mediate experiences of difference, exclusion and alienation in a period of huge social and political change.

Hybrid identities are central to Eva Kolinsky's chapter on identity among Turks living in Germany. Kolinsky's findings, based on interviews with several generations of Turks, have special resonance in the wake of the conservative backlash, framed as a defence of a German *Leitkultur*, against the efforts of the SPD-Green coalition to make outdated naturalisation laws more favourable to foreign residents. Her specific focus is on younger Turks and the manner in which they "insist upon visibility and upon an acceptance of their Turkish identity" whilst picking from each culture which experiences and customs they wish to incorporate into their own self-understanding. The key factor in each case is personal biography: individuals construct identity in accordance with variables such as region, customs, class, family, and social status as well as from key events such as parental migration or encounters with racism. The diversity and tendency to "perform" identity noted by Kolinsky, may well, in fact, come to present the most significant test of the normality of the Berlin Republic: will the state be able to integrate people with different ethnic, social, cultural and biographical experiences whilst respecting their right to be "different"?

Margaret Littler is also interested in the performance of identity in her piece on Emine Sevgi Özdamar, a Turkish author who has lived in Germany since 1965 and who writes in German. Littler's analysis adapts postcolonial theory to explore the complex relationship of the literary text *Mutterzunge* not only to Özdamar's adopted homeland, Germany, but also to her Turkish heritage and its complex interactions with Arabic Islamic culture, its Ottoman past, Kemalism and westernisation. Littler shows how Özdamar's suggestion that the "authentic" identity adopted by Turks is simply an acting-out of levels of identification, or over-identification, with parts of the overdetermined narrative of national history, is deployed within the work's presentation of Turks living in the FRG and their construction of their self-understanding. In her final remarks, Littler hints at the manner in which German-Turkish hybridity, confounding "attempts to fix [Turkish identity] in a simple dichotomous relationship *either* to the West *or* the Ottoman imperial past," might generate insights into "contemporary *German* identity." The "simple" dichotomy between a "German tradition" and the nation's own contested westernisation, most recently under the banner of "normality," may thus be more apparent than real.

Generation, gender and ethnicity are the central themes of Katharina Gerstenberger's chapter on the German-Turkish writer Zafer Şenocak and the novel *Gefährliche Verwandtschaft* and Monika Maron's *Pawels Briefe*, an autobiographically-inspired account of a family history which includes a Jewish grandfather murdered in the Holocaust and a mother married to the former Interior Minister of the former GDR, Karl Maron. Both texts, Gerstenberger argues, contribute to what academic Gerd Gemünden has called the "heterogeneity that *already* exists in Germany."[14] Equally, both reflect new ways of confronting German history that seek to incorporate ethnic, cultural and biographical diversity into a version of *Vergangenheitsbewältigung* now rooted in "cultural memory and trauma, memory and narrative [and] memory and mourning" in the place of the previous "politically oriented project of coming to terms with the past." Şenocak's "postmodern and post-national narrator" as much as Maron's less fanciful literary alter ego thus return to the theme of the Nazi past in a manner that reflects the new Germany's focus on individual conscience, genealogical complexity, the heterogeneity of biography and the meshing of complicity and innocence.

The "heterogeneity that *already* exists in Germany" is reflected in the debates regarding "German Literature Today" reviewed by Stuart Parkes in the final contribution to the volume. Parkes begins from the premise that "in comparison with Britain and the USA, the literature and literary life in Germany have been far more frequently linked with questions of national status and prestige" and examines the impact of globalisation, consequent transformations in the publishing market and the conglomeration of media concerns, on national culture and the identity of the new Germany. Despite widespread concerns about the "viability" of German writing in the age of globalisation, Parkes concludes that "German literature has come out of the national ghetto and moved much closer to other literatures": it has become less ideological, more interested in aesthetics than political critique, as the "Federal Republic increasingly becomes a democratic state like any other."

Concluding Remarks

Parkes's assessment of the state of literature in the new Germany coincides with the emphasis on diversity, hybridity, and multiculturalism as a response to the potentially homogenising consequences of globalisation for national cultures that is central to a good number of the other chapters in the volume. German literature, he argues, now embodies a previously absent regional, ethnic, gender, and cultural variety, including an openness to western, oriental and global influences. Where our authors differ, however, is in their judgments as to whether the new normality claimed for the Berlin Republic, in particular by the SPD-Green coalition, is capable of embracing this heterogeneity or attempts to subsume it within a version of German identity that is primarily shaped by the experiences of a generation of political leaders in possession of a particular vision of a *west* German history and *west* German values. Thus, the main challenge for the new Germany, as it faces elections in late 2002 (as this book goes to print) which might well see the return to power of more conservative forces, is to live up to its own rhetoric of inclusiveness, diversity, and transparency. In this way it may be able to shape a form of German identity that moves away from a narrow focus on ethnic homogeneity towards a new pluralism that can both profit from the country's openness to the outside world and resist the cultural one-dimensionality associated by many with global capitalism.

Notes

[1] Martin Walser, "Die Banalität des Guten. Erfahrungen beim Verfassen einer Sonntagsrede aus Anlaß der Verleihung des Friedenspreises des deutschen Buchhandels," *Frankfurter Allgemeine Zeitung* (12 October 1998): 15. See the chapter by Kathrin Schödel in this volume.

[2] See Stefan Berger's *The Search for Normality: National Identity and Historical Consciousness in Germany since 1800* for a discussion of the link between the New Right and "normalisation" (Providence: Berghahn Books, 1997).

[3] In his *Friedenspreisrede*, Walser cites his own eulogy for the Jewish-German patriot Victor Klemperer: "Ich habe gesagt: wer alles als einen Weg sieht, der nur in Auschwitz enden konnte, der macht aus dem deutsch-jüdischen Verhältnis eine Schicksalskatastrophe unter gar allen Umständen." ("Die Banalität des Guten," 15. The self-quotation is from *Das Prinzip Genauigkeit* [Frankfurt am Main: Suhrkamp, 1995], 34–35).

[4] Revisionist historians such as Ernst Nolte sought to historicise (or, in the eyes of his critics, relativise) National Socialism within a long German past stretching from the *Völkerwanderungen* and encompassing the Reformation and the Enlightenment as much as Auschwitz. For the documentation of this debate see Rudolph Augstein et al., *Historikerstreit: Die Dokumentation der Kontroverse um die Einzigartigkeit der nationalsozialistischen Judenvernichtung* (Munich: Piper, 1987).

[5] See Frank Brunssen's article in this volume.

[6] See Stephen Brockmann, *Literature and German Unification* (Cambridge: Cambridge UP, 1999), 115.

[7] See Bill Niven, *Facing the Nazi Past* (London: Routledge, 2001) for an excellent discussion of coming-to-terms with the past in unified Germany. See also the chapters in this volume by Frank Brunssen, Kathrin Schödel, and Ingo Cornils.

[8] See Nina Philippi, "Civilian Power and War: The German Debate about Out-of-Area Operations 1990–99," in Sebastian Harnisch and Hanns Maull, eds., *Germany*

as a Civilian Power? The Foreign Policy of the Berlin Republic (Manchester: Manchester UP, 2001), 49–67.

[9] See Hanns Maull, "Germany's Foreign Policy, Post-Kosovo: Still a 'Civilian Power?" in *Germany as a Civilian Power?* 106–27.

[10] Richard Schröder, "Was heißt: 'Ich bin Deutscher?'" *Zeitpunkte*, "Vereint, doch nicht eins. Deutschland fünf Jahre nach der Wiedervereinigung" 5 (1995), 14.

[11] See also the review article by Martin Filler, "Berlin: The Lost Opportunity," in *The New York Review of Books* (1 November 2000).

[12] See Stephen Brockmann's *Literature and German Unification* for an examination of the roots of conservative anti-capitalism in German Romanticism (109–36).

[13] Volker Hage, "Die Enkel kommen," *Der Spiegel* (11 October 1999): 244–54, 245 and 252. The second term derives from Botho Strauss.

[14] Gerd Gemünden, "Nostalgie for the Nation," in Mieke Bal, ed., *Acts of Memory* (Hanover, NH and London: U of New England P, 1999), 131.

Berlin

The New Self-Understanding of the Berlin Republic: Readings of Contemporary German History

Frank Brunssen

THE EAST GERMAN revolution of 1989 and the ensuing unification of the two Germanys in 1990 was the most significant caesura in recent German history. Since 1990 all those images and perceptions of Germany that had been established during the decades of the Cold War have had to be revised.[1] One of the most important changes that took place in the course of the transition from a divided Germany to the Berlin Republic concerned the way in which Germans see themselves and would want to be seen from outside. Since the *Wende* or turning-point of 1989/90, this changed perception has manifested itself in new readings of contemporary history and in new interpretations and public representations of the past.

In the immediate postwar years and the following decades of division, the caesura of 1945 dominated perceptions of German history and became the crucial reference point for historiographical examination. Initially, many Germans experienced 1945 as the collapse of the nation; intellectuals later conceived of the year as constituting a breach of civilisation; since the mid-1980s it has been widely perceived by postwar Germans as a liberation from National Socialism. Given the singularity of its crimes, the Nazi dictatorship was often read as the catastrophic climax of, or even as the synonym for, German history as a whole. From the beginning of their existence, the Federal Republic and the Democratic Republic were therefore eager to justify their democratic self-understanding and their historical legitimacy through the negation of their predecessor, the Third Reich.

This view of German history was subjected to substantial revaluation after the watershed of 1989/90, leading to a significant shift: the historiographical fixation on 1945 has been relaxed in favour of an ever-increasing affirmation of the Federal Republic. Its fifty-year history is now understood by many to be an "Erfolgsgeschichte"[2] — a word that can mean both success story and successful history. However, prominent critics, such as the philosopher Jürgen Habermas, have dismissed this revaluation as a new "historische Interpunktion,"[3] devised by conservative revisionists who seek to relativise the breach of 1945 for the sake of an uncritical normalisation of German identity, nationhood and history. The following discussion will, therefore, focus on the question as to what significance the two historical turning points of 1945 and 1989/90 might have for the new self-understanding of the Berlin Republic.

The Negation of History

Between 1945 and 1989/90, the rejection of Germany's National Socialist past constituted a key feature of the self-understanding of both parts of the divided nation. In the case of the Federal Republic, the negation of what Germany represented between 1933 and 1945 played a vital role in the newly emerging democracy.[4] In the early years of the new state the dismissal of the Third Reich manifested itself in the policies toward the past adopted by the Adenauer administration.[5] On the one hand, Adenauer's Government attempted a symbolic separation from National Socialism, through acknowledgements of responsibility or measures such as the Agreement on Compensation with Israel. On the other hand, it also aimed at drawing a final line under the past: the implementation of the Reinstatement Act of 1951, for example, returned over 55,000 former NSDAP members to the civil service. At the time, the ambivalent nature of this policy in many ways reflected the state of mind of those numerous Germans who had previously supported the Nazi state in one way or another. After the experience of defeat in 1945 many people distanced themselves from the Third Reich. Their rejection of National Socialism, however, was often not the result of self-critical reflection but rather an expression of the utter disillusionment they had felt after the collapse of the regime.

Yet numerous young Germans did respond after 1945 in a different way to the recent past. Those who had been indoctrinated under Hitler and had just reached maturity at the end of the war experienced the collapse of their National Socialist world-view. In due course, disillusionment with Nazi socialisation transmuted into a deeply sceptical and anti-ideological outlook.[6] The writer Günter Grass, for example, who initially had been driven by the "Unbeirrbarkeit des Hitlerjungen,"[7] adopted a "prinzipielle Antihaltung" after 1949 towards the new Conservative government, rearmament and the evident materialism of the Federal Republic on the one hand, and, on the other, towards the past, defining himself "selbstredend und ohne Risiko als Antifaschist" (13).

For those of Grass's generation who shared this gesture of negation, the disassociation from the immediate German present and the past did, however, create a serious problem, as their attitude fundamentally called into question their national identity as Germans. The historian Ernest Renan had already stressed in the late nineteenth century that history plays a crucial role in determining the features of a nation. Apart from a shared geographical terrain, a shared language, religion, and the commitment to living together, it is "la possession en commun d'un riche legs de souvenirs" of a "long passé d'efforts, de sacrifices et de dévouements"[8] that constitutes a nation's identity. Interestingly, Jürgen Habermas has expressed a similar view, describing "ein schwer entwirrbares Geflecht von familialen, örtlichen, politischen, auch intellektuellen Überlieferungen."[9] Hence, for Habermas, as for Renan, the identity of a person or a nation is constituted by a specific history that has given this person or nation its distinct profile. Yet the past only functions positively as the source of an individual's or a collective's identity for as long as a person or nation considers the traditions provided by history as commendable and as valuable for shaping the present. This means, as the writer Hans Magnus Enzensberger has put it: "Wer sich selbst verstehen und sich seiner Identität sicher sein will, der muß sich identifizieren."[10]

After 1945 this kind of positive identification with German history had become impossible for Grass's generation. Having been socialised under a dictatorship, the experience of his age cohort after the war served only to highlight the problem. The East German writer Christa Wolf, for example, noted how difficult it is to dissolve the ties of such a negative form of identification.[11] Moreover, she has pointed out how in those postwar years she had hoped fervently, like many of her generation, "keine Deutsche sein zu müssen."[12] When the monstrous extent of the crimes came to light, Germany appeared to offer its citizens only discredited historical traditions. In 1945, the generation of Wolf and Grass was thus confronted with nothing less than the disintegration of German national identity.

To the protest generation of the 1960s the critical negation of the National Socialist past and of its highly problematical repercussions for the present-day Federal Republic was of crucial significance. One of the major reasons for the generational conflict of that time was the widespread unwillingness of the older generation to reflect self-critically upon the Nazi legacy. This phenomenon was characterised by Margarete and Alexander Mitscherlich as an "Unfähigkeit zu trauern," to quote the title of their famous 1967 psycho-sociological study of the Germans. Hans Magnus Enzensberger similarly described the Federal Republic of the 1950s and 1960s as a "mördergrube" where "die vergangenheit in den müllschlukkern schwelt," where people put "fleckenwasser" on the past in order to live in an "ewigen frühling der amnesie."[13] It was the postwar generation, however, which then discovered the rhetorical means in the Critical Theory of the late Frankfurt School that enabled them to engage in the necessary "Kritik des Negativen."[14] To the members of this cohort neither their parents' and grandparents' past nor the present of the Federal Republic offered any major incentive to identify with the new German state; instead they attempted to establish some kind of "geschichtslosen Neuanfang"[15] outside of the German tradition. The journalist Thomas Schmid has thus pointed out that they regarded the "Existenz im toten Winkel der Geschichte" as the "Normalfall,"[16] a statement which explains why contemporary historians have detected a "eigentümliche Geschichtslosigkeit"[17] in the Germany of the 1960s. It was not German history but the opposition towards anything German that defined this generation. Many younger Germans sought identification elsewhere and turned towards a politically motivated internationalism or saw themselves primarily as cosmopolitan and European. In describing the self-understanding of his generation, Enzensberger hence stated at the time that the Germans were divested of their identity so thoroughly after the war, "daß man sich fragen muß, ob von einer deutschen Nation überhaupt noch die Rede sein kann."[18]

Yet the nation refused to disappear from people's minds. Just after the building of the Berlin Wall in August 1961, Enzensberger claimed that the only thing the two Germanys agreed on was the need to disagree.[19] This reciprocal negation, which had become programmatic in both states, made it impossible for East and West Germans alike to define themselves as Germans in the way that citizens of other states might define themselves as French or Polish, for example. Years after his forced expatriation from East Germany in 1976, the poet Wolf Biermann described the impossibility of a non-fragmented identity as a visceral experience:

> Noch bin ich wie drüben: bin ganz. und ganz
> zerrissen, ein rührend deutscher Deutscher
> verharre am rand, wo der große riss
> in Ost und West die reiche welt
> zerstückelt, so wie mein bleiches land
> zerstückelt die stadt. und das geht bis
> quer durch mein fröhliches gramgesicht.[20]

In comparison with neighbouring states, no normal standards could be applied to the divided Germany; it represented a "Grenz- und Sonderfall." The Wall, Enzensberger argued, not only divided Germans from Germans but also Germans from the rest of the world. The only thing that Germans shared, he claimed, was division: "Die Zerrissenheit ist unsere Identität."[21]

In the German Democratic Republic, the negation of National Socialism represented one of the foundations of the official self-understanding propagated by the SED. The notion of the anti-fascist tradition became a historiographical doctrine which was designed to detach the GDR from the phase of fascist dictatorship in German history. The writer Jurek Becker, who grew up in the GDR, has described the lie that was inherent in this self-understanding. The GDR, Becker claimed in the 1990s, invented a history of anti-fascism, proclaimed that fascism had had nothing to do with its citizens, who had, in fact, liberated themselves from Hitler with the help of the red army. Rather caustically he speculated that of the ten thousand anti-fascists that might have been active in the whole of Nazi Germany it seemed that at least eight million were now living in the GDR![22]

The anti-fascist imperative was also intended to raise the international profile of the GDR by means of the permanent ideological negation of the Federal Republic. GDR officials never tired of stressing that those ideological evils which had supposedly been eradicated in the GDR still prevailed in the FRG. Conformist intellectuals such as Stephan Hermlin, therefore, termed the GDR the "Antiglobkestaat,"[23] in which former Nazis such as Hans Globke, who had been a leading civil servant in the Ministry of the Interior under Goebbels, had written a commentary to Hitler's anti-Semitic laws in 1936, and then served as a senior advisor in Adenauer's Chancellery, were barred from public life. The GDR was indeed a "Gegenstaat"[24] because it needed the FRG as a "negative" counterpart in order to define its "positive" features. In this way the anti-fascist imperative was also intended to compensate for the GDR's inferiority complex, which originated from the territorial and economic asymmetry between the two states. In order to eliminate this unevenness and further ingrain the belief in the historical legitimacy of the GDR, the government began, in the 1960s, to eradicate the word "German" from public discourse and replace it with "GDR."[25] However, measures of this kind did not reflect the opinions or wishes of average citizens. In reality, GDR officials did not manage to remould the East Germans into a socialist, one-class nation because national identities are not simply created or changed overnight through political manipulation.[26]

There were arguably only two phases in the history of the GDR during which the possibility of an independent identity became feasible.

Firstly, the postwar years, when, as Christa Wolf has explained, the gradual identification of young people with what would later become the GDR[27] manifested itself; a development which was soon suffocated by the interventions of an increasingly repressive state. Secondly, the *Wende* years of 1989/90, when radical public criticism of "real existing Socialism" suggested the possibility of a self-determined GDR. According to the civil rights activist Friedrich Schorlemmer, for example, there existed a brief but successful GDR identity which emerged after Erich Honecker's resignation in October 1989.[28] The former activist Jens Reich similarly observed that it was only in the last year of the GDR's existence that he was able to identify with it.[29] Apart from these two phases, however, there was no identity specific to the citizens of the GDR; on the contrary, the number of people who left East Germany or applied for exit visas indicates that a great number of citizens could not identify with the state.

The division of the nation thus never permitted the formation of an identity that could be shared by all Germans. In the late 1970s the West German political scientist Dolf Sternberger began to promote a concept that accepted this division as a fact. In his reflections on "Verfassungspatriotismus" Sternberger did not hesitate to concede that the German nation was indeed a difficult concept.[30] Nevertheless, he argued, Germans lived in a "ganzen Verfassung," a kind of second fatherland in the shape of the Basic Law of 1949. Since this time there had developed imperceptibly "ein neuer, ein zweiter Patriotismus . . . der eben auf die Verfassung sich gründet."[31] Sternberger's model was welcomed by many West Germans, especially by left-liberal intellectuals, because it allowed for pragmatic accommodation with the identity problem. However, it also contained two substantial drawbacks: it obviously could not include the East Germans and, paradoxically, it might appear to be somewhat unhistorical, as German history prior to the implementation of the Constitution was not considered to be of major significance to the self-understanding of the West Germans.

In the mid-1980s, the critical negation of the past became the bone of contention in the so-called Historians' Controversy ("Historikerstreit"). This debate started when the historian Ernst Nolte questioned the singularity of the Holocaust by claiming a causal nexus[32] between Auschwitz and the *Gulag* network of Soviet labour camps, and by viewing Soviet crimes as the model for those of the Germans (45). Nolte's chief opponent, Jürgen Habermas, was determined to fight this apparent relativisation of the Holocaust. He was, however, no less committed to revealing and condemning the political intention behind Nolte's argument: "eine revisionistische Historie in Dienst [zu] nehmen für die nationalgeschichtliche Aufmöbelung einer konventionellen Identität."[33] Habermas feared that the German past would no longer be subjected to critical scrutiny but would instead permit a positive identification that could revive a conventional German national identity. Although in the end Habermas gained the upper hand and expressed support for Sternberger's constitutional patriotism, the Historians' Controversy did not lead to any resolution of the identity problem.

The Revaluation of the Federal Republic

The political eruptions at the end of the 1980s caused a fundamental shift in the historiographical perspective on Germany: increasingly affirmative perceptions of contemporary German history emerged. The titles of some recent international publications are instructive in this regard; they indicate, for example, an *Annäherung an Deutschland*[34] (David Schoenbaum/Elizabeth Pond), they give Germany a "zweite Chance"[35] (Fritz Stern), or betoken a "Liebeserklärung" to the "schrecklichen Deutschen"[36] (Angelo Bolaffi). Numerous domestic publications strike a similar tone. The political scientist Kurt Sontheimer states that the Federal Republic has earned a degree of careful praise[37] and the historian Arnulf Baring even feels free to proclaim: "Es lebe die Republik, es lebe Deutschland!"[38] In the more recent writings of many experts on Germany, therefore it is not so much the year 1945 as 1989/90 that has become the reference point for assessing contemporary German history.

There are several reasons for this new, more affirmative approach. The first is the "return of history" in 1989/90, when — for the first time since the uprising of June 1953 — the citizens of East Germany appeared to take their destiny into their own hands and subsequently liberated themselves in a peaceful revolution from a dictatorial regime. The ensuing unification process also seemed to demonstrate that the Germans were at last leaving the "waiting room of history": Chancellor Kohl's Ten Point Programme; the general elections of March 1990 in East Germany; the introduction of the Deutschmark in the GDR in the summer, and formal unification on 3 October of that year were acts of self-determination. Together, these events showed that Germans from East and West were starting to write the same history again for the first time since 1945.

The second reason was the belief that the end of political division would bring about the abolition of German dividedness, precisely that ideological, social, and cultural fragmentation which had haunted the country for centuries. In an impressive study the historian Fritz Stern has shown that it was the drama of German disunity[39] that had led Germany to play such a destructive role in the twentieth century, indeed which had allowed Hitler to gain power. In the light of 1989/ 90, however, Stern expressed the belief that the "old" Federal Republic had achieved something never previously accomplished, that is, the overcoming of disunity (23). The same conviction, shared by many Germans at the time, was voiced in Berlin by Willy Brandt after the opening of the Wall when he claimed outside the Schöneberg Town Hall that the two halves of Germany would now grow together.[40]

The third reason was the fact that unification appeared to transform Germany into a more normal state, that is, a state more similar to her European neighbours, a view expressed, for example, by the British historian Timothy Garton Ash.[41] There is no doubt, the political scientists Andrei S. Markovits and Simon Reich argue, that Germany had been "in no way normal"[42] before 1989. Yet since the Wende "the Berlin Republic has provided evidence that Germany has started on the road toward normalcy, at least in terms of growing sovereignty and autonomy" (10). Moreover, ordinary Germans regarded the amalgamation of the two states as a psychological normalisation, since the division had often been understood as a kind of sentence or punishment for the War and the Holocaust.[43] With the accession of the GDR to the Federal Republic's political system and the final definition of the nation's territorial limits, the German Question can indeed be regarded as having been resolved. For the first time in their history, most Germans respect or support the democratic system and its institutions, and the vast majority of citizens recognise the country's existing borders with its nine neighbouring states.

The final reason for the positive revaluation of German history is the emergence of a possible answer to the unresolved identity question. Before 1989/90, the National Socialist past and the division of the nation had ruled out even a controversial identification with history that included Germans from both sides of the Iron Curtain. The monstrous history before 1945 and two most dissimilar histories since 1949 had denied such a choice. The caesura of 1989/90, however, brought this anomaly to an end and enabled the Germans to begin writing a shared history, to which they can relate — if they so wish — in a positive fashion. This new history has only just begun and for the time being old and new disparities between East and West still pose massive problems. The Social Democrat Richard Schröder was therefore right in claiming that unification can only succeed if the Germans manage to unify their dissimilar histories. To achieve this, Schröder maintains, they should again understand themselves as one people, not by defining Germany against her neighbours and alleged enemies within — as was the case between 1871 and 1945 — but rather by following the principle that being German today should mean "nichts Besonderes, aber etwas Bestimmtes."[44]

In this context some attention should also be paid to the question of whether we should, in fact, continue talking about "German" or "national identity," or whether it might not be more appropriate to use the term "German self-understanding." Admittedly, the two notions cannot be completely separated, yet differences do exist both on the denotative and the connotative level. In one authoritative dictionary, "identity" is defined as the "same in substance," "oneness" or even "absolute or essential sameness."[45] Applied to the concept of the nation, the ideal of an essential sameness suggesting an absolute symbiosis of an individual with a nation appears anachronistic. Viewed against the background of European integration, definitions of this kind seem to ignore the existence and close interrelation of nations in the present-day world. As for Germany, one cannot ignore the uncomfortable associations with the National Socialist "Volksgemeinschaft" either. Stefan Berger is thus correct to claim that the "very concept of 'national identity' remains a fudged one . . . which tends to exist in conflict with the values of tolerance and pluralism."[46] Two reasons speak in favour of a more frequent use of the term "self-understanding." First, because it does not carry any dubious historical connotations; second, because it does not include the aspect of absolute or essential sameness. "There is no such thing as an 'essential' national identity,"[47] Mary Fulbrook writes in her summary of the most important scholarship, preferring to refer instead to "national identity construction" (23). Although the term "national identity" will be unavoidable in the debate about the Berlin Republic, it still seems more appropriate to make use of "self-understanding." This is because the term includes the notion of construction. Indeed, common dictionary definitions stress that "self-understanding" first and foremost refers to the "idea"[18] — that is, an intellectual construction — that a group or a person has of itself.

German Self-Understanding and "Normality"

Affirmative readings of contemporary German history have attracted fierce criticism from some critics associated with the political Left. Jürgen Habermas, in particular, has pointed out that, in the "old" Federal Republic, the caesura of 1945 had been regarded with good reason as the pivotal historiographical reference point. He believes that Auschwitz has indeed become the "Signatur eines ganzen Zeitalters."[49] It is only by virtue of self-critical reflection on this breach in civilisation, Habermas argues, that the Federal Republic has become a politically civilised state since 1949. In fact, he argues that a liberal political culture was only able to establish itself in Germany *because* of Auschwitz.[50] For this reason Habermas perceives 1945 in general, and the Holocaust in particular, as the supreme measure by which any assessment of contemporary German history should be made.

At the opposite end of the political spectrum, historians such as Arnulf Baring refuse to regard Auschwitz as the essence of German history.[51] It is wrong, he states, to believe "unsere Geschichte müsse und könne nur im Lichte der Vernichtungslager gesehen werden" (328). Instead, he advocates a more comprehensive perspective that takes into account the multifacetted nature, ambivalence and openness of German history. (336). Baring perceives the Holocaust as only one of many chapters in German history, although he concedes that the National Socialist past weighs heavily upon the Germans (327). Baring's reading does not focus on the Nazi years but highlights the democratic renewal of the last fifty years which grants the Germans the right to celebrate the kind of state in which they live (337). A remark by the chairwoman of the Christian Democrats, Angela Merkel, in the year 2000 illustrates to what extent this affirmative revaluation has become common currency, at least amongst politicians: "Wir sollten ein natürliches Gefühl für unsere *ganze* Geschichte entwickeln," Merkel maintained, "und dann sagen: Wir sind auch froh, Deutsche zu sein."[52]

The crux of these conflicting assessments is that Habermas and Baring alike are trying to determine what kind of "normality" should mark the new self-understanding of the Berlin Republic.[53] Seen from this angle, the controversy of the 1980s — just like the Historians' Controversy — revolves around hegemony over the interpretation of history. For Habermas, any German desire for a genuine normality is unacceptable because it presupposes the relativisation of the abnormal: the Holocaust. People in the "old" Federal Republic, he argues, had developed an awareness, "daß nur die Vermeidung eines auftrumpfend-zudeckenden Bewußtseins von 'Normalität' auch in unserem Land halbwegs normale Verhältnisse hat entstehen lassen" (171). He thus expresses concern about revisionist historians such as Michael Stürmer who, as Habermas claims, insinuate: "Um wieder eine normale Nation zu werden, sollten wir uns der selbstkritischen Erinnerung an Auschwitz erwehren."[54]

Other experts on German affairs, however, including the American historian David Schoenbaum and journalist Elizabeth Pond, see the

Federal Republic as "finally normal — 'stinknormal,' in the Berlin argot."[55] The country's "new normality," they state, "probably grants it the same tolerance for mistakes that others enjoy" (236). And, in Kurt Sontheimer's view, the differences which remain between Germany and her neighbours are minimal in the context of a shared European normality in which Germans have finally found their place.[56]

Conclusion

The historical caesura of 1989/90 is of crucial significance for the new self-understanding of the Berlin Republic. Since unification, the fixation on the National Socialist past has been relaxed in favour of a revaluation of the Federal Republic's history since 1949. Today, its fifty-year existence is widely understood as an "Erfolgsgeschichte," not least because the accession of the GDR represented something like the ratification of the Basic Law by the East Germans. The demise of the GDR seemed to verify the historical legitimacy of the Federal Republic following decades of ideological competition. It is for this reason that Fritz Stern has aptly described German unification as "eine Art zweiter Anerkennung der Bundesrepublik."[57]

Yet considering Germany's contemporary history on the whole, we must ask ourselves whether this new "historische Interpunktion" is actually justified or whether the watershed of 1945 should remain the pivotal historiographical reference point. There can be no doubt that the fundamental transformation of Central and Eastern Europe at the end of the twentieth century requires a critical revision of previous positions. For this reason, as Jürgen Kocka emphasises, "wird dieser große Umbruch nicht vorbeigehen an der Art, in der wir Geschichte schreiben."[58] This should not mean, however, that 1945 must be relativised or erased by 1989/90. Winston Churchill's assessment of 1946 that "crimes and massacres have been committed for which there is . . . no equal at any time in human history,"[59] is as true today as it was then. For the Germans, 1945 will continue to be a past that cannot be overcome, the monstrosities of which must be recognised as a warning from history — not least because they teach the Germans who they were and who they never wish to be again. Caught up in their enthusiasm for the German success story some conservative historians lose sight of this and advocate a position which attempts to "'normalise' Auschwitz, to render it part of Germany's pluralist political culture like any other issue."[60]

At the same time, however, some critics from the political Left do not strike the right balance either by turning 1945 into the lodestar of historiography. Although this view is understandable, especially when one considers that intellectuals such as Jürgen Habermas and Günter Grass belong to the "Auschwitz-Generation."[61] For some of this age group, and above all for the victims, the Holocaust has therefore become the measure of all things. At the same time, however, we cannot overlook the fact that the biographies of the vast majority of present-day Germans were not moulded by the National Socialist dictatorship. In fact, it was the years 1989/90 which left the more profound mark on many people's lives, first and foremost in East Germany where this recent caesura has fundamentally changed the lifestyles and careers of almost all citizens. A rational and realistic reading of contemporary German history should, therefore, take both dates into account. On the one hand, it is of crucial significance for the Germans to understand 1945 as a collapse, a breach in civilisation, and a liberation from outside. On the other hand, this insight should not minimise the importance of 1989/90 as the date upon which Germans finally carried out a peaceful self-liberation from dictatorship and set out on their self-determined history.

As has been noted, Richard Schröder voiced the opinion that being German today should no longer mean "etwas Besonderes." The Berlin Republic is indeed more normal, that is, more like its western neighbours, than any other German state has ever been in the twentieth century. The country has abandoned that notorious "Sonderweg" which had set the nation apart from the western world and culminated in an absurd "Sonderbewußtsein" under Nazism. Since unification Germany has also disposed of her bi-lateral and international "Sonderrollen" and no longer represents a "Sonderfall," as Hans Magnus Enzensberger once put it. Instead, the Federal Republic's Foreign Secretary, Joschka Fischer, today regards the completion of European integration as being in Germany's pivotal national interest.[62]

However, Richard Schröder also associates Germany's new self-understanding with "etwas Bestimmtes." For Germans, he argues, it is not sufficient to resort to a vague philanthrophy, since this does not promote any genuine understanding of the national sensibilities and histories of other people.[63] It is indeed their history that differentiates the Germans quite substantially from other peoples — despite the fact that lifestyles and mentalities in Europe are becoming increasingly similar. While the British, for example, define their self-understanding with reference to two victorious world wars and the remarkable continuity of their democratic tradition, Germans have become what they are today through two lost world wars and the Holocaust, four decades of division, the peaceful revolution in the GDR and the merging of the two states.

Among postwar Germans in particular, this ambivalent past marked by discontinuity has created an often more critical assessment of their history than is sometimes the case elsewhere. Self-critical reflection ("Aufarbeitung") on deeply questionable phases of German history has developed into a specific feature of Germany's political culture over the last three decades. Recent public debates have demonstrated that a sizeable number of citizens see the normality of the Berlin Republic in the light of that problematical German history. The controversies about the *Wehrmacht* exhibition (1996–98) or about Daniel Jonah Goldhagen's book *Hitler's Willing Executioners* (1996–97), for example, were not only restricted to intellectual circles (as was the case with the Historians' Controversy) but received widespread attention in the media, even in mass circulation newspapers such as *Bild Zeitung*.

The debate about the building of the Holocaust Memorial in the centre of Berlin demonstrates that public reflection upon 1945 forms part of the Berlin Republic's self-understanding. From its early beginnings in the late 1980s, this first all-German controversy showed that right up to the *Bundestag* vote of June 1999 politicians, academics, publicists, artists and average citizens do want to see the German past represented in a critical way in the present — and not somewhere remote, but in a prominent, central public location between the Potsdam Square and the Brandenburg Gate. The debate and the decision to build the Memorial temper Andrei S. Markovits's and Simon Reich's suspicion that Germany might give up its "collective memory" and entirely "normalise its relations with the past."[64] All in all, the Germans' self-understanding is not marked by the formation of an uncritical normality, as even Jürgen Habermas has conceded despite his numerous reservations.[65] Hence, where one finds that often quoted *Neue Mitte*, among the city's restored and brand-new sites, Peter Eisenman's field of pillars for the murdered European Jews will be ingrained on the features of the Berlin Republic like the mark of Cain.

Notes

[1] See, for example, C. Meier, "Über Deutschland und die Deutschen," in G. Kohler and M. Meyer, eds., *Die Folgen von 1989* (Munich/Vienna: Hanser, 1994), 47.

[2] See, for example, A. Baring, *Es lebe die Republik, es lebe Deutschland! Stationen demokratischer Erneuerung 1949–1999* (Stuttgart: Deutsche Verlags-Anstalt, 1999), 279; A. Schildt, *Ankunft im Westen: Ein Essay zur Erfolgsgeschichte der Bundesrepublik* (Frankfurt am Main: Fischer, 1999); H. Schulze, *Kleine deutsche Geschichte*

(Munich: Beck, 1996), 265; K. Sontheimer, *So war Deutschland nie: Anmerkungen zur politischen Kultur der Bundesrepublik* (Munich: Beck, 1999), 249.

[3] J. Habermas, "1989 im Schatten von 1945. Zur Normalität einer künftigen Berliner Republik," in J. Habermas, *Die Normalität einer Berliner Republik* (Frankfurt am Main: Suhrkamp, 1995), 171. Also see J. Kocka, *Vereinigungskrise: Zur Geschichte der Gegenwart* (Göttingen: Vandenhoeck und Ruprecht, 1995), 30, 33, 83.

[4] See C. Meier, "Verurteilen und Verstehen," in *"Historikerstreit": Dokumentation der Kontroverse um die Einzigartigkeit der nationalsozialistischen Judenvernichtung* (Munich/Zurich: Piper, 1988), 48.

[5] See N. Frei, *Vergangenheitspolitik: Die Anfänge der Bundesrepublik und die NS-Vergangenheit* (Munich: Deutscher Taschenbuch Verlag, 1999).

[6] See H. Schelsky, *Die skeptische Generation: Eine Soziologie der deutschen Jugend* (Dusseldorf: Diederichs, 1957).

[7] G. Grass, *Schreiben nach Auschwitz: Frankfurter Poetik-Vorlesung* (Frankfurt am Main: Luchterhand, 1990), 11.

[8] E. Renan, *Qu'est-ce qu'une nation?* (Paris: Calmann Lévy, 1882), 26.

[9] J. Habermas, "Über den öffentlichen Gebrauch der Historie. Das offizielle Selbstverständnis der Bundesrepublik bricht auf," in *"Historikerstreit": Dokumentation der Kontroverse um die Einzigartigkeit der nationalsozialistischen Judenvernichtung*, 247.

[10] H. M. Enzensberger [Büchner Prize Speech, 1963], in *Büchner-Preis-Reden 1951–1971* (Stuttgart: Reclam, 1972), 126.

[11] C. Wolf, "Überlegungen zum 1. September 1939," in C. Wolf, *Im Dialog: Aktuelle Texte* (Frankfurt am Main: Luchterhand, 1990), 72.

[12] C. Wolf, "Rede vom Auslöffeln. Zur Sache: Deutschland," in *Wochenpost* (3 March 1994): iv.

[13] H. M. Enzensberger, "landessprache," in H. M. Enzensberger, *Landessprache: Gedichte* (Frankfurt am Main: Suhrkamp, 1969), 9.

[14] *Philosophisches Wörterbuch* (West Berlin: Pädagogisches Zentrum, 1975), 857.

[15] F. H. Tenbruck, "Alltagsnormen und Lebensgefühle in der Bundesrepublik," in R. Löwenthal and H.-P. Schwarz, eds., *Die zweite Republik: 25 Jahre Bundesrepublik — Eine Bilanz* (Stuttgart: Seewald, 1974), 292.

[16] T. Schmid, "Glasklarer Durchblick," *Die Zeit* 13 (26 March 1993): 10.

[17] W. J. Mommsen, "Wandlungen der nationalen Identität," in W. Weidenfeld, ed., *Die Identität der Deutschen*, 179.

[18] H. M. Enzensberger, "Über die Schwierigkeit, ein Inländer zu sein (1964)," in H. M. Enzensberger, *Der Fliegende Robert: Gedichte, Szenen, Essays* (Frankfurt am Main: Suhrkamp, 1989), 37.

[19] See Enzensberger [Büchner Prize Speech, 1963], 124.

[20] W. Biermann, *Affenfels und Barrikade: Gedichte, Lieder, Balladen* (Cologne: Kiepenheuer & Witsch, 1986), 25.

[21] Enzensberger [Büchner Prize Speech, 1963], 130.

[22] J. Becker, "Mein Vater, die Deutschen und ich," *Die Zeit* 21 (20 May 1994), 58.

[23] S. Hermlin, "Antwort," in K. Wagenbach et al., eds., *Vaterland, Muttersprache* (Berlin: Wagenbach, 1994), 186.

[24] E. Jäckel, *Das deutsche Jahrhundert: Eine historische Bilanz* (Stuttgart: Deutsche Verlags-Anstalt, 1996), 305.

[25] See Christa Wolf, "Rede vom Auslöffeln. Zur Sache: Deutschland," iv.

[26] See W. J. Mommsen, "Wandlungen der nationalen Identität," 184.

[27] See C. Wolf, "Überlegungen zum 1. September 1939," 73.

[28] See F. Schorlemmer, "Vor den Trümmern einer gescheiterten Alternative," in F. Schorlemmer, *Bis alle Mauern fallen: Texte aus einem verschwundenen Land* (Berlin: Verlag der Nation, 1991), 21.

[29] See J. Reich, "Die organisierte Langeweile," *Die Zeit* 41 (7 October 1999): 12.

[30] See D. Sternberger, "Verfassungspatriotismus. Rede bei der 25-Jahr-Feier der "Akademie für Politische Bildung" (1982)," in D. Sternberger, *Verfassungspatriotismus*, Schriften Band 10 (Frankfurt am Main: Insel, 1990), 20.

[31] See D. Sternberger, "Verfassungspatriotismus (1979)," in D. Sternberger, *Verfassungspatriotismus*, Schriften Band 10 (Frankfurt am Main: Insel, 1990), 13.

[32] E. Nolte, "Vergangenheit, die nicht vergehen will," in *"Historikerstreit": Die Dokumentation der Kontroverse um die Einzigartigkeit der nationalsozialistischen Judenvernichtung*, 46.

[33] J. Habermas, "Eine Art Schadensabwicklung. Die apologetischen Tendenzen in der deutschen Zeitgeschichtsschreibung," in *"Historikerstreit": Die Dokumentation der Kontroverse um die Einzigartigkeit der nationalsozialistischen Judenvernichtung*, 73.

[34] See the title of the German edition of D. Schoenbaum's and E. Pond's *Annäherung an Deutschland: Die Strapazen der Normalität* (Stuttgart: Deutsche Verlags-Anstalt, 1997).

[35] F. Stern, "Die zweite Chance? Deutschland am Anfang und am Ende des Jahrhunderts," in F. Stern, *Verspielte Größe: Essays zur deutschen Geschichte des 20.* Jahrhunderts (Munich: Beck, 1996).

[36] A. Bolaffi, *Die schrecklichen Deutschen: Eine merkwürdige Liebeserk*lärung (Berlin: Siedler, 1995).

[37] K. Sontheimer, *So war Deutschland nie: Anmerkungen zur politischen Kultur der Bundesrepublik*, 253.

[38] A. Baring, *Es lebe die Republik, es lebe Deutschland! Stationen demokratischer Erneuerung 1949–1999.*

[39] F. Stern, "Die zweite Chance? Deutschland am Anfang und am Ende des Jahrhunderts," 17.

[40] See W. Brandt, ". . . und Berlin wird leben. Berlin, John-F.-Kennedy-Platz, 10. November 1989," in W. Brandt, *". . . was zusammen gehört": Reden zu Deutschland* (Bonn: Dietz, 1990), 39.

[41] T. G. Ash. in Jewgenij A. Jewtuschenko et al., *Reden über Deutschland* (Munich: Bertelsmann, 1990), 112.

[42] A. S. Markovits and S. Reich, *The German Predicament: Memory and Power in the New Europe* (Ithaca, NY: Cornell UP, 1997), 8.

[43] See, for example, P. Schneider, "Wenn die Wirklichkeit die Ideen verrät," in P. Schneider, *Vom Ende der Gewißheit* (Berlin: Rowohlt, 1994), 13; or M. Walser, "Über Deutschland reden (Ein Bericht)," in M. Walser, *Über Deutschland reden* (Frankfurt am Main: Suhrkamp, 1989), 82.

[44] R. Schröder, "Was heißt: 'Ich bin Deutscher?'" *Zeitpunkte*, "Vereint, doch nicht eins. Deutschland fünf Jahre nach der Wiedervereinigung," 5 (1995), 14.

[45] *The Oxford English Dictionary*, vol. 7 (Oxford: 1989), 620. Also cp. *Brockhaus / Wahrig Deutsches Wörterbuch*, vol. 3 (Wiesbaden and Stuttgart, 1981), 703.

[46] S. Berger, *The Search for Normality: National Identity and Historical Consciousness in Germany Since 1800* (Providence: Berghahn, 1997), 211.

[47] M. Fulbrook, *German National Identity after the Holocaust* (Cambridge: Polity/Blackwell, 1999), 15.

[48] *Brockhaus / Wahrig Deutsches Wörterbuch*, vol. 5 (Wiesbaden and Stuttgart: 1983), 731.

[49] J. Habermas, "Geschichtsbewußtsein und posttraditionale Identität. Die Westorientierung der Bundesrepublik," in J. Habermas, *Die Moderne — ein unvollendetes Projekt: Philosophisch-politische Aufsätze 1977–1992* (Leipzig: Reclam, 1992), 162.

[50] J. Habermas, "1989 im Schatten von 1945. Zur Normalität einer künftigen Berliner Republik," 170.

[51] A. Baring, *Es lebe die Republik, es lebe Deutschland! Stationen demokratischer Erneuerung 1949–1999*, 330.

[52] "'Ich habe gern den Kopf oben.' Die CDU-Vorsitzende Angela Merkel im Gespräch mit ZEIT-Chefredakteur Roger de Weck," *Die Zeit* 19 (4 May 2000): 3.

[53] J. Habermas, "1989 im Schatten von 1945. Zur Normalität einer künftigen Berliner Republik," 171.

[54] J. Habermas, "Aus der Geschichte lernen?" in J. Habermas, *Die Normalität einer Berliner Republik*, 9.

[55] D. Schoenbaum and E. Pond, *The German Question and Other German Questions* (Basingstoke: Macmillan, in association with St. Antony's College, Oxford, 1996), 230.

[56] K. Sontheimer, *So war Deutschland nie*, 239.

[57] F. Stern, "Die zweite Chance? Deutschland am Anfang und am Ende des Jahrhunderts," 22.

[58] J. Kocka, *Vereinigungskrise: Zur Geschichte der Gegenwart*, 60.

[59] W. S. Churchill, "The Tragedy of Europe," in W. S. Churchill, *His Complete Speeches 1897–1963*, ed. R. T. James, vol. 8, 1943–1949 (New York/London: Chelsea House, 1974), 7380 [*sic*].

[60] A. S. Markovits and S. Reich, *The German Predicament: Memory and Power in the New Europe*, 205.

[61] G. Grass, *Schreiben nach Auschwitz*, 19.

[62] Cp. J. Fischer, "Vorwort," in A. S. Markovits and S. Reich, *Das deutsche Dilemma: Die Berliner Republik zwischen Macht und Machtverzicht* (Berlin: Alexander Fest, 1998), 15.

[63] R. Schröder, "Was heißt: 'Ich bin Deutscher?'" 14.

[64] A. S. Markovits and S. Reich, *The German Predicament: Memory and Power in the New Europe*, 206.

[65] J. Habermas, "Der Zeigefinger: Die Deutschen und ihr Denkmal," *Die Zeit* 14 (31 March 1999): 42.

Filling the Blanks:
Berlin as a Public Showcase

Ulrike Zitzlsperger

Introduction

Das vereinte Berlin ist unbekannter als das geteilte Berlin.[1]

WHEN DISCUSSING THE ROLE of the general public in the Berlin of the 1990s it has to be remembered that events leading up to reunification were set in motion by ordinary people. Media soundbites such as "Ein Volk sprengt seine Mauern" serve to remind us that the memory of reunification does not just cast back to the political processes at work; it also entails a reflection on individual perceptions and experiences. A sense of having participated in the making of history thus shapes memory. The feeling of having played a part in events was bolstered by the media's documentation of each and every development.[2] Some of these images have by now been used so frequently that, taken together, they overwhelm individual memories.

In the early twentieth century, the critic Karl Scheffler observed that Berlin's tragedy lay in the fact that it was condemned "immer zu werden und niemals zu sein."[3] In recent years this formulation has frequently been used in attempts to explain and define the phenomenon of the city and its most recent fate: the merging of the two halves. Berlin's turbulent history during the twentieth century — from rapid development and European pre-eminence to apocalyptic destruction and Cold War division — has denied it a "normal" development. Yet today this very lack of continuity would seem to add to its appeal. Compared to any other metropolis Berlin appears to be far more malleable, a city that can be consciously shaped.

The numerous attempts in the 1990s to define Berlin, both in the popular press and in academic discussion, can be attributed to this phenomenon. The journalist Klaus Hartung was certainly correct when he claimed that nothing was more difficult than to describe what Berlin was, yet this did not prevent the search for just such an account from becoming a favourite pastime.[4] Berlin's self-perception and its preoccupation with the past have been analysed by Wolf Jobst Siedler:

> Am charakteristischsten ist, daß Berlin im Schatten der Mauer sich selbst historisch geworden war. Es denkt an die fünfziger Jahre, an die Epoche von Weimar oder an den Aufbruch des späten Kaiserreichs, wenn es von sich selber spricht. Dieser Widerspruch zwischen dem ständigen Reden von seiner glanzvollen Vergangenheit und seiner eher ernüchternden Gegenwart macht gerade jene mißmutig, die die Idee Berlins im Auge haben . . . Für was steht denn heute Berlin?[5]

Taking Siedler's theme as a starting point, this article will consider how Berlin dealt with the transitional period in the 1990s when the post-ideological vacuum had to be filled. It will focus in particular on how the public was deliberately drawn into a process that aimed to establish a new identity for the city and to restore its status as an international metropolis.

One strategy designed to stimulate public participation was to provide a variety of events that harnessed culture in the broadest sense of the term. These were organised by the civic authorities together with marketing strategists, and were intended to fill what was known as the city's physical "voids" — caused by the Second World War, division after 1961 and the subsequent alienation between East and West. The events were designed to communicate what was happening in the *New Berlin* — this was how the metropolis was to be marketed — and to make it more approachable. It was not just selective aspects that were to be opened up to the public and visitors alike, but the city centre as a whole. The culture of the city changed considerably in character during this process, and a lack of "normality" — in contrast to something permanent and unquestionable — was elevated into a popular topic and art form. This is perhaps best illustrated by the following three examples:

1. The *Stadtforum Berlin*, an interdisciplinary panel of specialists set up by the Berlin Senate in the early 1990s. It was costly and heavily promoted. Its remit included making planning processes transparent to both specialists and the wider public.

2. The *InfoBox*, a futuristic information centre situated near Potsdamer Platz. This was developed to provide information for Berliners and visitors from further afield about the reconstruction taking place in the city centre.

3. The *Schaustelle Berlin*, a project set up jointly in 1996 by the Berlin Senate and the agency *Partner für Berlin*. The scheme was launched in order to promote new sites, enhancing them with cultural events during the summer. It eventually turned the whole of the city centre into what might be termed an "interactive museum."

Berlin in the 1990s

At the beginning of the 1990s, the nature of society in Berlin, as in the newly united country as a whole, was being hotly debated: the stark contrasts within Berlin, which for more than forty years had been governed by two diametrically opposed ideologies, were still tangible. One of many comparisons was drawn during a meeting of the *Stadtforum* in 1991 when it was claimed that while West Berlin might have a public but no public space, East Berlin by contrast provided public space but no public.[6] "Public" and "urban space" (or "identity") were thus to become two of the most important keywords in the following years.

As a result of reunification the city itself had to be redefined, both as a capital and as a metropolis situated between East and West. The search for new images was accompanied by major changes in the topography of the city. While a high degree of sensitivity toward change could be observed, at the same time there was an obvious interest in uplifting mass events comparable — although with less impact, of course — to 9 November 1989, the day the Wall fell.

In his book "Capital Dilemma," Michael Z. Wise describes Berlin's self-conscious awareness of its public image. Thus he refers to the rebuilding of the government quarter:

> In Berlin, unified as it is under a liberal democratic order, the Chancellor's architect desperately wanted his work to win public approval. Although Schultes was alone among his colleagues in articulating the aim so explicitly, it stemmed from a widespread German impulse that surfaced repeatedly as officials planned the new Berlin.[7]

Thanks to the combination of this public demand and the strategy of the civic authorities, numerous events throughout the 1990s generated the specialist interests of experts and excited the curiosity of the public. Repeatedly, however, reactions diverged: the general public expected something spectacular and substantial, while the quality press looked on with a more discerning eye. Behind each event there lurked the question as to how relevant a contribution it had made to Berlin's prestige. High-profile examples of such events can be enumerated as follows:

1. In 2000 the seventh *Lange Nacht der Museen* took place as part of *Schauplatz Museum*. More than fifty museums and other cultural institutions participate in this increasingly popular annual event, which allows visitors to follow set itineraries during a given night, facilitated by a public transport shuttle service. On these occasions museums do not limit themselves to their exhibitions, rather they "heighten" the experience with the help of a supplementary programme including music, readings and refreshments. The aim is to provide a special experience by the unorthodox timing and by linking separate attractions.

2. The mooted rebuilding of the *Berliner Stadtschloß*, which had been razed to the ground under Walter Ulbricht's communist regime in 1951, attracted public attention after a rather unusual initiative started in 1993. A privately financed project by the Hamburg businessman Wilhelm von Boddien so explicitly evoked the illusion of a restored palace façade by means of a combination of scaffolding, fabric and a huge mirror that when the dummy façade was removed after two weeks its abrupt absence caused an immediate reaction amongst the public. This example illustrates how planning processes can be made accessible and how public interest can be steered with the help of events relying on visual impact.[8]

3. When the first *Love-Parade* took place in Berlin in 1989, it was the project of a small group of young people interested in "techno," at that time a little-known music fashion. Ten years later the Parade attracts not only up to a million music and dance enthusiasts but also political figures well aware of its popular appeal. The organisers' threats in 1999 to relocate to Paris because of the authorities' financial and environmental concerns were reversed only when the city realised what the potential loss of the Love Parade would mean for Berlin. The annual event, which has a new, popularist theme each year (in 2000, for example, "One world — One Love Parade"), had become central to the image of Berlin as a dynamic and youthful metropolis. The Love Parade's distinctive achievement lies in extending what was originally a narrow focus into the public sphere. Participants from home and abroad praise the special atmosphere, which has made it one of Berlin's prime attractions.

By 2000, however, the excitement of Berlin as a special location had begun to wane and the Techno-party looked to move on, with Leeds and Tel Aviv among the new locations. But the initial party atmosphere associated with post-unification Berlin will be hard to beat. More than any other 1990s event, the Love Parade epitomises the collective thrill of a peaceful mass event.

4. In 1995 there was a spectacular prelude to the renovation of the *Reichstag* when it was wrapped in shimmering silver fabric by the Bulgarian artist, Christo. The discussion that followed the transformation, and the special atmosphere it generated, marked the beginning of a whole calendar of unique events accompanying Berlin's attempt to secure undisputed status as a genuine metropolis.

The magazine *Stern* described the occasion as akin to a church service. Thus cultural acts in the public domain do not just have an immediate impact — they can also give expression to unspecified hopes and desires:

> Still ist es. Ehrfürchtig umrunden Tausende von Menschen das Gebäude, dem die silbrig glänzende Hülle eine Art von Heiligenschein verliehen hat. Ergriffen befühlen sie das schwere Tuch und tragen als Reliquie briefmarkengroße Stückchen nach Hause. Berlin hat eine neue Pilgerstätte bekommen, die alle eint.[9]

Today, visiting the cupola of the Reichstag seems to be the ultimate experience: both tourists and Berliners consider the building to be one of the most significant symbols of the city. Its accessibility, its importance, and its aesthetic qualities would appear to serve the interests of the people, the city, and the government alike.[10]

5. A spectacular light-show arranged for the millennium celebrations between *Großer Stern* and Brandenburg Gate was another attempt to attract the "masses." This time, however, the idea somewhat backfired. The (wholly accidental) similarities with Albert Speer's infamous Nazi spectacle were a stark reminder of the historical dimensions that need to be taken into account when planning such events. The show eventually went ahead in a revised and more appropriate manner, its success setting an example for years to come.[11]

6. A new interactive museum called *The Story of Berlin* uses similar effects, albeit on a different scale. Here, selected episodes

in the city's history are re-enacted "live." The very heritage of Berlin is on offer, although sometimes in somewhat bizarre form. In 1999, for example, a 24-hour residence in an original World War Two concrete bunker was available as a "meaningful" experience. In the *Story of Berlin*, history has been turned into a "visitor experience" with an immediacy appealing to all the senses; the claim of authenticity works with emotional effect.

In the 1990s, as well as various events of this kind, there were, as I shall now outline, also attempts to find alternative forms of public participation in discussions which were designed to create anticipation of planned developments and to flesh out how the new Berlin might be defined.

The *Stadtforum*

The first initiative of this kind was the *Stadtforum Berlin*, established by the then *Senat für Stadtentwicklung und Umweltschutz.*[12] Because of the division of the city and the complexity of the task ahead, it was not only experts such as town-planners and architects that were required, but also economists, social scientists, environmentalists, historians, artists and others. They were organised in so-called *Bänke*. The sheer number of issues facing Berlin meant that when the *Stadtforum* first met fortnightly sessions were necessary. Topics discussed included the rebuilding of *Potsdamer Platz* and the *Berliner Stadtschloß*, Berlin's bid for the Olympic Games in 2000, comparisons with other cities, and the role of Berlin as an industrial and commercial centre.

This interdisciplinary board, though essentially democratic in principle, functioned in practice only on the basis of some tight organisational restrictions. For example, it was the Senate — with the help of a so-called steering committee — that decided in advance on the list of speakers. After the opening speeches, only participants from the various specialist groups were allowed to take part in the discussion, with the result that participation by the public was limited to a passive role.

The *Stadtforum* was the first example of its type — although there was a similar institution in Holland — proving itself worthy of its name by initiating a public debate on the future of the city. The media provided regular and extensive information on meetings. Indeed, few institutions dealing with the subject of Berlin have been as comprehensively documented. Among its many publications, such as extensive "media dossiers" for individual meetings (minutes of contributions to the discussions, presentations, summaries, main ideas), there is a journal, and an interactive media archive — not to mention recordings of meetings and numerous books. Conferences and exhibitions underlined the importance of certain phenomena such as aspects of urban society. The large quantity of information reflects the character of a new — perhaps ephemeral — culture of debate that arose from the creative tension in a city caught between East and West during a phase of profound change.

The wide-ranging expertise of the members of the *Stadtforum* demonstrated that city-related issues were now being seen in a wider context and as relating to far more than architecture or town planning. Though the *Stadtforum's* self-imposed regulations were somewhat restrictive, its original structure proved that the city as a whole could become a theme of general interest, that debates on the topic are not merely subject-specific but multi-faceted, and that lack of consensus on questions relating to development can become a public issue. Last but not least, the *Stadtforum's* work gained international recognition. Thus it became one of the first exportable assets the city was able to offer after reunification. Yet arguably the most important achievement of the *Stadtforum* was that the public was now better informed than before. It went beyond "outstanding" events to encompass the whole future appearance of the city.

The success of the *Stadtforum* in stimulating a culture of debate meant that it was itself open to development. After it had been restructured in 1996, Klaus Hartung described it as the "laboratory of the future citizen."[13] Despite this, public interest in the forum has since waned. One reason was that the most decisive steps for Berlin's future had already been taken. Another was that a new attraction now demanded public attention.

The *InfoBox*

The *InfoBox* was set up to explain the future of the Potsdamer Platz and the Zentrale Bereich when the spectacular construction work began there in 1995. It was, by its very nature, more accessible to the public.

The controversial plans for redeveloping the square were already a widely discussed topic, highlighted as they had been since 1992 by the *Stadtforum* and the media. Controversy centred on the sheer scale of the project — after all, at a sensitive point in the so-called "heart" of the city — and on whether an "urban entertainment centre" was an appropriate use of the former "death strip" alongside the Berlin Wall. Curiosity, concern, and a general desire to be involved found a perfect outlet when the temporary and architecturally remarkable information-box, resembling a long red container on stilts, was sited on the nearby Leipziger Platz. The *InfoBox* was jointly financed by the Berlin Senate and the companies involved in the Potsdamer Platz development. At the same time these companies, which included DaimlerChrysler, Sony and the electricity supply company BEWAG, continued to advertise on their own behalf on nearby sites, presenting the rebuilding in terms of a countdown and establishing their particular relationship to Berlin.[14]

The *InfoBox* catered both for Berlin residents and for an increasing number of tourists. Multiple exhibition areas provided by the Senate, the Government, and investors were all intended to promote the future of the city. Mock-ups of the new centre, information films with dramatic background music, emotive artefacts such as coffee-cups from the famous Café Josty, once situated on the square, and the impressive view from the roof of the building all conveyed a sense of leaving the past behind and the promise of a new tomorrow. This vision was enhanced by selective historical details and up-to-the-minute computer simulations. The combination of architecture and information transmitted by the exhibition transformed building sites into something that simply could not be ignored.

The close link with the city was particularly emphasized. Michael Schumacher, one of the *InfoBox's* architects, is quoted as follows:

> Die "Kiste" steht auf dem ehemaligen "Todesstreifen" und repräsentiert sowohl die freche Berliner Subkultur während der Zeit der Isolation, als auch den Optimismus nach dem Mauerfall. Insofern ist die InfoBox . . . kein verallgemeinerbares Marketinginstrument für Investoren aus aller und in aller Welt, sondern eine originär Berliner Sache.[15]

Situated on one of the most lucrative sites in the city, the *InfoBox's* continued usefulness was inextricably linked to the redevelopment of the square. With Potsdamer Platz more or less complete by the millennium, it became obsolete and its future bleak — a situation that had been foreseen in 1995 in the conditions of the architectural competition. Transfer to another site was considered inappropriate, mainly because of the building's symbolic impact. So on 30 December 2000 about a thousand invited guests bade a fond, formal farewell to the red box.[16] The slogan for the evening, "Tschüß InfoBox — Hallo Berlin," was certainly fitting: the *InfoBox*, once advertising "Heute die Stadt von morgen sehen" and representing the process of unifying and rebuilding Berlin, had been superseded by the completed metropolis.

In the six years of its existence the *InfoBox* had become one of Berlin's most popular attractions after the Brandenburg Gate: approximately nine million people visited it to inform themselves about "tomorrow's world." It even made its way into contemporary German literature, since the building served as an ideal symbol of the transitional state of 1990s Berlin.[17]

The degree of public participation in this case can be attributed to a number of factors. Thus the *InfoBox* provided not just targeted in-depth information (including impressive statistical data, technical and logistical details) but an overview of a six-year development programme for Berlin. Its temporary nature, moreover, turned the exhibition into an "event," and the mixture of information and innovation helped reinforce the identity of the "New Berlin." The *InfoBox* became a source of civic pride; the fact that seventy thousand visitors now come to the Potsdamer Platz each day proves the success of the scheme.

The *Schaustelle*

Similar factors worked for the *Schaustelle Berlin*. Here the debate linked building work and culture even more closely together. In this context the term *Architainment* was coined. The *Schaustelle Berlin*, a joint project of the Senate and the agency *Partner für Berlin*, did not only follow the building work at Potsdamer Platz but also the development of the government quarter and other sites.[18] Throughout the summer months every stage of construction was made accessible to the public. Adults and children were informed about technical achievements — for example, how divers had to be used to lay the foundations for the future "Daimler City."

Readings and concerts on such foundations, thematic tours of the city, illuminated cranes and ballets surrounded by scaffolding provided a multitude of attractions, large and small. Since the public had been kept consistently informed over the years, they were able to associate certain locations with cultural events. The new interest in the aesthetic aspects of building sites led to a boom in postcards and books dealing with all stages of building work. This reflected both people's changed perceptions of what is "attractive" and the uniqueness of the "city of cranes."

While literature and film took their time in locating and describing the "healing" of the wounds, visitors found themselves presented with a magnificent and fast-paced spectacle, framed in culture and open to all.[19] With an end to construction work in sight, the "wear and tear" of the marketing drive became obvious. Picnics with builders, recycled parts of cranes covered with information, and a whole city disguised as a museum seemed jaded and showed that the theme was now hackneyed. Indeed, by the year 2000 anticipation of the "new" was out of date.

The still lavish, though ever thinner, brochures advertising events tell their own story of the recent history of the city. In 1997's *Schaustelle Berlin. Moving on: Das neue Berlin* we read:

> Take a closer look or you might miss something. That's the odd thing about Berlin. One day you make something new and yet you have a feeling that its always been there. So the best thing is to keep your eyes open. Then you will be able to remember later on how things used to be.[20]

The English summary in the brochure does not include the more realistic qualification that exists in the German text, "Vielleicht finden Sie nicht alles schön, was wir Ihnen vorstellen. Aber ganz bestimmt sehen Sie die Stadt hinterher mit anderen Augen."

One year later, in 1998, the mayor, Eberhard Diepgen, stated in the introduction to the brochure that

> The construction sites have long since risen from the depths and have soared to new heights. With grand openings taking place all the time. The new Berlin is unfolding before our very eyes. Our building sites serve as a show-case for a modern open city.[21]

The apparent emergence of Berlin from "cocoon to a stunning beauty" was, by 2000, far more institutionalised, less urgent: the "open city" was promoted as a museum, the *Schaustelle* divided up:

> The EXPO 2000 in Hanover and its 30 decentralised projects in Berlin are the thematic focal points of this year's "Schaustelle" . . . "Berlin: Open City — The City on Exhibit" is the name of the project that directs people through Berlin along ten different routes on foot.[22]

Promotion of the city has come full circle. The task ahead is clearly of a different magnitude, but once again Scheffler's view is brought into play:

> A newspaper in Berlin recently wrote: "What has become of the city over the past ten years, is incredibly beautiful, but also practically impossible to describe. One must open one's eyes wide in order to find it between the old and new lines of buildings: Berlin's subtle smile, somewhat proud, somewhat shy, fairly ironic, confident and certainly looking forward to the future. It has a mysterious air like Mona Lisa's smile and, in any case, fills pages and will continue to do so for a long time to come" . . . The vision of perpetual birth which Karl Scheffler identified as the capital's characteristic feature almost a hundred years ago is bound to remain with us in the coming century.[23]

The visual element is still of importance, but now for the sake of future interest some mystery must be added to the picture.

The Metropolis

Wer etwas erlebt hat, glaubt in der Regel, das Erlebnis sei aussage-kräftiger als intellektuell erschließbare Zusammenhänge.[24]

In the 1990s, thanks both to political and to business initiatives, Berlin succeeded in making use of the "voids" left after unification and in making the public feel included in developments. Its strategy was based on providing information, "events," and new communicative approaches. Terms such as *Infotainment* or *Architainment,* which became popular with the *InfoBox* and the *Schaustelle,* underline the extent to which "culture" took on a broader sense. It became more marketable, whether for the sake of more transparency and the establishment of a new identity, or simply to commercialise new trends. The once all-defining Berlin Wall was to be replaced by a *creatio ex nihilo,* and new contexts and images were stage-managed for this purpose. What the *Stadtforum,* the *InfoBox* and the *Schaustelle Berlin* have in common, however, is their attempt to develop organic understanding of change. Those who experienced the development of Potsdamer Platz between 1995 and 2000 have a different attitude to the new square than those confronted for the first time with the finished product. Here the careful handling of memory plays as important a role as the pleasure many took in the "time in between."[25]

What is the future of this kind of stage management? It could be assumed that with a return to normality setting in, the city as a forum will lose its attraction and relevance. Once daily life runs smoothly again the productive tension of the transitional years will no longer be present. The substantial cultural programme of the city depended on a period when more inside knowledge, more targeted acceptance, served a purpose. The city has been explained to the public, the new special locations and symbols have been established. Where once precise definitions of the new Berlin were lacking, now it has been opened up by events, relaying messages that remain general and therefore adaptable. By contrast with the specific aims pursued by advertising or with the subjective view presented through characters in imaginative literature, images and parameters were offered for the period when Berlin enjoyed a status of "no longer" and "not yet": it benefited from the provision of occasions to be talked about.

The price to be paid for the success of this process is a shift away from an established "culture" requiring constant fostering toward a much broader definition; individual institutions such as theatres, museums and libraries suffer from the comparison with "events." The image-orientated culture of the 1990s which focused on the idea of a metropolis and drew in as many inhabitants as possible was fast-moving, spectacular, inflationary and forward-looking. By its very nature this form of culture had a limited lifespan. Ideal for making a new start, it has now lost its validity in a Berlin that feels normal again.[26] This is certainly true of attempts to target the public as deliberately as the three projects discussed.

During the 1990s, moreover, literary attempts to treat the city have become less ambitious and more realistic, using it simply as background, while in 1999 advertising said goodbye to the much promoted "das Neue Berlin" and now focuses on more detailed aspects of life. The new keywords are: "Ost-West-Metropole," "Hauptstadt," "Kreative Stadt," "Junge Stadt," and "Lebenswerte Stadt."[27]

Thus we return to Siedler's statement quoted at the beginning of this essay. In dealing so thoroughly with the contemporary situation, Berlin has obviously overcome its past tendency to delve back into its history. As for what defines Berlin: in the 1990s it was a multitude of visual impressions, of definitions of the "transitional culture" focusing on what is "about to be," Berlin being "different," young, in flux. Certainly "Berlin" has been made a topic of public interest. The euphoria triggered by taking possession of post-*Wende* Berlin may well be replaced by a substantial metropolitan culture, which — as in other cities — is able to make do without "events" and constant soul-searching.

Notes

[1] K. Hartung, "Doppelgesicht. Über die Paradoxie in Berlin," *Kursbuch* 137 (Berlin, 1999): 12.

[2] The flood of information on television made its way into literature. See for example A. Ören, *Unerwarteter Besuch: Auf der Suche nach der gegenwärtigen Zeit VI* (Berlin: Espresso Verlag, 1995), 115, and C. Nooteboom, *Berliner Notizen* (Frankfurt am Main: Suhrkamp, 1991), 95 and 138.

[3] K. Scheffler, *Berlin — ein Stadtschicksal* (reprint Berlin: Fannei und Walz, 1989), 219. Other authors concur with this observation and a rota of thirty years can be observed when the particular historical changes are defined.

[4] K. Hartung, "Berliner Übergangszeit. Entwickelt sich in der Hauptstadt eine Stadtgesellschaft und eine neue intellektuelle Kultur?" in W. Süß and R. Rytlewski, eds., *Berlin. Die Hauptstadt: Vergangenheit und Zukunft einer europäischen Metropole* (Bonn: Bundeszentrale für politische Bildung, 1999), 835–67, 837.

[5] W. J. Siedler, *Phoenix im Sand: Glanz und Elend in der Hauptstadt* (Berlin: Propyläen, 1998), 22. On Berlin's having to redefine itself in the 1990s commentators' observations overlap. Werner Süß, for example, writes: "Die Kennzeichnung des neuen Berlin, seiner zukünftigen Rolle steht noch aus. Sie erfaßt alle Ebenen zugleich." (Süß, *Berlin*, 12). Michael Sontheimer states that "Seit die Doppelstadt wieder zusammengeworfen und ihrer surrealen Sonderheit beraubt ist, stellt sich ihren Politikern und ihren Bewohnern in verschärfter Dringlichkeit die Frage, was Berlin sein soll und werden wird." (*Berlin Berlin: Der Umzug in die Hauptstadt* [Hamburg: Propyläen, 1999], 84). Thomas Krüger establishes in his introduction that during reunification Berlin was a tabula rasa, offering itself as an expanse for all kinds of projections. (*Die bewegte Stadt: Berlin am Ende der Neunziger* [Berlin: FAB-Verlag, 1998], 21–26, 22).

[6] Senat für Stadtentwicklung und Umweltschutz, ed., "Stadtforum: Medienmappe," 15 Nov. 1991 (minutes).

[7] M. Z. Wise, *Capital Dilemma: Germany's Search for a New Architecture of Democracy* (New York: Princeton Architectural Press, 1998), 72.

[8] On the importance of the Schloß see Wise, *Capital Dilemma*, 114–16, and B. Ladd, *The Ghosts of Berlin: Confronting German History in the Urban Landscape* (Chicago and London: U of Chicago P, 1997), 60.

[9] Anja Lösel, "In Hülle und Fülle," *Der Stern* 27 (1995).

[10] The Reichstag has attracted much attention in recent publications. On the Wrapping itself it is worth mentioning: Christo & Jeanne-Claude, *Verhüllter/Wrapped Reichstag*, Berlin, 1971–1995 (Cologne: Benedikt Taschen Verlag, 1995). This publication documents the project, serves to promote the artist and establishes a sense of drama in the accomplishment of the plans. An exhibition in 2001 in Berlin concerned with Christo's work dedicated a whole floor to the history and the performance of this event.

[11] The millennium provoked particular interest in Berlin. By contrast with other cities, the year was promoted as part of a whole process that had started with reunification in the early 1990s. A marketing magazine was introduced leading up to the event: in three editions *99.01 Der Jahrhundertschritt* listed and commented on cultural events within that period.

[12] For a critical assessment of the work of the *Stadtforum* see H. Kleger, A. Fiedler and H. Kuhle, eds., *Vom Stadtforum zum Forum der Stadt: Entwicklung und Perspektiven des Stadtforums Berlin* (Berlin, Amsterdam: Verlag Fakultas, 1996); also press comments since 1991 assembled by the office of the *Stadtforum* itself. More recently an alternative "grassroots *Stadtforum*" has been founded, concentrating on social deprivation in the city. On the restructured *Stadtforum* see: Ch. v. Lessen, "Der Glanz der Sternstunden ist erloschen," *Tagesspiegel* (24 January 1998).

[13] *Stadtforum Journal* 6 (1997).

[14] For a critical account see U. Rada, *Hauptstadt der Verdrängung: Berliner Zukunft zwischen Kiez und Metropole* (Berlin: Schwarze Risse, 1997), 10. Rada interprets it as a "Brave New World." It might be more appropriate to speak about a carefully monitored *humanisation*. The catalogue *Infobox* (Berlin: Verlag D. Nishen, 1998) provides a summary of the exhibition areas. For a representative reflection of enthusiastic ac-

counts see U. Gellermann, "Geliebte rote Kiste," *Foyer* (Sonderausgabe November 1999): 22–23.

[15] Th. Krüger, *InfoBox Berlin* (Berlin: Stadtwandel Verlag, 1999), 20.

[16] On this occasion the final six (out of 300) red panels were successfully auctioned for a charitable purpose.

[17] For example F. C. Delius, *Die Flatterzunge* (Hamburg: Rowohlt, 1999) uses the InfoBox to reflect the protagonists' state of mind and as a focus for the preferred state of change and transition: "Auf einmal fühlte ich mich glücklich da oben, auf dem Dach der InfoBox thronend über der Geschichte" (53) or: "InfoBox, mein Zufluchtsort, kein schlechter Ort für einen Selbstmord. Man muß sich vorbereiten. Ich prüfte die Aussichtsterrasse" (33).

[18] For critical press reviews of the *Schaustelle* in recent years see: "Hurra, alles Kultur," *die tageszeitung* (18 July 1999), "Regisseure inszenieren die Stadt," *die tageszeitung* (28 July 1999) or "Berlin hat fertig," *die tageszeitung* (11 July 1999).

[19] Novels that make use of the image of wounds and the healing process in the city are: C. Nooteboom, *Allerseelen* (Frankfurt am Main: Suhrkamp, 1999) and P. Schneider, *Eduards Heimkehr* (Berlin: Rowohlt 1999).

[20] *Schaustelle Berlin: Weiter geht's/moving on: das Neue Berlin entdecken* (1997), ed. Partner für Berlin Gesellschaft für Hauptstadt-Marketing mbH, 4. The English texts given are quoted from the brochures.

[21] *Schaustelle Berlin* (1998), 2.

[22] *Schaustelle Berlin* (2000), 5.

[23] English text as found on the Internet under: http://212.204.43.41/cgi-bin/schaustelle2000/intro/grusswort.html (date of access 9 January 2001). This mythical air of a city's development being staged corresponds to the critics' account of individual performances, often highlighting the impact of locations such as tunnels or a bank vestibule.

[24] D. Diederichsen, *Der lange Weg nach Mitte: Der Sound und die Stadt* (Cologne: Kiepenheuer und Witsch, 1999), 82.

[25] Again there are numerous reflections in literature. For example: Evelyn Roll, ed., *Ecke Friedrichstraße: Ansichten über Berlin* (Munich: Deutscher Taschenbuch Verlag, 1997), 12.

[26] For different interpretations and tasks of culture in Berlin in the broadest sense see: K. Siebenhaar and St. Damm, *Berlin Kultur: Identitäten, Ansichten, Leitbild* (Berlin: FAB Verlag, 1995). Currently "Berlin Kultur" and "Hauptstadt Kultur" are associated with the argument about funding in the city.

[27] For more details see: http://www.berlin.de/home/land/Bundeshauptstadt/Partner/deutsch/framesets/fs_flash_dnb.html (date of access 1 Oct. 2001).

Das Kunsthaus Tacheles:
The Berlin Architecture Debate of the
1990s in Micro-Historical Context

Janet Stewart

THROUGHOUT THE 1990S, Berlin has been a city obsessed with architectural and planning issues. Exhibitions, television, video, film,
radio, literature, newspapers and magazines have all played their role in
stimulating and feeding public debate, not merely in Berlin, nor indeed
Germany, but throughout the world.[1] There have been myriad publications on the "New Berlin," most of which focus on the reconstruction
of the Potsdamer Platz, Europe's "largest building site."[2] Architects,
architectural historians, urban planners, cultural historians, sociologists
and others have been drawn to Berlin, fascinated by the chance to experience at first hand the massive reconstruction of a European capital city
for the twenty-first century and the consequences of the dramatic events
of 1989, signified most poignantly by the fall of the Berlin Wall.[3] In
Berlin, architecture and the politics of reunification quickly became
intertwined; in a time of rapid political change, the architecture of the
new capital has come to provide reassurance of Germany's national identity and its orientation to the West.[4]

In addition to its central role in (re)defining German national identity, however, the architecture of "New Berlin" has also come to be seen
as a test case for the role and nature of architecture at the millennium
and beyond:

> For all its problems, Berlin is the world's most potent crucible of
> thought about the nature of cities. With vast expenditure of wealth, the
> richest nation in Europe has generated projects designed to knit the
> fractured metropolis together. . . . They have much to teach.[5]

The image of a "fractured metropolis" in need of "knitting together" is
entirely pertinent, since Berlin's recent architectural history is not merely
the tale of massive building programmes on vacant lots, but also involves
the renovation of large swaths of the existing city. To facilitate effective

restructuring, the *Denkmalschutzamt* undertook a huge stock-taking exercise.[6] This not only brought numerous single buildings under its protection, but also entire areas such as the Spandauer Vorstadt (bounded by the Wilhelm-Pieck-Strasse in the North, the *S-Bahn* and the Spree in the South, the Karl-Liebknecht-Strasse in the East and the Friedrichstrasse in the West).[7] Declaring the Spandauer Vorstadt a "Sanierungsgebiet," has, however, had mixed consequences: "Als Sanierungsgebiet genießt es [die Spandauer Vorstadt] besondere Förderung durch das Land Berlin. Aber damit ist auch der Wandel zum Schickimicki-Quartier eingeläutet."[8] Preservation has, paradoxically, heralded sweeping changes in this part of the city, and given rise to an ongoing debate on the nature of urbanity.

Although the vigorous architecture debate which raged in and about Berlin in the early 1990s has since abated, the original battle-lines are still in place.[9] The cover of the September 1999 issue of *Der Spiegel,* which included a forty-page special on the "New Berlin," juxtaposes two views of "New Berlin" — first, as a city experiencing an "Aufbruch zur Weltstadt" and second, as a city functioning as "Deutschlands neue alte Metropole." Simplifying the actual debate, two clear positions can be discerned. On the one hand, there is the desire to create the space of global capitalism seen in the steel and glass skyscrapers, the shopping arcades and the *Mediathek* being built on Potsdamer Platz — signs of the dawning of the "global city." On the other hand, there is the desire to create a metropolis at once new and old. "Critical reconstruction," a direction in urban planning developed in Berlin in the 1980s, sets out to ensure that new buildings in the city are designed according to existing patterns and plans, so understanding and preserving Berlin's historic identity.[10]

The work of the Italian philosopher Massimo Cacciari on the dialectic of space and place and its role in the Metropolis suggests a way to formalise the co-ordinates of the debate over architecture in Berlin.[11] In constructing an image of the Metropolis, Cacciari turns to sources gleaned from the turn of the century, exploring the work of Georg Simmel, Max Weber, Adolf Loos and others.[12] Cacciari conceives space as the "making-space that establishes places" and place as a collection of things, "the arranging-harmonizing of things." In an ideal situation, space would be "a game of a combination of places." However, in the Metropolis we find something else — the "conquest of space" by the "technico-scientific project." This process represents "the liquidation of place as a collection of things."[13] According to Cacciari, the modern architectural project, concerned with planning, possessing and dominating space, thus has as its consequence what he calls an "*Ent-ortung* of space" (166). If one looks at one of the faces of "New Berlin," the new-look Potsdamer Platz, and in particular, the DaimlerChrysler and the Sony complexes which have been built to the rhythms of global capitalism, then it is not difficult to grasp what Cacciari means by this "*Ent-ortung* of space." As Andreas Huyssen argues, the "postnationalism of global corporate architecture à la Postdamer Platz . . . has neither memory nor a sense of place."[14]

However, Cacciari's highly nuanced account of the Metropolis is sophisticated enough to warn of the dangers of turning one's back on processes of "*Ent-ortung*" only to embrace "restorative nostalgia,"[15] the pitfall of the rather positivistic form of "critical reconstruction" championed by Berlin's *Senatsbaudirektor,* Hans Stimmann, for the rebuilding of Berlin Mitte after the *Wende*.[16] If today's Potsdamer Platz is an exemplary instance of the conquest of space by global capitalism, then the painstakingly rebuilt Hotel Adlon, situated on Unter den Linden not far from the Brandenburg Gate, is a prime example of the postmodern nostalgia encouraged by "critical reconstruction." The hotel, owned by the Cologne-based investors, Fundus, was described in a recent issue of the *Architectural Review* as a "strange threat to the fabric of Berlin," which was an example of "the fungus of retro architecture."[17] Taking issue with "critical reconstruction" as a whole, Brian Ladd questions whether this style of urban planning can justifiably be claimed to be "critical," since it is based on a selective form of engagement with the past which nostalgically focuses on an idealised "golden age": Berlin as the capital of a newly united Wilhelmine Germany. By romanticising this period, "critical reconstruction" fails to engage with the misery housed in the five-storey rental blocks which sprang up in Berlin at the turn of the century. Moreover, it cannot find a place for the original eighteenth century town-houses which many of the rental blocks replaced.[18] In other words, "critical reconstruction" is a doctrine which, while highlighting certain parts of the city's architectural and, by extension, social and political history, represses and silences others. There are concerns that reconstruction based solely on (real existing) "critical reconstruction" could, just like the construction programmes embarked upon on Potsdamer Platz, actually have the effect of erasing cultural memories. In particular, the East Berlin architectural critic, Bruno Flierl, has pointed out that in rebuilding the eastern part of the city, typical markers of GDR architecture and life are being devalued and deleted.[19]

Neither the contemporary architecture of Potsdamer Platz, nor the rebuilding of other parts of the city under the restrictions of "critical reconstruction," then, seem to provide an adequate exit from the impasse of contemporary debates on urban architecture and planning. While the new-look Potsdamer Platz represents what Cacciari has termed the radical "*Ent-ortung* of space," "critical reconstruction" seems to be based on a rueful and nostalgic gaze toward a selective vision of a lost past. In "The Voids of Berlin," Andreas Huyssen sets up a similar dichotomy, maintaining that, with the notable exception of Daniel Libeskind's Jewish Museum, the architecture of "New Berlin" falls into one of two categories: either it posits the past as past and creates a traditional tourist image of the city, or it posits the present as present and creates a new corporate global culture with which to attract international attention.[20] In the former, history is reified, while in the latter, it is denied. What these positions have in common, however, is their pretence toward totalization.

Toward the end of *Architecture and Nihilism*, Cacciari reveals his philosophical counterpoint to the architectural double-bind of either "*Ent-ortung*" or nostalgia: "the spirit of fulfilment" which

> implies neither the task of effecting solution nor that of effecting the end of all solution, but the idea of composition as a listening to the differences, [it] knows that the shattered cannot ever again be relived; for this reason, it does not overcome it or subsume it but rather listens to it in its specific being-there, seeks it out in the invisibility of its be-ing-for-death.[21]

The first step toward the realisation of this creative imperative consists in the disruption of totalization through the use of strategies based on differentiation, disunity and division. While the rhetoric employed in Berlin in the 1990s was largely founded on the idea of unification, Cacci-ari's thought suggests that the interesting areas for further exploration may be those sites which resisted the dominant call to unification, whether under the banner of global capitalism or "critical reconstruction" of a specific image of Berlin. In the remainder of this essay, we will turn to a micro-historical analysis of one such site, the Kunsthaus Tacheles, which has been identified as a potent signifier of the Berlin that existed between the revolution of 1989 and reunification:

> Das bloße Haus, bar jeden Programms, steht als Zeichen für die Iden-tität des Nachwende-Berlins, für eine Zeit, als Aufbruch alles war und die Hoffnung, mit Experimenten auf ungewohnten Feldern zur Metro-pole zu werden, sogar Landespolitiker teilten.[22]

Throughout the 1990s, the Kunsthaus Tacheles represented a prominent site of resistance to dominant architectural and political discourses. From its inception, it was "ein Ort der ungelösten Widersprüche,"[23] but it was precisely the myriad contradictions and tensions upon which it was constructed that allowed the building to disrupt the pretence toward totalization sweeping the city.

The Kunsthaus Tacheles is located at the junction of the Oranienburgerstrasse with the Friedrichstrasse and includes the largest unreconstructed parcel of land remaining in Berlin Mitte.[24] Although situated only a relatively short distance from Potsdamer Platz and the Regierungsviertel, the area is rather different in character. Tacheles stands at the edge of the Spandauer Vorstadt:

> das letzte zusammenhängende Reststück des historischen Zentrums . . . ein nicht herrschaftlicher Ort, der für die Identität Berlins von kaum zu überschätzender Bedeutung ist. Dieser Ort ist genausowenig ohne Makel wie die deutsche Geschichte selbst, er zeigt wie kein anderer Teil Berlins die Wunden und Narben einer mehr als hundertjährigen Stadterneuerung.[25]

In other words, it is located in an area which still displays, rather than disguises, historical fractures in the urban landscape. It is, however, an area undergoing rapid transformation. Now home to numerous art galleries, cafes and bars, the area has played on and transcended its former neglected appearance to become a definitive location of culture.[26] Ironically, the Spandauer Vorstadt owes a debt of gratitude to the Kunsthaus Tacheles for its most recent incarnation. Together with the Hackesche Höfe, located at the other end of the Oranienburgerstrasse, the Kunsthaus Tacheles has been identified as the catalyst for the reinvention of the Spandauer Vorstadt.

The Kunsthaus Tacheles, created from the ruined shell of a building occupied by squatters in 1989, quickly became a premier location for *off-Kultur*. Echoing a pattern established in the 1970s in Kreuzberg and repeated throughout Prenzlauer Berg and parts of Berlin Mitte after the *Wende*, the building was only the second in the former East Berlin to be occupied by a group of squatters, from both the West and the East of the city. The most pressing task facing the squatters was to prevent the remainder of the building from being demolished.[27] As early as 1977, a demolition order had been served on the building which lay in the path of a planned four-lane feeder road. However, the wheels of demolition ground slowly in the GDR, and although the building's imposing glass dome was destroyed in a controlled explosion in 1981, the remainder was still standing in 1989. In July 1990, after an intense battle with the building authorities in Berlin Mitte, a preservation order was placed on the ruin, preventing any further threat of demolition.[28] Once this had been accomplished, the newly formed "Verein Tacheles e.V.," supported by Berlin Mitte's Building Department to the tune of a million marks, set about making the ruin habitable. Amongst other things, they created studios on the third and fourth floors, changed the cinema to a theatre, opened a cafe on the ground floor and renovated the Blue Salon, located directly under the roof, so that it could be used for concerts and theatre performances. The cellar housed what was, by 1993, one of Berlin's most popular underground clubs. However, while at the opposite end of the Oranienburgerstrasse, the Hackesche Höfe (also housing a cinema, theatre, cafes, and shops) were being painstakingly restored to their former glory,[29] the group that had saved Tacheles from total destruction sought to remodel the available space in order to create something new which thrived on an atmosphere of provisionality. Among the squatters who took possession of the building in the early 1990s, the credo was: "Die Ideale sind ruiniert — retten wir die Ruine!"[30]

Yet while the day-to-day running of the Kunsthaus emphasised the provisionality of the present, the past was also ever-present in the shape of the imposing facade which was almost all that remained of the original building. Since this was a facade that had been identified as a listed building, it invited historical reconstruction. Indeed, this was an important part of the stock-taking exercise embarked upon by the *Denkmalschutzamt* after reunification in 1990. A historical reconstruction of the building housing Tacheles was begun by the Museum Mitte which traced the history of the building to its origins in 1908. The results of this work were displayed in an exhibition, "Vom Warenhaus zum Kunsthaus," shown in the Museum Mitte in the summer of 1999 and still accessible in the form of a virtual exhibition.[31] In other words, reconstruction here does not refer to processes of rebuilding, but to the textual and visual documentation of the changing use of a particular building over a century characterised by socio-political turmoil. This form of reconstruction is in marked contrast to the fate of the Hackesche Höfe, which underwent a meticulous process of restoration during the early 1990s. The renovated Hackesche Höfe is itself a kind of museum piece, while in documenting change without prioritising or returning to origins, the Kunsthaus Tacheles is attempting to avoid the trap of *Musealisierung* by allowing past and present to co-exist but remain strictly separated. Moreover, not only did the Kunsthaus Tacheles avoid becoming a museum piece, it also refused to take on the role of museum; the building's history was exhibited elsewhere, not in the Kunsthaus itself.

In documenting the pre-history of the Kunsthaus Tacheles, the exhibition revealed a number of tensions associated with the building. The first of these is neatly encapsulated in the title of the exhibition itself. Its juxtaposition of "Warenhaus" and "Kunsthaus" is suggestive of a radical division between commerce and art, but the repetition of "Haus" in the title may nonetheless indicate an underlying connection between the two. By the mid-1990s, the relationship of commerce to art had become a bone of contention among those closely associated with Tacheles. Voicing the fear of many, the former chair of the *Verein Tacheles*, Jochen Sandig remarked that "Tacheles wird sein eigenes Abziehbild und droht, im Sog der Touristenströme weggespült zu werden."[32] The tension between commerce and art is, however, not unique to the building in its 1990s incarnation. In GDR times, the building was denigrated as an example of bourgeois architecture and its fabric was more or less left to rot. At the same time, however, its cinema was still in use, showing alternative art films which would not have appeared in mainstream programmes.[33] And immediately before the rise to power of the National Socialists, the building was purchased by the electric company AEG, who styled it as a "House of Technology" that would function as a permanent exhibition space for the "New Berlin" created by modernist architects such as Peter Behrens.

However, the building itself was no 1920s' rationalist creation. It was built, not as a department store (*Warenhaus*), but as an arcade, or *Passage*. The Friedrichstrassen-Passage, as it was then known, was built between 1907 and 1909 to a design by the architect, Franz Ahrens. As an arcade built toward the end of the first decade of the twentieth century, the Friedrichstrassen-Passage was in some sense a ruin before it was completed, part of the prehistory of modernity before it could assert its own modernity. It was a type of building already on the brink of extinction — indeed, it had the dubious distinction of being the last arcade built in Europe — but at the same time, in its construction, Ahrens used entirely modern technical innovations both for the structure and for the organisation of the circulation of money in the interior. The Friedrichstrassen-Passage attracted much attention in architectural journals at the time it was being built, not least for its unique steel and glass dome which, because of new technological developments, could be built larger than any other glass dome previously.[34] There was more to the ambitious nature of this project, however, including large and sumptuous exhibition spaces: the red room, the blue room and the yellow room. These were designed for a rolling exhibition of commodities. The floor plan was that of an arcade and yet the central cash system installed, using pneumatics, was more suited to the department stores which were appearing in the area in and around the Friedrichstrasse in the first decade of the twentieth century.[35] The ambivalent status of a building which did not seem to know whether it was an arcade or a department store, or whether it was meant to concentrate on selling or exhibiting commodities, meant that in its original incarnation, the venture was ultimately unsuccessful, eventually succumbing to bankruptcy in 1914.

Yet the building's typology as *Passage* did continue to exert an influence on the use of space. As one of the artists involved with Tacheles wrote in *Alltag im Chaos*, a volume documenting life in the Kunsthaus in the early 1990s:

> Eigentlich wurde Tacheles als Passage gebaut, ist immer eine geblieben und ist immer als Passage gescheitert. Die jüdischen Kaufleute sind Pleite gegangen, AEG hatte ein Kaufhaus hier — und so die sind auch rausgeflogen. Jetzt sind wir drin, und es ist nichts anders als ein Warenhaus, ein Produktions- und Warenhaus. Man kann hier versuchen, was man will. Es ist nichts anderes als 'ne Passage, ist als das gebaut, immer nur zum Ausprobieren.[36]

This view not only accentuates a sense of tension between art and commerce. It also articulates an awareness of the elegiac existence of the arcade, which is always already a ruin, tempered by a persistent hope that the next fleeting experiment might well work out. It is significant that these contradictions are expressed in terms of building typology, focusing on the form of the *Passage*. This calls to mind the work of Walter Benjamin, whose unfinished *Passagenwerk*[37] is "an encyclopaedic display of the historical potential that lies dormant in the word 'Passage.'"[38] There are two dimensions of Benjamin's work which are of particular relevance here: first, the arcade as ruin and second, the arcade as a space which facilitates the circulation of individuals through the city by providing a connection between two points.

Part of Benjamin's interest in the *Passage* stems precisely from the fact that "these monuments built by the bourgeoisie to house and display the fetishized commodities of consumer capitalism . . . rapidly became obsolete and old-fashioned."[39] *Passagen* become the "lingering remains" which provide the key to the nature of modernity; they are the architectural ruins of the dreams of the nineteenth century.[40] What is of significance for Benjamin, however, is the function that these ruins can have in the present, preventing the past from being either forgotten or petrified. And indeed, we have seen how, through its ultimately untimely appearance, the Friedrichstrasse-Passage embraced its ruin-like existence throughout the twentieth century, to function finally as a visible and tactile challenge to the seamless representation of unification found elsewhere in Berlin's "Neue Mitte."

Equally, however, the Friedrichstrassen-Passage also functioned as a space in which the boundaries between interior and the exterior are blurred, a space which connected the noise and, at times, glamour, of the Friedrichstrasse to the Oranienburgerstrasse, and a space which facilitated the circulation of individuals and commodities. In the 1990s, the Kunsthaus Tacheles has assumed a similar role, yet there is a difference here between the role of the original *Passage* and the role assumed by the Kunsthaus Tacheles in describing itself as a "bridge" connecting City and Kiez.[41] Georg Simmel, a sociologist fascinated by the study of space, argues that a bridge is a construct which, in connecting two locations, highlights their separation as the necessary precondition for their connection.[42] The Kunsthaus Tacheles, inclusive of its "sculpture garden," might still connect City and Kiez, but it does so by disrupting the easy way in which the commercial city (Friedrichstrasse) flows into the cultural sphere (Oranienburgerstrasse and beyond). In other words, there is a tension here between connection and separation. This is a tension which has been recognised by those involved in the lengthy and complex debates on the future of Tacheles. Emphasising the strategic importance of the site, Mitte's *Baustadtrat*, Thomas Flierl, has gone on record as stating that whatever is built on the empty space must both build bridges between the quarter and the city and also function as a barrier between the monotonous blocks of the critically reconstructed Friedrichstrasse and the picturesque labyrinth of the Spandauer Vorstadt.[43]

It is partly as a consequence of the strategic importance of the site occupied by Tacheles, that its redevelopment has been hotly contested. In the 1990s, the tale was not merely one of a functioning but controversial art squat, based in the ruins and living for the provisionality of the present. Since the facade was listed in 1990, there have been a number of attempts to resolve the question of Tacheles' future by planning the renovation of the facade and the redevelopment of the open space that lies behind it. It has been the site of internal and external struggles between squatters, anarchists, artists, those involved with heritage, building authorities at both national and federal level, politicians, architects, and private investors.

Although saved from destruction and modelled as a Kunsthaus in the early 1990s, Tacheles' future has always been far from certain. In the early years, financial support for renovation work and the development of a cultural programme was forthcoming from both the building authorities in Berlin Mitte for initial renovations, and from the *Kultur-Senator*, Ulrich Roloff-Momin, who devoted DM 400,000 over two

years to the Kunsthaus.[44] There had been some confusion about ownership of the site, but eventually claims from both AEG and the Jewish
Claims Conference were dropped and it passed into the hands of the
state.[45] It was then offered for sale and a number of potential investors
came forward, including the Swedish Skanska-Group, who had plans for
the development of the site drawn up by the German architects' firm,
Kleihues.[46] However, the plans submitted were not popular with the
artists and others associated directly with Tacheles, and the firm ultimately failed in its bid.[47] In January 1993, a decision was taken in the
Berlin council chamber which meant that any future investor would be
forced to guarantee the Kunsthaus Tacheles a place in their long-term
plans.[48] Around the same time, representatives of Tacheles began to
negotiate with the Cologne-based investors, Fundus, with a view to
producing a blueprint for the site's redevelopment. In 1995, Fundus
looked ready to purchase the site.

In 1995, the Architektenkammer Berlin published a detailed "interim report" on the rebuilding of the city. This volume devotes only a
short paragraph to Tacheles, in which it states that

> Die heftigen, jahrelangen Auseinandersetzungen um diesen Verkauf sind
> inzwischen abgeschlossen. Das künftige, relativ differenzierte Nut-
> zungskonzept des neuen Eigentümers, des Kölner Investment-Fonds
> Fundus, ist nicht mehr so bedrohlich wie das anderer Investoren.[49]

However, the reassuring tone adopted here functions only to conceal the
ongoing disputes about the future of the Kunsthaus Tacheles and about
the redevelopment of the site. In 1996, Fundus agreed in principle to
rent out the Kunsthaus Tacheles for a period of ten years at a symbolic
rent of $1DM/m^2$ subject to contract (in particular, Fundus was looking
for financial commitment to the Kunsthaus from the *Senatsverwaltung
für Kultur* in Berlin). The dispute dragged on, culminating in a pro-
tracted legal battle, after a court order, in the name of the Federal Republic of Germany, was served on the Kunsthaus Tacheles in April 1997,
requiring the whole site to be cleared. At the same time, internal disputes
suggested that the art squat itself was finding it difficult to adapt to the
rapid changes which had taken place in Berlin Mitte since 1989.[50] Finally,
in 1999, an agreement was reached between Tacheles and Fundus and in
summer 2000 renovation of the Kunsthaus Tacheles began. Fundus
invested DM 6.5 million to create an international modern Kunsthaus
with contact to similar ventures in Prague, Vienna, and Palermo.[51]

While Fundus was prepared to compromise on the Kunsthaus
Tacheles, it was not prepared to give any ground on the development of

the remainder of the site, over which it retained complete control.[52] So, while reconstruction of the *Kunstruine* at least appears set to be carried out in co-operation with art, commerce retains complete control over construction. This does not mean, however, that the development of the empty site behind Tacheles has been uncontroversial. Since the early 1990s, the future of this open space has been fiercely debated, with a focus on issues of public versus private space, empty versus built space, intimacy versus anonymity. Particular concerns also reflect wider issues such as the nature of urbanity and are, indeed, inextricably linked to debates on the reconstruction, or otherwise, of the "no-man's land" at Potsdamer Platz.

It should not come as a surprise that debates centred on the nature of public and private space, since the typology of the original building, as *Passage*, is predicated on a tension between public and private space, interior and exterior, since "the arcades form a transition zone between the 'outdoor' world of the street and the interior space of the home."[53] The Kunsthaus Tacheles, too, thrived on being a space simultaneously public and private, offering the interplay of anonymity and intimacy.[54] A number of blueprints had been drawn up for the redevelopment of the site, before the Fundus-Gruppe announced an architectural competition to generate new ideas for this contested urban space. The short list, when it was revealed, was nothing short of eclectic, including both Patschke (who was responsible for the Hotel Adlon) and Daniel Libeskind. Both have been regarded for years as representing the two extremes of the Berlin architecture debate. However, the choice was then whittled down to either Libeskind or Rob Krier. While Libeskind had composed a labyrinth of buildings and passageways with the motto "Jazz," Krier envisaged a shopping arcade, complete with a large hotel like the Adlon. In the end, however, neither Krier's nor Libeskind's design was chosen. Instead, the Fundus-Gruppe commissioned a Miami-based firm of architects, Duany Plater Zyberk, representatives of a movement called "New Urbanism" to draw up the final plans for redevelopment of the site.[55]

"New Urbanism" is an architectural philosophy developed in the USA which posits a return to the idealised "historical city" as a way of countering the bleak urban landscapes created from the empty homogenous space of the modernist city. As such, it signifies a movement which, according to Cacciari's philosophy of architecture, falls into the trap of nostalgia for a lost past. And what is more, the past it yearns for is an entirely imagined one — Duany Plater-Zyberk's projects include the Miami town, "Seaside," made famous as the set for the motion picture,

The Truman Show. Their plans for the Tacheles site, which include buildings that are to be up to nine storeys high and historicist facades in "amerikanischem Zuckerbäckerstil" complete with "üppiger Fensterverzierungen, Erkern und Türmchen,"[56] are likely to fall foul not only of those pushing for a brave new architectural world, but also of those committed to "critical reconstruction." Most significantly, their plan deviates from previous versions by losing any commitment to retaining a public space devoted to the cultural sphere as a counter-point to the Tacheles facade. Instead, the complex boasts two narrow courtyards and four interior courtyards.[57]

Why have the plans by Jeff Speck from Duany Plater-Zyberk been chosen? It may have been an attempt to circumvent further intense debate on the nature of architecture and urbanity in the twenty-first century which choosing either Libeskind or Krier could have caused:

> Befürchtet wird offenkundig, dass eine Libeskind-versus-Krier Debatte den mittlerweile verdrängten Architekturstreit der 90er Jahre neu entfachen und ausgerechnet im Minenfeld Tacheles zur Explosion bringen könnte.[58]

It is significant that this report recognises the potential for disruption still held by the "minefield" which is the Kunsthaus Tacheles. Its capacity to take the lid off repressed debates is connected with the numerous paradoxes which it still houses. As such, the *Kulturruine* is not only a paradigmatic signifier of the revolutionary hope of 1989, but also of the continuing tension between construction and reconstruction, art and global capitalism, public and private space, intimacy and anonymity, which characterises the contemporary urban environment. The latest reports suggest that big business is set to move into the Spandauer Vorstadt,[59] but it seems that culture, space and power may remain in tension here, preventing the fractured metropolis from being too tightly knitted together. Where art still retains the power to disrupt the seamless fiction of unification, there is perhaps the hope that, by following Cacciari and "listening to the differences,"[60] a new "New Urbanism" may be found in the twenty-first century which would give up any pretence toward totalization and offer a way out of the architectural double-bind of "*Entortung*" or nostalgia.

Notes

[1] Although these publications are too numerous to mention here, two major exhibitions in particular are of importance — first, the *InfoBox* situated in the centre of Potsdamer Platz during the period of reconstruction and second, *Berlin: Offene Stadt*, which is based on the idea of the city itself as exhibition. R. Enke et al, *Berlin: Offene Stadt. Die Stadt als Ausstellung* (Berlin: Nicolai, 1999).

[2] See, for example, B. Flierl, *Berlin baut um — Wessen Stadt wird die Stadt?* (Berlin: Verlag für Bauwesen, 1998); A. Huyssen, "The Voids of Berlin," *Critical Inquiry* 24/1 (1997): 57–81; E. Schweitzer, *Großbaustelle Berlin: Wie die Hauptstadt verplant wird* (Berlin: Nicolai, 1997).

[3] The decision to make Berlin the capital of the reunified Germany was by no means a foregone conclusion. See A. Ritchie, *Faust's Metropolis: A History of Berlin* (London: HarperCollins, 1998), 850–58.

[4] M. Mönninger, "Die politische Architektur der Hauptstadt," in T. Scheer, J. P. Kliehues and P. Kahlfeldt, *Stadt der Architektur der Stadt: Berlin 1900–2000* (Berlin: Nicolai, 2000), 397.

[5] P. Davey, "Building Berlin," *The Architectural Review* 205/1223 (January 1999): 28–30, 28. The caution expressed in this passage, however, turns into the pessimism at the hand of Andreas Huyssen who suggests that "Berlin may be the place to study how this new emphasis on the city as cultural sign, combined with its role as capital and the pressures of large-scale developments, prevents creative alternatives and thus represents a false start into the twenty-first century" (Huyssen, "Voids," 59).

[6] On the ongoing debate over the role and function of *Denkmalschutz* in Berlin see M. Kotzur, *Denkmalpflege nach dem Mauerfall: Eine Zwischenbilanz* (Berlin: Schelzky & Jeep, 1997).

[7] H. Bodenschatz et al., *Berlin auf der Suche nach dem verlorenen Zentrum* (Berlin: Junius, 1995), 181.

[8] J. Bauditz, "Aufbruch gegen Abriß. Die Bürgerinitiative Spandauer Vorstadt," in Gesellschaft Hackesche Höfe e.V., *Die Spandauer Vorstadt: Utopien und Realitäten zwischen Scheunenviertel und Friedrichstrasse* (Berlin: Argon, 1995), 47.

[9] There are a number of published collections of contributions to the debate including: A. Burg, ed., *Neue Berlinische Architektur: Eine Debatte* (Berlin: Birkhäuser, 1994); A. Balfour, ed., *Berlin* (London: Academy Editions, 1995); G. Kähler, ed., *Einfach schwierig: Eine deutsche Architekturdebatte* (Braunschweig: Viehweg, 1995).

[10] G. Kähler, "Als der Dampf sich nun erhob....," in T. Scheer, J. P. Kliehues and P. Kahlfeldt, *Stadt der Architektur der Stadt: Berlin 1900–2000* (Berlin: Nicolai, 2000), 383.

[11] M. Cacciari, *Architecture and Nihilism* (New Haven: Yale UP, 1993).

[12] The Berlin mythologised by "critical reconstruction" is precisely the pre-1914 version (see B. Ladd, *The Ghosts of Berlin* [Chicago: U of Chicago P, 1997], 231–32). It is therefore not only illuminating, but also entirely justified to use Cacciari's work on the Metropolis as a framework through which to view the contradictions and

conflicts structuring the debate on the reconstruction of Berlin at the turn of the next century.

[13] Cacciari, *Architecture and Nihilism*, 167.

[14] Huyssen, "Voids," 81.

[15] Cacciari, *Architecture and Nihilism*, 210.

[16] Kähler, "Als der Dampf," 383–84.

[17] P. Davey, "Adlon Hotel. Unter den Linden, Berlin," *Architectural Review* 205/1223 (January 1999): 25.

[18] Ladd, *Ghosts*, 108–10.

[19] Flierl, *Berlin baut um, passim*.

[20] Huyssen, "Voids," *passim*.

[21] Cacciari, *Architecture and Nihilism*, 209–10.

[22] C. Wahjudi, *Metroloops: Berliner Kulturentwürfe* (Bremen: Ullstein, 1999), 213.

[23] J. Sandig, "Tacheles. Titanic oder Arche Noah?" in Gesellschaft Hackesche Höfe e.V., *Die Spandauer Vorstadt: Utopien und Realitäten zwischen Scheunenviertel und Friedrichstrasse* (Berlin: Argon, 1995), 85.

[24] The site covers a total of 25,000m^2 (U. Clewing, "Nichts für schwache Nerven. Das Tacheles — ein Berliner Gegenmodell," *Bauwelt* 84/44 [1993]: 2389–95, 2394).

[25] Bodenschatz et al., *Berlin auf der Suche*, 184.

[26] R. Schneider, "Früher Fisch — heute Kunst," *Berliner Illustrirte Zeitung*, 5 March 2000.

[27] Clewing, "Nichts für schwache Nerven," 2389.

[28] The irony of squatters, situated officially outside the law, using regulations to achieve their aims has not escaped commentators on Berlin's architecture in the 1990s. Andreas Huyssen ("Voids," 68) demonstrates a deep scepticism about the role of squatters, dismissing their efforts in West Berlin as "leftist romanticism" which embraced a nineteenth century view of the city, that was then adopted by the city planners in the 1980s and led directly to the ideology of "critical reconstruction" paradigmatic for 1990s Berlin. Brian Ladd (*Ghosts*, 107) is rather more careful in his analysis, showing how the efforts of the squatters had ramifications for architectural and social history, altering the face of the city. Finally, however, he too draws connections between nostalgia and the efforts of the squatters in the 1970s and early 1980s.

[29] For a detailed account of the restoration of the Hackesche Höfe see Gesellschaft Hackesche Höfe, *Die Hackeschen Höfe: Geschichte und Geschichten einer Lebenswelt in der Mitte Berlins* (Berlin: Argon Verlag, 1993).

[30] A. Rost, et al., *Tacheles: Alltag im Chaos. Ein Fotobuch von Andreas Rost mit Texten von Annette Gries, Heinz Havemeister und Peter Moors* (Berlin: Elefantenpress, 1992).

[31] http://www.dhm.de/museen/berlin-mitte/einf.htm (accessed 3 March 2001).

[32] Sandig, "Tacheles," 87.

[33] http://www.dhm.de/museen/berlin-mitte/nachk.htm (accessed 3 March 2001).

[34] See K.P. Kloß and D. Ahmadi, "Einkaufszentren und Ladenzeilen," in K. K. Weber and P. Güttler, eds., *Berlin und seine Bauten: Teil VIII Bauten für Handel und Gewerbe. Bd. A Handel* (Berlin: Wilhelm Ernst und Sohn, 1978), 261–63; "Die Friedrichstrassen-Passage in Berlin," *Zeitschrift für Bauwesen* 59 (1909): 18–42.

[35] Messel's Wertheim department store on the Rosenthalerstrasse was, for example, built in 1903.

[36] M. Berg, cited in A. Rost et al., *Tacheles: Alltag im Chaos* (Berlin: Elefanten Press, 1992).

[37] W. Benjamin, *Das Passagenwerk* (Frankfurt am Main: Suhrkamp, 1982).

[38] H. Heynen, *Architecture and Modernity* (Cambridge, MA: MIT Press, 1999), 103.

[39] G. Gilloch, *Myth and Metropolis* (Cambridge: Polity, 1996), 111.

[40] Benjamin, *Passagenwerk*, 59.

[41] In an exhibition of the results of a virtual architecture competition organised by Tacheles to marshall ideas for the empty site adjacent to the building, Tacheles' position "zwischen Kiez und City" was highlighted. See: http://www.tacheles.de/archiv/1996/architektur/architektur_index.html (accessed 9 March 2000).

[42] G. Simmel, "Bridge and Door" in D. Frisby and M. Featherstone, eds., *Simmel on Culture* (London: Sage, 1997), 170–4.

[43] P. Schubert, "Neues Tacheles zwischen allen Stilen," *Berliner Morgenpost* (5 February 2000).

[44] Clewing, "Nichts für schwache Nerven," 2392.

[45] Clewing, "Nichts für schwache Nerven," 2392.

[46] Clewing, "Nichts für schwache Nerven," 2393.

[47] See Sandig, "Tacheles," *passim*; Clewing, "Nichts für schwache Nerven," *passim*. Tacheles' own web-site includes a chronology of their struggles: http://www.tacheles.de/situation/verhandlungen/chronologie.html (accessed 11 Sept. 2000).

[48] Sandig, "Tacheles," 88.

[49] Bodenschatz et al., *Berlin auf der Suche*, 182.

[50] Wahjudi, *Metroloops*, 215–7.

[51] M. Nercessian, "Auf zu Kunst und Kommerz: Die Sanierung des Tacheles hat begonnen," *Berliner Morgenpost* (25 July 2000).

[52] P. Schubert, "Neues Tacheles zwischen alten Stilen," *Berliner Morgenpost* (5 February 2000).

[53] Heynen, *Architecture*, 103.

[54] U. Rada, "Der Streit um die Bebauung der Tacheles" in *TAZ-BERLIN* (19 July 1996).

[55] P. Schubert, "Kubaner aus Florida plant Quartier am Tacheles," *Berliner Morgenpost* (24 June 2000).

[56] T. Veihelmann, "American Gemütlichkeit," *Berliner Zeitung* (30 November 2000).

[57] "Begrüntes Paradies für Stadtflaneure. Der Masterplan für das Tacheles-Areal steht," *Berliner Morgenpost* (22 November 2000).

[58] "Begrüntes Paradies für Stadtflaneure. Der Masterplan für das Tacheles-Areal steht," *Berliner Morgenpost* (22 November 2000).

[59] P. Schubert "Big Business auf der geilen Meile," *Berliner Morgenpost* (12 December 2001).

[60] Cacciari, *Architecture and Nihilism*, 209.

Normalising Cultural Memory?
The "Walser-Bubis Debate" and Martin
Walser's Novel *Ein springender Brunnen*

Kathrin Schödel

T HE CONTROVERSY WHICH FOLLOWED Martin Walser's speech on
receipt of the *Friedenspreis des deutschen Buchhandels* in the *Paulskir-che* in Frankfurt on 11 October 1998 was one of the first major debates
on practices of remembering the Third Reich and the Holocaust in
Germany after the era of Helmut Kohl (1982–1997). It was also the first
full-scale discussion among intellectuals attempting to define a new
German national identity — or resisting that aim — in what is now often
called the Berlin Republic.

In this context it is less important, perhaps, to do full justice to the
complex, self-reflexive structure of Walser's speech than to set forth the
issues contested in the course of the debate, more or less irrespective of
whether Walser actually intended to raise them or not. Key terms and
themes of the debate are thus discussed in an analysis that looks in detail
at the controversy that ensued rather than the *Friedenspreisrede* itself.[1]

Walser's speech was largely concerned with a critique of the frenzy
of media hype and political advantage-seeking that the author sees as
characteristic of the public sphere and especially of public reflections on
the Shoah. For Walser, the murder of European Jews has thus been
instrumentalised by large sections of the media and by an apparently
dominant left-liberal intelligentsia as a means of denying German national identity and maintaining the position of a cultural and political
elite.

The novel *Ein springender Brunnen*, also published in 1998, but
largely ignored in the debate, perhaps offers a clearer idea of Walser's
notion of what a *private*, that is, supposedly non-instrumentalised form
of memory might look like. A semi-autobiographical account based on
the author's childhood and youth in Wasserburg on the Bodensee between 1932 and 1945, *Ein springender Brunnen* challenges the conven-
tion that depictions of the Nazi period should focus on the Shoah and

its moral and political consequences. In metafictional comments in the novel, the narrator — most likely standing in for Walser — hence claims that he is trying to establish an aesthetic position outside of a public sphere dominated by political correctness, moral coercion and instrumentalisation. Yet can this distinction between *public* and *private* memory really be sustained? In other words, can the novel itself truly be free of the political manoeuvring Walser disparages in his speech? In fact, the novel attempts a normalisation of German history. Walser's fictional depiction of the Nazi period links the novel to the most controversial aspect of the debate: the search for a normal German national identity. This connection is explored in the final section of this chapter following a discussion of the broader debate on individual conscience and public memory initiated by the *Friedenspreisrede*.

Individual Conscience and Collective Memory

The style of the *Friedenspreis* speech is one of self-reflexive introspection, as is already suggested by the title "Erfahrungen beim Verfassen einer Sonntagsrede."[2] Walser begins with two long paragraphs which focus ironically on the problem of delivering a speech in the manner of his own "Sonntagsrede," staging the paradox of criticising public utterances within a public utterance. Many statements are qualified and clearly marked as the author's opinion, and most points are made indirectly: "Bei mir stellt sich eine unbeweisbare Ahnung ein" (11), "Könnte es sein?" (11), "[ich] bin fast froh, wenn ich glaube, entdecken zu können . . . " (12). Yet the speech is not merely a "Selbsterkundung"[3] characterised by a "vorsichtigen Sprachgebrauch" (12). Hence the headline under which it was published in the *FAZ* the day after it was delivered, "Die Banalität des Guten,"[4] immediately draws attention to its most explosive topic: Walser's criticism of the nature of public discourse on the National Socialist period.

Walser most probably employed this allusion to Hannah Arendt's famous report, *Eichmann in Jerusalem* (1963), in order to describe what he sees as the simplistic manner in which the memory of the Nazi past is (con)fused with moral exhortation (13). His adaptation of Arendt's term is also an example of the provocative style of parts of the *Friedenspreisrede* insofar as it uses a formulation describing National Socialist crimes to characterise contemporary practices of remembering. Indeed Walser's speech contains a number of arguments, and especially terms, metaphors and phrases, which are clearly intended to attack long-standing taboos regarding discussions of the Nazi period. "Wegschauen" (8), "Moralkeule" (13) and "Instrumentalisierung" (12) are the most obvious examples, and those most commented on by Walser's critics, in particular Ignatz Bubis (1927–1999), the now deceased president of the *Zentralrat der Juden in Deutschland*. It was mainly the use of these terms which caused Bubis to brand the speech as "geistige Brandstiftung."[5] Indeed "wegschauen" is associated with the behaviour of the majority of Germans during the Third Reich, a meaning that Walser appears to trivialise when he used the word to describe his own attitude toward over abundant "Filmsequenzen aus Konzentrationslagern" (11). "Moralkeule" and "Instrumentalisierung" are terms reminiscent of the attacks on the memory of the Holocaust voiced by the extreme right.

Thus Walser was accused of making socially acceptable arguments that had previously been restricted to far-right fringe groups. According to Bubis, and many others, his remarks on the instrumentalisation of the past equated to a call for an end to public remembrance of the Nazi period.[6] Walser himself later spoke of the liberating intent of his speech.[7] Bubis took this to imply a liberation from memory of the Nazi past, but most commentators — at least of those who made it into Schirrmacher's volume, *Die Walser-Bubis-Debatte* — understood the author to mean a liberation of the memory of the Nazi period from empty rituals.[8] Whatever Walser's own intentions may have been, his speech had both effects. It was applauded by the far right[9] and may well have contributed to an atmosphere in which anti-Semitic attacks became more frequent.[10] Yet, at the same time, the Walser debate was part of a search for new forms of remembering the Holocaust and National Socialism in a unified Germany which is increasingly inhabited by members of generations born after the Third Reich.

Walser's attitude of introspection in such a controversial speech on remembering the Nazi past might seem to be part of a stylistic game, but it is in fact closely tied in with the central argument of the speech: Walser's view of public memory as "Gewissensproblematik" (10). The author describes individual conscience as solely responsible for remembering the Nazi past, and demands that it should be free of external influences (13). In reactions to this notion, a perhaps unsurprising pattern can be observed. Accordingly, it is possible to isolate three types of response: emphatic disagreement, emphatic agreement, and more complex views which discuss Walser's thoughts critically without either completely dismissing or embracing them.

Those who disagreed most strongly described individual conscience as an easy place to dispose of the uncomfortable memory of the Holocaust. In an early comment on the *Friedenspreis* speech in *die tageszei-*

tung, for instance, Micha Brumlik ironically employs the euphemistic vocabulary usually applied to the disposal of nuclear waste to describe Walser's attitude to the Nazi past: "Die Auseinandersetzung mit einer nach wie vor wirksamen Vergangenheit soll dorthin entsorgt werden, wo sie endgelagert werden kann: ins individuelle Gewissen."[11] By making personal conscience responsible for memory, it is claimed, Walser is in fact demanding that a line be drawn under the past.

Emphatic agreement was expressed in many letters to the author, subsequently collated in the volume *Die Walser-Bubis-Debatte*.[12] But one of the most problematic aspects of Walser's notion of individual conscience and memory came to light most clearly in a very prominent defence of his position, that is, in Klaus von Dohnanyi's controversial contribution to the debate.[13] By taking a closer look at Dohnanyi's line of argument it can be shown that if it is primarily personal conscience that is concerned with the memory of the Nazi period, it is not only left to the individual's discretion as to how often the past should be remembered, but *what* is remembered and *how* it is remembered is also affected. Dohnanyi wrote in an article in the *FAZ*:

> Allerdings müßten sich natürlich auch die jüdischen Bürger in Deutschland fragen, ob sie sich so sehr viel tapferer als die meisten anderen Deutschen verhalten hätten, wenn nach 1933 "nur" die Behinderten, die Homosexuellen oder die Roma in die Vernichtungslager geschleppt worden wären. (148)

Apart from the tactlessness of this question, and its obvious exculpatory intentions, it is misleading in its exclusive focus on onlookers who lacked the courage to resist, but did not support the system in any way. The issue Dohnanyi is attempting to raise — life under a totalitarian regime — is, of course, vital. His approach, however, disregards the fact that it was Germans who persecuted Jews, disabled people, homosexuals, Roma, and others, and not Germans and Jews who together persecuted others.[14] Dohnanyi hence turns the reality of concrete historical events into an abstract speculation on human nature.

The Walser debate thus touches on questions of re-reading history. Different practices of remembering have an impact on the version of the past that is remembered. If personal conscience is seen as the main instrument of remembering, memory becomes merely a depoliticised and ahistorical process of self-examination.[15] Dohnanyi's remarks, as cited above, demonstrate how this might lead to an apologetic view of general human weakness. This, in turn, might preclude historical analysis and could make accounts of the past limited and distorted.

On the other hand, it is surely the case that historical facts *do* have to be seen in relation to individual behaviour. Accordingly, it has been argued that Walser's emphasis on personal conscience was especially important for young people today in that it highlighted the fact that it was individuals, rather than anonymous powers, who made decisions, acted or failed to act in the Third Reich.[16] It is indeed one of the dangers public memory faces that it might become too far removed from individual experience to allow generations born long after the historical period, in particular, to relate to events in the past. It is, therefore, necessary again and again to find new ways of involving people in acts of memory, and Walser's concept of individual conscience might be seen to be one of them. Yet there are also obvious contradictions in the notion of individual conscience. First, individual conscience is always influenced by social factors. Second, in the not so distant future everyone will have to depend on some form of contribution from public institutions and the media before the National Socialist past can become an object of their conscience.[17]

Recent theories of collective memory have, consequently, described the essential role of public, ritualised acts of memory in all societies.[18] The most prominent exponents of German *Kulturwissenschaft*, Aleida and Jan Assmann, argued during an interview on the Walser debate that "Kultur" might even be defined as "Gedächtnis." There is no social group without some form of collective memory, including stories handed down in oral or written texts, memorials, museums, and commemoration days. At the same time, individual memory is always "kulturell geformt."[19] Personal and public memory are thus interdependent. In the light of these current theories of memory, Walser's notion of a dichotomy between public ritualised memory and individual conscience might well appear as an over-simplification.

Walser comments provocatively on practices of remembering Auschwitz: "Was durch solche Ritualisierung zustande kommt, ist von der Qualität Lippengcbct." (13) Salomon Korn, amongst others, concurs with the view that public forms of memory in Germany have become all too fixed, especially official acts with their "Reden zu Gedenktagen mit ihren immergleichen Formulierungen."[20] Walser, however, expanded these thoughts in his contribution to the debate surrounding the planned national Holocaust memorial in Berlin, describing it as "einen fußballfeldgroßen Alptraum" (13), and "die Monumentalisierung der Schande" (13). He also criticises "'negativen Nationalismus'" for being no better than its opposite (13). For Walser, the memorial and other public forms of memory represent an attempt to force Germans to develop a bad conscience about their past: "In der Diskussion um das Holocaustdenkmal in Berlin kann die Nachwelt einmal nachlesen, was Leute anrichteten, die sich für das Gewissen von anderen verantwortlich fühlten" (13).

The manner in which public memory functions, however, needs to be analysed in a more differentiated way. Aleida Assmann explains in the interview quoted above:

> Ich meine, ein solches Mahnmal muß auf drei Ebenen funktionie-ren. . . . Da gibt es die politisch-symbolische Ebene. . . . Auf dieser Ebene ist das Mahnmal ein Zeichen, daß man sich in die Rechtsnach-folge des "Dritten Reiches" stellt und auch ein diplomatisches Zeichen für andere Staaten setzt. . . . Da ist . . . zweitens die gesellschaftliche Ebene. . . . Wir brauchen . . . die Erinnerung an den National-sozialismus als einen negativen Maßstab, an dem wir messen können, wie es um die deutsche Zivilgesellschaft bestellt ist. Und die dritte Ebene ist die persönliche. . . . Es muß Raum geben für die individuelle Annäherung an diese vielen, vielen Toten.[21]

It is not only Walser's demand for "Gewissensfreiheit" (14) that is prob-lematic, but his very conception of conscience as the single human faculty concerned with memory. This ignores the role of rational analysis as well as sympathy or grief, for instance — these are emotions that are not auto-matically linked to a guilty conscience. Public memory of the Nazi past is not maintained because Germans today are still, as Walser says, on the side of the "Beschuldigten" (11), but because there is a political and social responsibility, and will, to remember the Holocaust in the country that brought it about.

Yet the letters to Walser published in the volume *Die Walser-Bubis-Debatte*, with their frequent references to guilt, accusations and atonement in connection with their criticism of public memory,[22] in particular, reveal the necessity that, as the author Louis Begley writes, "wir alle lernen, zwischen Erinnerung und Schuld zu unterscheiden."[23] This cannot be achieved by focusing exclusively on the connection between conscience and memory, which neglects the need for public forms of memory. To insist, as Walser did, that public acts of remembrance simply function as an accusation, is clearly an exaggeration. Yet the author's attack on left-liberal intellectuals as self-righteous "Gewissenswart[e]" (15) who use the mem-ory of the Nazi past in order to pass judgement on others, might be taken as a challenge to rethink outdated forms of referring to the past, particu-larly those rooted in the student revolt of 1968 during which a generation born after the war confronted their parents' complicity.

Many commentators agreed with Walser that it is necessary to look at the ways in which the Nazi past is used in the present. Indeed, we might mention here the frequent references to the Holocaust during the Kosovo war six months after the Walser debate in early 1999 made by members of the SPD-Green government. The Berlin Republic had not ceased to describe itself in relation to the Nazi past, but Auschwitz was now used to justify the first participation of the German *Bundeswehr* in military action, which dissolves the traditional connection between anti-fascism and pacifism in left-liberal views. In this context, in an article warning of the dangers of comparing Serbia with Nazi Germany, Frank Schirrmacher approvingly quoted Walser's criticism of the instrumentalisation of Auschwitz.[24]

Walser's condemnation of the use of Auschwitz in public discourse is, however, narrower in its focus: he concentrates on the notion that negative historical reflection could be harmful to German identity. For this reason he appears to condemn any use of history for "gegenwärtige Zwecke" (12). From a theoretical point of view, it has been shown that public memory is always established or maintained because it serves a purpose in the present.[25] At the same time, it is indispensable for modern democratic societies to reflect on the content, forms and functions of their collective memories, on the way in which they construct and appropriate collective histories, that is, to reflect on how they instrumentalise the past.

Ignatz Bubis was outraged because he misinterpreted Walser's criticism of instrumentalisation as directed against the claims for financial compensation lodged by former forced labourers.[26] Walser's speech does not in fact refer to those issues, as he later confirmed.[27] The "gegenwärtige Zwecke" he talks about are related to the Third Reich in a much less direct way. But Walser's language was vague enough to encourage such misreadings at a time when discussions about the forced labourers were topical. Bubis's misunderstanding is in fact indicative of an important aspect of the Walser debate. On the one hand, the beginning of the Berlin Republic, with a government dominated by politicians who grew up after 1945, was often described as a watershed in a now united Germany's relationship to its Nazi past. Equally, the preponderance of people born after the Nazi period in present-day Germany was also frequently stressed. On the other hand, the debate took place when many survivors of the Holocaust were still alive, and it was almost exclusively conducted by members of Walser's generation, born in the late 1920s, the so-called *Flakhelfer Generation*, that is, the last generation that had an active involvement in the Third Reich. The fact that the Nazi past was still connected to their own experience meant that the tone of the debate often became very personal, perhaps sometimes to the detriment of the quality of the arguments.[28] This personal dimension, in fact, may have been the starting point for Walser's attack on instrumentalisation: criticism of his literary works, especially *Ein springender Brunnen*, which denounced them for either not stressing the Holocaust enough or not mentioning it at all (12).

The Normalisation of Memory and National Identity

Walser's primary example of the instrumentalisation of the past is the warning from many on the left, most prominently Günter Grass, that a unified Germany might make possible a new Auschwitz (12). Walser not only criticises such generalising and undifferentiated arguments, but also insists that the memory of the Holocaust is used in a way that makes it impossible to refer to the Germans of today as "ein normales Volk, eine gewöhnliche Gesellschaft" (13). The author does not specify what he means by "normal," but his speech makes clear what he thinks it is that prevents Germany from defining itself and being perceived as a normal country: media representations of concentration camps and ritualised public acts of commemorating the Holocaust. He focuses specifically on the planned Holocaust memorial in Berlin, the depiction of racist attacks in Germany today (10–11), and on the negative nationalism of both left-wing intellectuals and left-wing media (13).

In the public discourse on remembering the Nazi period and on present-day German identity the term normal has distinct overtones. It was one of the central terms in the 1980s *Historikerstreit* and was used in connection with attempts to historicise National Socialism. During this debate, *Historisierung* was taken to mean the attempt to shift the focus of historiography away from the central Nazi crime, the extermination of the Jews of Europe, towards the normality of every-day life in Germany. As a result, it was argued, the Nazi period would be incorporated into a normal historical narrative and become simply another historical period. The foregrounding of the abnormal monstrosity of its crimes would thereby cease.[29] Saul Friedländer, the most strident critic of such positions in the *Historikerstreit*, warns that this form of historicisation would result in one-sided exculpatory accounts of German history.[30]

In Walser's speech and during the Walser debate normality was principally discussed with regard to Germany today and the ways in which it commemorates the past, rather than the past itself. Since the controversy surrounding Botho Strauß's "Anschwellender Bocksgesang" (1993) and the so-called New Right the term has been primarily associated with the definition of a unified Germany as a normal nation with a new sense of self-confidence.[31]

Walser's criticism of the "Gewissenswart" (15) is very similar to Strauß's attack of the "Gewissenswächter,"[32] both aimed at left-liberal intellectuals in Germany. Nowadays, however, perhaps ironically after the election of an SPD-Green government in 1998, the search for a new positive national identity is no longer restricted to the right of the political spectrum. The call for normality in Germany no longer necessarily equates to reactionary views.[33] Walser's construction of an intellectual discourse dominated by references to Auschwitz and negative depictions of Germany, and Austria (11), therefore, does not quite reflect the current situation, and it is no surprise that he had to resort to a quote from more than fifteen years before to demonstrate his point.[34] At the same time, it does not seem appropriate to class Walser as a proponent of the New Right, even though parallels can be drawn.[35] The Walser debate, therefore, cannot easily be described in the traditional categories of left and right.[36]

Among left-liberal intellectuals, an anti-national stance based on arguments using Auschwitz, which had turned into an almost automatic reaction, is now being called into question. A more positive attitude towards patriotism and *Heimat* can be found, for instance, in the *Kursbuch* 141, *Das gelobte Land*, published in September 2000.[37] These topics are now approached with fewer preconceptions. Although this is not an entirely new development even among Germany's left, it now seems to be more widely accepted. At the same time, negative German self-images are coming under scrutiny as being a form of national identity in themselves, rather than being the opposite of nationalism.[38] The traditional left-wing view, voiced most recently by Günter Grass, whom Walser quotes in his speech, that German division was a just punishment for the crimes committed by the German nation, and that Germany should never become one nation again, is generally being rethought.[39] Foreign commentators in particular have also agreed that Germany today is normal in the sense of no longer having to prove that it is a functioning democratic state much like other European countries.[40] Yet is a form of normality desirable that involves, as Stuart Taberner writes, "the same unpleasantly chauvinistic nationalism that has been prevalent in countries such as England and France"?[41] And should we indeed accept racist attacks as normal as Walser seems to suggest (10–11)?

Many commentators have pointed out the paradox of normality[42] — the more normality is talked about the less it is actually present because, obviously, what is normal is precisely that which does not need to be talked about at length. Such a paradoxical discussion of the normal might, however, be a first step towards what Jan-Holger Kirsch in his essay on the Walser debate calls reflexive normality: "eine *reflexive Normalität*, bei der gewisse gesellschaftliche Übereinkünfte als feste Basis gelten, die aber der Diskussion ausgesetzt bleibt und dabei auf konkrete Wertideen bezogen wird."[43] In the Walser debate it was Ignatz Bubis, but also, for instance, Thomas Assheuer and Moshe Zuckermann, who questioned normality and related it to concrete values. Zuckermann thus asked: "Zu fragen wäre freilich, was heißt es eigentlich, ein 'normales Volk' in einer Welt zu sein, in der 'das Normale' zum Argument derer geworden ist, die ihre Macht und objektive Stärke den Erniedrigten und Beleidigten dieser Erde gegenüber gewahrt wissen wollen."[44] Bubis and Assheuer focus on the question of the relation of a normal Germany to its past.[45] Assheuer claims that Walser "unternahm den polemischen Versuch, das kulturelle Gedächtnis der nationalstaatlichen Normalität [of a unified Germany — K.S.] anzupassen." (134) In his speech Walser does not make any concrete suggestions as to what a normal way of relating to Germany's past might be, but he had, of course, published his own contribution to German cultural memory a few months previously, that is, his autobiographical novel, *Ein springender Brunnen*.

Ein springender Brunnen

In his *Friedenspreisrede* Walser describes literature as situated outside the sphere of *Meinung* and political machinations he criticises. Similarly, in the metafictional passages in *Ein springender Brunnen* the narrator expresses what he calls a "Wunschdenkens Ziel: Ein interesseloses Interesse an der Vergangenheit,"[46] that is, a form of memory in art that is not dominated by present interests — moral, political, didactic or self-justificatory.[47] In order to achieve such a relation to the past Walser tries to free himself of all later judgements about the time of his childhood and youth, and attempts to recreate the perspective that would have been most natural to the boy at the time. Walser succeeds in showing, rather than explaining, the various ways in which National Socialism penetrated the life of a young boy in a small town as well as how he was immune to some of its ideological manipulations. In the protagonist and his family, Walser depicts what it means to live within a historical period apparently in ignorance of what would later be seen as the defining events of that period, and without knowing how it would end.

The narrative is, however, by no means free of present aims. The paradoxical "interesseloses Interesse an der Vergangenheit" can only be "Wunschdenkens Ziel." Every approach to the past is influenced by present moods (see *SB*, 281), and the interest which prompted it. Firstly, there is the perfectly understandable wish to preserve personal, in parts idyllic, childhood memories despite the shock of the later realisation of what took place at the same time. Yet this is embedded in a more general aim: Walser fulfils in fiction what was demanded by conservatives for historiography in the *Historikerstreit*. Historicising the Nazi period meant depicting it not solely by describing the social and political developments that led to World War II and the mass exterminations, but by showing what is supposed to be German *Alltagsgeschichte*, the lives of ordinary people during the period without applying pre-established moral categories. This allows new perspectives on different degrees of involvement and suffering in social groups that were neither the direct victims of Nazi crimes nor their perpetrators. In *Ein springender Brunnen*, therefore, characters are shown in their different relations to National Socialism. There are active members of the *NSDAP* as well as, for example, a clown who criticises the regime in a circus performance. With the death of the protagonist's older brother in the war, suffering in an ordinary German family is depicted. Yet, the main character's childhood is in large part described without reference to the historical period in which it takes place. Such an emphasis on the normality of life under Hitler, in historiography or fiction, can serve a specific purpose. It can provide a version of the German past that allows a normal German identity in the present that is not based on having to come to terms with the catastrophic and criminal developments in German history, but can draw on the continuity of normal life. The main objection to a re-reading of this kind is that it might entail a distorting relativisation of the Holocaust and generate dangerously apologetic attitudes towards "Mitläufertum" and "Wegschauen."

As Walser pointed out in his defence, the conscious limitation to one perspective — "Perspektivität" (*WBD*, 12) — is a common literary device. But that does not mean that the effects of this narrative form in Walser's novel should not be analysed. The chapter "Der Eintritt der Mutter in die Partei" tells how Johann's mother came to decide to become a member of the National Socialist Party. Because Johann's family is in financial difficulties his mother wants the "Parteiversammlungen" to be held in the family restaurant (*SB*, 91). This may certainly have been the reason for Walser's mother to join the party, and it is an interesting example of the way such decisions may often have been taken without considering anything other than the well-being of oneself and one's family. But the scene invites generalisations along the lines of what Walser once said about his project for a novel entitled "Der Eintritt meiner Mutter in die Partei": "Wenn es ihm [Walser] zu erzählen gelänge . . . warum die streng katholische Mutter, keineswegs eine Nationalsozialistin, einst in die Partei eingetreten sei — 'dann hätte ich die Illusion, ich hätte erzählt, warum Deutschland in die Partei eingetreten ist.'"[48] In this way, a view of the Nazi past might be encouraged that concentrates on those who adapted to the regime without believing in it at all. While this aspect should not be neglected, it would be falsifying if it replaced one of the most important, and shocking, elements of the memory of the Third Reich today: the images and accounts of wide spread enthusiasm for Hitler.

In the protagonist, Walser also defends postwar "Wegschauen" from the crimes that came to light. It may be true that after 1945 it would have been unbearable to live on in Germany without sometimes "thinking away" (*SB*, 401). A sudden full realisation of what had happened, of the barbaric crimes the whole country had been complicit in, would have been impossible. But the thrust of Walser's depiction of that attitude is somewhat different. Although Auschwitz itself is not mentioned in the novel, which was criticised in "Das literarische Quartett,"[49] Walser does not completely leave out all references to the persecution of the Jews. Johann's Jewish friend Wolfgang starts talking about his family's situation (*SB*, 397), but Johann decides that he does not want anything to do with the fear with which the Jews in his village were forced to live (*SB*, 400, 401). In order to be free, Johann believes he has to be free of their fear and their possible accusations. The victims thus appear as a threat to the protagonist's freedom. Johann does not say he has to free himself of his own past involvement with the Nazi regime, or of the reality of the crimes that were committed, but of the victims' memories. Accordingly, the ending of *Ein springender Brunnen* touches on what was the most sensitive issue in the Walser debate: if a normal German identity is to be constructed through a normalisation of history, what happens to the memory of the victims?

Both *Ein springender Brunnen* and the Walser-Bubis debate showed how the attempt to normalise German national identity might involve a turning-away from the victims and their descendants, above all German Jews. The issue of German-Jewish relations is, quite understandably, still very sensitive, and the most damaging accusation levelled against Walser and others was that of being anti-Semitic.[50] Blatantly anti-Semitic clichés appeared in very few of the contributions to the debate published in the major newspapers and magazines.[51] It was usually more subtle forms of exclusion that can be seen as discriminatory, and the line between important differentiations and discrimination proved to be very thin.

Both non-Jewish and Jewish Germans welcomed the fact that Walser's speech and Bubis's reaction to it destroyed the illusion of a single

German "Gedächtniskultur."[52] Salomon Korn in the *FAZ* argues that in acts of commemoration a "Jargon der Betroffenheit"[53] is used, which ultimately serves to avoid looking for "die unbequeme Wahrheit" (306), and glosses over the issue of the different interests in remembering on the side of the victims' and the perpetrators' descendants. He suggests that the Walser debate might have been "ein schmerzlicher, aber notwendiger Umweg" (307) towards mutual understanding and an open dialogue between these groups. Taking an even more positive view on the debate, the German-Jewish author Rafael Seligmann writes in *Die Welt:* "Auf diese Weise lebt der deutsch-jüdische Dialog wieder auf. Ein Ende des Streits zu verlangen, wäre kontraproduktiv."[54]

Some attempts at defining German and Jewish approaches to remembering, nevertheless, may themselves have been counter-productive, in that they may have cemented clichéd images rather than established a dialogue. Although cultural differences should not be ignored,[55] the contrast between two forms of memory that Manfred Fuhrmann outlines in "Jüdisches Gedenken. Eine Nachbetrachtung zur Debatte Walser-Bubis," for instance, appears to suggest that there is an opposition between Walser's supposedly modern concept of memory — "Walsers moderner, ethisch fundierter und an das Individuum gebundener Erinnerungsbegriff" — and an archaic, mythical form of Jewish memory — "die jüdische, in die Religion und in den Kult eingebundene Tradition des Gedenkens."[56] It is certainly useful to reflect on the cultural and biographical background of the opponents in the debate, especially in order to understand some of the more personal and also the more insulting contributions and how they were received. Yet Bubis's criticism should not be explained away by relating it to a different concept of memory, and one which is seen as less advanced as Walser's. Collective memory is important in the Jewish religion, but it is also a constituent part of every social group, as Fuhrmann himself stresses in the same article (*WBD*, 665).

Far more openly discriminatory than Fuhrmann's remarks is a line of argument that blames Jews and their insistence on remembering for the appearance of anti-Semitism, identifying the victims of racial hatred as its cause, and consequently expecting them to change rather than those with racist views.[57] Rafael Seligmann, on the other hand, interpreted Bubis's outspoken criticism of Walser as an escape from that logic, which had forced German Jews to act as "Musterjuden," who stay quiet about their own feelings in fear of an upsurge of anti-Semitism (*WBD*, 199).

Walser's speech and his novel could similarly be seen as examples of a new honesty about the feelings of non-Jewish Germans. But Walser's construction of German identity goes beyond merely being more open to individual memories that differ from the official version of the past, and even beyond establishing a positive national identity. Although the author criticises public acts of memory for encouraging the illusion of being "für einen Augenblick . . . näher bei den Opfern als bei den Tätern" (11), he develops his own version of German victimhood. With metaphors such as "Gewissenswart" (15), "Meinungssoldaten" (15), he draws a parallel between Nazi terror and the call for remembrance today, thus himself instrumentalising the past. Johann, in *Ein springender Brunnen*, likewise compares the National Socialist regime and the victims' fear: "Er wollte nie mehr unterworfen sein, weder einer Macht noch einer Angst" (*SB*, 402). Both, National Socialism and the requirement to remember it, thus appear as outside forces subjugating Germans. Such a concept of German identity is based on a one-sided, falsified version of history, as well as being in danger of creating anti-Jewish resentment and defining Germanness above all in opposition to, and indeed as threatened by, the victims of the Third Reich. It is to be hoped that a normal democratic society can exist without a national identity of this kind.

Notes

[1] For a detailed chronological account of the Walser debate see Wilfried Scharf and Martina Thiele, "Die publizistische Kontroverse über Martin Walsers Friedenspreisrede," *Deutsche Studien* 36 (1999): 147–209.

[2] Martin Walser, "Erfahrungen beim Verfassen einer Sonntagsrede," in Frank Schirrmacher, ed., *Die Walser-Bubis-Debatte. Eine Dokumentation.* (Frankfurt am Main: Suhrkamp, 1999), 7–17. (Further references to this volume appear as *WBD*).

[3] Martin Walser, "Wovon zeugt die Schande, wenn nicht von Verbrechen. Das Gewissen ist die innere Einsamkeit mit sich: Ein Zwischenruf" (*Frankfurter Allgemeine Zeitung* (28 November 1998), *WBD*, 252–260, 252.

[4] Martin Walser, "Die Banalität des Guten. Erfahrungen beim Verfassen einer Sonntagsrede aus Anlaß der Verleihung des Friedenspreises des deutschen Buchhandels," *Frankfurter Allgemeine Zeitung* (12 October 1998): 15.

[5] "Geistige Brandstiftung. Bubis wendet sich gegen Walser" (dpa/*Frankfurter Allgemeine Zeitung* [13 October 1998]), *WBD*, 34–35.

[6] Micha Brumlik, "Vom Alptraum nationalen Glücks" (*taz* [15 October 1998]), *WBD*, 49–51, 49; Klaus Harpprecht, "Wen meint Walser?" (*Die Zeit* [15 October 1998]), *WBD*, 51–53, 52; Eva Demski, "Martin Walsers Neubiedermeier. Leserbrief" (*Frankfurter Allgemeine Zeitung* [16 October 1998]), *WBD*, 54.

[7] Martin Walser, "Wovon zeugt die Schande, wenn nicht von Verbrechen. Das Gewissen ist die innere Einsamkeit mit sich: Ein Zwischenruf" (*Frankfurter Allgemeine Zeitung* [28 November 1998]), *WBD*, 252–260, 259.

[8] See among others: Siegfried Unseld, "Brief an Ignatz Bubis" (13 Oct. 1998), *WBD*, 36–37, 37; Michael Wolffsohn, "'Von Brandstiftung kann keine Rede sein.' Geschichte als Falle: Bubis, Walser und die jüdische Welt" (*Frankfurter Allgemeine Zeitung* [18 October 1998]), *WBD*, 61–64, 62; Jörg Magenau, "An der Kranzab-wurf-Stelle. Zum Streit über Martin Walsers Friedenspreis-Rede" (*Appenzeller Zeitung* [27 Oct. 1998]), *WBD*, 87–88, 87; Andrea Köhler, "Entschädigung oder Absolution? Die Erinnerung ist nicht teilbar — die Walser-Debatte" (*Neue Zürcher Zeitung* [5 Dec. 1998]), *WBD*, 343–347, 343; Daniele Dell'Agli, "Zwischen einander" (*taz* [5 Dec 1998]), *WBD*, 350–359, 351–352; Günter de Bruyn, "Diese Debatte wird auch noch weitergehen, wenn wir nicht mehr sind" (*Frankfurter Allgemeine Zeitung* [7 December 1998]), *WBD*, 366–369, 367; Frank Schirrmacher, "Ein Gespräch" (*Frankfurter Allgemeine Zeitung* [14 December 1998]), *WBD*, 436–438, 437.

[9] See Martin Dietzsch et al., eds., *Endlich ein normales Volk? Vom rechten Verständnis der Friedenspreis-Rede Martin Walsers. Eine Dokumentation.* (Duisburg: Diss., 1999).

[10] Most obviously related to the debate was an incident with a pig with Bubis's name written on it that was brought into *Alexanderplatz* in Berlin. See on this and other incidents: Jan-Holger Kirsch, "Identität durch Normalität. Der Konflikt um Martin Walsers Friedenspreisrede," *Leviathan* 27 (1999): 309–354, 340, with further references.

[11] Micha Brumlik, "Vom Alptraum nationalen Glücks" (*taz* [15 October 1998]), *WBD*, 49–51, 49; see also Robert Leicht, "Warum Walser irrt. Auch die Nachgeborenen haften für das Erbe von Auschwitz" (*Die Zeit* [3 December 1998]), *WBD*, 327–329, 327.

[12] Walser stresses this in the talk with Bubis that Frank Schirrmacher arranged: Ignatz Bubis, Salomon Korn, Frank Schirrmacher, Martin Walser, "Wir brauchen eine neue Sprache für die Erinnerung. Ein Gespräch" (*Frankfurter Allgemeine Zeitung* [14 December 1998]), *WBD*, 438–465, 455. Examples of such letters can be found in *WBD*, 33, 41–42, 83, 103.

[13] Klaus von Dohnanyi, "Eine Friedensrede. Walsers notwendige Klage" (*Frankfurter Allgemeine Zeitung* [14 November 1998]), *WBD*, 146–150.

[14] See for a detailed critique of Dohnanyi's remark: Jan Philipp Reemtsma, "Worüber zu reden ist" (*Frankfurter Allgemeine Zeitung* [26 November 1998]), *WBD*, 227–229.

[15] Klaus von Dohnanyi, "Jeder prüfe sein Gewissen. Eine Antwort auf Ignatz Bubis und Jan Philipp Reemtsma" (*Frankfurter Allgemeine Zeitung* [30 November 1998]), *WBD*, 282–285, 282.

[16] Volker Schulte, "Erfahrungen jenseits des Lehrplans. Leserbrief" (*Frankfurter Allgemeine Zeitung* [26 November 1998]), *WDB*, 240.

[17] Walser conceded in the talk with Bubis: "Ich habe vielleicht zu wenig deutlich gemacht, daß es öffentliche Erinnerungspflege geben soll" (*WBD*, 446).

[18] Jan Assmann, *Das kulturelle Gedächtnis. Schrift, Erinnerung und politische Identität in frühen Hochkulturen.* (Munich: C. H. Beck, 1992); Aleida Assmann, *Erinnerungs-räume. Formen und Wandlungen des kulturellen Gedächtnisses.* (Munich: C. H. Beck, 1999); and with reference to the Walser debate: Aleida Assmann in: Aleida Assmann and Ute Frevert, *Geschichtsvergessenheit — Geschichtsversessenheit. Vom Umgang mit deutschen Vergangenheiten nach 1945.* (Stuttgart: Deutsche Verlags-Anstalt, 1999), 79–80.

[19] "Niemand lebt im Augenblick. Ein Gespräch mit den Kulturwissenschaftlern Aleida und Jan Assmann über deutsche Geschichte, deutsches Gedenken und den Streit um Martin Walser," *Die Zeit* (3 December 1998): 43.

[20] Salomon Korn, "'Es kommt darauf an, wie man Rituale mit Leben erfüllt'. Interview" (*Frankfuter Rundschau* [11 December 1998]), *WBD*, 403–406, 404.

[21] "Niemand lebt im Augenblick. Ein Gespräch mit den Kulturwissenschaftlern Aleida und Jan Assmann über deutsche Geschichte, deutsches Gedenken und den Streit um Martin Walser," *Die Zeit* (3 Dec. 1998): 43.

[22] See *WBD*, 42, 93, 171, 172, 431, 468, 480, 512, 514, 554.

[23] Louis Begley, "Die Gräber sind noch immer offen" (*Die Zeit* [22 December 1998]), *WBD*, 521–523, 523. See also William Niven, *Facing the Nazi Past: United Germany and the Legacy of the Third Reich* (London and New York: Routledge, 2001), chapter 7. Niven, to whom I am very grateful for letting me read this text before its publication, makes a similar point on "the existence of an irrational sense of guilt in many youngsters."

[24] Frank Schirrmacher, "Luftkampf. Deutschlands Anteil am Krieg," *Frankfurter Allgemeine Zeitung* (14 April 1999): 41.

[25] "Niemand lebt im Augenblick. Ein Gespräch mit den Kulturwissenschaftlern Aleida und Jan Assmann über deutsche Geschichte, deutsches Gedenken und den Streit um Martin Walser," *Die Zeit* (3 December 1998). See also Moshe Zuckermann, "Von Erinnerungsnot und Ideologie. Warum Martin Walsers Rede keine geistige Brand-stiftung ist, sondern nur Ausdruck des Zeitgeists" (*Der Tagespiegel* [28 November 1998]), *WBD*, 263–268, 265–266.

[26] Bubis in the talk with Walser, *WBD*, 438–465, 438–439.

[27] Walser 444.

[28] See, for example, Klaus von Dohnanyi, "Wir sind alle verletzbar" (*Frankfurter Allgemeine Zeitung* [17 November 1998]), *WBD*, 164; Klaus von Dohnanyi, "Schuld oder Schulden? Ignatz Bubis' unerhörtes Interview" (*Frankfurter Allgemei-ne Zeitung* [30 November 1998]), *WBD*, 278–281.

[29] For a differentiated analysis of "normalisation" and "historicisation" see: Nicolas Berg, "'Auschwitz' und die Geschichtswissenschaft — Überlegungen zu Kontrover-sen der letzten Jahre," in Nicolas Berg et al., eds., *Shoah. Formen der Erinnerung. Geschichte, Philosophie, Literatur, Kunst.* (Munich: Fink, 1996), 31–52, 38–42.

[30] Saul Friedländer, *Memory, History, and the Extermination of the Jews of Europe.* (Bloomington, IN: Indiana UP, 1993), 64–84.

[31] Heimo Schwilk and Ulrich Schacht write in the introduction to *Die selbstbewusste Nation*: "Normalität, also selbstbewußte Nation" (Heimo Schwilk/Ulrich Schacht,

eds., *Die selbstbewusste Nation: "Anschwellender Bocksgesang" und weitere Beiträge zu einer deutschen Debatte.* [Frankfurt am Main, Berlin: Ullstein, 1994], 12).

[32] Botho Strauß, "Anschwellender Bocksgesang," 19–40, 25.

[33] Patrick Bahners, "Total normal. Vorsicht Falle: Die unbefangene Nation" (*Frankfurter Allgemeine Zeitung* [3 November 1998]), *WBD*, 99–101, 100.

[34] Walser quotes Thomas Bernhard as "ein . . . bedeutender Dichter" (10) with his negative view of Salzburg with people dreaming of "Ausrottung und Gaskammern" (10); the quote comes from an interview with Bernhard in 1983: Jean-Louis de Rambures, "Alle Menschen sind Monster, sobald sie ihren Panzer lüften," in Sepp Dreissinger, ed., *Von einer Katastrophe in die andere. 13 Gespräche mit Thomas Bernhard.* (Weitra: Bibliothek der Provinz, 1992), 104–113, 111.

[35] For Walser and the "New Right" see: Stuart Taberner, "A Manifesto for Germany's 'New Right'?: Martin Walser, The Past, Transcendence, Aesthetics, and *Ein springender Brunnen*," *German Life and Letters* 53 (2000): 126–141.

[36] The most prominent example is Klaus von Dohnanyi, former SPD mayor of Hamburg, defending Walser.

[37] See, for instance, Hans Magnus Enzensberger, "Ach Deutschland! Eine patriotische Kleinigkeit," in *Das gelobte Land. Kursbuch* 141 (2000): 1–4.

[38] See Daniele Dell'Agli, "Zwischen einander" (*taz* [5 December 1998]), *WBD*, 350–359, 356; Aleida Assmann, in Aleida Assmann and Ute Frevert, *Geschichtsvergessenheit — Geschichtsversessenheit. Vom Umgang mit deutschen Vergangenheiten nach 1945.* (Stuttgart: Deutsche Verlags-Anstalt, 1999), 66–67.

[39] See Aleida Assmann 64.

[40] For instance, Avi Primor, "Der Fleck auf dem Rock. Keine Frage der Schuld, sondern der Verantwortung — meine Antwort an Walser" (*Frankfurter Allgemeine Zeitung* [9 Dec. 1998]), *WBD*, 381–383, 383.

[41] Stuart Taberner, "'Wie schön wäre Deutschland, wenn man sich noch als Deutscher fühlen und mit Stolz als Deutscher fühlen könnte': Martin Walser's Reception of Victor Klemperer's *Tagebücher 1933–1945* in *Das Prinzip Genauigkeit und Die Verteidigung der Kindheit*," *Deutsche Vierteljahrsschrift für Literaturwissenschaft und Geistesgeschichte* 73 (1999): 710–732, 732.

[42] Patrick Bahners, "Total normal. Vorsicht Falle: Die unbefangene Nation" (*Frankfurter Allgemeine Zeitung* [3 November 1998]), *WBD*, 99–101, 99; see also: Paul Scheffer, "Das Mißtrauenskapital schwindet. Die Walser-Bubis-Kontroverse zeigt, daß die Zeit der Vormundschaft über Deutschland vorbei ist" (*Frankfurter Allgemeine Zeitung* [12 December 1998]), *WBD*, 411–418, 411; Michael Mertes, "Schamschwellen beginnen zu sinken" (*Rheinischer Merkur* [18 December 1998]), *WBD*, 506–508, 507.

[43] Jan-Holger Kirsch, "Identität durch Normalität. Der Konflikt um Martin Walsers Friedenspreisrede," *Leviathan* 27 (1999): 309–354, 349.

[44] Moshe Zuckermann, "Von Erinnerungsnot und Ideologie. Warum Martin Walsers Rede keine geistige Brandstiftung ist, sondern nur Ausdruck des Zeitgeists" (*Der Tagespiegel* [28 November 1998]), *WBD*, 263–268, 267.

[45] Ignatz Bubis, "Rede des Präsidenten des Zentralrates der Juden in Deutschland am 9. November 1998 in der Synagoge Rykerstraße in Berlin" (9 November 1998), *WBD*, 106–113, 112; Thomas Assheuer, "Ein normaler Staat?" (*Die Zeit* [12 December 1998]), *WBD*, 134–138, 134–136.

[46] Martin Walser, *Ein springender Brunnen*. (Frankfurt am Main: Suhrkamp, 1998), 283. Further references to the novel appear as *SB*.

[47] Walser's aesthetics corresponds to the criticism of "Gesinnungsästhetik," that is, aesthetics governed by convictions rather than its own inherent laws, voiced in another debate in Germany after the unification, the "Literaturstreit." See Stuart Taberner, "A Manifesto for Germany's 'New Right'?: Martin Walser, The Past, Transcendence, Aesthetics, and *Ein springender Brunnen*," 127–128.

[48] Volker Hage, "Königssohn von Wasserburg," *Der Spiegel* 31 (27 July 1998): 148–150, 149.

[49] For a summary and extensive quotes from the programme see Jochen Hieber, "Unversöhnte Lebensläufe. Zur Rhetorik der Verletzung in der Walser-Bubis-Debatte," in Michael Braun et al., eds., *"Hinauf und Zurück/in die herzhelle Zukunft": Deutschjüdische Literatur im 20. Jahrhundert. Festschrift für Birgit Lermen* (Bonn: Bouvier, 2000), 543–559, 544–547.

[50] See "'Moral verjährt nicht'. Ignatz Bubis über die Auschwitz-Debatte und seine Auseinandersetzung mit Martin Walser und Klaus von Dohnanyi," *Der Spiegel* 49 (1998): 50–54, 52 regarding the imminent publication of Walser's *Der Tod eines Kritikers*, which Frank Schirrmacher, Walser's erstwhile champion at the *FAZ*, had dismissed as anti-semitic.

[51] Augstein's reference to Bubis as "Frankfurter Baulöwe," and his suggestion that Bubis might be too "befangen" to be concerned with planning a national Holocaust memorial, and that his involvement might cause sentiments against the "Weltjudentum" as "eine jroße [*sic!*] Macht" (Augstein is quoting Adenauer), are examples of the more direct forms of anti-Semitism in the debate (Rudolf Augstein, "'Wir sind alle verletzbar'" (*Der Spiegel* [30 November 1998]), *WBD*, 283–289, 286 and 287).

[52] Ulrich Raulff, "Das geteilte Gedächtnis. Ignatz Bubis attackiert Martin Walser" (*Frankfurter Allgemeine Zeitung* [10 November 1998]), *WBD*, 122–124, 123.

[53] Salomon Korn, "Es ist Zeit. Die andere Seite des Walser-Bubis-Streits" (*Frankfurter Allgemeine Zeitung* [1 December 1998]), *WBD*, 304–307, 306.

[54] Rafael Seligmann, "Endlich streiten wir uns. Walser contra Bubis: Der deutschjüdische Dialog befreit sich aus dem Angstghetto" (*Die Welt* [2 November 1998]), *WBD*, 198–200, 199.

[55] See Amir Eshel, "Vom eigenen Gewissen. Die Walser-Bubis-Debatte und der Ort des Nationalsozialismus im Selbstbild der Bundesrepublik," *Deutsche Vierteljahrsschrift für Literaturwissenschaft und Geistesgeschichte* 74 (2000): 333–360, 348.

[56] Manfred Fuhrmann, "Jüdisches Gedenken. Eine Nachbetrachtung zur Debatte Walser-Bubis" (*Berliner Zeitung* [8 May 1999]), *WBD*, 662–665, 663.

[57] See, for instance, Augstein as quoted above, and Dieter Breuers, "Opfer und Täter. Auch Ignatz Bubis sollte sich zurücknehmen" (*Kölnische Rundschau* [10 November 1998]), *WBD*, 128–130, 129.

Political Formations

"Glücklose Engel": Fictions of German History and the End of the German Democratic Republic

Karen Leeder

> "Who knows what an angel would be doing in
> a century like this one"
>
> — Patrick McGrath[1]

I SHALL START WITH A QUOTATION from Wolf Biermann's "Barlach-Lied":

> Was soll aus uns noch werden
> Und droht so große Not
> Vom Himmel auf die Erden
> Falln sich die Engel tot.

Biermann's 1965 song, warning of imminent threat, diagnoses the darkening times by referring to a fall of angels. They fall dead from the heavens like insects or birds in a hostile climate.[2] And similar, if less poetic, obituaries have been issued by a number of commentators in different fields. Gerhard Bott, former Director of the Walraff-Richartz-Museum in Cologne, in an examination of the angel in Western art, speaks of a "Verfall der Engel": a fall certainly; but he is also pointing to the degeneration of the image.[3] Modern angels have been debased as the result of a long process of vulgarised aesthetic humanisation, socialisation and sexualisation, which began perhaps with the painters of the Italian Renaissance. Paradoxically, as angels became less substantial in eyes of theologians, they became more so in eyes of artists and writers, with the result that in representations they began to obey the laws of nature and science. That process has continued, with every age more or less producing the angels it needs. And, as that has happened, the figure of the angel has fallen to earth — becoming more and more a reflection of the time it represents, and less a reflection of an immutable and divinely-sponsored universe.[4] It would be pertinent then to ask, with Patrick

McGrath, what an angel is doing in a (secular) century like ours. The answer is complicated. And it would certainly be wrong to underestimate the power these icons have in contemporary times, even, or precisely, to diagnose their own decline. Lutz Niethammer treats "verblasene Engel" as exiles of *posthistoire*, and for Peter Sloterdijk, "die leeren Engel unsere Zeit" illuminate the problem of contemporary humankind in its insecurity and fragmentariness.[5] However, even as they have been marginalised and mechanised, it is clear that angels have invaded the structures and forms of our thinking — certainly at the level of popular culture. These manifestations may simply testify to the fact that the angel is no more invulnerable to domestication and trivialisation in the market place than any other remnant of cultural heritage. The image of the angel has, however, also proved potent in any number of works of art and literature: from, to take a very small range of examples, Tony Kuschner's *Angels in America,* James Merill's epic poem *The Changing Light at Sandover,* Wim Wenders's and Peter Handke's *Himmel über Berlin* and *In weiter Ferne so nah!,* to the French photographer Louis Jammes' life-sized photographs of winged, war-dazed children posted around Sarajevo during the Bosnian war and a wave of recent poetry in German and English. This is neither a unique nor an entirely ephemeral manifestation. Historically, none of the monotheistic religions have constructed their narratives of divinity without the aid of the angel mediator. And in much the same way that modern physicists have reformulated models of the atomic orders, so in their very different ways, spiritual cartographers of sorts have refined our understandings of the angels and recast topographies of the angelic orders — from the author of the apocryphal book of Enoch, to Dionysius the Areopagite whose *Celestial Hierarchies* establishes the tiers of the angelic hierarchy, to literary formulations, which have been almost as influential: Dante, Milton, Blake, Klopstock and, in the twentieth century, Rilke.

The first point to make then, is that the vision, and the desire to interpret it, flourishes in some eras, and falls away in others, but at some level it abides. But why do artists and writers in a secular society find angels such a persuasive trope? And how are we to understand the continuities and shifts between the various sightings and citations? The question itself is a fashionable one: few major theorists have been without a pronouncement on angels: Foucault, Lacan, Derrida, Kristeva, Irigaray, Wittig, or Grosz. More recently the French Philosopher of science Michel Serres's *La Légende des Anges* (1993), published in English as *Angels: A Modern Myth* (1995), argues that traditional images of angels foretell the preoccupations of modern life: particularly in their function as go-betweens or message-bearers. They foreshadow, he claims, the extent to which vast interconnecting message systems govern contemporary understandings of physics, communications theory, geography, society and language.[6] Serres exploits the double meaning of the word "légende" to understand angels as the key to a map of an emphatically contemporary existence. In quite a different tone, Harold Bloom's 1996 *Omens of Millennium: The Gnosis of Angels, Dreams and Resurrection* argues that what he identifies as four dominant concerns of the 1980s are necessarily fused: angelology, prophetic dreams, an epidemic of near-death experiences and the approach of the millennium.[7] The central figure of his polemical theology though is the angel. Bloom's gnostic angels are creatures born of a disabling malaise of belatedness, typified by the anxiety of the so-called Generation X and rendered acute by the advent of the millennium. Different as they seem, both writers propose some kind of cross-pollination between information technology and ancient spirituality.

But beyond arguments about the relevance of angels for the contemporary moment, there are more general reasons why this image remains so compelling. In religious terms angels express what the Biblical scholar Henry Corbin calls the "paradox of monotheism": only the angel allows God to express himself through the word but to remain unspeakable. Angelology then becomes the attempt to solve the crisis of proximity and distance. However, translated into aesthetic terms, the angel comes to represent the limits of epistemology, and of representation, by pointing beyond itself to the unknown — one might say toward the sublime — or what Benjamin famously claimed for the aura of the work of art: "die einmalige Erscheinung der Ferne so nah sie auch sein mag." As Cathrin Pichler sums up:

> Der Engel ist mehrdeutig; er erscheint nicht definierbar, eine Art Zwischenwesen — zwischen den Zeiten, zwischen den Räumen, zwischen Himmel und Erde, Himmel und Hölle, zwischen Lebendigem und Totem, zwischen Geist und Materie . . . Der Engel ist etwas Fragliches.[8]

But also, more specifically, angels exist not by dint of essence, but of function. The Greek word for angel, "angeloi," means messenger, as does the Hebrew "Mal'akh," the Arabic "Malak," and the Persian "ferehht," or "angaros" (courier). Angels offer a way into a discussion of mediation, a philosophy of difference and relation, but also, in a more specifically literary vein, the function of metaphor (in that they manifest the Logos) and translation, in being the messenger between realms — ideas at the heart of the literary and artistic enterprise.

This is not to say, however, that different angels and different interpretations of the angel figure are not bound up intimately with their times. One might argue that, like significant mythological figures, the angel tends to appear in periods of transition and crisis. As Heiner Müller explained in 1991:

> Die Engel tauchen ja immer auf, wenn man keine Chance mehr sieht, daß die Hoffnung sich realisiert. Dann braucht man solche Figuren. . . . Engel sind Figuren jenseits von Hoffnung und Verzweiflung.[9]

In the rest of this chapter I want to examine the particular function of a crop of angels which appeared in the late 1980s and early 1990s. However, first I shall look back briefly to the angels of Modernism. There are two reasons for this. Firstly it can be argued that the figure of the angel functions as a "necessary fiction" for the contemporary moment, in a way that can only be understood when set against the Modernist fictions which it cites and extends. Secondly, the poems to be discussed here are all responses to the most famous Modernist angel: the only truly new angel, a very German angel, that is, the angel of history.[10]

The thought that there was a moment in the first two decades or so of this century which produced an extraordinary efflorescence of angels is not a new one. Hugo Friedrich in his *Struktur der Modernen Lyrik* of 1956 comments upon what he calls an empty transcendentalism in much modern poetry, citing Rimbaud's recourse to "angels without God and without a message" as a kind of archetype.[11] In his *The Truth of Poetry* (1969), Michael Hamburger observes that a whole genealogy of such angels could be traced from Rimbaud to Hofmannsthal, George, Rilke, Valéry, Wallace Stevens and the Spanish poet Rafael Alberti.[12] It has been argued that many of these writers were responding to a crisis overshadowed by the spiritual depression which followed the "death of God."[13] The rationalisation and intellectualisation of the public sphere in the late nineteenth and early twentieth century, which caused Max Weber to speak of a "disenchanted world," had forced manifestations of the sublime, the divine, the imaginary, the symbolic, and the affective, into a private space. The corollary of this depletion of the public sphere was then a paradoxical animation of the private and ultimately aesthetic sphere. The effect was to shift the balance of the relationship: in the face of such radical marginalisation, artists managed to turn historical necessity into a spiritual advantage, and became utopian. In the same way the social marginality of the artist was also converted to a spiritual centrality, and art became the mouthpiece of the infinite (in that being no-where can be converted to being everywhere). But in that process of conversion, artists were faced with another crisis: classical culture had lost its unique authority, and artists were forced to shift through the bric-à-brac of traditional systems, with their conflicting claims, in order to create for themselves some semblance of meaning. The willed act of creation of self, and the creation of that self's authority, is a profoundly Oedipal act in that the artist is both destroyer and creator: severing him/herself from origins and a world of transcendence, but also sponsoring a sphere of immanence within their own work. This is, to speak with Heller again, "a poetry of achievement" rather than a "poetry of return (166)." In this process the artifice of creating a fictional world is analogous to the artifice of constructing the human world — the convergence of literary and existential fictions is clear. Modernist angels have generally been interpreted in the light of this fiction — not as angels of theology; rather as secular angels, the functionaries, not of faith, but of the imagination.

The preoccupation with fictions has been regarded as one of the characteristic hallmarks of Modernist literature.[14] Like the "angel of reality" in Wallace Stevens's poem, who proclaims: "Yet I am the necessary angel of earth, / Since, in my sight, you see the earth again," the angel has been understood as a "supreme fiction,"[15] the symbol for the ability of art to rescue material existence, no matter how negative or repulsive, and to redeem it by dint of an alchemical transformation: finally that of poetry itself. This does not quite do justice to the writers concerned, however; it would be more accurate to see this understanding as one half of the equation. They are better seen as part of a struggle between the transcendental and the earthly, sublime and secular, genetic fallacy and moment of artistic self-realisation — between fiction and conviction. And angels of this period, both in the iconographic and literary manifestations, represent an acute *agon* between the authority of the old and the creation of the new. They stand somewhere between nostalgia for confident intermediaries of the divine voice and frustrated allegories of an emptied heaven. The figure of the angel is a means then of fixing the urgent dialectic at the heart of Modernism.

Even a truncated sketch of some of the issues suggests fascinating parallels with the more contemporary angels to be discussed here and the fin-de-siècle crisis of the twentieth century, which also saw the implosion of the GDR and the emergence of the new German state. It is unsurprising then that in the midst of this crisis, writers and artists should turn to perhaps the most famous symbol of the earlier crisis as a way of confronting history.

In November 1921 Walter Benjamin acquired Paul Klee's *Angelus novus* (1920), one of the artist's fifty or so paintings, aquarelles, and etchings to figure angels.[16] He kept it for the rest of his life — even cutting it out of its frame and taking it with him into exile. Benjamin's mediation of the angel figure is complex and varied, but one of the key passages for understanding it is the famous ninth thesis from his "Theses on the Philosophy of History":

> Es gibt ein Bild von Klee, das *Angelus Novus* heißt. Ein Engel ist darauf dargestellt, der aussieht, als wäre er im Begriff, sich von etwas zu entfernen, worauf er starrt. Seine Augen sind aufgerissen, sein Mund steht offen und seine Flügel sind ausgespannt. Der Engel der Geschichte muß so aussehen. Er hat das Antlitz der Vergangenheit zugewendet. Wo eine Kette von Begebenheiten vor *uns* erscheint, da sieht *er* eine einzige Katastrophe, die unablässig Trümmer auf Trümmer häuft und sie ihm vor die Füße schleudert. Er möchte wohl verweilen, die Toten wecken und das Zerschlagene zusammenfügen. Aber ein Sturm weht vom Paradiese her, der sich in seinen Flügeln verfangen hat und so stark ist, daß der Engel sie nicht mehr schließen kann. Dieser Sturm treibt ihn unaufhaltsam in die Zukunft, der er den Rücken kehrt, während der Trümmerhaufen vor ihm zum Himmel wächst. Das, was wir den Fortschritt nennen ist *dieser* Sturm.[17]

I cannot discuss this text here (it has been widely discussed elsewhere),[18] nor is there space to deal more broadly with the reception of Walter Benjamin in the GDR. In the late years, especially, he became a kind of "Anzapf-Säulenheiliger" (Adolf Endler) for GDR authors.[19] However, the obvious explosive potential of this text in the state that saw itself as the "Sieger der Geschichte," but was increasingly faced with crippling historical stagnation, is clear. Indeed many writers turned to the figure to explore and express their frustrations. I want, however, to turn straight to a text by Heiner Müller, "Der Glücklose Engel" of 1958, which functions in relation to Benjamin, rather as Benjamin does to Klee, as a kind of *Bildüberschreibung.*[20] Müller's poem is significant because a number of the later poems take issue as much with Müller as they do with Benjamin. The interest lies in the fact that all these texts are allegories of history more or less, and appear at moments of crisis: Benjamin's reflections of 1940 comment upon the immanent horror of Fascism: Müller's text from 1958 comes at a time of crisis of identity for Communism with the advent of neo-Stalinism in the late 1950s; and the later poems come in the wake of 1989 and the collapse of socialism. As such they offer a seismograph of the historical development of the twentieth century.

Müller's text came about when he was asked by Paul Dessau in 1958 to write a libretto for Brecht's opera fragment *Die Reisen des Glücksgotts* (itself inspired by Benjamin). This was never completed though there are a number of scenes and texts, the last of which is "Der Glücklose Engel".[21]

> DER GLÜCKLOSE ENGEL. Hinter ihm schwemmt Vergangenheit an, schüttet Geröll auf Flügel und Schultern, mit Lärm wie von begrabnen Trommeln, während vor ihm sich die Zukunft staut, seine Augen eindrückt, die Augäpfel sprengt wie ein Stern, das Wort umdreht zum tönenden Knebel, ihn würgt mit seinem Atem. Eine Zeit lang sieht man noch sein Flügelschlagen, hört in das Rauschen die Steinschläge vor über hinter ihm niedergehen, lauter je heftiger die vergebliche Bewegung, vereinzelt, wenn sie langsamer wird. Dann schließt sich über ihm der Augenblick: auf dem schnell verschütteten Stehplatz kommt der glücklose Engel zur Ruhe, wartend auf Geschichte in der Versteinerung von Flug Blick Atem. Bis das erneute Rauschen mächtiger Flügelschläge sich in Wellen durch den Stein fortpflanzt und seinen Flug anzeigt.

Müller's angel, takes up Benjamin's and refers it to his own political situation, becoming as Wolfgang Heise has claimed, a "Gegenmetapher" to Benjamin in the process.[22] Like Benjamin's, it appears to have a kind of secular redemption — or utopia — as its goal. As in Benjamin's text, the past is a catastrophe of history mounting up like rubble: "Geröll auf Flügel und Schultern." But unlike the "Angelus Novus" whom Benjamin sees as being driven into the future, despite himself, by the storm of progress, Müller's angel has undergone "an about turn of 180 degrees."[23] Benjamin's angel is prevented by the storm from redeeming the past; Müller's angel, facing the future, is caught up by history, so that it comes to a standstill and is buried by the rubble of the past: "versteinert." The historical reference here is to the period of retrenchment (following the brief liberalisation in the wake of Stalin's death) which was referred to as "Versteinerung" (Weber 258). Even the key which Benjamin so often calls upon — the "Augenblick" of "Jetztzeit"[24] — is explicitly closed off in Müller: "Dann schließt sich über ihm der Augen-/ blick." The angel is trapped then in a present without a future — a kind of ahistorical limbo between history and future — and is condemned to fall out of time: "wartend auf Geschichte." This compelling image signals Müller's profound interrogation of Benjamin's philosophy of history, from the point of view of a later historical subject; but it also works pointedly against the teleological schemes and historical optimism of the GDR.[25] However the text goes further; for the moment is one of discontinuity, but also of blindness and silence — "das Wort umdreht zum tönenden Knebel" — a further phrase with political implications for the GDR. Müller is writing, as Peter Böthig suggests: "an der Schwelle zum Verstummen."[26] "Daß es 'so weiter' geht ist die Katastrophe" (1, 683;

5 592) wrote Benjamin: "Daß es nicht weiter geht ist die Katastrophe" is, as it were, Müller's response here. And of course he is speaking of official GDR notions of historical progress, really existing socialism and the idea of the future as a guarantee of utopia more generally. The angel is not dead; however, its attitude, or rather Müller's, has changed. It does not seek to reach the future, nor look to messianic intervention in order to break through the petrified present. The angel waits for a new movement of wings in the stone, though it is doubtful whether the logic of the poem would allow him any agency at all. But his goal is to dissolve the "Versteinerung von Flug Blick Atem"; his goal then is subversion of the present. In 1992 Müller described the end of this earlier piece as "eher schon manchmal ein bißchen flach optimistisch."[27] In fact the poem does not say anything about the quality of history to come and there is little optimism. For as Müller has said (see above), angels are beyond hope or despair. At its best the very passivity of this blind and faceless angel might function as a kind of call to action on his behalf. However, from the perspective of post-unification Germany, some thirty-three years after the first text, Müller's disappointment can be seen in a seven-line poem first published in *Sinn und Form*: "Glückloser Engel 2":

> Zwischen Stadt und Stadt
> Nach der Mauer der Abgrund
> Wind an den Schultern Die fremde
> Hand am einsamen Fleisch
> Der Engel ich höre ihn noch
> Aber er hat kein Gesicht mehr als
> Deines das ich nicht kenne.[28]

The relation to Benjamin's thesis, and Müller's own earlier text, is clear from the title and also from the wind and the facelessness. In contrast to the allegorical place-lessness of the first text there is a fairly immediate context suggested in the phrase "Zwischen Stadt und Stadt," of post-1989 Berlin. Instead of the aspiration toward Utopia, there is the reality of the abyss: "Abgrund."[29] The next lines evoke the contingency of contemporary living, especially in the newly unified east — "Die fremde / Hand am einsamen Fleisch" — suggesting perhaps the loveless transactions of a prostitute, of the kind documented elsewhere in Müller's poetry of these years, and indeed in any number of post-*Wende* German poems.[30] Is the angel of history a whore? One could compare the whore "es war einmal" of the "Bordell des Historicismus" of Benjamin's sixteenth thesis (1/2 705); or the story of the Viennese actor meeting an angel/whore in Ernst Bloch's *Spuren*, or indeed the marked sexuality of

Müller's own earlier angel figures.[31] But the poem is difficult to pin down. The line "Der Engel ich hör ihn noch" suggests some kind of hope. It might suggest that angel had freed itself from the stone. This is the line taken by Erdmut Wizisla: "Er tritt nicht zum Fluge an, aber die Erinnerung an eine Bewegung lebt und bleibt ein Stachel. Müllers Bild ist der präziseste Ausdruck der geschichtlichen Situation."[32] This would seem to be supported by an interview of 1989 with Müller in which Gorbachev's reforms are compared to "das Rauschen der Flügel-schlägen."[33] However, one can read the lines more negatively. The sound might imply nostalgia: not movement, but the subject's desire to hear it. This is an angel that seems to have little in common with the one which once flew. It appears to have no face, which could suggest a continuation from the previous poem: the caved-in eyes and the gagged mouth. But much depends on how one reads the curious "als / Deines" at the end of the poem. It could imply a hitherto unknown face of the angel; it could be addressed to an intimate, perhaps the self, and imply a face not (no longer?) recognised ("welches Grab schützt mich vor meiner Jugend");[34] it could imply a future reader, whom it appears Müller trusts to have a face. In this it surely echoes Brecht's great poem "An die Nachgeborenen" which also looks to a future which will look back "mit Nachsicht" to the compromises of those who have had to fight for a better world in the present.[35] Either way however, the end is tentative to say the least: the possibility of subversion or change in the present is deferred to a future which might be hoped for (against hope), but which nothing in the poem guarantees.

Poems about the angel of history by Andreas Koziol, who was born in 1957 and is associated with the Prenzlauer Berg scene, and Thomas Martin, who was born in 1963, also appeared during the period 1989–1992.[36] They respond to Müller's 1958 angel as much as they do to Benjamin. However, theirs is an emphatically different generational experience, as indicated by Martin's title: "Steinenkel." But there is also a different take on the possibility of progress and aspirations toward utopia. One of the dominant moods is that of irony. It is no coincidence that in Koziol's *Bestiarium literaricum*, in the tradition of Franz Blei, "der Heinermüller" is also given the characteristics of a Benjaminian angel:

> Der Heinermüller ist auch aus dem Holz jener Schamanen geschnitzt, die auf den "Brettern, die die Welt bedeuten" die Aschen der Visionen säen. Bitternis und Trauer haben ihm einst schmerzbetäubende Flügel verliehen, von denen ihm aber der Rechte immer wieder unter die Rä-

der des Weltgeschehens gerät, woraufhin er immer wieder mit dem
Linken in "Richtung Deutschland" abwinkt. Was ganz natürlich ein
Wind erzeugt, der die Aschen immer wieder zu den Horizonten des
Bühnen- wie Weltbilds emporjagt.[37]

And Koziol's poem is in effect a caricature; not so much of the angel of
history, but of the discourses about it: "der engel der situation (ein
freistilcartoon)."

> er hockt auf den zehenspitzen am fuß einer rolltreppe,
> die aufwärts zum museum der westöstlichen langeweile führt.
> mit seinen schulterblättern ist ein buch verwachsen, in
> dessen seiten die winde aller utopien blättern. er selber
> kann den text nicht fassen, den er transportierte, ohne
> mit den händen weit über sich zurückzugreifen.
> in seiner kehle brennt das gas des traums von einer welt,
> dir für ideen nicht entflammt, ein dunkler stern am himmel
> zentralistischer fiktionen. er schreit vor wißbegier und
> schmerz in sich hinein. ein echo rollt, als kindliches
> gerücht durch seinen steiß zur alten welt, um sich im
> wind der tiefen sonne zu verblasen. es reißt ihn hin, er
> fällt auf das gesicht, den stempel der datierung seines
> doppelten geschlechts: jetzt erdet er sich selbst in seinem
> teufelskreis der zeit, von grund zu essen seiner sehnsucht
> nach dem paradies, die nach den formgesetzen eines gotts,
> der menschen fraß, aus jedem stein, der ihm im weg lag,
> tritt.[38]

The poem thus describes a situation of historical limbo. The angel does
not seem unduly distressed or uncomfortable: "er hockt auf den zehen-
spitzen am fuß einer rolltreppe." There is no storm, or rubble. Instead,
once again, he is confronted with a kind of abyss. Here it appears in the
"museum westöstlicher langeweile," or in the escalator as the symbol of
endless return: "ein teufelskreis der zeit."[39] The winds of all the utopias
rustle the pages of a book which he wears on his back instead of wings,
suggesting that all the utopian aspirations of history are comparable. But
he, with a finely poised double meaning, "kann den text nicht fassen, den
er transportierte." The authority of "origins," in Benjamin's terms, or of
the founding aspirations of the GDR, to speak in more political terms,
are without meaning for him in the here and now. This is a time with no
ideas, no ideals, no possibility of redemption, and certainly no message.
One is reminded of Günter Kunert's "B.B.s spät gedenkend," also from

1992 (and also a response to "An die Nachgeborenen"): "Keine Nachrichten / mehr an Nachgeborene."[40] Benjamin's storm from paradise returns in this poem, but in a deeply satirical form, as a kind of wind (ll. 10–11). Koziol's poem is not without melancholy, in the angel's cry (the only thing any of these angels actually say) and its reluctant "sehnsucht" (ll. 15–16), and in this it chimes in with a mood of loss and despair which appears in a great many poems of the period. It is also critical of the "gott der menschen fraß" which emerged from the stone as a grim and barbarous distortion of the once longed-for paradise. However, it would be wrong to exaggerate the force of either of these lines of thought. The poem refuses to cohere to any message or meaning, or to open a historical perspective. It is resolutely set against the notion of a "zentralistische fiktion," and deconstructs the angel figure while citing it. Goethe, Erich Arendt, Müller and Benjamin are all cited, and played off against one another. In one sense, they could be seen as representatives of that tradition which the angel must bear without having access to it: that is, a progressive critical vision. The result, however, is a text which refuses hierarchies of meaning and chooses instead to splice fragments together in a playful way. There is no message, just as the only movement is simply self-conscious movement between quotations.

In Martin's text, "Steinenkel," everything that points to the possibility of movement in Brecht or Müller is reversed.

Plattgewalzt. Unter den Platten das Signum (Brigade Datum Qualitätspaß) liegt er oder sie im Fundament auf dem Rücken, die unnatürlich wachen Augen eingetrocknet, die Flügel zerknickt, medikamentengrün umrahmt von Erbrochenem und Kot. Spuren im Sand, ein Fossil, dessen Karikatur der Arme Mensch wäre unter der Walze im Straßenverkehr, plattgedrückt im Comicstrip. Unter sich die versteinten Gezeiten, über sich Stein, der ihn einschließt mit dem Augenschlag der Gegenwart; die Zukunft sein Haus, das ihm auf den Füßen steht. Er schläft, aber unruhig vom Gang der Lebenden oben, ahnt seine Auflösung im endversorgenden Bauprogramm. Wir reproduzieren uns über ihm oder ihr, das mit Röntgenaugen die Platten durchmißt. Die Lücken im Bau sind verwachsen, Regen schneit Gips, blüht tropfsteinnasengleich ins Zimmer auf den Tisch, wird Wand zwischen uns im Bett. Aus dem (versehentlich) beigetretcnen Insekt ist ein Engel mit den Augen Samsas geworden. Dieser Engel, vom Leben erwacht, frißt Stein in gleichem Maß wie der ihn schluckt, verdaut, gibt ihn von sich in verzweifelt leichten Klängen einer Mozartsinfonie MOLTO ALLEGRO g-Moll; schüttelt die Flügelstümpfe ab von den Suhlen, Betonbrocken ihm aus den Kiefern, den Knebel aus Mörtel speiend ins Fernsehprogramm, die Augen glühn blau wie die Röhre. Das Paar Flügel versengt, oder von

Ratten benagt, erhebt er sich unsicher flatternd, jetzt wackeln die
Wände, dröhnts im Geschoß und klein, eine Flugmaus, spritzt er nach
oben, nach vorn durch die Schächte im Block, paradiesig taumelnd gen
Himmel, ruht kurz auf der Antenne, hebt an, verschwindet und ist
vergessen. Am Saugnapf des Fortschritts ziehts ihn nach oben, er
verfängt sich im Staubnetz, weht über Grenzen, scheinbar verloren, setzt
sich als farbloser Niederschlag nach dem gescheiterten Experiment. Im
Bild sehn wir ihn wieder: lustige Person, harmloser Schalk, alt, fast
sterblich geworden, flurrt er oder sie im Kreisverkehr um uns, vergeblich
winkend, blinde Mechanik überholter Signale.[41]

Here the "Steinenekel" is flattened, wings broken, eyes dried up, lying
in vomit and excrement like a drug addict or drunkard. Although Benjamin's and Müller's angels are written in as fossils, memories of past
times and past ways of thinking, this broken remnant has become the
archetypal "Ungeziefer": Gregor Samsa. The angel/insect has been
cemented (ll. 7–8) to the "Augenschlag der Gegenwart." And this is a
present again not much interested in history. Once again the potential
threat of the creature rising from the earth and unsettling the foundations is played with, but then revealed at the end of the poem to be
nothing. With singed, rat-gnawed wings it arises like a bat that is caught
up blindly and against its will ("paradiesig taumelnd"), only to fall again
"als farbloser Niederschlag nach dem gescheiterten Experiment." This
could refer to the ashes of the socialist experiment, but also carries the
possible darker sense of radioactive rain. In fact the text is full of potential threats which are cited but then almost immediately rendered harm-
less, random or banal. In the final lines, the angel returns: but again it is
"sinnlos," part of a meaningless "Kreisverkehr" of a mechanism which
has long since been overtaken.

The dialectic of catastrophe and progress which marks Benjamin's text
and indeed Müller's own earlier poem, seems, in these more recent works,
to have lost its power. All of them open onto a void of sorts; all of them take
catastrophe as a given. This is comprehensible. Müller, speaking of the
Wende, described the shock of that moment of collapse of past and present
as a "sehr Benjaminische Erfahrung":

Dieses Zusammenfallen von Zukunft und Vergangenheit, diese Beset-
zung mit der totalen Gegenwart, die hier nie funktioniert hat. Und
jetzt ist plötzlich die Zukunft die Vergangenheit, wenn man so alt ist
wie ich.[42]

All these have become an undifferentiated present — an "Abgrund" as he calls it in "Glückloser Engel 2," or in the interview, referring to Benjamin, an "Inferno."[43] This of course is not so very far from the meaningless circles of no-time which appear in Koziol and Martin. All the poems then refuse the notion of history — "Geschichte" — and in this seem symptomatic of a postmodern scepticism about meta-narratives of the kind that appears explicitly in the Koziol poem as the rejection of "centralising fictions." One could, however, argue that the poems look to more modest and singular structures — "Geschichten." All suggest a narrative framework as a kind of account of, or containment for, identity. Nevertheless, these are narratives which do not go anywhere, deliberately undermining or evacuating themselves. Moreover, they are excruciatingly aware of their own status as belated reproduction (Müller), "cartoon" (Koziol), or "Comicstrip" (Martin) — as fictions. The distinguishing characteristic of that self-consciousness is that each could best be read as "eine (Lektüre-)situation" — Müller on Müller and Benjamin, Koziol's reading angel echoes Goethe, Erich Arendt, Müller and Benjamin, and Martin takes up Müller, Kafka, various idioms, and popular music.[44] They are reading angels who are simultaneously read; and they speak of a very particular moment. But in the refusal of history and the turn to self-conscious fictions, they are symptomatic of broader tendencies in the literature of the first years of the new Germany.

However, these characteristics also bring the angels discussed here very close indeed to the most famous angels of postwar Germany: the angels of Wenders's *Himmel über Berlin* (1987) and *In weiter Ferne so nah!* (1993). There is not sufficient space here to treat these angels in detail. Suffice it to say that these too are "glücklose Engel" who have been exiled as a punishment — in Wenders's film treatment — to the "worst place in the world" (postwar Berlin) by a God who has then disappeared.[45] They are recording angels who cannot partake in the experience they witness; reading angels who haunt the libraries of human knowledge (and the Benjamin quotation along with references to Rilke's *Duino Elegies* make an appearance in these scenes), but also angels who wander a desolate no-place and no-time in search of humble human stories. In the sequel, they are part of the dominant cycles of history (in the recurring circular images) and are also subject to the intervention of Time itself (Emit Fletsi played by Willem Dafoe) who will turn back the wheel of progress into a meaningless now. However, they also seek meaning through a fall into the human.[46] There is one important difference, however. For Wenders, redemption of sorts is to be found in the grand mythmaking of the artistic medium: story-telling, and ultimately cinema: "Das Kino könnte der Engel sein."[47] For Müller,

Koziol and Martin, however, artistic forms offer little possibility beyond that of documenting the catastrophe.

But the final comments must return to the figure of the angel. All of these texts (from Klee on) produce a very human angel. Moreover it is an angel without a message, faceless, meaningless or dead, who acts as a comment on, or lament for, a lost history. Patrick McGrath's short story "The Angel," from which the motto for this chapter was taken, seems to come to the same conclusion. The narrator looks on as the down-and-out Harry reveals his true self, his body foul with putrescence, in a kind of living death. He comments: "This is what it means to be an angel . . . in our times at least."[48] McGrath identifies the paradox between the eternal and utopian aspirations, which the figure of the angel inevitably calls up, and its sordid contemporary reality. That paradox is compelling, and of course is very close to the struggle that the angel came to embody in texts from the beginning of the twentieth century. What is fascinating, however, is that so many writers still use the figure of this angel as a symbol for, or a fiction of, that struggle, particularly in those crisis years leading up to and after the *Wende*.[49] And if the "Angel of History" does not find its way into so many poems later in the decade with the same intensity, there are nevertheless a large number of other angels. Not so much angels of history; but angels of otherness. This is already hinted at here in all three authors, especially in the emphasis on sexuality (Müller, Koziol, and Martin each place the gender of the angel in question) but also on textuality. However, there are also new angels of the sublime. That too would seem to be a symptom of broader tendencies: which one might summarise as the shift from a concern with history to one with aesthetics in some modern German literature. While there might be many problems with such a shift — not least of which is the way political reticence can be deemed to be support for the status quo — as far as angels go it is perhaps no bad thing. It is after all a very odd idea to take an angel — the quintessential being of timelessness — as a representative of history. While in Benjamin and (I would argue) in Müller, there is a productive tension at work — that is allegory in a Benjaminian sense (1/2 338) — too often in the more recent poems the angel is a simple allegory, and a very reduced allegory. And there is nothing that kills poetry so much as allegory.

Notes

[1] Patrick McGrath, "The Angel," in *Blood and Water and Other Stories* (London: Penguin, 1989), 1–16, 13.

[2] Wolf Biermann, *Die Drahtharfe: Balladen Gedichte Chöre* (Berlin: Verlag Klaus Wagenbach, 1965), 37. Biermann's song diagnoses the troubled times in which it was written, of course, accurately.

[3] Gerhard Bott, "Introduction," in James Underhill, *Angels* (Shaftesbury: Element Books, 1995), 8–23. Also quoted in Cathrin Pichler, ed., *:Engel :Engel: Legenden der Gegenwart* (Vienna, New York: Springer, 1998), 34.

[4] On angels see Peter Lamborn Wilson, *Angels* (London: Thames and Hudson, 1980), or Heinrich Krauss, *Die Engel: Überlieferung, Gestalt, Deutung* (Munich: Beck, 2000).

[5] Lutz Niethammer, *Posthistoire: Ist die Geschichte zu Ende?* (Reinbek bei Hamburg: Rowohlt, 1989), esp. ch. 6, "Der verblasene Engel: Über die Posthistoire einer Historik der Gefahr," 116–53; Peter Sloterdijk, *Sphären*, vol. 1, *Blasen* (Frankfurt am Main: Suhrkamp, 2000), especially ch. 6, "Seelenraumteiler," 419–79, 420.

[6] Michel Serres, *Angels: A Modern Myth*, trans. Francis Cowper (Paris, New York: Flammarion, 1995).

[7] Harold Bloom, *Omens of Millennium: The Gnosis of Angels, Dreams and Resurrection* (London: Fourth Estate, 1996).

[8] Cathrin Pichler, ":Engel :Engel," in *:Engel: Engel*, 69.

[9] "Jetzt sind eher die infernalischen Aspekte bei Benjamin wichtig. Gespräch mit Heiner Müller," in Michael Opitz and Erdmut Wizisla, eds., *Aber ein Sturm weht vom Paradiese her: Texte zu Walter Benjamin* (Leipzig: Reclam, 1992), 348–52, 350.

[10] The reception of this figure is not anything like as concentrated in the English tradition, for example. I have been inspired by the excellent little anthology Erdmut Wizisla and Michael Opitz, eds., *Glückloser Engel: Dichtungen zu Walter Benjamin* (Frankfurt am Main: Insel, 1992).

[11] Hugo Friedrich, *Die Struktur der modernen Lyrik: Von Baudelaire bis zur Gegenwart* (Hamburg: Rowohlt, 1956), 127.

[17] Michael Hamburger, *The Truth of Poetry: Tensions in Modern Poetry from Baudelaire to the 1960s* (London: Weidenfeld and Nicholson, 1969), 28. In fact one could extend that list many times over (Baudelaire, Claudel, Giraudoux, Proust, Cocteau, Anatole France, Edgar Allen Poe, Bulgakov, Else Lasker Schüler, Georg Trakl, Franz Kafka, Walter Benjamin, and — as a fascinating rider to this from the real world — the "Angel of Mons" who appeared to soldiers in the Battlefields of the First World War.

[13] Erich Heller, *The Disinherited Mind: Essays in Modern German Literature and Thought* (London: Bowes and Bowes, 1952; 3rd ed., 1971), 160.

[14] Indeed a comparison of Rilke, Paul Valéry, and Wallace Stevens as "great modern fictionalists" (also of course writers who famously use the angel figure) forms a chapter

of Malcolm Bradbury's and James McFarlane's standard text: *Modernism: A Guide to European Literature 1830–1930* (London: Penguin, 1976, reprinted 1991).

[15] Wallace Stevens, "Angel Surrounded by Paysans," and "Notes Toward a Supreme Fiction," in *Collected Poems* (London: Faber, 1984), 496–97 and 404.

[16] Compare Mark Luprecht, *Of Angels, Things and Death: Paul Klee's Last Painting in Context* (Frankfurt am Main: Peter Lang, 1999).

[17] Walter Benjamin, "Über den Begriff der Geschichte," in Rolf Tiedemann and Hermann Schweppenhäuser, eds., *Gesammelte Schriften* vol. 1/2 (Frankfurt am Main: Suhrkamp, 1980), 691–704, 697–98.

[18] Compare Ralf Konnersmann, *Erstarrte Unruhe: Walter Benjamins Begriff der Geschichte* (Frankfurt am Main: Fischer, 1991), esp. 121–27, or Robert Alter, *Necessary Angels: Tradition and Modernity in Kafka, Benjamin and Scholem* (Cambridge, MA: Harvard UP, 1991).

[19] Adolf Endler, "Alles ist im Untergrund obenauf; einmannfrei . . .," in Torsten Metelka , ed., *"Alles ist im Untergrund obenauf; einmannfrei…": Ausgewählte Beiträge aus der Zeitschrift KONTEXT 1–7* (Berlin: Kontext Verlag, 1990), 58. More generally, see Graham Jackman, "Walter Benjamin in the GDR: An Introductory Survey," *German Monitor* 25 (1992): 1–24.

[20] Compare Thomas Weber, "Glücklose Engel: Über ein Motiv bei Heiner Müller und Walter Benjamin," in *Das Argument* 35 (1993): 241–53, 242.

[21] Heiner Müller, *Werke*, ed. Frank Hörnigk, vol. 1, *Die Gedichte* (Frankfurt am Main: Suhrkamp, 1998), 53.

[22] Wolfgang Heise, quoted in Weber 242.

[23] Erdmut Wizisla, "Glückloser Engel: Der Angelus Novus als literarischer Gegenstand," in *Namen, Texte, Stimmen: Walter Benjamins Sprachphilosophie*, ed. Thomas Regehly and Iris Gniosdorsch, *Hohenheimer Protokolle* 44 (Stuttgart, 1993), 155–70.

[24] Benjamin, "Über den Begriff der Geschichte," 1/2: 701 and 703.

[25] Compare Frank Hörnigk on Müller's interest in history: "Texte die auf Geschichte warten: Zum Geschichtsbegriff bei Heiner Müller," in Hörnigk, ed., *Heiner Müller Material: Texte und Kommentare* (Leipzig: Reclam, 1989), 123–37.

[26] Peter Böthig, *Grammatik einer Landschaft: Literatur aus der DDR in den 80er Jahren* (Berlin: Lukas Verlag, 1997), 45.

[27] Müller, "Jetzt sind eher . . .," 350.

[28] First published in *Sinn und Form*, 43, 5 (1991): 852 and in Müller, *Werke*, 1, 236, where it appears with a lower-case 'd' on the word "die" in line 3.

[29] This is a common motif in post-*Wende* poetry and also cites other angel texts by Müller: "Der Engel der Verzweiflung" from the play *Der Auftrag*, which is reprinted in *Werke*, 1, 212, and his essay "Die Einsamkeit des Films," on Syberberg's *Hitler — Ein Film aus Deutschland,* in Müller, *Rotwelsch* (Berlin: Merve, 1982).

[30] Compare, for example, "Herz der Finsternis nach Joseph Conrad" or Müller's poetic text: "Mommsens Block," *Werke*, 1, 234 and 257–64 respectively.

[31] Ernst Bloch, *Spuren* (Frankfurt am Main: Suhrkamp, 1969), 80.

[32] Wizisla, "Glückloser Engel," 163.

[33] "Dem Terrorismus die Utopie entreißen," in Müller, *Zur Lage der Nation* (Berlin: Rotbuch, 1990), 9.

[34] Compare Müller, "Selbstkritik," *Werke*, 1, 236.

[35] Brecht, "An die Nachgeborenen," in *Werke*, 30 vols. (Berlin, Weimar, Frankfurt: Suhrkamp, 1989–98), 12, 87.

[36] As Erdmut Wizisla points out, a number of writers including Christoph Hein, Klaus Körner and Hans-Eckardt Wenzel took up the angel in the late 1980s (Wizisla, "Glückloser Engel," 69). One could go further and compare Barbara Köhler, Durs Grünbein, Harald Gerlach etc.

[37] Andreas Koziol, *Bestiarium literaricum* (Berlin: Galrev, 1991), 58.

[38] Andreas Koziol, *mehr über rauten und türme: gedichte* (Berlin and Weimar: Aufbau — Außer der Reihe, 1989), 68. An earlier, longer version appeared in *ariadnefabrik* 1 (1989): 2.

[39] Not that far from the use of the Paternoster motif in *Grass's Ein weites Feld* (Göttingen: Steidl, 1995).

[40] Günter Kunert, "B.Bs spät gedenkend," in John Willett, ed., *Brecht damals und heute / Brecht Then and Now, The Brecht Yearbook 20* (Madison, U of Wisconsin P, 1995), 31.

[41] Printed in Opitz and Wizisla, *Aber ein Sturm*, 94.

[42] Müller, "Jetzt sind eher . . .," 351.

[43] Müller, "Jetzt sind eher . . .," 352.

[44] Peter Böthig makes this point about Koziol's text (in Böthig, *Grammatik einer Landschaft: Literatur aus der DDR in den 80er Jahren*, 57), but in fact it applies to all these texts.

[45] Compare Wenders, "Erste Beschreibung eines recht unbeschreiblichen Filmes," in Wenders, *Die Logik der Bilder: Essays und Gespräche*, ed. Michael Töteberg (Frankfurt am Main: Verlag der Autoren, 1988; 2nd ed. 1993), 93–104, 99.

[46] Compare Roger F. Cook, "Angels, Fiction, and History in Berlin: Wings of Desire," in Roger F. Cook and Gerd Gemünden, eds., *The Cinema of Wim Wenders: Image, Narrative and the Postmodern Condition* (Detroit: Wayne State UP, 1997), 163–91.

[47] "Das Kino könnte der Engel sein: André Müller spricht mit Wim Wenders über seinen Film *Der Himmel über Berlin*," *Der Spiegel* 43 (1987), 230.

[48] Patrick McGrath, "The Angel," 15.

[49] Compare, from the same period: Holger Teschke, "Für Paul Klee," in *Jasminder Felder Windschlucht New York: Gedichte* (Berlin and Weimar: Aufbau, 1991), 80 and Harold Gerlach, "Angelus Novus," in *Einschlüsse. Aufbrüche: Blätter zu sechs Monaten deutscher Geschichte* (Rodolstadt: Burgart, 1991) [no pagination].

Successful Failure? The Impact of the German Student Movement on the Federal Republic of Germany

Ingo Cornils

Introduction

IN 1993, MATTHIAS KOPP'S film essay "Erfolgreich gescheitert," broadcast on *Deutsche Welle-TV*, cemented the dual view of the impact of the German student movement on the Federal Republic of Germany. The movement was seen to have succeeded because — in spite of opposition to American capitalism and global power politics — it secured West Germany's orientation toward the West. Thus it promoted sexual liberation, a tolerant multicultural society, equality, a sense of hope, and thriving subcultures. The student movement was seen to have failed because it was remarkably ineffective regarding any change in the political system, the economy, or the workplace. Moreover, it was, and still is, associated with allegedly disastrous antiauthoritarian education practices, terrorism, and drug abuse.

The term "successful failure" was introduced during the first of the increasingly ritualistic anniversary debates on the movement in 1988,[1] but the matter-of-fact tone in which this paradoxical verdict was delivered by Kopp in 1993 suggested that the formula, which allowed former adversaries to save face, had now become widely accepted. Each side could claim victory: the 68ers for conquering the imagination, the conservatives for conquering reality.

In 1998, this uneasy co-existence was shattered by a plethora of new books, essays and editorials. The battle for cultural hegemony and the exclusive right to interpret the past in the Federal Republic erupted again in full force, with the added spice that whilst for the first time historians attempted to argue that 1968 had indeed become history, a new government had been elected whose ministers had their roots in the radical politics of that period. This government, according to some observers, at least, threatened to put the utopian dream back on the agenda.

In an article of 1999, Reinhard Mohr analyses the demise of the German Left and its loosening grip on the political and cultural hegemony in Germany.[2] He argues that the historical advantage of the Left, bolstered by the notion that it was responsible for a second founding of the Bonn Republic[3] and a fundamental liberalisation and democratisation (a view put forward by Jürgen Habermas in 1988), has disappeared. And even though the Right have their own identity crisis,[4] the position of the 68ers as founding fathers *wider Willen* is gradually eroding. Their copyright on "progressiveness" appears to have lapsed.

The most obvious reason for this shift in perception is that the 1960s have become a distant and increasingly incomprehensible era, one which fewer and fewer people can remember clearly. We may vaguely feel that the era was of cultural significance in terms of a fundamental shift in popular culture and changing attitudes to state authority.[5] Yet its broader political significance is far more difficult to determine, particularly after the collapse of communism in the early 1990s which ended the model of antagonism which the war and postwar generations had internalized so well. Today, the gulf between the 68ers and the modern observer seems almost unbridgeable. Looking back to thirty years ago, Tariq Ali wrote:

> To those reading about it today, that world might appear to be like a submerged continent. However, it is difficult for us to believe that we live now in a world where hope is gone for ever and where self-contemplation and self-interest have replaced the belief in a world of equality. Humanity still possesses all the facilities to effect such a change, but the system that has triumphed in the last years of this century would rather render our very being null and void than give up its privileges.[6]

Success

Yet there are still many voices that claim that the German student movement was successful,[7] or at least that it had a significant impact on German society.[8] Helmuth Kiesel argues that the movement's true achievement lies in helping to realise the modern pluralistic society that had always been intended by the fathers of the Basic Law:

> Sie [die Protestbewegung — IC] hat die traditionalistischen Drapierungen der Bundesrepublik und ihrer Gesellschaft, Talare und Uniformen, Konventionen und Reglements, moralische Gebote und strafgesetzliche Verbote, so weit wie möglich abgeschafft und hat dadurch deutlich werden lassen, was zwischen 1945 und 1949 auf den Weg gebracht worden war: ein demokratischer Staat mit einer autono-

men und pluralistischen Zivil- und Bürgergemeinschaft, getragen von einer Bevölkerung, die sich mehrheitlich keineswegs nach alten Zeiten sehnte, sondern mehrheitlich demokratisch und modern sein wollte.[9]

Lutz Schulenburg maintains that 1968 marks the beginning of an era of revolutionary rebellion against a capitalist system and consumer society which ignore the real needs and desires of the individual. In his view, what the student movement has taught all subsequent movements is that spontaneity and grass-roots democracy, however frustrating and slow, are the basis of an alternative political culture characterized by the transparency of the decision making process, the end of subordination, the practice of wide consultation, and the delegation of tasks and authority.[10]

The student movement's most dedicated scholar is Wolfgang Kraushaar of the Hamburger Institut für Sozialforschung, who is best known for his *Protestchronik* (1996) and *Frankfurter Schule und Studentenbewegung* (1998). He believes the successes outweigh the failures: the students may have failed in their radical attempts to change society, but they were successful in their emancipation from their parents, in sensitising society to the Nazi past, and in their demands for an expansion of education, for sexual self determination, women's emancipation, and democratisation of some institutions. While the movement has had negative side effects, it has demonstrated that a minority can make a significant difference:

> Das Jahr 1968 hat in der Bundesrepublik alles verändert. Auch wenn die APO in ihren unmittelbaren politischen Zielsetzungen fast überall gescheitert ist, so hat sie die Einstellungen, Haltungen und Mentalitäten doch nachhaltig verändert. Das, was Menschen in ihrer Subjektivität ausmacht, ist erst durch sie in den Mittelpunkt des öffentlichen Interesses gerückt worden. Der tradierte Politikbegriff ist um entscheidende Dimensionen erweitert worden. Politisches Handeln ist nicht länger mehr obrigkeitsstaatlich geprägt und auf Regierungen, Parlamente und Parteien beschränkt. Selbstinitiative, Mündigkeit, Zivilcourage, Nonkonformismus und kollektive Verantwortlichkeit haben einen unverzichtbaren Stellenwert erhalten.[11]

Failure

Critics of the student movement, predictably, continue to deny that it has any positive legacy at all. The 68ers are blamed for a significant fall in standards in the schools brought about by their antiauthoritarian ideas on education.[12] They are seen to be responsible for the loss of "German virtues" such as diligence, order, honesty and punctuality, thus contributing to a general weakening of the national fibre.[13] They are accused of creating a myth, of artificially keeping themselves in the public consciousness via "Ursprungslegende," "Fundamentalopposition," "Führer- und Opferkult," to guarantee them the "Diskurshoheit" long after their ideological sell-by-date.[14] Former activists like Frank Böckelmann[15] and critics such as Günter Grass[16] unite in questioning the consensus of the lasting impact of the student revolt. Worst of all, the 68ers stand accused of not knowing how to answer today's problems: their iconoclasm, according to Reinhard Mohr, has turned into an ideological conservatism which views social and technological changes predominantly as a threat, while their response to the debate about how to remember the Holocaust has been conspicuous by its absence: "Da, wo die 68er Linke ihren hoch moralischen Anfang genommen hatte — wo sie auch heute geistig gefordert wäre — da hörte man fast nichts von ihr."[17]

It is interesting to note that the 68ers are simultaneously accused of having held the *Deutungshoheit* too long and of not having any answers for today's problems. This indicates a certain romantic expectation on the part of later generations that indeed the 68ers know "where it's at." However, any residual dependence on them is certainly well hidden. The 68ers have become "strangers in a strange land," their icon, the magic year 1968, is, according to Armin Thurnher, "eine Chiffre der Diffamierung im ganz normalen Generationen-Kannibalismus."[18] Achim Schmillen, a member of the Green Party working in Joschka Fischer's office, thus gained the admiration of his peers by publicly ridiculing the "myth of 68."

New generations are jostling for their place, and they are not always appreciative of the "Zukunftsverantwortung der Linken." Matthias Horx was one of the first to assert the emancipation of the generations after 1968,[19] but their prime spokesperson is Reinhard Mohr, who has formulated his generation's grudge against the 68ers as having imbued them with a rebellious spirit whilst taking off to Tuscany and the fleshpots of tenured university posts.[20]

What is true is that the generation of 1968 has received a disproportionate amount of attention and is still seen as the decisive generation in the history of the Federal Republic. A unique set of circumstances, according to sociologist Heinz Bude,[21] make it distinctive, effective, and so long lasting in its identity and consciousness. Factors that glue its members together are the birth around the end of the Second World War, their moral upbringing in the "Nie wieder Krieg" mould, their abhorrence at the silence and materialism of their parents, and their willingness to engage in collective protest.[22]

The fact that some members of the 68 generation once played a catalytic function is not questioned by the generations now in their thirties. They are simply fed up with the fact that the 68ers are in their "Prominenzphase,"[23] that they have joined the establishment and become the representatives of the system they once tried to destroy.[24]

Machtwechsel

The move of the seat of government to Berlin in the summer of 1999 was most certainly not a return to the protest tradition in that city. Rather, it freed the younger generation from the historical baggage of the Bonn Republic. The "Generation Berlin" cares little for Rudi Dutschke,[25] and is trying to dissociate itself from the 68ers. Younger German parliamentarians recently announced a "cultural revolution" against "die staatstragenden Yesterday Heroes der 68er." In a polemic of some vindictiveness, they declared their independence from the "subversiven Grundimpetus radikalen Kritisierens bestehender Verhältnisse, der seit der 68er-Revolte in der bundesrepublikanischen Gesellschaft vorherrschend geworden ist."[26] Richard Herzinger points out that this protest is simply part of the "Anpassungsmechanismen" of young party members in power. By attacking their elders, they are compensating for their own lack of purpose. But he feels they have missed their target, since the 68ers are no longer a homogeneous group.[27]

While it is a fact that some politicians who have taken over the key posts in the new German government are members of the 68 generation, they do not intend to follow the agenda of the German student movement. Joschka Fischer indicated this break with the past before the Federal elections:

> Daß das politsche System und die demokratische Kultur heute weit durchlässiger, anpassungsfähiger und offener gegenüber neuen Herausforderungen geworden sind, als dies für das damalige System Westdeutschland galt, ist eine bleibende Leistung des magischen Jahres 1968. Ansonsten riecht die heutige Zeit nach großen Veränderungen und damit nach Zukunft, und das ist gut so.[28]

Even the Springer press, one of the prime targets of the students' protest against "the establishment" felt there was no cause for concern. On the day after the election, *Die Welt* commented:

> Der 27. September ist ein Tag des Siegs der 68er Generation. Mit Schröder werden zum ersten Mal die Kämpfer der außerparlamentarischen

Opposition in den höchsten Ämtern des Staates sitzen. Der "Marsch durch die Institutionen" war erfolgreich, die Truppe ist ganz oben angelangt. Doch Schröders Wahlsieg ist ein Struktursieg, kein Sieg der 68er Ideologie. Die wurde still und leise entsorgt. Doch an die Stelle eines Wandels trat in vielen Fällen eine Art weltanschauliches Vakuum. Pragmatismus für eine Politik der Popkultur. Das gibt dem Generationensieg etwas Hohles.[29]

The new Chancellor Gerhard Schröder, intent on making the *neue Mitte* as wide as possible, made the most of his own affinity with the year 1968, but was careful not to give the impression that his government saw itself as following in the footsteps of the revolution:

Der Umzug nach Berlin ist mit einem Generationswechsel verbunden. Das gilt für die Politiker, und das gilt für die Politik. Die Generation, die zum Ende des Jahrzehnts in den Entscheidungszentren angelangt ist, ist zusammen mit dem Land erwachsen geworden. Wir haben es mit Biographien erlebter — und ertrotzter — Demokratie zu tun: in der Auseinandersetzung mit autoritären Strukturen im Westen, im Aufbegehren gegen ein diktatorisches System im Osten Deutschlands. Diese Generation ist angekommen und muß schon wieder den Stabwechsel zur nächsten vorbereiten.[30]

Historisation

If 1968 has become the "Gradmesser, mit dem das Selbstverständnis der Republik überprüft werden kann,"[31] then we need to know exactly what 1968 actually stands for. This is becoming increasingly difficult if we do not want to depend entirely on the unreliable and partisan memory of the greying 68ers. The era has received intense media attention, but, because of its anti-establishment attitude, its constantly changing agenda and essentially ephemeral nature,[32] the real debates and discussions within the student movement (as opposed to its media image) have until recently been poorly documented. To help scholars, researchers and archivists are now locating and documenting the resources scattered around libraries and private collections. One of the first was a small guide put together by Phillipp Gassert and Pavel A. Richter.[33] Another resource for researchers is the recent publication of a "Quellenkunde" by German archivists Thomas Becker and Ute Schröder.[34]

There is no doubt about it — 1968 is facing historisation. Historians and sociologists feel it is time for closer investigation. Ingrid Gilcher-

Holtey[35] and her colleagues want to get away from the memories of the activists in order to move toward a critical, analytical view of the protest movement, and hope this can yield "die Erfassung der Wirkung dieser Bewegung." Gilcher-Holtey's approach is superficially plausible: she argues that the German student movement was a social movement, in that a large number of individuals aimed for social change. Unfortunately, the sociologists offering their opinions in her book do not yet possess the instruments or methods of interpretation that would allow them to arrive at objective, specific conclusions. Ingeborg Villinger thus basically follows Barbara Sichtermann's ten-year-old argument when she pronounces: "die durch die 68er provozierte Politisierung des Alltags leitete eine Veränderung der Wahrnehmungsperspektive ein, deren inhärente Dynamik Folgen zeigte."[36] What these consequences might be is left distinctly vague, amounting, it seems, only to a cryptic concept of a "Verflüssigung der Normalität." Kristina Schulz admits that when it comes to interpreting the impact of the German student movement the sociologist's tools are simply not precise enough:

> Die gesellschaftsverändernden Impulse der Protestbewegungen können nicht getrennt von den anderen Faktoren sozialen Wandels bestimmt werden, was die direkte Zuschreibung von Folgen sozialer Bewegungen erschwert.[37]

What good, then, is a historical view of 1968? Robert Frank lists a number of myths about the German student movement which a closer historical study, he claims, reveals as nonsense.[38] One example of this is the myth that 1968 was anti-totalitarian in nature. He argues that almost the opposite was true, both in terms of individual and collective behaviour. But the biggest myth of all, according to Frank, is the "Gründungsmythos," that is, the myth that 1968 was the time when a miraculous "Nachgründung der Bundesrepublik" took place. Unfortunately, as with several other writers in Gilcher-Holtey's book, he does not supply any evidence for his view.

Historians do not have a monopoly on the truth when it comes to the evaluation of the impact of 1968, and even though research into the sixties promises to give us a better understanding of the "deep socio-historical processes of transformation," the "natural enmity"[39] between participants and historians prevents, for the time being, a final assessment.

This is not to say that a historical approach cannot yield any results. Andrei Markovits's and Philip Gorski's study of the German Left[40] successfully explores the metamorphoses of the left political spectrum from orthodox Marxism via sectarian, anti-authoritarian movement to ecological mass movement. Ingo Juchler's "historiographische Untersuchung" of the influence of third world liberation movements and theories on the US and German student movements pulls together a wealth of information on this particular aspect,[41] while Sabine von Dirke's recent study traces the aesthetic and social challenges to the "hegemonic culture" by the West German counterculture(s) from the 1950s to the 1980s.[42]

Wolfgang Kraushaar has recently written a review of new publications about the German student movement, and included a helpful listing of the "Publikationsschübe" from 1967 to the present.[43] While also conceding that a final verdict on the impact of the movement is impossible as long as the diagnostic uncertainty remains, he believes there are some trends to be made out in the research:

1. Cultural interpretations of the impact of the movement have taken over from political, economic or social interpretations. For the time being, there is agreement about the short-term political failure and long-term socio-cultural effects. However, these are difficult to determine.

2. Even though there is no conclusive explanation for it, the global character of the phenomenon of 1968 is generally accepted.

3. The disparity of influences and groupings which have converged in the 68-movement is increasingly the object of research. There was no unity of purpose on the ideological or organisational level.

4. The symbolic significance of scenes, individuals and situations appears to have played a greater role than hitherto assumed. The activists were part of a media-led and informal self-stylisation. This has led to the increased use of terms like "myth," "idol" and "icon."

5. The metatheoretical coordinates for a discussion of the movement which existed in the first fifteen years after the events are no longer uncontested. New, postmodern interpretations compete with the old ones, but they have until now not been able to gain the upper hand. This increases the uncertainty about the categorical framework within which a valid analysis could be reached.[44]

For his own part, Kraushaar is satisfied that the 68-movement was not only one of the strongest political challenges of the Federal Republic, but that it caused a socio-cultural "Bruch" which had a fundamental impact. Announcing his latest book,[45] he observes:

> Die Frage steht im Raum, ob eine grundlegende Veränderung der Mentalitäten, Lebensstile und Lebensentwürfe, die Ausbildung zivil-gesellschaftlicher Normen, die Fundamentalliberalisierung der neuen Mittelschichten . . . ohne die von der antiautoritären Bewegung frei-gesetzten Schubkraft überhaupt denkbar gewesen wären.

The significant word in this rather hopeful collection of suggested effects is "denkbar." Kraushaar implies that the socio-cultural changes and value shifts which have undeniably taken place after 68 could not even have been contemplated without the 68ers who first created the impetus for change.

Kraushaar's view is echoed by another surviving and politically un-compromised 68er, Peter Schneider. The author of *Lenz* (1973) has over the last decade produced a number of seminal essays on German identity, German unification and, most recently, growing xenophobia in Ger-many.[46] In a "defense of the 68ers against the wire-fence-generation," Schneider writes:

> ich rufe es euch, unseren lebensneidischen Krittlern und Sargträgern zu: Nicht einmal ihr würdet in der Gesellschaft leben wollen, die ihr hättet, wenn es unseren Aufbruch nicht gegeben hätte — nicht die Eroberung der Körper durch die neue Musik, die Erweiterung der sexuellen Gren-zen, das Aufbegehren der Frauen! Dass dieser Kampf auch zu barbari-schen Verirrungen geführt hat, muss ich hier nicht noch einmal beschreien, nur orthodoxe Dummköpfe bestreiten es, dass sie massenhaft und vielleicht für immer mit der Kultur des Gehorsams gebrochen ha-ben.[47]

Memory and Reality

A wealth of coffee-table books, biographies and cultural histories combi-ne to send the message: this was the most exciting period in West Ger-man history, on a par with the "Roaring Twenties" in the Weimar Republic. We want to know more about this period because we may feel that our present is too safe and predictable, or because we can escape from reality in the accounts of the 60s: in them we find abandon, free-dom, iconoclasm, challenge and intensity. There is something about the unfulfilled promise which leaves us wondering what might have been. In the legendary and literary representations of the German student movement, we find preserved the experience of liberation which we might need again like the frozen genes of an extinct species.[48]

Taking stock, however, the question must be whether the "long march through the institutions"[49] actually had any verifiable impact on the Federal Republic. If so, was it successful in terms that the marchers can agree on, and in terms that we today could agree on? In other words, we need to decide whether we want to take the students at their word and judge their impact by what they openly campaigned for,[50] or whether we believe that their impact has to be seen in their collateral influence, which could be measured by examining collective memory, media attention, public discourse, and the political sphere. Both strategies depend on whether we believe the 68ers, who have, until recently, held the monopoly on the interpretation on the German student movement, and whether we can disentangle myth and reality. It is fascinating to see how easy it is to redefine an entire era. We have seen this phenomenon in the re-branding of the SPD as a counter-cultural force in the 1972 election,[51] in the re-evaluation of Rudi Dutschke from "rebel rouser" to moral icon, and the latest incarnation of "68" as "training ground" for our new, level-headed political leaders.

Like the Greens, the students set out to do more than they could actually achieve, and in the process, they lost what cannot be regained: their youth, their innocence, their idealism, and their utopian dream. This loss, in my opinion, has influenced the political and cultural climate for the last thirty years. The experiences of the German student movement led to a much more sober and focussed protest by the feminist movement, the green movement and the peace movement. None of these movements were on the agenda in 1968, not even the support for Willy Brandt, his *Ostpolitik,* and eventually unification. The mobilisation of "Otto Normalverbraucher" to vote for the Social Democrats for the first time after the war may have had something to do with the *Zeitgeist,* but, as far as the students were concerned, the SPD was no more likely to rock the boat than the CDU, a fact that had become clear for all to see when the SPD helped to pass the Emergency Laws in May 1968.

Judged by their own ideals, demands, plans and aspirations, the students have failed miserably. The economic system they despised now rules supreme, the one-dimensionality of mankind continues apace on television and the internet. The slogan of the "successful failure" with regard to the aims, aspirations and utopian dreams of the German student movement appears to be little more than well-rehearsed apologetics. By accepting this compromise, we do not need to decide, we do not need to destroy the dream, and we do not need to answer the questions the students asked either. The students often quoted Hermann Hesse's dictum that in order to achieve the possible, one has to demand the impossible. At the beginning of the new millennium, Germans seem barely bold enough to attempt the possible — the programme of change promised by the red-green coalition: the creation of a truly "civil society," has run out of steam in the face of reality.

But, of course, the "struggle" is not over yet, and the alternative to the 68ers in their *Prominenzphase* is not exactly preferable. Does that mean that the "historic mission" of the 68ers has been fulfilled? The *Spiegel* believes that there is still more to do:

> Vielleicht müssen die 68er erst zu Großvätern werden, um mit ihren Enkeln eine neue gesellschaftliche Synthese einzugehen, die sich zuweilen schon andeutet — zwischen den klugen Kindern der Postmoderne und den desillusionierten Vätern der Revolte, die immer noch neugierig sind auf eine Zukunft, die sie nicht von früher kennen.[52]

So what *can* we say? Six Theses

1. The impact of the German student movement on the Federal Republic is contested. It is a struggle for *Interpretationshoheit* between the 68er generation, their critics, and the generations that followed. It is also a game with very few permanent players.

2. The impact of the German student movement is being re-evaluated because generations post 68 seek to gain influence and power in the Berlin Republic.

3. The impact of the German student movement is played down by the "losers" in the shift to more liberal, more transparent and more democratic practices in the Federal Republic. This includes, paradoxically, a number of former activists and participants of the movement.

4. The impact of the German student movement is overstated by those who stand to gain from the cultural shift. This includes, paradoxically, conservative voices, scaremongers, people who did not have anything to do with the events while they were happening, and those who simply wish that the German student movement had been successful.

5. The intense debate about the impact has itself changed the impact — the German student movement is accorded a mythical

status and significance because it still holds the interest of the media and, because of its diverse nature, has become a rich field for academic research. While we are trying to analyse the impact, we contribute to the impact.

6. All the nostalgic accounts of the German student movement capture the mood of the time, and preserve it. This in itself is an important legacy and demonstrates the impact on the public psyche, in that we may wish for a return of that intensity, even though its actualisation would be impractical and embarrassing in the present climate.

Postscript: Joschka's *Wilde Jahre*

Since the conception of this essay in Spring 2000, a chain of events occurred that has brought the antagonism between the two opposing interpretations of the German student movement's impact on German life to the fore again, in quite an unexpected manner.

In January 2001, Bettina Röhl, daughter of Ulrike Meinhof, posted an accusation on her website stating that Joschka Fischer, the Foreign Minister and Vice-Chancellor of the Federal Republic of Germany, had committed serious crimes as a militant "sponti" during and in the aftermath of the German student movement.[53] He was accused of having beaten up a policeman at a demonstration and, more seriously, of supporting the *RAF*. The timing of these "revelations" (Fischer's past is reasonably well documented in biographies both sympathetic and unsympathetic) was crucial: the CDU opposition could hope to deflect public attention from their own party finance scandal and put the Schröder Government under pressure.

The ensuing debate — held publicly and with surprising ferocity considering that the events in question took place almost thirty years ago — brought all the old antagonists into the ring again. New accusations were made daily and were eagerly debated both in the sensationalist as well as the serious press.[54] While British voices analysed events with a certain detachment (Lord Weidenfeld felt that the debate showed that Germany had learned from the past and that the debate itself was a good thing for democracy;[55] *The Guardian* described it as being ultimately about the moral use of force[56]), the debate in the German media (especially *Focus* and *Bild*) hit hysterical levels, but ran out of steam by the end of February 2001. The majority of the population looked on in mild amusement and wanted Fischer to remain in office, seeing him as a man who has learned from his experiences and accepting that his "historical baggage" is actually a positive attribute in an otherwise bland political landscape.

As to the "serious debate" about the alleged catastrophic impact of the German student movement on German society, as demanded by some observers, it has yet to yield anything new. The discussion, a minor *Kulturkampf* between proponents of *Leitkultur* and *Subkultur*, is still dominated by the continuing struggle for cultural hegemony — is the capitalist reality allowed to destroy the idealistic legacy of the 68ers? Apparently not. Not only has the campaign of the CDU run its course — Angela Merkel's demand in the *Bundestag* that Schröder, Fischer and Trittin should once and for all renounce their 68 past[57] was generally considered ill-informed and hypocritical. Ms Röhl's publisher dumped her forthcoming book (they also publish Fischer's autobiography), and even Roland Koch's attempt to put Fischer on trial in Frankfurt (the scene of the alleged crimes) for making false statements is seen as an obvious ploy motivated by party-political interests.

What has been termed by *Die Zeit* as the "dritte Vergangenheits-bewältigung" never really took place, not because there is nothing to come to terms with (Fischer did apologise for his violent acts and stressed that he had moved away from militant action by the mid-seventies), but because the 68ers once again closed ranks. In their view, 1968 must be preserved as necessary part of our past, and the lessons learnt must be carried into our present in order to fend off the alternative: a meaningless, purely materialistic existence, which Rudi Dutschke once described as "gut konsumieren und trotzdem vor sich hin vegetieren."

The new discussion has shown that Germans are mostly realistic about the limitations of the German student movement. At the same time, the debate, which may flare up again if new allegations are put forward in the run-up to the Federal elections in 2002, has demonstrated that 1968 is far from history — it is still a presence in our political, social and cultural reality. The myth of 1968 is showing further cracks, but the chiffre 1968 continues to be "eine Münze im Kampf um das politische Selbstverständnis dieser Republik."[58]

Notes

[1] See Wilhelm Bittorf, "Träume im Kopf, Sturm auf den Straßen," *Der Spiegel* 14–21 (1988); Ronald Fraser, *1968: A Student Generation in Revolt* (London: Chatto & Windus, 1988); Barbara Sichtermann, "1968 als Symbol" (in Lothar Baier et al., *Die Früchte der Revolte: Über die Veränderung der politischen Kultur durch die Studen-*

tenbewegung (Berlin: Wagenbach, 1988); Knut Nevermann, "Die naive Rebellion," *Süddeutsche Zeitung* (9 April 1988); Hermann Rudolf, "Halb Treibsatz, halb Rohrkrepierer," *Süddeutsche Zeitung* (9 July 1988).

[2] Reinhard Mohr, "Von der Revolte zur Denkstarre," *Der Spiegel* 48 (1999): 164–74.

[3] See Claus Leggewie, "Der Mythos des Neuanfangs. Gründungsetappen der Bundesrepublik Deutschland," from the website: http://nakayama.org/polylogos/philosophers/arendt/arendt-mythos.html.

[4] Nicknamed "Der Marsch aus den Institutionen," as opposed to the students' "Marsch durch die Institutionen."

[5] For an overview of the era — excluding Germany — see Arthur Marwick, *The Sixties* (Oxford: Oxford UP, 1998).

[6] Tariq Ali and Susan Watson, *1968: Marching in the Streets* (London: Bloomsbury, 1998), 13.

[7] See Michael Ruetz, *Sichtbare Zeit* (Frankfurt: Zweitausendeins, 1995), 209, and Rolf Uesseler, *Die 68er: "Macht kaputt, was euch kaputt macht"* (Munich: Heyne, 1998), 354.

[8] Hermann Glaser believes that it led to the political victory of the SPD/FDP coalition in 1969 (*Kleine Kulturgeschichte der Bundesrepublik Deutschland 1945–1989* [Munich: Hanser, 1991]). Marcel Reich-Ranicki feels that it forced society to deal with the Nazi past (*Mein Leben* [Stuttgart: Deutsche Verlags-Anstalt, 1999], 461).

[9] Helmuth Kiesel, "Literatur um 1968. Politischer Protest und postmoderner Impuls," in *Protest! Literatur um 1968* (Marbach: Deutsche Schillergesellschaft, 1998), 627–28.

[10] Lutz Schulenburg, ed., *Das Leben ändern, die Welt verändern!* (Hamburg: Nautilus, 1998), 9.

[11] Wolfgang Kraushaar, *Das Jahr, das alles verändert hat* (Munich: Piper, 1998), 323.

[12] One of the most vocal exponents of this view is Dietrich Schwanitz, author of bestsellers like *Der Campus*, *Bildung* and *Der Zirkel*. In a recent interview, Schwanitz claims that the anti-authoritarian movement caused a politisation of the German education system, which allowed more and more students to enter *Gymnasien* and universities without expecting them to work to the traditional standards ("Wenn das Blöde Kult wird," *Stormarner Tageblatt* [1 July 2000]: 6).

[13] See Ingo Cornils, "The German Student Movement. Legend and Legacy," *Debatte* 4:2 (1996): 36–62. For a longer discussion of the attempt by the "New Right" to vilify the 68ers see Michael Schneider, "'Volkspädagogik' von rechts: Ernst Nolte, die Bemühungen um die 'Historisierung' des Nationalsozialismus und die 'selbstbewußte Nation,'" (Bonn, 1995; electronic ed. Bonn: Bibliothek der Friedrich Ebert Stiftung, 1998).

[14] Richard Herzinger, "Die Kulturrevolutionäre von 1968 — Garanten der liberalen Kultur in Deutschland?" http://www.oeko-net.de/kommune/kommune12–96/AHERZING.htm.

[15] Frank Böckelmann, "Offene Türen eingerannt," in Claus-M. Wolfschlag, ed., *Bye-bye 68* (Graz: Leopold Stocker Verlag, 1998), 76–77.

[16] The latest German winner of the Nobel Prize for Literature, himself an active participant at the time, dutifully covers the German student movement in *Mein Jahrhundert* (Göttingen: Steidl Verlag, 1999). His anchor for the years 1966–68 is a failed revolutionary turned academic, who fled the action in the city to study in peace in quiet Freiburg. The implication is that today's 68ers may not have been the revolutionaries we are supposed to take them for, and that they did not know what they were doing. Grass acknowledges that it was an intense time, but the verdict at the end is devastating when a young student tells her professor: "Von Ihnen kommt sowieso nichts mehr" (252).

[17] Reinhard Mohr, "Von der Revolte zur Denkstarre," *Der Spiegel* 48 (1999): 173–74.

[18] Armin Thurnher, "Die Schrift leben," *Der Standard* (11 April 1998): 35.

[19] Matthias Horx, *Aufstand im Schlaraffenland* (Munich: Hanser, 1989). Horx credits the "real 68ers" with imbuing the following generation with the courage to stand up to their parents, to experiment with drugs and sex, and to discuss every aspect of life extensively and openly. However, he draws a distinction between the "klassischen 68er" with their focus on abstract theorising, and his own generation, which practised "Politik in der ersten Person" within a network of subcultures and held a desire to be even more radical than their heroes (15–19).

[20] Reinhard Mohr, *Zaungäste: Die Generation, die nach der Revolte kam* (Frankfurt: S. Fischer Verlag, 1992). See also *Kursbuch* 121, Berlin, 1995: *Der Generationenbruch*, especially Eckart Britsch, "Jede Jugend ist die dümmste" (159–65).

[21] Heinz Bude, *Das Altern einer Generation: Die Jahrgänge 1938–1948* (Frankfurt am Main: Suhrkamp, 1995).

[22] Daniel Cohn-Bendit and Reinhard Mohr, *1968. Die letzte Revolution, die noch nichts vom Ozonloch wußte* (Berlin: Wagenbach, 1988).

[23] At least in terms of age group. Karl Heinz Heinemann and Thomas Jaitner, eds., *Ein langer Marsch: '68 und die Folgen* (Cologne: PapyRossa-Verlag, 1993) and Oskar Negt, *Achtundsechzig: Politische Intellektuelle und die Macht* (Göttingen: Steidl Verlag, 1995) argue that the "real 68ers" do their "Maulwurfsarbeit" in less prominent places.

[24] See also: "Die Mächtigen von morgen," *Der Spiegel* 18 (2001).

[25] The Körber Foundation (Hamburg) recently held a school competition "Aufbegehren, Handeln, Verändern. Protest in der Geschichte" and invited winners to Berlin for a conference and a discussion with Rudi Dutschke's widow, Gretchen Dutschke:

> "Was ist von damals geblieben?," will Schülerin Sandra wissen. "Oh, das wollte ich von euch wissen." "Ich glaube, dass gar nichts erhalten ist," sinniert ein Schüler. Keiner widerspricht. Die schmerzliche Erkenntnis tritt ausgerechnet in der so heiß umkämpften TU Berlin zutage: Die 18-Jährigen von heute wissen nicht, dass viele Dinge, die ihnen und ihren Eltern selbstverständlich sind, damals erst buchstäblich losgetreten wurden.

Matthias Schmook, "Zeitreise — Schüler trafen Gretchen Dutschke," *Hamburger Abendblatt* (10 February 2000): 17.

[26] At the launch of their new political magazine "Berliner Republik" in Berlin, October 1999.

[27] "Die 68er haben sich längst selbst von den rebellischen Träumen ihrer Jugend verabschiedet und sich in die verschiedensten Richtungen wie Utopienostalgiker, kulturpessimistische Untergangsdiagnostiker und liberale Reformisten ausdifferenziert." Richard Herzinger, "Berliner Mief," *Die Zeit* 39 (1999). See also: Stiftung für die Rechte zukünftiger Generationen, ed., *Die Achtundsechziger: Warum wir Jungen sie nicht mehr brauchen* (Freiburg: Kore, 1998). The message is that the "great ideals" have either been realised or died long ago.

[28] Joschka Fischer, "Ein magisches Jahr," *Spiegel special* 9 (1998).

[29] Matthias Döpfner, "Der Sieg der Achtundsechziger," *Die Welt* (28 September 1998). The paper's fascination with the generation of 1968 is due to its new editor, Thomas Schmid, a former student activist. In various articles the paper now acknowledges that 1968 did indeed have an impact, in that the generation of 1968 is controlling the state ("Sieg der Achtundsechziger"), is responsible for the "morally justified" NATO intervention in Kosovo ("Der Krieg der Achtundsechziger" [31 July 1999]) and is responsible for a redefinition of the relationship between Europe and the USA ("Die Achtundsechziger als neue Atlantiker" [30 March 1999]).

[30] Gerhard Schröder, "Meine Berliner Republik," *Der Stern* 36 (1999).

[31] Wolfgang Kraushaar, "'1968'. Das Jahr der Rebellion," *Der Spiegel* 13 (1999).

[32] Compare Margaret Atack, *May 68 in French Fiction and Film* (Oxford: Oxford UP, 1999), 3:

> There is [. . .] a "hall of mirrors" aspect to the lived experience of May. The event is lived as completely outside normal experience. It is unique, other, and immediate. It is therefore, by definition, ephemeral, a fact registered in the number of books gathering and preserving documents, the collection of photographs, the special issues with photographs and quotations. The inscriptions would be effaced, the actions would not be repeated.

[33] Phillipp Gassert and Pavel A. Richter, 1968, in *West Germany: A Guide to Sources and Literature of the Extra-Parliamentary Opposition* (Washington: German Historical Institute, 1998).

[34] Thomas Becker and Ute Schröder, eds., *Die Studentenproteste der 60er Jahre. Archivführer — Chronik — Bibliographie* (Cologne: Böhlau, 2000).

[35] Ingrid Gilcher-Holtey, ed., *1968: Vom Ereignis zum Gegenstand der Geschichtswissenschaft* (Göttingen: Vandenhoeck & Ruprecht, 1998). See also David Farber, *The Sixties: From Memory to History* (Chapel Hill: U of North Carolina P, 1994).

[36] Ingeborg Villinger "Stelle sich jemand vor, wir hätten gesiegt. Das Symbolische der 68er Bewegung und die Folgen," in Gilcher-Holtey, 251.

[37] Kristina Schulz, "Macht und Mythos von '1968,'" in Gilcher-Holtey, 256.

[38] Robert Frank, "1968 — ein Mythos?" in Gilcher-Holtey, 301–7.

[39] See Christoph Classen, "Die sechziger Jahre als Suchbewegung — Ein Symposium in Kopenhagen über soziale Kultur und politische Ideen in beiden deutschen Staaten," in *Potsdamer Bulletin für Zeithistorische Studien* 13 (13 July 1998), 46.

[40] Andrei Markovits and Philip Gorski, *The German Left: Red, Green, and Beyond* (New York: Oxford UP, 1993).

[41] Ingo Juchler, *Die Studentenbewegungen in den Vereinigten Staaten und der Bundesrepublik Deutschland der sechziger Jahre* (Berlin: Dunker & Humblot, 1996).

[42] Sabine von Dirke, *"All Power to the Imagination!" The West German Counterculture from the Student Movement to the Greens* (Lincoln and London: U Nebraska P, 1997). Von Dirke explores an interesting aspect of the German student movement that goes beyond the scope of this article, namely, the extent to which the counterculture's alternative politics and its aesthetic concepts and artistic practices impacted on the dominant "hegemonic" culture of the Federal Republic (31–66 and 209–18).

[43] Wolfgang Kraushaar, "Der Zeitzeuge als Feind des Historikers? Neuerscheinungen zur 68er-Bewegung," *Mittelweg 36, Zeitschrift des Hamburger Instituts für Sozialforschung,* No. 6/99, 49–72.

[44] Kraushaar 70–71 (translation IC).

[45] Wolfgang Kraushaar, *Neunzehnhundertachtundsechzig (1968) als Mythos, Chiffre und Zäsur* (Hamburg: Hamburger Edition, 2000).

[46] Peter Schneider, "Der Zerfall des Zivilen," *Die Zeit* 32 (2000).

[47] Peter Schneider, "Ausbruch aus der Käseglocke," *Der Spiegel* 21 (2000).

[48] See Ingo Cornils, "Romantic Relapse? The Literary Representation of the German Student Movement," in Chris Hall and David Rock, eds., *CUTG Proceedings 1999* (Bern: Peter Lang, 2000), 107–23.

[49] See Ingo Cornils, "The Struggle Continues. Rudi Dutschke's Long March," in Gerard J. DeGroot, ed., *Student Protest: The Sixties and After* (London, 1998), 100–114.

[50] See Mager and Spinnarke, *Was wollen die Studenten?* (Frankfurt am Main: Fischer, 1967); Günter Gaus's famous interview with Rudi Dutschke, 3 December 1967; and Hans Magnus Enzensberger's interview with Rudi Dutschke, Bernd Rabehl and Christian Semler in *Kursbuch 14* (Berlin, 1968).

[51] For example in their election poster depicting Willy Brandt and Walter Scheel as the heroes from the 1969 cult film *Easy Rider.*

[52] "Die neuen Deutschen," *Der Spiegel* 21 (2000).

[53] See Alexander Smoltczyk, "Die letzte Gefangene der RAF," *Spiegel Reporter* 3 (2001); Hannah Cleaver, "Germany is shaken by daughter of Meinhof," *Daily Telegraph* (3 March 2001).

[54] The following contributions give an overview of the debate. Further links can be found on my webpage: http://www.german.leeds.ac.uk/gsm/gsm1.htm. Gunter Hofmann, "Joschka und Jochen. 1968, noch einmal besichtigt — wie die Bundesrepublik beginnt, sich zu historisieren," *Die Zeit* 4 (2001); Michael Naumann, "Fischer in der Geschichtsfalle," *Die Zeit* 4 (2001); Reinhard Mohr, "Zorn auf die roten Jahre," *Der Spiegel* 4 (2001); Wolf Biermann, "Komm mit angeln . . . sagte der Fischer zum Wurm. Anmerkungen zur Vergangenheitsbewältigung von 1968," *Die Welt* (19 January 2001); Klaus Hartung, "Runter mit dem Zeigefinger." *Die Zeit* 5 (2001); "Ein Segen für dieses Land." Interview with Daniel Cohn-Bendit, *Der Spiegel* 5 (2001); Karl Heinz Bohrer, "Fantasie, die keine war," *Die Zeit* 7 (2001);

Hans-Jürgen Fink/Irene Jung, "Verteufeln hilft nicht." Interview with Joachim Gauck, *Hamburger Abendblatt, Wochenend Journal* (10 February 2001); Gerd Koenen, "Ach, achtundsechzig. Fischer, das 'rote Jahrzehnt' und wir," *Kommune: Zeitschrift für Politik, Ökonomie, Kultur* No. 5 (2001).

[55] Lord Weidenfeld, "Mutmaßungen über Joschka Fischer," *Die Welt* (25 January 2001)

[56] John Hooper, "Fischer's troubles an affair of state," *The Guardian* (27 February 2001).

[57] "CDU wirft Fischer Verharmlosung vor," *Süddeutsche Zeitung* (18 January 2001).

[58] Wolfgang Kraushaar, *1968: Das Jahr, das alles verändert hat* (Munich: Piper, 1998), 313. See also Edgar Wolfrum, "'1968' in der gegenwärtigen deutschen Geschichtspolitik," *Aus Politik und Zeitgeschichte*, B 22–23/2001, 28–36

The PDS: "CSU des Ostens"?[1] — *Heimat* and the Left

Peter Thompson

"Wer hätte jemals gedacht, daß die Heimat das letzte Bindemittel des Marxismus-Leninismus sein könnte?"[2]

IN CHARACTERISTICALLY POLEMICAL manner, Christian von Ditfurth thus presents the recent stance adopted by the *Partei des demokratischen Sozialismus* on the national question and the social coherence of the five new states as the worst of all worlds. By using the term Marxism-Leninism he reinforces the impression that the PDS is an unreconstructed Stalinist party, and by describing *Heimat* as a "letzte Bindemittel" he also gives the impression that the party is using this term as a desperate and cynical ploy. The PDS's use of *Heimat,* therefore, is presented by von Ditfurth as a bad thing — because the concept is limited only to the ex-GDR and because it might appear to flirt with sinister, hard-right nationalist policies. In one sentence the PDS is thus described as both neo-Stalinist and proto-fascist. It is the modern equivalent of the Cold War description of the SED and other left wingers as "rot-lackierte Faschisten."

The aim of this essay is to go beyond the polemical and to investigate to what extent the PDS's attitudes toward regional and, indeed, modern German identity are rooted in the different social structures of east and west Germany. I will also ask whether the PDS can make any worthwhile contribution to the debate on the national question and challenge Ditfurth's assumption that *Heimat* — in its east German form at least — is inherently reactionary. These questions derive from the three-fold political reality of post-1990 Germany. Thus united Germany is a country which a) is attempting to create a sense of national coherence, b) is simultaneously seeking to build a *post-national* consensus, c) has never even truly become a nation in the first place.

In a liberal version of the theory of permanent revolution, much of the west German left-liberal intelligentsia since the 1960s has imagined that it is possible to skip over — or at least ignore — the nation in Germany and go straight to the utopia of a liberal-bourgeois internationalism. Apart from its polemical intent, Ditfurth's comment also ignores the fact that questions of *Heimat* and national identity have long played a role — if a considerably neglected one — in the socialist movement.[3] It also touches in very real terms upon one of the central issues of contemporary political debate, namely that of the *socio-ideological* rather than merely the more commonly addressed *political* character of PDS support.

The debate about the nation within the PDS was initiated around the time of the 1998 election when the leadership, and in particular Lothar Bisky, raised the question of national identity in Germany and what the relationship between the Left and the national question should be. As a result the PDS was attacked for being akin to the National Bolsheviks or the Strasserite Left-Nazis.[4] Since then there have been further examples of an attempt to address the question which have caused deep divisions both within and outside the party. These have culminated in Gregor Gysi's comments during the run-up to the Berlin election about the PDS and the five new states playing a healing role in Germany's struggle with the national question and Gabrielle Zimmer's (Gysi's successor as leader of the PDS) contention that the younger generation of Germans socialised in the GDR have fewer problems with national identity than west Germans and that it is possible for them to say that they love Germany and are proud to be German. The cynic might argue that this is a political tactic designed to win over the socially conservative vote to the PDS rather than see it go to the hard-right and this issue will be dealt with extensively below. What is to be demonstrated here, however, is that the debate actually reflects a different social agenda in the ex-GDR which cannot be ignored and which contributes considerably to the continued division of Germany.

Liberalism, Collectivity and Identity

The primary reason for the apparent difference in values between eastern and western Germany lies in the discrepancy between the fifty-year tradition of political liberalism and the more recent growth of economic liberalism in the west, on the one hand, and the tradition of social conservatism and collectivity in the east on the other. Paradoxically there are some on the Right who have argued that the GDR was in fact the better of the two Germanies in that it represented the continuity of "German" values under the guise of Stalinism rather than the "decadent" and liberal refounding of society which took place in the Federal Republic. Equally, the propounders of totalitarian theory could equate the socially authoritarian nature of the GDR with the Nazi dictatorship. The central reason for this interpretation lies in the fact that both socialism as well as the various forms of orthodox conservatism through to fascism tend to challenge individualistic liberal tenets and to put the interests of the collective above those of the individual.[5] From here it is only a short step to equating all forms of collectivity and branding them all as reactionary. It is this sort of undifferentiated analysis which also leads to the horse-shoe theory of political analysis which sees left and right as meeting up somewhere round the back of the "acceptable" spectrum.

An example of how the desire for *Heimat* can be interpreted as reactionary can be found in the response, both inside and outside the party, to Gabrielle Zimmer's statement in an interview with the *taz* in October 2000, just after her election as Gysi's successor:

> Ich will keine neue DDR, das ist Quatsch. Ich bin auf der Suche nach einer neuen Identität. Man kann Thüringerin, Europäerin, Weltbürgerin sein, wie man will — für mich gibt es darüber hinaus eine nationale Identität. Mir fällt es leichter als Gysi und Bisky, zu sagen, dass ich Deutschland auch liebe. Die beiden sind kurz vor beziehungsweise nach dem Krieg geboren, sie haben den Kalten Krieg der 50er- und 60er-Jahre bewusst miterlebt, sie haben sich an der DDR ganz anders gerieben als wir Jüngeren. Ich — und da steht meine Person für viele der jetzt jüngeren Leute in der PDS-Führung — hatte ein durchaus positives Verhältnis zur DDR. Ich habe mich zu ihr als meinem Land bekannt. Jetzt, wo es sie nicht mehr gibt, bin ich ein bisschen auf der Suche nach einem Ersatz.[6]

This one quotation demonstrates quite remarkably the changes in attitude in the GDR toward society and nation which took place within the space of two generations. It shows quite clearly that the older generation, growing up in an ideological framework of ideological monumentalism or high Stalinism, are still largely conditioned by those values, whereas the younger generation, socialised during the conservative and antiquarian period under Honecker, have a far more de-ideologised and non-political attitude toward their own history.[7]

For Zimmer the "national" identity created in the GDR was something completely normal; the equivalent generation in the West still finds the concept of national identity very difficult.[8] As a result, her ability to come to terms with being German is far greater than that even of many west Germans. For her, and this is also the basis for much *Ostalgie,* it is a question of seeking an identity in place rather than ideology. Paradoxically, the collapse of Stalinism as an ideology has emptied the GDR of its political content and left a shell of memories of *Heimat,* order and stability. These are all concepts which the west German Left has spent many decades resisting in the name of socialist liberation. Equally paradoxically therefore, Zimmer's generation of east Germans may well play a role in helping to normalise west German attitudes to their own nation. Those who grew up under the welfare dictatorship of the "Brezhnev social contract" are much more likely to want to defend the welfare democracy of the Brandt years than the neo-liberal social dislocation implicit in Schröders "neue Mitte."

The major error in trying to identify the continuing social and psychological division of Germany and the lack of an all-German identity lies in focussing entirely on the *Wende* of 1989 rather than what preceded and gave rise to it. Since 1989 we have been preoccupied with a sense of disappointment with the *Wende* itself and are constantly tempted to conclude that this disappointment lies in the nature of the "Revolution" of 1989 and its consequences. 1989 is given a primary causative status, with symptomatic ripples emanating directly from it.

However, the *Wende* is in fact itself merely a ripple: a symptom of a deeper and wider historical turning point which can be located in the shift to the re-economisation of society and the neo-liberal wave around the mid-1970s. In consequence the socio-economic situation in the ex-GDR is therefore primarily related not to the mechanisms of transition since 1989 (in which the GDR has apparently been colonised by an unchanged West German society) but to the nature of economic transition which has embraced the world economy for a quarter of a century and which itself gave rise to unification. This means that East Germans demonstrated for unification with the auto-mythology rather than the changing reality of the Federal Republic. They imagined they would get the West Germany of the 1950s, but got that of the 1990s. They wished for the *Wirtschaftswunder* but got the *Standortkrise* instead. As Dieter Klein puts it, "die Ironie der Geschichte besteht ja darin, daß just als die Ostdeutschen hoffnungsvoll aufbrachten, um endlich des bundesdeutschen Wohlstandsstaates teilhaftig zu werden, dieser gerade dabei war, beschleunigt zu entschwinden."[9]

In terms of the consequences for contemporary politics and the relationship between the SPD and the PDS, Rolf Reisig maintains that "die neue, eher neoliberale Linie [of the SPD] verkörpert nicht den im Osten vorhandenen sozialdemokratischen Wertehaushalt."[10] In this context, the GDR then becomes for many east Germans a socially secure retrospectively "imagined community" rather than a dictatorship, and the PDS the party of the defence of the collective values of that society rather than simply "the successor party to the SED." The PDS's dilemma, therefore, is how to assume that role as a social defence organisation while at the same time demonstrating its readiness to take on responsibility for a system which is increasingly anti-collective. Even André Brie, the most vocal of those wishing for a social-democratisation of the PDS and a more serious orientation toward the west recognises the limitations facing the party:

> Die neue Verantwortung der PDS besteht darin, dass ihre Wählerinnen und Wähler sie nicht mehr nur als Adressatin ostdeutschen und linken Wir-Gefühls und legitimen Protestes sehen, sondern von ihr wirksame Interessenvertretung, politische Veränderung und kompetente Mitgestaltung erwarten . . . Sie wird zunehmend eine Partei werden müssen, die ein modernes und für die Öffentlichkeit erkennbares sozialistisches Profil entwickelt und zugleich zu kompetenter Realpolitik und zur Übernahme konkreter politischer Verantwortung bereit und in der Lage ist.[11]

However, despite the attempts of the Gysi-Bisky-Brie group to reorientate the party toward the west, in general we can say that the PDS continues to represent a part of the Left historically anchored in the collectivist values of the five new states and that if it wishes to survive as a distinctive force it has no alternative. As Yvonne Kaufman, Deputy Chair of the PDS, maintains, "Die PDS ist eine systemalternative Partei. Das ist ja identitätsstiftend für die Partei. Sonst wären wir überflüssig."[12] What the most recent turn of the PDS since the election of Gabriele Zimmer has shown is a new attempt to provide an alternative to the status quo within its electoral fortress of the ex-GDR rather than the whole of the Federal Republic. This demonstrates that the basic values of the PDS, although still of the Left, are actually fundamentally different to those of the western Left. Its 1968 was primarily that of the Prague Spring rather than the Paris events and it did not grow up in the context of the Anglo-Saxon individualism which so characterises the mainstream western liberal Left. For this reason its roots are in a more orthodox Marxism along with a regionalist nationalism in which values of order and community take precedence over individualism.

In order to prosper in the west, the PDS will have to adapt to the very values which are so distant from its own traditions and yet at the same time try to bring its own eastern values of collective socialism into the political agenda of the Federal Republic. The success of this strategy depends as much on the objective development of the economy and society as on the subjective processes of party policy. It is therefore the uses and disadvantages of history for the PDS — the contents as well as the specific weight of the "Rücksack der Geschichte" it has to carry — which lead us to ask questions as to whether *Heimat* and a retrospective obsession with the GDR can indeed function positively in a united Germany. This means that the Stalinism debate within and about the PDS is not primarily about the past and culpability for the running of a Stalinist state but much more about political orientation for the future. Neugebauer and Stöss, therefore, make a fundamental mistake in maintaining that the retrospective view is its main problem:

> Die Lautstärke der nun ausgetragenen ideologischen Kontroversen übersteigt deren gesellschaftlich-politische Relevanz bei weitem. Die Partei diskutiert nach wie vor rückwärtsgewandt, vernachlässigt ihre Profilierung als moderne sozialistische Partei und koppelt sich damit vom Modernisierungsdiskurs in der Bundesrepublik ab.[13]

The point is that the retrospectively imagined community of the GDR takes on different significance for different purposes. There is a large constituency, in both east and west, which understands the term *Modernisierungsdiskurs* entirely negatively. To them it means the end of community, stability and *Überschaubarkeit* in favour of flexibility, globalisation and economic liberalisation. What is shown here is that history has both uses and disadvantages which exist in a complicated dialectical relationship and, as Jarausch points out, the debate about their significance is clearly defined by the political preferences of the participants.[14]

An example of this complex relationship can be found in Dieter Klein. Klein was one of the founders and main theoreticians of the reformist group "Dritter Weg" in the late 1980s within the SED. He remains a reformist within the PDS and was, until the Cottbus conference in October 2000, a member of its leadership as well as a member of the *Moderner Sozialismus*[15] group at the Humboldt University in Berlin. In that sense he is well aware and critical of the history of Stalinism in the German workers' movement and its role in deforming the GDR. And yet he too takes a view of that history which is not entirely negative and is designed to rescue historical legitimation for the future of the PDS:

> Nachdem das Berliner Programm der SPD mit seinen demokratisch-sozialistischen Grundforderungen nur noch eine marginale Rolle in der sozialdemokratischen Politik spielt und besonders von Schröder de facto ad acta gelegt wurde, bewirbt sich die PDS um die in Deutschland vakante Rolle einer sozialistischen Partei. Sie ist in ihren historischen Wurzeln in der Arbeiterbewegung, ihrer Programmatik und ihren Wählerinteressen entsprechend — und begünstigt durch den Ausschluß

aus allen Machtkartellen der etablierten Parteien — besonders ausge-
prägt die Partei der sozialen Gerechtigkeit.[16]

What these three points demonstrate is that even in somebody determined to push the PDS in a more social democratic direction and who
is broadly in favour of the removal of pro-SED elements from the party,
there is a need to emphasise the sense of continuity of a working class
tradition and acknowledge the existence of the GDR as a social alternative to capitalism.

The main difference between the PDS and the other main parties in
the present climate is that it is still predominantly a *political* party,
whereas all of the others have become *economic* parties. This does not
mean that the other parties have decided to control the economy but
that they have, to a greater or lesser degree, allowed market economic
considerations to control them. On the other hand a *political* party such
as the PDS sees its role as that of attempting to control the economy in
the name of social imperatives. In that sense *Ostalgie* and attachment to
Heimat do not represent a call for the return to the authoritarianism of
a Stalino-Prussian dictatorship but a desire for protection against the
neo-liberal tides of recent times. Regional defence of the ex-GDR can
therefore be seen as synonymous not with conservatism but with a radical
political opposition which may, at some point in the future, be extended
to the whole of Germany.

The Right has recognised this east German potential as well and
campaigns there with slogans which are as anti-capitalist as they are
xenophobic.[17] It is this recognition, I believe, which lies behind the
policies developed by the new Zimmer leadership to attract support in
the west and the paradoxical though concomitant emphasis on German
national identity. In a very dismissive article, Klaus Hartung argues the
same when he describes the sort of atmosphere the PDS offers in eastern
Germany:

> Die PDS bietet Osttrotz und flotte Sprüche, Teilhabe an der Macht
> und Jobs für den frustrierten Teil der DDR-Intelligenz; sie bietet Par-
> teileben, Nestwärme und Harmonie angesichts der kalten zerstrittenen
> Westparteien. . . .[18]

As with Ditfurth, a clever use of rhetoric implies that "Nestwärme and
Harmonie" are actually worse than anomie and disharmony. The real
question is whether this is entirely negative and whether it is possible to
defend the idea of community and "communism" in a Germany dominated by the compounded ideologies of abstract anti-nationalism and an

increasingly neo-liberal economic outlook, without appearing socially authoritarian. If so, what sort of problems does this cause for the PDS in its relationships with a predominantly libertarian western Left and an increasingly neo-liberal SPD? The PDS is increasingly described as a nationalist and socialist party, if not yet a National Socialist one. As Stefan Berg has pointed out there now exists in the ex-GDR the *Menschengemeinschaft* of which Ulbricht once dreamed.[19] The PDS tends to represent those who have a memory (false or not) of social cohesion or those who feel that one should be regained against the tide of individualism sweeping in from the west. Too often though, this desire for a *Menschengemeinschaft* is misidentified as a desire for a Nazi *Volksgemeinschaft*.[20]

Community or Society?

Paradoxically, it could be argued that the nostalgia for the GDR is more similar to the American theoretical tradition of the civil society, according to Friedrich Jaeger, "die als Summe sozialer Gemeinschaften die Elemente der kulturellen Integration selber erzeugt und ständig erneuert, von den sie als Gesellschaft zehrt,"[21] than it is to the ideal of the west German "bürgerliche Gesellschaft." As Jaeger goes on to point out, within the social community, economic rationale and cultural identity are seen as indivisible whereas in the concept of the "bürgerliche Gesellschaft" they are often treated as separate entities. Neo-liberalism rests ideologically on an absolute delinking of economics and culture. The idea that "there is no such thing as society" is the prime example of this approach. In the case of German unification the attempt to impose a "bürgerliche" form of west German identity onto a social tradition rooted more in notions of civil community in which the maintenance of political authority and social stability is seen as superior to, and determining of, economic policy is bound to cause friction and fundamental misunderstanding.

The sense of social isolation and confusion which is now undoubtedly present in the ex-GDR is therefore clearly represented in opinion poll and survey data conducted in the east. The most exhaustive surveys conducted to date are analysed in Neugebauer/Stöss where the traditional Left/Right axis for determining social values is replaced with intersecting Authoritarian/Liberal and Social Justice/ Free Market axes. With this repositioning and reinterpretation of social values we find in many cases that PDS voters and members are revealed as being "authoritarian" and heavily orientated toward social justice rather than the free market. With this presentation of data it is also apparently easy to show that in terms of social values, PDS voters can hardly be distinguished from those of the *Republikaner*.[22] Again however, this sort of interpretation of raw data fundamentally distorts the thinking and motivation behind the apparent overlap of superficial responses to public opinion surveys. The social psychology of the average east German is not determined by some Prussian-fascist authoritarian personality trait but by their experience of unification, conflated with their ever-fading memories of the reality of the GDR.

In a sort of mirror image of west Germany, east German identification with the GDR is with its socio-economic structures, with its collectivist and non-market orientated values and not with the political dictatorship of the party elite. If the West Germans had the economic miracle and a form of patriotism rooted in the strength of the German mark as a substitute identity then the East Germans had their antiquarian so-called niche existence. What both had in common was a propensity not to examine the underlying geo-strategic and historical conditions for their social and economic systems.

However, another reason for the perception of the PDS as an authoritarian party is more to do with the political heritage of those doing the analysis than with the subjects of that analysis. In this case the typical western post-1968 anti-authoritarian perspective is applied to a society which had no 1968 and which — for good or ill — is not obsessed with retrospective anti-Nazism and abstract anti-nationalism in the same way as its western counterpart. The view, therefore, that the PDS is close to right-wing values is based in a criticism of its adherence in eastern Germany to what are seen as values traditionally associated with the Right in western Germany. But again, what are seen as negative values in a capitalist society — discipline, law and order, thrift and an identification with *Heimat*[23] — are not necessarily negative when felt by those socialised in a society which considered itself a *sozialistische Menschengemeinschaft* with a high degree of collective identification and social cohesion.

Of course it can be argued that values such as these, in themselves and regardless of their socio-historical context, tend toward exclusivist or xenophobic attitudes. The rise of neo-Nazi movements and anti-foreigner attacks are often pointed to as prime examples of this.[24] And yet every study shows that those engaged in such activities are not of the generation which is traditionally associated with the above values but are carried out by the young disaffected generation socialised in the closing years of the GDR and the ten years since the fall of the Berlin Wall.

Those of the older GDR-nostalgic generation may well be conservative in their outlook but one has to ask what it is they wish to conserve and whether or not they have a point in doing so. That they vote PDS should be held neither against them nor the PDS.

Hubertus Schmold, a prominent member of the DGB, in recognising the trend toward increasing instability of employment and its political consequences, has called for a more prominent role for social security as a necessary corrective to flexibility. However, even this is done in the name of *increased* flexibility: "Wir müssen die Menschen mitnehmen. Wer für Flexibilität wirbt, aber nicht genug Sicherheit bietet, der wird keine Flexibilität erreichen."[25]

This is the real *Wende* from which all the other changes detailed here have issued. In this sense the political change of direction of the mid-seventies was of far greater significance than the *Wende* of 1989, and, moreover, the latter issued directly out of the former. As Roger de Weck enquired, somewhat belatedly, in *Die Zeit:* "Die linken Ideologen wollten die völlige Kontrolle der Politik über die Wirtschaft. Kommt jetzt das Gegenteil?"[26] It is my contention here that this reversal has been coming since at least 1974 and that the end of the Long Cold War from 1917–1989 was brought about by, but has also deepened, that economisation of society. Uwe-Jean Heuser, for example, states in *Die Zeit* that "Das erste Jahrzehnt der Einheit war auch das Jahrzehnt der Globalisierung"[27] as though the two events or processes were entirely autonomous features of late capitalism. The point, however, is that globalisation and the re-unification of Germany are intimately intertwined. The former gave rise to the latter and the latter in turn accelerated the former. To paraphrase Horkheimer, "wer von der deutschen Einheit spricht, soll auch nicht über die Globalisierung schweigen." To oppose globalisation, therefore, is almost inevitably to withdraw into community and safety. *Ostalgie,* brought down to its simplest level, represents the east German version of the "spirit of the Blitz." Nobody in Britain seriously wants the Second World War back any more than anybody in eastern Germany wants a return to dictatorial SED rule, but the sense of social solidarity of those days is often appealed to as a means of orientation in difficult times. What people look back to is the antiquarian, somewhat cosy nature of the GDR. As Volker Braun puts it in his poem *Nachruf,* "was ich nicht hatte, werde ich ewig missen."[28]

So the most that can be said about the PDS is that it has certain trends and tendencies as well as supporters and voting groups which can be seen as relatively authoritarian. In the words of Neugebauer and Stöss, however, all this shows is that the PDS is a "ganz normale Partei."[29]

Where it is different to the other parties, including the Greens, is in its continuing commitment to a radical analysis of social phenomena and a totalising theory based in Marxist historical materialism. The problem for the PDS is that in these post-modern days of neo-liberal individualism, all totalising theories are automatically seen as authoritarian.

The PDS and History

It is not so much that the ex-GDR, and therefore also the PDS, are primarily victims of their own history but that they have become victims of everybody's present. We all experience disunity within our own lives and societies, whether it is between class or race or nation or region or gender but the disunity is one of a socio-historical rather than an essentialist one. Truth is not in that sense decentred but merely disrupted. Class, racial, national, regional or gender disunification is a characteristic of the modern age and its possible transcendence is therefore to be located in much larger questions than simply those of problems of communication between east and west Germans.[30]

At the Münster PDS conference in 2000 Lothar Bisky maintained: "Die PDS ist keine Geschichtspartei."[31] In saying this he was attempting to reorientate the PDS away from the eternal discussions about the history of the German workers' movement and the GDR and toward a debate about the future. This is a hopeless task though, for the PDS is a party which is, by its very nature, rooted in the past and, in eastern Germany survives largely on a diet of identificatory nostalgia only washed down with small drafts of policies for the future. The code contained within Bisky's statement, however, is that the proportions in this relationship between past and future have to change in order to win over more voters in western Germany. The difficult task facing the PDS is that it has to appeal to the past and the future at the same time and yet still have a presence in contemporary political activity. This is both its strength and its weakness. However, the PDS's preoccupation with history is not based simply on psychological identification with the GDR past but is conditioned by an identification with great figures, ideas and concepts from the past based in monumentalist, antiquarian and critical approaches. This identification has a pre-eminently contemporary purpose and cannot be seen simply as nostalgia.

We can conclude from this that the preoccupation with the past has a basis in unresolved social questions. A purely future-orientated policy can only be arrived at by wrenching politics out of history and reducing it to a purely contingent phenomenon based in a depoliticised and deideologised context of supply and demand politics — the terrible fate of most "modern" parties and one probably responsible for low voter turn-out everywhere. The PDS's problem, if it can be seen as such, is that it remains a political and an ideological party which bases itself in a specific tradition — namely a Marxist one — of historical analysis. Leadership attempts to move it away from a Marxist approach must, by definition then, start with an attack on the historical context and analytical approach of major parts of the Party.

On the other hand, what is disadvantageous about the antiquarian values of many PDS voters and members is that the conditions which created the social cohesion, namely productivist models with clear class boundaries and social structures, were produced not out of the exigencies of the socio-economic development of a socialist society and economy but out of the political inflexibility and social stagnation of Stalinist political hegemony. The question we are left with in the end, therefore, is if there ever was a Marxist baby, has it not long since drowned in the Stalinist bathwater of instrumentalised historical analysis? To continue the metaphor, is there any point in trying to resuscitate the baby at all? Would it not be easier to jettison all adherence to an oppositional position toward capitalism and, as Brie puts it, "endlich ankommen in die BRD"? The answer, of course, is that if the PDS were to do this, as some in the leadership seem to wish, then there would be no reason for its continued existence alongside the SPD.

Alternatively, there is the scenario in which it becomes a purely regional party, such as the CSU in Bavaria in which it would gradually lose its critical ideological edge in favour of a regionalist-nationalist conservatism. The parties of the Right such as the CSU have the advantage that they can explicitly base their whole programme on conservative concepts of nation, religion and tradition, i.e. monumentalism and antiquarianism, and be proud of it. The Left, however, must always apologise for doing the same. For that reason Stalinism tended to fall back on concepts of nationalism transmuted into Greater-Russian chauvinism, of religion transmuted into Marxist-Leninist dogma, and of tradition transmuted into the functional manipulation of history. Yet Stalinism also had to rest on the collective ownership — if not control — of the means of production. Stalinism minus economic control equals right-wing social authoritarianism, a development seen all too clearly in post-Soviet Russia. Separating out the positive defensive elements of *Ostalgie* from the negative and reactionary elements of Stalinist thinking is therefore the major problem facing the leadership. Perhaps, at base, this is the reason for the new emphasis on community over history. Of an abstract collectivism over forced collectivisation.

This is where André Brie's statement about finally arriving in the Federal Republic is, in my view, wrong. In the long term, the only way the PDS can ever really "arrive" in the Federal Republic is by maintaining an alternative profile as a distinctive political and ideological party of opposition to the prevailing socio-economic system. To arrive without that alternative would be to arrive with no luggage — or no rucksack, as Yvonne Kaufmann put it — and be, therefore, at the mercy of others and the vagaries of western political beauty contests. Despite all of the problems of Stalinism in the Long Cold War, the PDS tends still to hold to the view that socialism remains the only viable alternative to the rule of capital. Where Brie and the rest of the leadership are right, however, is in their insistence that the PDS must jettison its adherence to those Stalinist ideologies of the past before it can build on the positive traditions of the workers' movement. What is necessary, however, is a rejection of deideologised Stalinist monumentalism and antiquarianism in favour of a re-politicised critical praxis. This oppositional Marxist strand has existed within the workers' movement throughout the dark years of the Long Cold War in various forms and the PDS has no alternative but to build upon it in order to remain distinctive. What the PDS needs to do is indeed "endlich ankommen in die BRD" but as a rather unwelcome squatters rather than a fully paid up member of the property-owning democracy.

This brings us to the central important point about understanding the GDR — and therefore the PDS. What is often misunderstood is that — especially in the period of antiquarian neo-Stalinism after the 1960s — emphasis was not only placed on ideological training and indoctrination but primarily on social security and communality. The GDR under Honecker during the period of the "Einheit der Wirtschafts- und Sozialpolitik" was a depoliticised state in which ideology was merely about administration and not agitation. Retrospective identification with the GDR is therefore an identification with the social and economic stability of that antiquarian and depoliticised reality and not with the agitation and ideological propaganda of the monumentalist years. Western observers often ignore this distinction. They believe that PDS voters are looking back nostalgically to some revolutionary communism when in fact they are looking back to a relatively conservative communalism. What the West judges to have been a stagnated society is often seen by those who experienced it as a stable one. In turn it was stable because its

politics were antiquarian ones, designed to consolidate rather than criticise.

Conclusions

Gregor Gysi once asked; "Die Kernfrage ist: Stellen wir das Primat der
Politik wieder her?"[32] However, the primacy of politics in the twentieth
century had both a negative and positive dialectic. On the one hand a
return to the deideologised politics of the Long Cold War in which
dogma replaced critique cannot be desired. On the other hand a return
to the subordination of political and social control to the primacy of
economics would be equally damaging. What the PDS is striving to
achieve is a new type of politicisation of the ideological agenda which
takes a radical approach to globalisation and its consequences for people
and environment but which does so in a critical and self-critical fashion.

It is sometimes argued that the ex-GDR is actually best placed to
prevail in a globalised economy because of the way in which the old
hyper-social and hyper-political structures of the GDR regime were so
completely destroyed in 1989. The destruction of the socio-economic
structural base of society was certainly radical and has indeed created the
objective conditions for transition to a fully marketised and dynamic
economy. However, as Anton Ackermann and the SED discovered after
1945, the creation of objective economic conditions for social transformation is only a very small part of the task of bringing about a change in
people's identities and loyalties. Just as the Stalinists thought in vulgar
economistic categories in 1945, so the marketisers and globalisers think
today. The subjective conditions for transition are always at least as
important as the objective ones. At the moment the PDS profits from the
fact that those subjective conditions have not yet fully changed in the
direction of an acceptance of economic primacy. A recent opinion poll
had the following results:

> Kürzlich sagte jemand: "Wenn man will, dass in unserem Land linke
> Politik gemacht wird, dann muss man die PDS wählen. Die PDS ist die
> einzige Partei, die noch linke Politik vertritt." Finden Sie, der hat
> Recht, oder der hat nicht Recht?[33]
>
> Bevölkerung

	gesamt	West	Ost
Hat Recht	30	26	44
Nicht Recht	38	42	24
Unentschieden	33	32	32

This poll shows the extent to which the PDS is identified as an ideological rather than just as a geographical party representing the ex-GDR. In this context, André Brie makes the following statement:

> Während alle anderen Parteien inzwischen erklärtermaßen die "Unternehmergesellschaft" zum Leitbild für die Zukunft bestimmt haben und ihre Politik vom Primat der Wirtschaftsinteressen leiten lassen, obwohl die derart machtvoll sind, dass sie der Parteien kaum noch bedürfen, will und muss die PDS die Interessen der Menschen und insbesondere die Interessen der sozial Schwachen, sozial Benachteiligten und sozial Ausgegrenzten zum Ausgangspunkt ihrer Politik und Strategie machen.[34]

This raises questions about whether the tactics which Brie promotes for the PDS in the short term — i.e. social-democratisation and preparation for real political responsibility within government — are compatible with these long-term strategic considerations. One is forced to ask the old question of whether the Left is able to play a role in the government of a capitalist state and remain on the Left. The tragedy of the twentieth century is that the experience of Stalinism raises the question of whether it is possible for the Left to exercise power in a post-capitalist state either. The consequence of this analysis would appear to suggest that the Left in general can only ever play a critical and radical role in opposition. As soon as it takes power either through revolution as in Russia or parliamentary means as in the West, its critical energies are absorbed into administrative procedures and the maintenance of power at all costs. In this sense both social-democratic and Stalinist stagnation can be seen as almost inevitable consequences of the exercise of the power gained from critical praxis. As Jean Améry puts it:

> Mag sein . . . daß die Linke ihrem Wesen nach niemals Macht sein kann. . . . Als Macht negiert sie ihren fundamental bestreitenden Charakter. . . . Die negative Dialektik der Linken ist ihre raison d'être und ist auf paradoxe Weise die aussichtslose Chance der Gesellschaft.[35]

This has obvious consequences for an analysis of the PDS since 1990. Its position has been one of a mixture of opposition to the system as a whole combined with participation in coalition governments in Mecklenburg-Vorpommern and toleration of an SPD-Green Government in Sachsen-Anhalt which have been less than radical or revolutionary in their activities. What this all means for the PDS is that its strategic decision-making has to respond to what are apparently disparate impetuses and traditions. As we have seen, the debate as to which direction to take is essentially tied up with questions of history and identity of the Party, the SED, the GDR and the history of the Left and socialist theory and praxis. This is not because of some ideological nostalgia or addiction to doctrinal debates but paradoxically because amongst voters questions of identity and social position have become depoliticised and transmuted into a form of left-communitarianism. When politics itself is seen as necessarily authoritarian because it challenges the metaphysics of social contingency upon which economic liberalism is based, then to return to a deeper level of politics even than the one which was left behind with the fall of the wall becomes increasingly difficult.

In conclusion we can say that the PDS has mobilised around the idea of *Heimat* and identity for two reasons: Firstly there is the shared experience and retrospectively imagined community of the GDR. Secondly there is the recognition that ideas of *Heimat* and identity exist purely in the political realm and it is here that the primacy of politics over the economisation of society can more easily be maintained.

Perhaps, therefore, Ditfurth is right and *Heimat* is the last refuge of the socialist. In a world hostile to collective thinking and social action, though, this may be no bad thing.

Notes

[1] Toralf Staud, "Auf dem Weg zur CSU des Ostens," *Die Zeit* (19 October 2000): 6.

[2] Christian von Ditfurth, *Ostalgie oder linke Alternative: Meine Reise durch die PDS* (Cologne: Kiepenheuer & Witsch, 1998), 63.

[3] See Christoph Dieckmann, *Temperatursprung: Deutsche Verhältnisse* (Frankfurt am Main: Suhrkamp, 1995).

[4] See Johann M. Möller in *Die Welt* (29 September 1998): 4, and also "Die Duldung der rechtsextremen Szene in der DDR ist zu verurteilen," an interview with Lothar Bisky in *Der Tagesspiegel* (3 November 1998): 16.

[5] The CDU has begun to realise the potential of this reality and has started to emphasise traditional right-wing political solutions such as nationalism and the concept of the *Leitkultur*. The *Spiegel* points out that the CDU's candidate for Prime Minister of Brandenburg in the elections of 4 September 1999 tried to take some of the wind out of the DVU's sails by saying in *Junge Freiheit* (an extreme right-wing weekly journal) that in the past there had been a fear of using the concept of the nation in the old Federal Republic and that this had led to a "gewissen verkrümmten Haltung." *Der Spiegel* 35 (30 August 1999), 27

[6] *taz* no. 6282 (28 October 2000), 3. Interview with Jens König. For further contributions to this debate see: http://www.pds-online.de/partei/aktuell/0010/zimmer_taz.htm

[7] For a discussion of the terms monumentalism and antiquarianism as applicable to the history of Stalinism see Peter Thompson "The PDS: Marx's Baby or Stalin's

Bathwater? or Vom Nutzen und Nachteil der Historie für das Leben der PDS." In Peter Barker, ed., *The GDR and Its History, German Monitor* 49 (Amsterdam: Rodopi, 2000), 97–113.

[8] Winfried Wolf, for example, expresses a typically radical abstract rejection of German national identity found on the Western Left in his article: "PDS-Deutschtümelei. Kann es 'linken Patriotismus' geben? Eine Antwort auf Klaus Höpcke," *Junge Welt* (4 November 2000): "Diese PDS-Debatte findet statt in einer Bundesrepublik Deutschland, in der ein Großteil derjenigen, die sich gegen den nationalen Terror von rechts wehren, sich als 'antinational' und 'internationalistisch' verstehen und sich von einer PDS, die ein deutsches Vaterland entdeckt, abgestoßen fühlen. So kamen wir als PDS zwar in die Schlagzeilen — aber als Negativ-Werbung" (6).

[9] Dieter Klein, "Zwischen Ideologie und politischer Realität," in Peter Barker, ed., *The Party of Democratic Socialism in Germany: Modern Post-Communism or Nostalgic Populism? German Monitor* 42 (Amsterdam: Rodopi), 1998, 109–27, 117.

[10] *Der Spiegel* 35 (30 August 1999), 25.

[11] André Brie, *Die PDS im Ost und West — Fakten und Argumente statt Vermutungen* (Berlin, August 2000). As a web page: http://www.pds-online.de/partei/ aktuell/0008/brie-studie.pdf, 6.

[12] Author's interview with Yvonne Kaufmann, Karl Liebknecht Haus, on 26 September 1998.

[13] Gero Neugebauer and Richard Stöss, eds., *Die PDS: Geschichte. Organisation. Mitgliederstruktur* (Leske+Budrich, Opladen, 1996), 301–2.

[14] Konrad Jarausch, "Beyond Uniformity: The Challenge of Historicizing the GDR," in Konrad Jarausch, *Dictatorship as Experience: Towards a Socio-Cultural History of the GDR* (New York/Oxford: Berghahn, 1999), 3–14.

[15] For an extensive analysis of the *Moderner Sozialismus* tendency see Eva Sturm, *"Und der Zukunft zugewandt"? Eine Untersuchung zur "Politfähigkeit" der PDS* (Forschung Politik Wissenschaft, Leske+Budrich, Opladen, 2000), 15–20.

[16] Dieter Klein, "Zwischen Ideologie und politischer Realität," in Peter Barker, ed., 112

[17] See, for example, the NPD *Partei Programm*: "Wir Nationaldemokraten setzen uns mit Entschiedenheit für eine neue Gemeinschaftsordnung ein, die in nationaler Solidarität vorhandene Gruppenegoismen überwindet und zu sozialer Sicherheit und Gerechtigkeit führt" and "Die NPD lehnt die in der kapitalistischen Wirtschaftsordnung systematisch betriebene Internationalisierung der Volkswirtschaften entschieden ab. Diese Globalisierung der Wirtschaft beruht auf dem überholten und falschen Ziel der maximalen Ausbeutung der Erde durch Schaffung von wirtschaftlichen Monokulturen gemäß dem sogenannten 'Gesetz der komparativen Vorteile.' Die NPD lehnt die Globalisierung der deutschen Wirtschaft auch deswegen ab, weil die unmittelbar zur Massenerwerbslosigkeit geführt hat." Website: http://home.t-online.de/home/National /programm.htm

[18] Klaus Hartung "Partei des beliebigen Sozialismus," *Die Zeit* 41 (1999), http://www.zeit.de/1999/41/199941_hartung.html.

[19] Stefan Berg, *Das Lange Leben der DDR* (Berlin: Wichern Verlag, 1995), 15.

[20] For a good example of this suspicion on the Left toward the concept of the nation see the analysis and collection of documents in *Die Linke und die "soziale Frage." Wie rechte Wahlerfolge, Nationalismus und Rassismus zusammenhängen:* http://www. nadir.org/nadir/periodika/bahamas/auswahl /web40.htm.

[21] Friedrich Jaeger, "Gesellschaft und Gemeinschaft. Die Gesellschaftstheorie des Kommunitarismus und die politische Ideengeschichte der 'civil society' in den USA," in Thomas Mergel and Thomas Welskopp, eds., *Geschichte zwischen Kultur und Gesellschaft: Beiträge zur Theoriedebatte* (Munich: Beck Verlag, 1997), 306.

[22] See Neugebauer and Stöss, 290.

[23] "schnell ans Meer," *Der Spiegel* 47 (1995): 50.

[24] *Die Linke und die "soziale Frage."*

[25] Werner A. Perger, "Die bange Linke" *Die Zeit* 48 (23 November 2000): 3.

[26] *Die Zeit* 36 (2 September 1999): 10.

[27] *Die Zeit* 45 (4 November 1999): 1.

[28] "Nachruf" in *Neues Deutschland* (4/5 August 1990): 4.

[29] Neugebauer and Stöss, 286.

[30] The Election result in Sachsen-Anhalt on 26 April 1998 in which the DVU obtained 13% of the vote and the CDU was reduced to 22% giving a structural majority to the left parties (even though they were unable to form a government) was a first indictaion of the way in which class conflict returned to the German political stage some ten years after the fall of the wall.

[31] Lothar Bisky, January 1999. Quoted in: Klaus Hartung "Krise im Treibhaus." *Die Zeit* 3 (1999), http://www.zeit.de/1999/3/199903_pds.html

[32] Gregor Gysi "Nach neuen Wegen Suchen," *Der Spiegel* 40 (4 October 1999): 61.

[33] André Brie, *Die PDS,* 12.

[34] André Brie, *Die PDS,* 23.

[35] Jean Améry, "Rechts = zeitgemäß? Links = passé?" in *Vorgänge: Zeitschrift für Gesellschaftspolitik* 15/1975 (Beltz Verlag, Basel 1975), 31.

"An Helligkeit ragt in Europa vor allem mei' Sachsenland vor": Prime Minister Biedenkopf and the Myth of Saxon Identity

Chris Szejnmann

THIS ESSAY DEALS with Saxon identity and broadly with how this identity has developed over the last two hundred years. It summarises and assesses the validity of certain "positive" stereotypes that have been used in descriptions of Saxon people and analyses how contemporary politicians, most importantly the state's first post-unification Prime Minister, Kurt Biedenkopf, have used them.

When the German Democratic Republic (GDR) joined the Federal Republic of Germany (FRG) and ceased to exist in October 1990, the *Freistaat* Saxony was reconstituted and became a state (*Land*) within the federal structure of the newly unified country. After the Second World War, this federal structure was imposed upon western Germany, later the FRG, by the victorious western Allies as a central part of their strategy for a democratic re-structuring of the country. The German states — a total of sixteen since unification — enjoy considerable power. Most importantly, their parliaments control education, communal affairs, police and radio. However, they are not entirely autonomous, and the Basic Law takes precedence over state constitutions. At the same time, however, states (*Länder*) such as Saxony have striven to forge an identity within the new Germany, and most often an identity that reflects supposedly unique and positive aspects of their respective cultures and pasts.

Saxony's Prime Minister, Kurt Biedenkopf, for example, set out in his 1990 government statement the constituents of what he regarded as the state's main contribution to a united Germany:

> Wir bringen zunächst das Wichtigste ein, was wir haben, nämlich uns selbst. Unser Land mit seinen Menschen, unsere Geschichte, unseren Unternehmungsgeist, unsere Phantasie, unseren Witz, aber auch unsere reiche Kultur- und Industrietradition des Freistaates Sachsen.[1]

Six years later, in an interview with the news magazine *Der Spiegel*, Biedenkopf was convinced that inhabitants of the free state "sind stolz darauf, Sachsen zu sein." He explained that this pride derived from the "tausendjährige staatliche Verfaßtheit der Region . . . die Sachsen, ähnlich wie Bayern, von vielen anderen Regionen unterscheidet."[2] Additionally, Biedenkopf frequently refers to a genuine "Pioniersinn" and "Bürgersinn" amongst Saxons. According to him, these have their roots in the history of the industrial development and the cultural landscape of the state.

A number of important aspects have contributed to the development of a Saxon identity. Mary Fulbrook's observation that "a sense of national identity is shaped in part by a common past, the perception of shared memories; often a sense of community in adversity; and a sense of common destiny,"[3] would also seem to apply at a regional level. Saxon identity is linked with the long history of its dynasty — the Wettins — who ruled the region for more than eight hundred years until 1918. This experience was enhanced by the fact that Saxony was one of the heartlands of the Reformation, and that it bordered Slav lands. In fact, a Slav minority (the Sorbs) lives within its territory. Additionally, Saxony underwent a specific economic development from the twelfth century onwards, with the mining of silver, iron ore and coal bringing wealth and economic skills into the region.

In the eighteenth century, Johann Kaspar Riesbeck travelled through Saxony and described the people in glowing terms by emphasising their ethnic and economic superiority compared to their Slav neighbours:

> Es ist, als wenn der hohe Rücken des Erzgebirges und des Thüringer Waldes eine Scheidewand zwischen Licht und Finsternis, Arbeitsamkeit und Indolenz, Freiheit und Sklaverei, Reichtum und Bettelei wäre. Vielleicht findet man in der ganzen Welt keinen in der Nähe so auffallenden Abstich zweier Völker als zwischen den Sachsen und Böhmen . . . Ein fleißigeres Volk als die Sachsen habe ich noch nie gesehen . . . ihr empfindsamer und reger Geist ist unermüdet und unerschöpflich.[4]

Saxony was one of the first central European regions to experience the industrial revolution at the beginning of the nineteenth century. From this point on it developed into the most industrialised, urbanised and most densely populated state in Germany. Industrialisation and modernisation helped to shape Saxon society, and a number of important manufacturing centres developed as the region became the cradle of the German working-class movement. Machines from Chemnitz — the "Saxon Manchester" — motor vehicles and motorbikes from Zwickau, Plauen and Chemnitz, lace from Plauen, and textile products from Crimmitschau all spring to mind in this context. Other related phenomena that contributed to a sense of Saxon identity were the stable borders the state had enjoyed since the Congress of Vienna in 1815, and the setting up of nature organisations, *Heimat* associations, history clubs and local museums. In addition, the historian Karl Lamprecht founded the *Seminar für Landesgeschichte und Siedlungsgeschichte* at the University of Leipzig in 1906, the first of its kind in Germany. Moreover the poets Lene Voigt and Anton Günther popularised the Saxon dialect, and Saxony was celebrated in the paeans to their homeland that were published by local writers in the 1920s, such as the poem *Mein Sachsenland*:

> Schirm euch Gott, ihr Sachsenkinder!
> Unsrer Väter stolzer Ruhm,
> Sachsenfleiß und Sachsentreue
> Sei der Söhne Heiligtum!
>
> Fremder Neid soll ferner schauen
> Sachsens Volk stets Hand in Hand,
> Treu der Schille, treu der Heimat,
> Treu dem deutschen Vaterland! . . .
>
> Laßt sie leuchten, unsre Farben, Sachsenbanner weiß und grün.[5]

And Hans Reimann's *Sachsenlied* of 1929 is similarly effusive:

> Ich will mal mein Sachsen besingen,
> das Land voller Witz und Humor;
> an Helligkeit ragt in Europa
> vor allem mei' Sachsenland vor.[6]

Given the self-evidently "patriotic" sentiments that both poems contain, it is not difficult to imagine the ease which these expressions of "love" for a Saxon homeland and exclusion of outsiders were subsequently exploited and perverted for ideological reasons during the Third Reich.

Saxony's integration into the GDR after the Second World War delivered a number of significant blows to the tradition of Saxon state history and the proclamation of a specific Saxon identity. According to the SED (Socialist Unity Party = Communist Party) rulers, this kind of regional identity was a typical product of the bourgeois class enemy. In 1952 the SED dissolved the old states and replaced them with districts. Then it promoted its alternative to bourgeois state history: Marxist regional history.[7] Nevertheless, Saxony did not disappear into oblivion during the GDR, thanks, not least, to the activities of a few local historians — particularly Karlheinz Blaschke, Karl Czok and Hartmut Zwahr — and a "anhaltenden Interesse an Publikationen zur Geschichte Sachsens bei einem großen Leserkreis."[8] Specific descriptions of the character of Saxon people also continued to be published. The most prominent promoter of this was Karlheinz Blaschke, who suffered in professional terms because he proclaimed himself a "bourgeois historian" within the GDR. At the end of the 1980s, he described the Saxons in typical fashion:

> So fallen seine zur Findigkeit und praktischen Anwendung neigende Intelligenz, sein Fleiß, seine Rührigkeit und Wendigkeit auf, auch werden ihm Sparsamkeit, der Hang zur Gemütlichkeit und eine bis zur Selbstverleugnung gehende Bereitschaft zur Verträglichkeit und Anpassung nachgesagt.[9]

On the other side of the Iron Curtain, in West Germany, some who had left Saxony after the Second World War propagated a similar image. The poet Rudolf Hagelstange (born in 1912) argued that the geographical location of Saxony and Thuringia in central Germany shaped its people in specific ways:

> Er [der Mitteldeutsche] kommt . . . mit allen gut aus; er ist entgegenkommend und außerhalb seiner Landesgrenzen anpassungsfähig, ja anpassungsfreudig. . . . Er lächelt gern über sich und seinesgleichen und über die eigene nachgiebige Art. . . . Er lebt aus der Mitte: er liebt die Mitte . . . Er fühlt die große Freiheit, die der Mitte innewohnt.[10]

The discussion so far has shown how a variety of people — from a traveller in the eighteenth century to the current Prime Minister Biedenkopf — have emphasised a number of positive characteristics supposedly inherent amongst Saxons. According to these narratives, Saxons are hard working, open, good-natured, humorous, balanced and peaceful. Such descriptions, of course, draw on familiar myths and stereotypes, serving mostly to enforce them, and do not stand up to serious scrutiny, as the following examples reveal.

In Imperial Germany the Saxons tended to emphasise their cultural activities and tolerant society compared to the authoritarian and militaristic Prussians. In reality, their own state, however, surpassed Prussia in its repression of the organised working class and restrictions on the electoral franchise. Additionally, Saxony pursued comparatively repressive policies toward its two minority groups, the Sorbs and the Jews.[11] In the Weimar Republic, the free state was a centre of the "racial hygiene" movement and home to some of the greatest Nazi bastions. During the Third Reich Saxony possessed a number of notorious concentration camps, killing centres, and in NSDAP *Gauleiter* Martin Mutschmann a particularly violent antisemitic state governor. And there were other depredations. Most importantly, around 15,000 people were murdered in a gas chamber in Sonnenstein sanatorium in Pirna, and in the Zeithain camp for prisoners of war (near Riesa) between 33,000 and 40,000 Soviet citizens died of starvation, illness, exhaustion, or were murdered from mid-1941 onwards.[12] While dissenting voices against these barbaric crimes are hard to come by, there is ample documentary evidence of popular support for the ruthless subjugation of other nations during the Second World War (this included the conquering of Slav land and the demand for "England's total destruction").[13]

In this context, it seems extraordinary that a significant number of historians, politicians, professionals, officials, and others have consistently put forward the "positive" stereotypes summarised in the foregoing. However, a variety of factors can be adduced by way of explanation. In the period before 1945, for example, these included a general attempt to preserve Saxon identity within the framework of an increasingly centralising and modernising German nation state;[14] an attempt to blame socialists, trade unions or Reich governments for economic problems rather than admitting to local economic incompetence or backwardness, and a bourgeois strategy to rally voters against the powerful working-class movement with an exaggerated threat of a "Bolshevik" Saxony.[15] Attempts were made to bolster the claim of a common past and the superiority of the Germanic race by claiming that Germans, and not Slavs, were responsible for the settlement and cultural development of the region, and efforts were made to justify territorial claims against the Czechs in the Ore Mountains. Much of this was part of the general idealisation of one's own *Heimat* for emotional or materialistic reasons (e.g. the promotion of myths and stereotypes in travel journals and brochures about Saxony designed to attract visitors and tourists to visit the state).

Returning to Kurt Biedenkopf's many references to a genuine "Pioniersinn" and "Bürgersinn" amongst Saxons that supposedly stemmed from the industrial and cultural history of the state, one needs to remember how he and other local CDU leaders have accounted for Saxony's current precarious economic situation. The first argument put forward is that eastern Germany, because it never received the equivalent of Marshall Aid from the USA, suffered far more from the consequences of the Second World War than western Germany. Moreover, it had to pay reparations to the USSR and lost a considerable part of its economic base in the period after 1945.[16] Second, the policies and actions of the SED-regime caused immeasurable damage to its economy. Arnold Vaatz, for example, former Minister for Environment and Development in the Free State of Saxony, has argued in an interview:

> Die wesentliche Ursache, daß in Ostdeutschland jetzt eine höhere Arbeitslosigkeit als in Westdeutschland ist, liegt darin, daß die gesamte industrielle Infrastruktur im Jahre 1990–91 nicht mehr konkurrenzfähig war. Dafür tragen ausschließlich diejenigen die Verantwortung, die diese Wirtschaft in Ostdeutschland an den Baum gefahren haben. Das ist die SED, heute unter dem Namen PDS firmierend.[17]

Both arguments seem to suggest that things went wrong for Saxony and that the positive character of Saxons was suppressed in the period between 1939 and 1989. The evidence of Saxony's actual industrial development suggests a rather different picture. By the second half of the nineteenth century Saxony's economy had already lost its pioneering role in the process of modernisation to the *Ruhrgebiet* and other regions. In fact, one of the main reasons why Saxony's economy suffered from the highest rates of unemployment of any German state between 1929 and 1936 stemmed from the failure of the majority of Saxony's industrialists to modernise their economic infrastructure. In short, most industrialists did not prove sufficiently flexible, adaptable and forward-looking to be able to compete in an environment of rapid modernisation, shifting markets and changing products. Similarly, it is not possible to detect a generally shared "public spirit" amongst Saxons. Between the foundation of the German Empire in 1871 and the Nazi seizure of power in 1933 there was no tradition of compromise and harmony between the middle classes and organised labour in Saxony, rather a deep-rooted dislike, suspicion and hatred. The result was an extremely polarised society that radicalised and drifted more and more away from the belief in democracy during the Weimar Republic.[18]

While it is difficult to see what kind of common identity Saxons shared in the first half of the twentieth century, it seems even harder to trace what might have survived of this to the present day. By the mid-1950s Saxon society had already changed dramatically as compared with that of the early 1930s. This was mainly due to the large number of casualties and the extent of destruction during the Second World War, with Dresden being the most obvious example. Other factors include substantial Soviet dismantlement of industrial plants; the influx of nearly one million displaced Germans from the east into Saxony; the disintegration of the Social Democratic milieu in the face of SED coercion following its revival immediately after the defeat of Nazi Germany; the change in the social composition of the industrial elite owing to the nationalisation of industries, demilitarisation and denazification, and, finally, new attitudes and policies toward women and young people.

One could continue with this list, not least by mentioning the dramatic changes that have taken place in Saxon society since 1989. Why, then, does Biedenkopf still deploy what are little more than well-worn myths? And, of equal importance, why do Saxons let him get away with it? First of all, of the three main political parties in Saxony — CDU (Christian Democratic Party), SPD (Social Democratic Party) and PDS (Party of Democratic Socialism) — the CDU is not the only one that subscribes to the view that a special type of human being lives in Saxony. In fact, before the state election in September 1999 the SPD's slogan under its party leader Karl-Heinz Kunkel was that "the SPD in Saxony is a special party in a special *Bundesland*."[19] Kunkel explained his party's distance toward the PDS — which contrasted with a SPD-PDS coalition government in the state Mecklenburg-Vorpommern — with the strong SPD tradition in Saxony, the bitter feuds between Social Democrats and Communists during the Weimar Republic, and the particularly harmful effects of the SED rule on Saxony's economy. Furthermore, Kunkel argued that the CDU — with its Christian name and neo-liberal economic policy — would fail to establish firm roots in Saxony's specific cultural landscape. These views are based on the assumption that there is a clear continuity between the "Red Kingdom" of 1903, when the local SPD achieved an overwhelming victory in the Reichstag election, and post-1989 Saxony. In reality, however, the hopes among Social Democrats that they might be able to exploit their traditions in the region could not have been dashed more dramatically. Nowhere in the new *Länder* has the SPD received worse election results than in Saxony.[20]

Of the established political parties, only the PDS rejects the notion of a special Saxon character. This does not fit with socialist dogma and is in line with the stance of the SED. Moreover, the PDS rejects the view that east Germany has been transformed and diversified since 1989. The PDS justifies itself as a party that emerged in the crisis brought about by the process of unification. According to this view, the GDR's economy was "not ailing. It was sick, but not dying." On the contrary, the economy and the new political structures that emerged during the revolution of 1989 were deliberately destroyed, and West Germany's economic and political structures were imposed on the east.[21]

Biedenkopf gained 56.9 percent of the vote in September 1999, securing an absolute parliamentary majority for the third consecutive time. To what extent have Biedenkopf's effusive statements about Saxons contributed to his electoral success? Of course, it is impossible to answer this question precisely. It seems beyond doubt, however, that much of Biedenkopf's popularity amongst Saxons stems from the fact that he is perceived as representing, in a particularly effective way, the state (and more generally, the common interests of the new *Länder*) in Germany and Europe.[22] Moreover, Biedenkopf's deployment of mythic and symbolic discourses helps to assert his legitimacy and strengthens his authority. Indeed, Biedenkopf and his wife greatly enjoy their role as state patrons (*Landesvater* and *Landesmutter*) and this is cultivated and endorsed in some official publications.[23]

George Schöpflin has pointed out that mythic and symbolic discourses "are a primary means by which people make sense of the political process, which is understood in a symbolic form. Attitudes are, therefore, shaped more by symbolic forms than by utilitarian calculation."[24] Biedenkopf's folksy style, one could argue, helps to cover up a significant number of unpleasant realities. Noteworthy in this context are persistently high unemployment rates in the region;[25] the fact that Saxony's economy has recently not performed well compared to some of the other new *Länder;* that local communities in Saxony have the highest level of debt in eastern Germany;[26] the lack of interest in politics amongst the population;[27] the lack of identification by young people with political parties;[28] and the lack of firm roots the CDU has in Saxony (in fact, Biedenkopf himself has complained publicly that the PDS in this state is still able to mobilise more members and activists than all other parties put together).[29] When CDU politicians declare that the GDR regime was plainly evil and damaging, that there are no distinctions between SED and PDS, and that extreme right-wing parties are as dangerous as the PDS, they seem to offer a clear explanation for current problems and to deploy a sharp weapon against their main political rivals in the region, the PDS. Thus Biedenkopf recently told party colleagues:

> auf der rechten Seite [sind] die DVU, die Republikaner, die NPD und andere Splittergruppen, auf der linken Seite [ist] die PDS/SED. Beide sind aus Quellen entstanden und beziehen einen Teil ihrer Ideologien aus Quellen, die ihre Unmenschlichkeit bereits demonstriert haben: die Rechten aus der menschenverachtenden Praxis, die im historisch einmaligen Verbrechen der Zeit des Nationalsozialismus zum Ausdruck kam, die Linken aus der Zeit des Kommunismus im realen Sozialismus und aus dem Unrechtsregime der DDR.[30]

However, it needs to be emphasised that for a myth to be effective in organising and mobilising opinion, it must have a certain resonance. It has to have some relationship with the memory of the collectivity that has fashioned it.[31] Biedenkopf, it seems, has been cleverly exploiting the special situation he found in Saxony. The emergence of a powerful state identity (*Landesbewußtsein*) immediately after the fall of the Berlin Wall was linked with the particular GDR past and the often painful process of unification. Without doubt, this development was a symptom of relief after Saxon identity had been suppressed during the two central dictatorships between 1933 and 1989. One could also add the argument that Saxony's economy suffered in particular during the GDR. However, the extraordinarily strong revival of Saxon identity (the widespread public display of green-white Saxon flags, mass participation in popular festivals, and the great demand for popular literature about Saxon history) was enhanced because unification triggered a crisis of identity. Many Saxons did not want to identify any longer with their GDR past, while a smooth identification with a West German identity was difficult to accomplish overnight. In fact, the ruthless criticism of the GDR society from the west and the disastrous crisis after the events of 1989 made the latter less and less likely to happen. An "escape" into a Saxon identity has arisen and it has been skilfully fostered by the Saxon government under Biedenkopf.

The reactions of Munich citizens after the defeat of the Nazi regime and the occupation by US troops in 1945 bear some interesting similarities to the situation in Saxony immediately after the fall of the Berlin Wall:

> As they rolled through the smashed streets, American soldiers encountered virtually no opposition; instead, amid the rubble, they found people busy trying to clear away signs and symbols of Nazi control . . . Cast off Nazi medals, party membership booklets, and pictures of the *Führer* littered the streets. Thousands of blue-white flags fluttered from windows, as if to say, "This is *Bavaria*, not Germany."[32]

One could even argue that the enormous efforts to restore the buildings from the period before the First World War — in particular the architectural heritage of the Wettins — have also been aimed at restoring the continuity between the pre-1933 and post-1989 period.[33]

Is the Saxon example unique or commonplace within Germany? It seems clear that the Saxon CDU has imitated its *volkstümlich* style from its political neighbour and coalition partner in Bonn, the Bavarian CSU. The extent of this is unique, for none of the other parties in power in the new *Länder* has done anything similar, and it is difficult to see on what grounds they might have done so. The disappearance of Prussia in 1945 has left a hole in the state histories of Mecklenburg-Vorpommern, Brandenburg, and Sachsen-Anhalt. Additionally, the local strength of the SPD and PDS is another significant factor. Finally, the CDU-led Thuringia was only created as a result of the merger of seven principalities in 1920 and lacks the long historical traditions of Saxony. The so-called old *Länder* (*alte Bundesländer*) in the west are not particularly old either. Lower Saxony, North Rhine-Westphalia and Rhineland-Palatinate only arose out of administrative-political necessity after the Second World War. In these states politicians face enormous problems whenever they attempt to deal with state history or state identity (the slogans "We in North Rhine-Westphalia," and "The Palatinate leads," exemplify the clumsy attempts in this direction) and probably envy the position in which Biedenkopf finds himself.[34]

Comparing the web sites "Sachsen-Online" and "Bayern-Online" — which are evidently maintained by their respective state chancelleries — Saxony surpasses its southwestern neighbour in its *volkstümlich* style.[35] Even allowing for the local patriotism that is common to such sites around the world the level of misleading and idealised promotion of the state is embarrassing and at times absurd. Thus, for example, a psychiatrist concludes that the Saxons are "der geniereichste deutsche Stamm" and apparently "im ganzen Land spielt Musik" because of the "Harmoniebedürfnis der Sachsen."[36] Furthermore, under the heading "Sachsen allgemeiner Trendsetter in Sachen Pazifismus," it is maintained that

> Sachsen ist immer arm an bedeutenden Feldherren gewesen. Darum haben die Armee und das Land in Kriegen fast immer auf der falschen Seite gestanden. Umso größer aber ist die Zahl der Gelehrten, Künstler, Dichter, Musiker, Erfinder und Kaufleute, die aus Sachsen stammen oder hier ihre Hauptwirkungsstätte hatten.[37]

To conclude, myths are often described as half-truths. While one might be able to detect the "pioneering spirit" that Biedenkopf evokes amongst Saxon industrialists in the first half of the nineteenth century, thereafter this is more and more difficult to establish. The argument that Saxons shared specific characteristics over the last two centuries is not tenable. Rather than treating these and the other stereotypes discussed in this piece as amusing examples of *Volkstümelei*, however, we need to engage with them and take them seriously, not least because in one form or another they appear in a large number of official statements and publications and often dominate the shelves in bookshops between Plauen, Leipzig and Zittau. An excerpt from a leaflet from the Saxon State Chancellery — printed in German, English and French — serves to underline how those who govern the state deploy a mythical Saxon identity:

Saxony's reputation throughout the world has always been based more on peaceful developments in trade, business, and the intellectual and cultural fields than on military might. And it was here, in the oldest German free state that the peaceful revolution of 1989 began. In demonstrating on the streets of Leipzig and Dresden, the people's call of "We are the people," which later became "We are one people," put an end to Communism in Germany.[38]

Here and in similar publications no attempt is made to engage in a more subtle analysis. Leipzig's special role in fomenting civil opposition that led to the process of unification cannot be explained without reference to resentments that had built up before October 1989 due to the high degree of pollution, the particularly bad condition of the old housing stock, and a miserable supply situation.[39]

As this essay goes to print a political turning point seems to be emerging in Saxony. During the local elections in June 2001 the CDU lost control of all major cities in the state. Most significantly, an alliance of PDS, SPD, Greens and FDP toppled the CDU's long-held control of Dresden. Shortly afterwards, in mid-September, Georg Milbradt, Saxony's former finance minister who had lost his job because of a clash with Biedenkopf on the question of the latter's succession, was voted new chairman of the Saxon CDU. Milbradt comprehensively beat Biedenkopf's candidate and chosen successor to his throne, Steffen Flath.[40] Biedenkopf's ability to distract from all the deficits of his rule was vanishing. Instead, his entanglement in widespread nepotism has become the focus of attention. Eventually Biedenkopf opted to throw in the towel. Rather than sticking to his originally expressed wish to retire in the middle of his current term of office, at the end of 2002, he retired on 17 April 2002. A day later Georg Milbradt became his successor. Milbradt will probably avoid repeating the claim Biedenkopf made before the state elections in September 1999, that if the great German socialist leader August Bebel (1840–1913) were alive today he would vote for the CDU.[41]

Notes

[1] "Regierungserklärung Prof. Dr. Kurt Biedenkopf, 8 November 1990," *Der Sächsische Landtag: Von der Wende zum Parlament* (Dresden, 1991), 56–58.

[2] Quoted from W. Bramke, "Wenn Politiker die Sachsen für sich und ihre Politik einspannen," *Frankfurter Rundschau* 9 (12 January 1999), 8.

[3] Mary Fulbrook, "Myth-Making and National Identity: The Case of the GDR," in G. Hosking and G. Schöpflin, eds., *Myths and Nationhood* (London: Hurst & Company, 1997), 72–87, 73.

[4] "Sachsen ist ein herrliches Land, Bruder!," J. K. Riesbeck, ed., *Briefe eines reisenden Franzosen über Deutschland* (Berlin: Rütten & Loening, 1976). Quoted from M. Kluge, ed., *Sachsen: Ein Lesebuch* (Munich, 1993), 15.

[5] "Mein Sachsenland," *Heimatblätter für Sachsen und Thüringen* 5 (July 1924).

[6] "Sachsenlied," in *Sächsische Miniaturen* (Munich, 1929), quoted from Kluge, *Ein Lesebuch,* 13.

[7] K. Blaschke, "Die sächsische Landesgeschichte zwischen Tradition und neuem Anfang," *Neues Archiv für sächsische Geschichte* 64 (1993): 7–28, 24.

[8] W. Bramke, "Einleitung," in W. Bramke and U. Heß, eds., *Wirtschaft und Gesellschaft in Sachsen im 20. Jahrhundert* (Leipzig: Leipziger Univ.-Verlag, 1998), 10. Quoted from C-C. W. Szejnmann, *Vom Traum zum Alptraum: Sachsen in der Weimarer Republik* (Leipzig: Kiepenheuer Verlag, 2000), 6.

[9] See K. Blaschke, "Eigenarten und Leistungen sächsischer Landesgeschichte," *Jahrbuch für Regionalgeschichte* 14 (1987): 33–54, 37. For more on this see C.-C. W. Szejnmann, "Landesgeschichte versus Regionalgeschichte? Konflikte, Gefahren und Möglichkeiten am Beispiel Sachsens im 20. Jahrhundert," in R. Witt, ed., *Im Spannungsfeld zwischen Landes- und Regionalgeschichte* (Schleswig: Landesarchiv Schleswig, 2002).

[10] R. Hagelstange, "Die Kraft der Mitte," *Die Kraft der Mitte in Thüringen* (Frankfurt, no date); quoted from Kluge, *Ein Lesebuch,* 23–27.

[11] For this see S. Lässig and K. H. Pohl, eds., *Sachsen im Kaiserreich: Politik, Wirtschaft und Gesellschaft im Umbruch* (Weimar: Böhlau, 1997); P. Kunze, *Kurze Geschichte der Sorben: Ein kulturhistorischer Überblick in 10 Kapiteln* (Dresden: Sächsische Landeszentrale für politische Bildung, 1995); S. Lässig, "Emancipation and Embourgeoisement: Jews, the State, and the Middle Classes in Saxony and Anhalt-Dessau," in J. Retallack, ed., *Saxony in German History: Culture, Society, and Politics, 1830–1933* (Ann Arbor: U of Michigan P, 2000), 99–118.

[12] C.-C. W. Szejnmann, *Nazism in Central Germany: The Brownshirts in "Red" Saxony* (Oxford: Berghahn Publishers, 1999), 24.

[13] J. Noakes, *Nazism 1919–1945. Volume 4: The German Home Front in World War II* (Exeter: Exeter UP, 1998), 528; quoted in Szejnmann, *Nazism in Central Germany,* 188.

[14] For the relationship between regional identity and the development of German nationalism, see C. Applegate, *A Nation of Provincials: The German Idea of Heimat* (Berkeley: U of California P, 1990).

[15] For this and the following see especially Szejnmann, *Nazism in Central Germany;* Szejnmann, *Vom Traum zum Alptraum;* Szejnmann, "Landesgeschichte versus Regionalgeschichte."

[16] Biedenkopf in a speech to the Saxon parliament, 24 June 1999.

[17] A. Vaatz "Zum Wahlverhalten der Ostdeutschen," interview with the "Deutschlandfunk," 5 June 1998.

[18] See Szejnmann, *Nazism in Central Germany.*

[19] For this and the following see K.-H. Kunkel, "Wie die SPD ihr historisches Erbe pflegt," *Frankfurter Rundschau* 267 (17 Nov. 1998), 20. Kunkel resigned as SPD leader in Saxony after his party only gained 10.7 percent of the vote in the state elections in September 1999. Subsequently, however, the local SPD did not alter its stance toward the PDS.

[20] See F. Walter, "Sachsen — Ein Stammland der Sozialdemokratie," *Politische Vierteljahrsschrift,* 32:2 (1991), 207–31.

[21] E. Lieberam and R. Wötzel, "Zehn Jahre nach der Wende (Thesen)." *Schriften aus dem Liebknecht-Haus Leipzig 4,* ed. PDS-Stadtvorstand Leipzig (Leipzig, October 1999), 7, 13–14.

[22] Biedenkopf famously defied a decision by the Commission of the European Union and paid high subsidies to the car manufacturer Volkswagen in Saxony. See also "Herbst-Politbarometer für Sachsen," *Die Presseschau* 16 (17 December 1997).

[23] See for example Saxon State Ministry of Agriculture, Food and Forestry, *Saxony Offers Products from the Farm to the Table* (February 1995), 40.

[24] George Schöpflin writes: "Politics is an aspect of the overall cultural system. Every political action is embedded in a wider cultural context. Cultural presuppositions and values may not be seen as narrowly political — influencing political action — and symbolic action is not perceived as a central means of interaction between political elites and public opinion, yet they do have this role. In this sense, myth creates a field in which interests are conveyed in a symbolic fashion or with considerable symbolic baggage. Mythic and symbolic discourses can thus be employed to assert legitimacy and strengthen authority. They mobilise emotions and enthusiasm. They are a primary means by which people make sense of the political process, which is understood in a symbolic form. Attitudes are, therefore, shaped more by symbolic forms than by utilitarian calculation. The potency of symbols in the political process derives from the fact that they are vehicles for conceptualization." See Schöpflin, "The Functions of Myth and a Taxonomy of Myths," in Hosking, *Myths and Nationhood,* 19–35, 27–8.

[25] There were 381,878 unemployed (16.6 percent) in Saxony in late August 2000. See *Leipziger Volkszeitung* 209 (7 September 2000). Additionally, a questionnaire in late 1997 showed that there was widespread pessimism regarding the employment situation. The majority of those questioned believed that there would be higher unemployment rates within the coming year. A substantial minority (37 percent) of those questioned expressed the opinion that none of the political parties would be

able to solve the problems according to the needs of the citizens. See "Herbst-Politbarometer für Sachsen," *Die Presseschau* 16 (17 December. 1997).

[26] Lisa Erdmann, "Kurt Biedenkopf (CDU): Der 'König' der Sachsen," *Der Spiegel* (19 September 1999), Spiegel ONLINE 36/1999.

[27] E.g., only 7,000 people visited the stand of the Saxon Parliament out of a total of 436,000 visitors during the *Tag der Sachsen* in Hoyerswerda in 1998. See "Tag der Sachsen," *Landtagskurier* 4 (1998). Additionally, the electoral turnout in state elections declined from 72.8 percent in October 1990 to 61.1 percent in September 1999.

[28] A study in 1997 showed that only a minority of young people felt close to a political party. Of the youth questioned, 12 percent felt close to the CDU, 9 percent to the Alliance 90/The Greens, 7 percent to the SPD, 6 percent to the PDS, 3 percent to the Republicans (Republikaner), 2 percent to the NPD (National Democratic Party of Germany), 2 percent to the FDP. Accordingly, 59 percent did not identify with any political party. See "Studie 97: Lebenszufriedenheit bei Sachsens Jugendlichen ungebrochen," *Die Presseschau* 1 (15 January 1998).

[29] Biedenkopf appealed to Saxon citizens with the following words: "Liebe Sachsen, Frauen wie Männer, durch die friedliche Revolution, die von Sachsen ausging, wurde die Vereinigung unseres Vaterlandes in Frieden und Freiheit erreicht. Die Freiheit bleibt aber nur dann erhalten, wenn sich genügend Menschen engagiert dafür einsetzen. Vor 1990 waren sich viele einig in der Ablehnung des SED-Regimes. Heute fällt es den meisten schwer, sich von dieser inneren Haltung gegen "die Herrschenden" zu lösen und sich für bestimmte politische Ansichten einzusetzen, auch wenn sie diese teilen. So kommt es, daß die Kommunisten hierzulande immer noch mehr Mitglieder und Aktivisten auf die Beine bringen, als alle demokratischen Parteien zusammen. Das kann doch nicht so bleiben! Die Demokratie braucht eine starke Basis. Die Sächsische Union hat ihre Wurzeln in der auf christlicher Tradition ruhenden Kultur und der eigenständigen, heimatverbundenen Lebensart der Sachsen. Daraus erwächst unser Engagement für die Gesellschaft von morgen, die fortschrittlich und zugleich menschlich sein soll. Machen Sie mit, kommen Sie zur sächsischen CDU — damit die mühsam errungene Freiheit erhalten bleibt, damit's weiter aufwärts geht! Ihr Kurt Biedenkopf." See http://www.cdu-sachsen.de (February 2000).

[30] Prof. Kurt Biedenkopf, speech to the state party conference in Riesa, 12 December 1998.

[31] Schöpflin, "Functions of Myth," 25–6.

[32] D. C. Large, *Where Ghosts Walked: Munich's Road to the Third Reich* (London: W. W. Norton & Company, 1997), 345–46.

[33] Similarly, Large observed in his study of Munich: "If the official celebration of the resistance legacy promoted a more positive interpretation of Munich's place in the Third Reich, the city's physical reconstruction in the postwar era aimed at establishing continuity with the pre-Nazi past, especially with the architectural heritage of the Wittelsbachs." See Large, *Where Ghosts Walked*, 356.

[34] Heinrich Best reminds us: "Only in the central zones of their territories did the German dynasties in the middle of the nineteenth century possess rights of rule that reached back into the middle ages. The single states, in contrast, largely only formed

in the wake of the Napoleonic wars due to the secularization of the religious territories and the absorption of small Reich estates." See H. Best, "Politische Regionen in Deutschland: Historische (Dis-) Kontinuitäten," in D. Oberndörfer and K. Schmitt, eds., *Parteien und regionale politische Traditionen in der Bundesrepublik Deutschland* (Berlin, 1991), 39–64, 48.

[35] See http://www.sachsen.de/; http://www.bayern.de/. Both websites were investigated in February 2000.

[36] See "Einwohner," http://sachsen.de/

[37] See "Persönlichkeiten," http://www.sachsen.de/

[38] Sächsische Staatskanzlei, 'Freistaat Sachsen' (second revised edition, June 1999). Brochure printed in English, French and German.

[39] See K.-D. Opp, "DDR 98. Zu den Ursachen einer spontanen Revolution," in H. Joas and M. Kohli, eds., *Der Zusammenbruch der DDR* (Frankfurt am Main: Suhrkamp, 1993), 194–221, 214–15. See also C. Liebold, "Zwischen zentralistischer Abhängigkeit und demokratischem Neubeginn. Leipziger Kommunalpolitik in der Wende 1989/90," in A. Fischer and G. Heydemann, eds., *Die politische 'Wende' in Sachsen* (Weimar: Böhlau, 1995), 71–116, 71.

[40] See *Die Woche* No. 27 (29 June 2001), 5.

[41] See "Worte der Woche," *Die Zeit* 39 (1999).

Unifying a Gendered State: Women in Post-1989 Germany

Sabine Lang

Introduction

THE PRE-UNIFICATION Federal Republic of Germany had the dubious reputation of being arguably one of the most gendered societies within the European Union (then the Europe Economic Community). Neither in its economy nor in its political culture and institutional make-up had the constitutional right to equality been realised. In the world of employment, for example, the vast majority of women dropped out of the workforce for several years to enable them to become the primary caregivers in the family, resulting in a severe narrowing of their career horizons once they decided to re-enter the labour market. Working mothers with small children were, in particular, widely regarded as neglecting their children and, therefore, as a threat to social stability. The few women who, by the 1980s, had risen to leading positions in politics and business were often perceived as having done so at the expense of their private lives. In addition, West German society still generally thought that senior women managers were a danger to conventional notions of female identity as well as the androcentric, corporate culture in which they had achieved success.[1]

Unification initially seemed to pose a challenge to the hegemonic, masculine culture in West Germany. East German women had possessed a strong voice during the political transformation of the German Democratic Republic (GDR) in 1989/90. This derived from their ideological and economic strength and the sheer number of political activists. As feminist researchers have noted, the centrality of East German women to the events of 1989 offered a striking contrast to the male-dominated revolutions in other Eastern European societies.[2] Yet East German women's activism crumbled under the pressure of economic, social and psychological upheaval. So did most of the institutions in the East German arena of gender politics, such as the *Demokratischer Frauenbund*

Deutschlands (DFD),[3] which had transformed itself from an "official" GDR organisation into a reform movement in March 1990, or the *Unabhängiger Frauenverband* (UFV), which had emerged in December 1989 as an umbrella organisation for women activists. For all the evidence we have on specific aspects of this demobilisation, the question remains as to why women from both east and west were not able to capitalise on the process of political and social transformation in 1989/90 in order to destabilise prevalent male cultural and political paradigms and set a new agenda for the united Germany.

This essay does not primarily address the defensive battle of East German women before and during 1989. Instead, it will focus on the questions of why and how Germany was reconstructed as a gendered state after unification. Emphasis will be put on the regulatory capacity of the unified German state in terms of its gender- and gendered-agenda. This focus does not imply a merely top-down imposition of politics, policies and political appointments, rather I maintain that the regulatory capacities of the state are interwoven with continuous attempts by other producers of cultural and political meaning — such as the media — to sustain male, hegemonic discourses and androcentric practices.

Thus, unifying the gendered state in Germany can be seen as an ongoing project with a number of intersecting voices and arenas of discourse. Yet it is also a project which exemplifies the power of established political structures in defining those discourses and policies. By the same token, that which at present appears to be the solid, regulatory success of androcentric politics in the unified German nation state is in fact a continually precarious constellation that is prone to be challenged by demands from marginalized women or through structural changes that are brought about, for example, by the Europeanisation of German politics.

The Transformation Process Seen Through a Gendered Lens

While the East German revolution of 1989 and the ongoing processes of transformation within German society and the state have been hailed as a paradigmatic and successful test of the peaceful exercise of democracy, there remains a powerful sub-discourse that identifies east German — and, at times, all German — women as the losers or victims of unification. The most convincing indicators cited by advocates of this position are levels of labour market participation, political representation, family policies, and domestic violence. The employment situation for women has indeed undergone a drastic change, given that the GDR enjoyed the highest female employment rate in the world. Thus before unification, 91% of those between the ages of 15 and 65 held jobs, as opposed to only 55% of West German women.[4] The East German government offered an impressive array of vocational training possibilities for women, so that only 10% of working women in 1989 had no vocational training or college degree. East German women also worked in a much wider range of occupations, including traditionally male professions, than did West German women. Training policies in the 1960s and 1970s had drastically diminished the worst segregations of the labour market, so that in East Germany women engineers, technicians or builders were not considered to be exotic.[5]

With unification, this structure of opportunities for women that had been created by the policies of an interventionist state changed rapidly. Women lost jobs on a far greater scale than men and they less frequently found new jobs. Between 1989 and 1992, for example, one third of all jobs held by women in the GDR were lost.[6] By 1996, after the first shockwaves of the restructuring of labour markets in the *Neue Länder,* women remained unemployed at a considerably higher rate (20.6%) than men (16.8%).[7] Labour market studies of the last decade indicate two trends: first, that the official unemployment rate for women remains higher than that for men, and second, that women now work in jobs below their qualification far more often than men and are more frequently forced to accept part-time jobs. Over the past few years the unemployment rate for women in the *Neue Länder* has consistently been around the 20% mark. This is about 5% higher than the corresponding rate for men and about double the rate for both women and men in the western states of Germany.[8]

The reality of severe competition for limited job opportunities was exacerbated for women by a public, political discourse that was centred around the dominant ideology of the male breadwinner model. In 1995 Saxony's Prime Minister, Kurt Biedenkopf, delivered a particularly telling example:

> Der Prozeß, in dem Frauen Männer aus angestammten Arbeitsplätzen verdrängen, ist bereits in vollem Gange und wird sich weiter fortsetzen. Im Westen Deutschlands drängen Frauen mit Macht in den Arbeitsmarkt und verdrängen dadurch die Männer. Im Osten wollen die Frauen im Arbeitsmarkt bleiben und erschweren dadurch den Männern den Zugang. In beiden Fällen wäre es eine Illusion anzunehmen, daß die Spannungen, die sich aus dieser Entwicklung ergeben, allein durch mehr Arbeitsplätze oder staatliche Beschäftigung im zweiten Arbeitsmarkt be-

wältigt werden könnten. Die mit der Umverteilung von Arbeit im beste-
henden Arbeitssystem verbundenen Veränderungen der gesellschaftlichen
Rollenerwartungen vor allem der Männer werden voraussichtlich nicht
ohne soziale Auseinandersetzungen ablaufen.[9]

Biedenkopf's remarks oscillate between the attempt to merely describe
realities and a specific framing of a social and economic problem, which
reinforces the already severe stigma attached to women who want to
either keep their jobs or actively pursue a career in the labour market.

Representative national polling data in 1991 indicate that 49% of
men in the western states at the time thought that a small child would
inevitably suffer if its mother was employed in the labour force.[10] By
contrast, only a quarter of men and women from the *neue Bundesländer*
held this view. More strikingly, only 6% of men from the *alte Bundesländer* in 1991 thought that a child would benefit from the fact that its
mother was not wholly engaged in child-rearing. Trends since 1991
indicate that the number of men in the new and old federal states who
see the role of women primarily within the family and not on the labour
market is increasing. This increase, moreover, closely corresponds to
men's changing assessments of macroeconomic developments within the
country (676).

High levels of income insecurity had reverberations in a second
sphere where east German women had been accustomed to different
standards of family policy, including state incentives to combine work
and family. Integration in the labour market and a high level of state
support for motherhood were a major priority in the GDR. At the time
of unification, aggregate data from a lifespan analysis showed that nearly
90% of all East German women could expect to give birth to at least one
child, whereas in West Germany the proportion was 74% of all women.[11]

State support for working mothers in East Germany included a one-
year, fully paid period of parental leave and a paid reduction of regular
working hours for women with more than one child. Childcare for children of all age groups was offered on a fulltime basis, and there was no
stigma attached to working mothers with infants. By contrast, east German women were confronted after unification with a West German
tradition of double standards. This included official policies based on the
male breadwinner model, such that women were encouraged into treating motherhood as a profession and were given economic incentives to
foster no more than only part-time involvement in the labour market. As
employment in the former East Germany deteriorated — some regions
today suffer rates of up to 40% — and as childcare provision decreased,

women started to react by "economising" on babies.[12] Thus, birth rates in eastern Germany dropped by over 50% after 1990 and still remain less than one child per woman.

In post-unification Germany, women (and also men, although women make up over 98% of the recipients) are allowed to take parental leave for three years without wage compensation but with a maximum flat rate subsidy of 600 marks per month. The granting of a subsidy, which is not enough to live on, yet attractive to women with working partners because they thus receive an independent wage, has been criticised by many social policy analysts as reinforcing androcentric traditions in Germany.[13] Practicable alternatives, such as full state support for taking care of an infant for a shorter period of time, combined with considerable public investment in adequate childcare facilities, or adoption of the Swedish model of obligatory participation of the father in paternal leave policies, have been discussed by academics but have yet to be considered in parliament. The claims of parliamentary representatives that there is a lack of financial resources reflects androcentric value systems within parliamentary decision-making.

The pressure on women with children to forego a career in order to stay at home with the family does not decrease with the age of the children, quite the contrary. While an entitlement to part time (half-day) childcare was introduced at federal level in August 1996, adequate financial resources were not made available to enhance its availability. Instead, many states complied with the stipulation by merely carving up available places for full-time childcare in order to create enough overall half-time provision. And the situation for career oriented women gets even worse once their children reach school age. For the first four years in primary school, German children and their parents are faced with highly irregular and flexible timetables and with classes that usually end around noon. Women thus find it hard to commit to even part-time jobs. Moreover, particularly in rural and suburban areas of Germany, provision of organised, after-school activities is not common.

It should therefore come as no surprise that, on average, mothers in Germany withdraw from the labour market for between six and eight years, thereby interrupting their careers for the sake of their families for a longer period of time than in any other European country, with the exception of the Netherlands and the Republic of Ireland.[14] When women re-enter the paid labour market, they take jobs that are for the most part below their appropriate skill levels, and they have foregone many possibilities for career planning and higher level jobs. It is also no accident that only 6% of upper-tier management jobs in Germany are currently held by women. In higher education, for example, only 8% of tenured university professors are female.[15] Yet economic and social pressures do not fully explain why East German women activists were not able to sustain their public involvement and political leverage beyond unification, given, as was noted earlier, the role that feminist activists played in the German civil rights movement which itself was a major political player in the unification process. As a consequence, additional variables need to be considered in order to be able to fully comprehend the marginalization of women's issues during that period.

Analysing the Legacy of 1989

Social movement analysis has produced differing accounts of German women's lack of influence and power during the transformation period before and after unification. The political opportunity approach has merit in that it identifies the narrow structural gateway within which mobilisation among women and for women's issues could occur in both the western and eastern states.[16] Resource mobilisation theory, by contrast, focuses on the lack of organised and reliable capacities within the movement that made it difficult for women to sustain a public voice during unification.[17] While movement analysis identifies the absence of organisational capacity and a consistent ideology, as well as instrumental thinking as contributory factors, I would like to concentrate on a different set of variables which militated against the ascendancy of feminist agendas within public discourse and the state, namely the structure of political processes and the framing capacities of the German media.

The centre of political processes in the eastern part of Germany shifted from movement-based politics before unification to a dominance of state-based politics after 1989. The Independent Women's League (*Unabhängiger Frauenverband,* UFV) which was founded and organised by about 1,200 women as a movement that would transform society from a feminist perspective was neither altogether willing nor sufficiently well equipped to negotiate with the representatives of the West German government. The reasons for this lack of bargaining power are not only to be found in the UFV's insistence on the politics of radical transformation. Certainly, these were in conflict with the transformation scenario envisaged by the ruling West German Conservative coalition and coincided with the economic collapse of the East German system. Yet the decline of feminist advocacy during and after unification is also the result of a long-standing, closed bargaining structure within the West German state, which Brigitte Young has termed the *Fraktionsstaat*. "Fraktionen" refers to the parliamentary parties within the German legislature, and it is here — and not among the ranks of ordinary party members in the country — that the political decision-making processes during unification were located. Since Germany has a parliamentary system in which the Chancellor is elected by the majority party, or parties, in parliament, the core of decision-making power within the political system rests with the parliamentary group of the ruling party in co-operation with the *Bundes-kanzleramt* — the executive office of the Chancellor.

The various layers of negotiation and discourse that are wrapped around this statist core tend to lack public transparency. Young demonstrates how German unification was primarily negotiated within this core power structure which, in turn, was an almost exclusively male domain: the "centre of German power is inaccessible and antithetical to feminist concerns," she argues, maintaining that there is "an inaccessible kernel around the very structure of German power, despite its 'edges' becoming more open to the entrance of women into power positions."[18] This inaccessible kernel, the masculinist *Fraktionsstaat,* does not only represent a strong, positional power of male politicians, it also constitutes — by analogy with Max Weber's use of the term *Versachlichung* — a "versachlichte Männlich-keit"[19] pointing to the sedimentation and rationalisation of male power within political organisations. Thus, we perceive mainly male actors and — more importantly — the tradition and persistence of masculinist value structures and normative orientations that neither actively promote women's agendas nor make an effort to integrate women's issues into policy processes.

For the feminist agenda of the UFV, the striking and lasting implications of this structural feature of the West German political system can be perhaps best exemplified with reference to the conduct of the abortion debate, which was the most contested women's issue at the time. It meant that west German women in parliament did not have a strong voice in the negotiations for the unification treaty and that the support of women within the west German Social Democratic Party (SPD) for the liberal East German trimester abortion law did not have a broad impact on policy.[20] A number of west German women parliamentarians tried to build a multi-party coalition around the so-called *Gruppenantrag.* The *Gruppenantrag* was considered by the public as a progressive, legal proposal in that it underlined women's freedom to choose an abortion, yet it also had strong, conservative elements to appease the Conservative parties and protect it from being overturned by the German Constitutional Court in Karlsruhe. In particular, the feminist movement regarded the attempts to regulate the specifics of the counselling process for women, which were set out in the new paragraph 219, as a setback for a liberal women's agenda. Most importantly, the proposed paragraph 219 stressed the high value of the foetus and emphasised its protection as the primary goal of counselling, and the counsellors themselves were supposed to be bound by law to provide such an interpretation.[21]

Ultimately, the west German Conservatives within their parliamentary group were able to control and steer the abortion discussion. Even though the *Gruppenantrag* was passed by the *Bundestag* with a total of 356 votes for, 282 votes against and 18 abstentions, the CDU/CSU fraction announced immediately that it would take the issue to the Constitutional Court, thus trying to re-open the public and legal debate under the banner of the "protection of life" and mobilising opinion against what they presented as the self-indulgent self-determination of women that was propagated by feminists and that was now evident in the passing of the *Gruppenantrag.*[22] On May 28, 1993, the German Constitutional Court declared the reform of 1992 to be invalid and asked Parliament to revise it with greater emphasis on the protection of unborn human life.

The project of unifying a gendered state thus did not just entail the incorporation of women from eastern Germany in a pre-existing gendered economic and social structure. It also made use of institutional and procedural venues within the masculinist parliamentary *Fraktionsstaat* to marginalize a liberal feminist agenda within the parliamentary system. The fact that women's issues were absorbed within the narrow confines of parliamentary power and male-dominated judicial structures was complemented, as I shall now outline, by the masculinist bias of the West German media system and its failure to provide an adequate public forum for women's issues and feminist positions during and after unification.

Up until the mid-1980s, the West German established media were overwhelmingly male dominated and male centred. In 1970, women made up only 12.3% of daily newspaper journalists.[23] As late as 1984, women held only 17% of the jobs requiring journalists within the public broadcasting system of West Germany. Women's voices were concentrated within a proliferating feminist subculture of publications like the bi-weeklies *Courage* and *Emma* that became the forum for the political advocacy of women.

Today, the German media is somewhat better at incorporating women but there is increasing evidence that breaking up the structures of positional masculinity — that is, in the first instance, by physically integrating women — does not necessarily lead to a breakup of traditional gate-keeping and agenda-setting processes. By the late 1980s, an increasing number of women had gained middle-ranking positions and visibility within the German media. A comprehensive study of women in the German media immediately after unification, in 1992, demonstrates that women are making inroads into the magazine sector, in particular where they now make up 41.3% of the employees, but also within news agencies (36.5% women) and in the daily newspaper journalism, with 30% women.[24] In the feminised fields of "service" and "entertainment," women make up 64% and 51.8% respectively.[25] Newspapers, radio and TV appreciate the power of women consumers and since the mid-1980s they have established a number of prominent newspaper sections, radio and TV programs geared at women's issues. Yet many of those initiatives were short lived. Newspapers, for example, such as the progressive Berlin-based *tageszeitung* decided in 1990 that a special women's page perpetuated and increased the segregation, stigmatisation, and marginalization of women's issues, and the majority of this democratically organised newspaper collective decided to "mainstream" women's topics within the paper.[26] All of the papers editors were advised to pay special attention to women's issues and to make sure that they were incorporated into all news reporting. Four years later, it had become clear that this strategy had failed, with none of the sections having really achieved their goal. Women's issues were simply neglected, and in the daily competition for what was considered newsworthy and what would get priority treatment, a women's agenda all too often lost out to other, seemingly more pressing, issues. Feminist journalists in the *tageszeitung* realised that the strategy of mainstreaming would only work when forced through all the sections of the newspaper by a critical mass of women. Other newspapers changed their women's sections from political orientation to lifestyle issues or reframed them in terms of family-related topics.

While the media of the women's movement had been a substantial part of mobilization during the 1980s, the former GDR did not have a comparable set of publications and programmes. It was actually as late as during the first phase of the *Wende* in December 1989, that the initial effort to launch a women's programme was put forward by Bärbel Romanowski, a journalist from the *Deutscher Fernsehfunk*.[27] Since women at that time were major players on the activist political stage, the DFF took to the idea, and Bärbel Romanowski soon became a well known spokesperson for women's issues. After a year of successful airing, with unification the programme was incorporated into the newly created public broadcasting ARD Länder channel ORB and has since been modified to cater also to a more lifestyle oriented audience. The second, widely visible women's media voice during unification was the women's magazine *Für Dich*, which was originally created by the SED as a mobilisation tool for women within the socialist system.[28] During the revolution, *Für Dich* assumed the position of voice for the newly created independent women's movement. After a number of re-launches and heavily declining readership, however, the magazine was closed down in June 1991. It thus fell victim to the general trend toward depoliticisation and could not compete with the broad range of west German women's publications catering to the lifestyle generations.

In sum, women's voices in East Germany had no strong media platform during unification and after. Women's issues were hardly raised within the mainstream media, and special women's formats had neither the broad support needed economically nor an attachment to a strong political movement that were needed to be an accepted voice. A central element of mobilisation during the unification process, that is, consistent and strong reporting on women's activities and agendas as well as the highlighting of specific issues, was thus foreclosed by the majority of the German media.

Conclusion: Implosion from Outside?

Neither the structure of the German state and its decision-making centres nor the structure of the media as framers of public opinion are likely to be welcoming toward progressive claims for women's representation and participation. A recent example is the legal initiative to encourage private business to enhance women's participation in the economic sphere. The passing of a so-called *Gleichstellungsgesetz für die Privatwirtschaft* (Affirmative Action Law for the Private Sector) was part of the coalition treaty between the Social Democrats and the Green Party in 1998. It was hailed as a central policy initiative for the advancement of women in business by many women's groups in the country. Yet it very soon became obvious that Chancellor Schröder and influential members of the parliamentary party of the SPD were opposed to a law. The Green party adopted a stronger language in favour of an initiative, yet failed to develop adequate strategies within the coalition to keep the issue on the agenda. Germany's federal minister for women's issues, the SPD's Christine Bergmann, tried to develop a negotiating base within the cabinet by having the well known feminist professor of law, Heide Pfarr, produce a first draft of a *Gleichstellungsgesetz*. Yet by the time this draft version was presented, the major business associations of Germany had already signalled publicly and unequivocally that they would never accept a binding law that increased women's participation in the labour market.

Their opposition did not change even after the proposed law was basically redrafted into a declaration of intent within a two-phase policy model: it introduced a voluntary first phase in which businesses could define ends and means of affirmative action initiatives themselves and act according to specific interests and needs. Only after a negative evaluation of progress regarding women's participation in the workforce after three years would the mandatory part of the law take effect — with no set guidelines for what a "negative" evaluation would mean in practice. Yet business even rejected this two-phase model and in July 2001 only agreed to Cabinet proposals for voluntary measures to increase women's participation in the workforce.[29]

Feminist advocates within the Social Democratic parliamentary party have declared this agreement "ein Trauerspiel" (5), yet were quite obviously not able to summon up enough political pressure in order to have any influence on the issue. It comes, therefore, as no surprise that German feminist advocates in recent years have begun to look beyond the confines of the nation state in order to re-engage the political culture "at home" in debate. This is also true regarding a *Gleichstellungsgesetz* for the private sector. Irmingard Schewe-Gerigk, the Green parliamentary spokesperson on women's issues, has confidently predicted that in the wake of the new equal opportunity measures of the European Union, the German voluntary agreement is unsustainable.

There is indeed increasing evidence that the German political system will be forced to fall into line with European Union policies. This is by no means a recent phenomenon. Some of the most central advances in gender policies in West Germany were shaped by the insistence on the part of European Union institutions that national governments comply with their standards. Germany, for example, did not act on income discrepancies until the European Community passed Equal Pay Legislation in 1975 and an Equal Treatment Law in 1976. Forced to convert these European laws into national legislation, the federal government delayed implementation until the European Commission threatened to sue Germany in the European Court in 1980. But while some advocates perceive the European Union to be a less structurally closed and therefore more "gender aware" institution, others caution against the presumption that EU policies will act as the radical vanguard of the promotion of gender equality. Fears at present focus on the downsizing of social services and on the effects of "mainstreaming," that is, the growing assumption on the part of officials of the European Union that special treatment and special programmes for women are either not necessary or even counterproductive as far as advancing women's issues is concerned. Instead, "mainstreaming" refers to the notion that interests and agendas of women will be an integral and explicit part of all European legislation and processes. Essential to such an approach, many concerned feminists argue, is an adequate representation of women in all of the institutions of the European Union. Additionally, such a concept requires that member states apply the same standards of group representation in their executive institutions that implement European programmes. In Germany there is considerable doubt for example, whether the demise of special women's programmes will sustain an adequate representation of women's issues in the funding of regional development and social agendas.

One of the crucial questions for the future will be whether the institutional reshaping of national politics will have a strong counterpart in civil society. Will the various remaining components of national women's movements become Europeanised or globalised as they encounter different aggregates of political decision-making power? Evidence is currently too scant to allow speculation. Yet the fate of women's advocacy during the transformation period of the early 1990s suggests not simply that the women's movement was too weak to act, but that institutional frameworks and discursive power generators, such as the media, influence incorporation or marginalisation. Learning from that history could be of great advantage during the process of the Europeanisation of gender politics.

Notes

[1] Christiane Schiersmann, "Führungspositionen — vom männlichen Privileg zur weiblichen Domäne?" in *Beiträge zur Arbeitsmarkt- und Berufsforschung* 179 (2000), special edition ed. Petra Beckmann and Gerhard Engelbrech, *Arbeitsmarkt für Frauen 2000 — Ein Schritt vor oder ein Schritt zurück? Kompendium zur Erwerbstätigkeit von Frauen*, 307.

[2] See for example Brigitte Young, *Triumph of the Fatherland: German Unification and the Marginalization of Women* (Ann Arbor: U of Michigan P, 1999) and Nanette Funk et al., *Gender Politics and Postcommunism* (New York/London: Routledge, 1993). See also Anne Hampele, "Der Unabhängige Frauenverband," in Helmut Müller-Enbergs, Marianne Schulz and Jan Wielgohs, *Von der Illegalität ins Parlament. Werdegang und Konzept der neuen Bürgerbewegungen* (Berlin: Links, 1993), 221–82.

[3] See Julia Teschner, "Demokratischer Frauenbund Deutschlands: Socialist Mass Organisation and Western Charity?" in Elizabeth Boa and Janet Wharton, eds., *Women and the Wende: Social Effects and Cultural Reflections of the German Unification Process* (Amsterdam: Rodopi, 1994), 53– 63.

[4] Ellen Sessar-Karpp and Elke Harder, "Erwerbstätigkeit, Arbeitslosigkeit und Weiterbildung von Frauen in den neuen Bundesländern," in Beckmann and Engelbrech, 569.

[5] Virginia Penrose, "Vierzig Jahre SED-Frauenpolitik: Ziele, Strategien, Ergebnisse," in *Frauenforschung: Informationsdienst des Forschungsinstituts Frau und Gesellschaft* 8:4 (1990), 67.

[6] Beckmann and Engelbrech 19.

[7] See Bundesanstalt für Arbeit, *Eckwerte des Arbeitsmarktes für Februar 1996*, Abteilung Statistik (Nürnberg: 1996).

[8] See *The Economist* (17 July 1998), 5. See also Statistische Monatsberichte der Bundesanstalt für Arbeit, Nürnberg: www.arbeitsamt.de/hst/services/statistik/.

[9] Kurt Biedenkopf, *Anmerkungen zur politischen Lage: Strategiepapier für den CDU-Bundesvorstand* (Dresden, 27 May 1995); Ingrid Kurz-Scherf, "Krise der Arbeitsgesellschaft: Patriarchale Blockaden," *Blätter für deutsche und internationale Politik* 40:8 (1995): 976.

[10] See Michael Braun, "Entwicklung der Einstellung zur Rolle der Frau nach der Vereinigung," in Beckmann and Engelbrech, eds., 675.

[11] See Ellen Sessar-Karpp and Elke Harder 584.

[12] *The Economist*, 5.

[13] Gisela Notz, "Frauen nun doch an den Herd? Erziehungsgeld, Erziehungsurlaub und die Auswirkungen auf die Lebens- und Arbeitssituation von Müttern," in Claudia Gather et al., *Frauen-Alters-Sicherung* (Berlin: Orlanda, 1991), 106–19.

[14] See Schliersmann 314.

[15] Helga Ebeling, "Zur Förderung von Wissenschaftlerinnen in der Bundesrepublik," in Sabine Lang and Birgit Sauer, eds., *Wissenschaft als Arbeit — Arbeit als Wissenschaftlerin* (Frankfurt am Main: Campus 1994), 39–56, 40.

[16] See Dieter Rucht, "German Unification, Democratization, and the Role of the Social Movements: A Missed Opportunity?" *Mobilization* 1:1 (1996): 36–52.

[17] See Herbert Kitschelt, "New Social Movements in West Germany and the United States," *Political Power and Social Theory* 5 (1985): 273–324.

[18] Young 20.

[19] See Birgit Sauer, *Die Asche des Souveräns: Staat und Demokratie in der Geschlechterdebatte* (Frankfurt am Main: Campus, 2001).

[20] See Elizabeth Clements, "The Abortion Debate in Unified Germany," in Boa and Wharton 38–52.

[21] Clements 44.

[22] For an analysis of this discourse, see Birgit Sauer, "'Doing Gender.' Das Parlament als Ort der Geschlechterkonstruktion. Eine Analyse der Bundestagsdebatte um die Neuregelung des Schwangerschaftsabbruchs," in Andreas Dirner and Ludgera Voigt, eds., *Sprache des Parlaments* (Berlin: de Gruyter, 1994), 94.

[23] Margret Lünenborg, "Direkte und indirekte Benachteiligung? Journalistinnen in Deutschland — Eine Studie der Universität Münster im Auftrag der IG Medien," in

AK Politik und Geschlecht/Netzwerk politikwissenschaftlich und politisch arbeitender Frauen, eds., *Rundbrief* 5:10 (1996): 58.

[24] *Rundbrief* 5:10 (1996): 60.

[25] See IG Medien, ed., *Frauen im Journalismus*. Gutachten über die Geschlechterverhältnisse bei den Medien in Deutschland. Erarbeitet von Siegfried Weischenberg u.a. (Münster 1996), 20.

[26] See *tageszeitung* (21 April 1990).

[27] For an analysis of women's media during the *Wende* see Andrea Rinke, "'Wende-Bilder': Television Images of Women in Germany in Transition," in Boa and Wharton, eds., 124–38.

[28] See Martha Wirsching, "Für Dich and the Wende: Women's Weekly between Plan and Market," in Boa and Wharton, eds., 139–54.

[29] See Marianne Heuwagen, "Gleichstellungsgesetz ist beerdigt," in *Süddeutsche Zeitung* (4 July 2001): 5.

Difference

"Zugzwang" or "Stillstand"? — Trains in the Post-1989 Fiction of Brigitte Struyzk, Reinhard Jirgl, and Wolfgang Hilbig

Simon Ward

THIS ARTICLE EXAMINES how three authors with GDR backgrounds, Wolfgang Hilbig, Brigitte Struyzk and Reinhard Jirgl, exploit the literary potential of the railway network in recent novels which take stock of the situation in Germany since 1989. In using the railway as a setting these writers are engaging with a topos whose cultural significance has its roots in the material presence of the railways as a major form of communication in Germany since the 1830s. That significance has not diminished to mere nostalgia in the meantime, as is seen, for example, in the role trains have played during times of transition, such as after 1945, or in the literature of the GDR in general. The three books under discussion demonstrate that the period of transition after 1989 also attracts writers to the railways as a potent setting for an examination not only of where Germany is headed and where it has been, but also of the role of literature itself.

Reconnections: Railways and the East German Revolution of 1989

The railways were always a potent symbol of both connection and division between the two Germanies during the Cold War. The practical consequences of that division became all the more apparent when social and political developments in the Warsaw Pact countries began to accelerate in 1989. One of the most striking images from that period was the train-loads of East Germans en route from the embassies in Prague and Warsaw to the Federal Republic. In the climate of euphoria after 9 November 1989, the railway lines provoked trains of thought which went beyond the merely practical. This was seen in the second of the ten points made by the then Chancellor of the Federal Republic, Helmut

Kohl, in his speech "zur Überwindung der Teilung Deutschlands und Europas" outlined to the *Bundestag* on 28 November 1989.

> Über den Ausbau der Eisenbahnstrecke Hannover-Berlin wird weiter verhandelt. . . .
>
> Vierzig Jahre Trennung bedeuten ja auch, daß sich die Verkehrswege zum Teil erheblich auseinanderentwickelt haben. Das gilt nicht nur für die Grenzübergänge, sondern beispielsweise auch für die traditionelle Linienführung der Verkehrswege in Mitteleuropa, für die Ost-West-Verbindungen. Es ist nicht einzusehen, weshalb die klassische Route Moskau-Warschau-Berlin-Paris, die ja immer über Köln führte und zu allen Zeiten große Bedeutung hatte, im Zeitalter schneller Züge . . . nicht mit eingebracht werden sollte.[1]

Kohl's vision of a reconnected Germany as a part of a reconnected Europe (in true Adenauerian fashion he did not forget the Rhineland) appealed to a vague historical tradition ("traditionelle Linienführung," "klassische Route"), conveniently forgetting that such East-West connections had also been central to carrying out a war on two fronts. Kohl's grand perspective is perhaps indicative of a haste in reestablishing "traditional" connections (akin to the desire to reconstruct the "traditional" centre of Berlin) while losing track of the cultural and economic effects of forty years of division.

Nevertheless, with the fall of the Wall, many reconnections were to be made. At the beginning of his contemporary reflections on the state of the unified nation, the East German writer Günter de Bruyn recalls a moment of epiphany at Berlin Alexanderplatz underground station:

> jetzt aber, als ich an Ort und Stelle hörte, daß nicht mehr Thälmann-platz oder Grotewohlstraße als Ziel genannt wurden . . . spürte ich eine Fröhlichkeit in mir aufsteigen, die Ähnlichkeit mit meinem ungläubigen Staunen, das wenige Jahre zuvor die Öffnung der Mauer begleitet hatte, das aber jetzt sofort seiner Zweifel beraubt wurde — durch den einfahrenden, deutlich mit Ruhleben bezeichneten Zug.[2]

The material reality of the train provides the evidence of reconnection for de Bruyn. He is writing ten years after Kohl's speech, however, and immediately points out that such "Vorzüge" have to be tempered with an appreciation of the realities of the post-unification situation in the East. The reconnected Germany provokes ambivalent, difficult emotions.

Railways and the (German) Imagination

The symbolic potential of the interlinking network of rails, recognised in their differing ways by Kohl and de Bruyn, represents one of the powerful resonances which the train has had ever since the prospect of such lines of connection gave birth to the "Vernetzungstraum."[3] Such feelings were particularly strong within the German context, given the absence of a powerful unified state in the first half of the nineteenth century. Goethe famously remarked to Eckermann in 1828: "Mir ist nicht bange, daß Deutschland nicht eins wird . . . unsere gute Chauseen und die künftigen Chauseen werden schon das Ihrige thun."[4] For the young liberal, Karl Beck, writing in 1837, only two years after the opening of the Nuremberg-Fürth line, progress toward a democratic, united Germany was embodied in the rail network.

> Diese Schienen — Hochzeitsbänder,
> Trauungsringe — blankgegossen,
> Liebend tauschen sie die Länder,
> Und die Ehe wird geschlossen.[5]

The political process of linking up the principalities is implicitly connected in Beck's poem with industrial, economic advancement. Indeed, the train as a "cultural metaphor" has a wide range of symbolic resonances.[6] Constructed of iron and steel, the railway's primary symbolic resonance is as the embodiment of industrial progress: it was the form in which the experience of industrialization was first available to the majority who were not working in the new factories.[7] "The machine ensemble, consisting of wheel and rail, railroad and carriage, expanded into a unified railway system, which appeared as one great machine covering the land."[8] As it connected up disparate places and imposed the need for a reliable timetable, the train also represented the standardization of time, the homogenization of spatial experience, as well as the relentless forward momentum of time passing and the transience of modern life.[9]

This wide range of resonances found their expression in nineteenth-century literary reflections on the impact of the railways. The texts of the time are marked by ambivalence toward the speed of this modernization and its effects on the individual, along with the sense of inevitability that the train's unstoppable progress seems to suggest.[10] According to Johannes Mahr, the train plays "eine untergeordnete Rolle"[11] in texts from the start of the twentieth century onwards, since it was "ein leicht austauschbares Exempel für die moderne Arbeitswelt und für die moderne Technik, während es solche Austauschbarkeit in den vorangegangenen Jahrzehnten

nicht gab."[12] According to Gerhard Rademacher, the train became "natu-
ralised": it was merely one in a repertoire of symbols to be employed in
literary works which either dealt with a specific *Lebensabschnitt* or used the
railway journey as a "paradigm for human existence."[13]

Railways and Societies in Transition:
Post-1945 German Literature

Although, within an industrialised society, the train is no longer an alien
presence, it nevertheless retains certain characteristics that lend it a symbolic potential that attracts writers throughout the twentieth century.
There is space here only to look briefly at two of those aspects in the
context of German literature since 1945: the train journey as a collective
experience, and as a signifier of transition.

As Walter Benjamin recognised in his *Passagen-Werk*, whereas the car
and aeroplane only carried small groups of passengers, the historical
significance of the train lay in the fact it was the last "Verkehrsmittel, was
Massen formiert."[14] What were for Benjamin the masses, was for Hans-
Werner Richter a community "unterwegs" as he looked at the situation
in Germany in 1946:

> Der Schienenstrang, der kreuz und quer durch ein Land läuft, ist die
> Lebensader eines Volkes. An ihm und auf ihm widerspiegelt sich der
> Geist eines Volkes, seine Mentalität, seine inneren und äußeren Sorgen,
> seine Furcht und seine Hoffnungen. . . . Wo sich ein Volk auf Reisen
> begibt, wird das Gesicht der Zeit sichtbar.[15]

At a time of collective transition in the period immediately after 1945,
everyday experience was deeply marked by the railways, principally because it was one of the few possible means of communication and
travel.[16] Richter used the train to denote both a collective experience and
movement and transition.

Whereas the *Nibelungen Express* heading for Bonn in Wolfgang Koeppen's 1953 novel *Das Treibhaus* denotes the arrival at restoration in the
West, in East Germany the period of transition — on the path to communism — was conceived from a long-term perspective. In the context of the
"Bitterfelder Weg," the conformist literature of the GDR took to its heart
the image of the train as the embodiment of the state and its historical
mission. Irmtraud Morgner's first major work, the programmatically socialist realist story, *Das Signal steht auf Fahrt* (1959), opens and closes
with scenes presenting a brigade of railwaymen as a collective. In particular
it shows how the apolitical conformist *Kleinbürger* Hans Hübner learns

the responsibilities of the train driver in a socialist collective.[17] The story concludes with a resounding resolution that establishes a harmony not only among the brigade, but also between the regular uniformity of the locomotive and the less predictable human hand, as the locomotive pulls out of the shed decked out with a banner: "mit weißen unregelmäßigen Buchstaben beschrieben: 'Der Sozialismus siegt.'"[18]

Christa Wolf's *Der geteilte Himmel*, published in 1963, is set for the most part in a train factory. Like Morgner's story, Wolf's novel is based around the trials, tribulations and ultimate success of a single brigade. The central protagonist, the trainee teacher Rita, joins the brigade and is gifted an insight into the industrial process: "Diesem Wagen, der äußerlich glatt und glänzend war, sah sie unter die Haut. Sie war froh darüber. Ich gehöre dazu, dachte sie" (9). The train is, however, a more ambivalent symbol of progress; for it is trains, "die da von rechts und links auf mich zukamen," in front of which Rita collapses at the factory.[19]

The trains coming from both directions are surely a conscious echo of Jakob Abs's death in Uwe Johnson's *Mutmaßungen über Jakob* (published in the West in 1959).[20] In contrast to Jakob's fate, Rita is rescued by her brigade. Even the unsuccessful test of the new brakes of the train in Wolf's novel (representing the fact that the GDR is heading too fast down the line of socialism for its own good) runs synchronically with Gagarin's successful first space flight, which suggests to Rita that the ultimate goal is assured.[21] By contrast, Jakob's complicated attempts to ensure the running of the GDR's rail passenger system are thrown off track by the overriding command to ensure the smooth passage of the military trains running south to quell the uprising in Budapest in 1956.[22]

In Morgner's and Wolf's early novels, the transitional period, manifested in the conflicts within the individual, are ultimately resolved for the good of the state, as embodied by the train. By contrast, Johnson's novel uses the train to exemplify more pessimistic perspectives on the autonomy of the individual within the historical process.

Railways in Post-1989 German Fiction

In this context it is striking that authors from the GDR writing after the *Wende* have turned to the railway network as a setting for the examination of the position and potential of the individual within a society in transition.

In Brigitte Struyzk's semi-autobiographical text, *In vollen Zügen* (1994), a railway journey sets in train a series of loosely connected personal reflections, primarily concerned with the lives of herself and her deceased daughter. These reflections interwine, however, with a commentary on the history of the GDR which is the background for Struyzk's experiences. Reinhard Jirgl's *Abschied von den Feinden* (1995) is a complex story principally based around two brothers' competing attempts to narrate each other's stories. These stories are based in the GDR past, but the act of narration takes place in post-unification Germany. The book makes manifold use of train and railway motifs.[23] Principally, however, the setting for the elder brother's reflections for the first two-thirds of the book is a train travelling between western and eastern Germany that comes to a standstill in the former border region. Wolfgang Hilbig's *Das Provisorium* (2000) follows the crises of its protagonist, the GDR-born writer C., who has been granted a visa to travel to West Germany. His provisional status, having left the east but not yet at home in the west, is continually underlined by his habit of waiting at train stations and travelling on innumerable trains between women and cities in the still-divided Germany of the late 1980s.

In all three texts, the train line connects the two political systems of East and West Germany. The railway network is the setting in which all three examine the period of transition around the *Wende* in late 1980s and early 1990s Germany, while also taking stock of their characters' GDR pasts (all three authors have their backgrounds in the GDR).

"Lokwechsel im Rückzug. Intercity."[24] In a book which frequently plays with the train motif, this opening sentence from *In vollen Zügen* alludes to the historic change as it happens: the locomotive, the driving force and former embodiment of the GDR state, is being replaced.[25] Yet, although it provides the frame for the reflections, the political transition is not in the foreground of Struzyk's book. This opening section closes with Struzyk drifting into a state of reverie and memory in which her poetically associative prose constructs the paradoxical state of time in which the book's narrative is generated: "Im Zug der Zeit vergeht sie, die Zeit, entsteht sie, die Zeit, die weit zurückliegt" (*IVZ,* 9). As time passes, so memories come into view — Struzyk's train of thought is a "Rückzug," a retreat into the past, or, as the book's subtitle puts it, the fragments are "Rücksichten," sitting with one's back to the direction of the train and looking back at places that have already been passed.

This fragmented text is not bound by a linear narrative. Instead, the sections resemble a series of snapshots in loosely chronological order, with the result that many different trains roll through her story as she looks back on a personal history which is also a history of the GDR. For example, we are reminded that the train was a material part of the everyday experience of living in a divided Germany. A trip to the West is ultimately a disappointment:

> Mit fünf über die grüne Grenze. Und dann in vollen Zügen, und stundenlang auf dem Bahnsteig gestanden, als Kontrolle war . . . Es war eine Ent-Täuschung wie eine Ent-Tarnung. Der gleiche Wald, die gleiche Sprache, die gleiche Eile. (*IVZ*, 46–47)

As this excerpt reminds us, the railway was also a material part of the walled-in world of the GDR.

She travels from West Germany to Berlin on the night of 9 to 10 November 1989, when her fellow travellers in the compartment become a microcosm of GDR history. A young man is returning to the GDR some years after being expelled for beating up a policeman. Struzyk is simply an observer of his tirade against the state, which is directed toward an elderly man. The young man's position is put into perspective by the fact that his interlocutor was himself a victim of Stalinist measures in the period following the war.

Struzyk also addresses the transitions taking place in the contemporary situation. In "Streifen" the discovery of a driver's timetable reveals how "Lokführer drosseln das Tempo, wenn sie den Bahnhof Friedrichstraße westwärts verlassen. Der Unterbau hält nur bei gedrosseltem Tempo die Belastung aus" (*IVZ*, 112). The "Unterbau," Marx's term for the economic base, is not secure enough to deal with the transition to the market economy. Struyzk underlines this connection in the next paragraph:

> Meine erste Fahrt in Richtung Bahnhof Zoo: Das Largo des Hinausgleitens suggerierte: Langsam verläßt man sein Land, mit gesammelten Sinnen. Der Fernzug, hier und heute, am 16. Juli 1991, hält auf offener Strecke, vor der Pathologie. (*IVZ*, 112)

The idea of leaving one's country in careful, thoughtful manner is surely meant ironically considering the manner in which many left the GDR once it was possible to do so freely. The pathology unit of the Charité becomes a symbol for the sick GDR, and the train of progress to the western side comes to a stop. Indeed the text twice brings a train to a halt. On the second occasion, in the playfully-entitled penultimate section "Zugzwang": "[der] Zug bleibt stehen auf der Höhe des Antennenwaldes von Nauen," Nauen having been a communications centre in the GDR. Perhaps this is the site from which Struzyk aims to broadcast her text.

Struzyk's book is not immediately concerned with the direction which the train is taking, however, but rather with breaking out of the "Zug der Zeit," the train of linear time. The second half is a dialogue with her daughter who has taken her own life. The final section, "Kein Text allein," attempts to confront that death in the book's most allusive fragment. She cites the doctor's judgement on her daughter's condition:

> Du wärst ernsthaft krank weil Du damals als Du in die deutsch-deutscher Binsen gegangen bist Dich nicht entscheiden konntest gehst Du zurück in ein zum Vergehen verurteiltes Land wo Deine Freunde sind oder bleibst Du in der Zukunft die Dir so schal und fremd erschien. (*IVZ*, 167)

The doctor's clinical analysis is marked by the subjunctive to rob it of its all-too definitive quality. Nevertheless it describes the permanently liminal condition "in between" states which was the fate of Struzyk's daughter and which, less cataclysmically, is also that of the narrator, whose journey "endet an Deinem Grab" and whose narrative has no clear lines into the future. Struzyk's train of thought consciously eschews any clear point of arrival.

Reinhard Jirgl's novel, *Abschied von den Feinden,* also examines this condition of being "in between" states. Having travelled from western to eastern Germany, returning, "[nachdem] die Grenze verschwunden war innerhalb I Nacht,"[26] for the first time in over eight years, the elder brother is now on his way back to the West. The journey is already enough in itself to unsettle his sense of location:

> Bereits während der Fahrt war er nicht mehr sicher, von Bekanntem sich zu entfernen u einer Fremdnis sich zu nähern; die Umkehrung wäre ebenso denkbar gewesen. (*AF,* 17)

To add to this sense of spatial liminality, he spends the journey (alone in his compartment with only his leather jacket on the peg opposite for company), looking at a series of photographs from his past. His memories are thus structured in a manner akin to Struzyk's procedure in *In vollen Zügen.* The train then stops in the middle of nowhere. After some time, the conductor explains, in Jirgl's inimitable orthographical style, that the "Strecke wird jetzt endlich ausgebessert . . . Unndann der neue Fahrplan: Der I. Wieder für Gans-Deutschland" (*AF,* 69). Ultimately, though, this unexpected stop opens up a possibility for the elder brother, whose desires are described by the younger brother:

> Über lange Jahre hinweg weiß ich einen Wunsch in ihm: Während einer Reise aus dem Zug, dessen Fahrt auf der Strecke ins Stocken geriet,

einfach auszusteigen — an beliebigen Orten, irgendwo dort, wo das Halten grad geschah. Das I, festgelegte & geplante Ziel wäre aufgegeben zugunsten der Möglichkeiten von vielerlei Wegen. (*AF,* 260)

As the elder brother leaves the train and steps out into the countryside, this is explicitly described as a moment outside the process of history — "*Ein Atemholen der Geschichte, (dachte er) wo Zeit in Landschaften sich kehrt*" (*AF,* 261). He is not "irgendwo," however, but rather in a place outside the relentless forward movement of time, for in this apparently empty countryside he comes across a deserted village that had been evacuated because it had become part of the ever extending border region of the GDR, and thus necessary for military occupation. Here the brother finds the ruins of the village, containing fragments reminiscent of his childhood that he tries to piece together for his own personal narrative:

> Nicht von ungefähr hatte ihn vordem beim Halten auf freier Strecke der Anblick dieser Landschaft zum Aussteigen verleitet. . . . Er erinnerte sich an diesen Ort, an das Geschehen hier, einst in unserer Kindheit. (*AF,* 288)

His speculations about the past remain provisional (*AF,* 319–20), but the return to the ruins of the past is nevertheless an ambiguously positive moment on which the novel concludes.

> Er war kein Reisender mehr. Er war an einem Ort, der seinen Namen verloren hatte & der niemals I Namen wieder bekommen würde. Der vielleicht zerfallenen, in Dreck, Stein & Staub sich zurückverwandelnd, und schließlich verschwinden würde; ein Ort also, an dem er nicht gewesen wäre. Dort, in diesem langsam erbleichenden Ort, würde er, unvereinbar mit-sich u: seinen Bildern, I blinder Punkt sein, I Fleck. Der würde bleiben. (*AF,* 322)

Cosentino is right to read this conclusion as highly ambivalent.[27] It is, however, Jirgl's peculiar orthography that allows him to stage this utopia of non-identity, balancing permanence and flux. The brother is "unvereinbar" but connected "mit-sich," and connected with, yet different from, his images (this is the meaning of the "u:"). This is not the overcoming of the provisional condition. Rather, the provisionality of the subject trapped in a teleological, mechanical historical process has been exchanged for a provisional state of "non-identity," caught between past and present in a place that simultaneously exists and is disappearing. What remains are the ruins of the historical process: "Fleck," "Punkt," the ruins of the past bypassed by the speeding time of linear progress westwards. In the final paragraph of his bleak novel, Jirgl presents the possibility of a "Stillstand" to be achieved in a place that was a victim of the GDR's regime's vain attempt to establish its immortality.[28]

The texts by both Struzyk and Jirgl stage the break from linear narrative — as represented by the train — into a more complex awareness of time. Provisionality is the enabler of an autonomous space which, although it may leave them in a no-man's land, nevertheless allows them to gain more complex understandings of the historical process. By contrast, for the protagonist of Wolfgang Hilbig's *Das Provisorium* (2000), the absence of a sense of home is aggravated by a sense of being "out of time." Although the most recently published of the three, Hilbig's novel is the only one that is narrated in the pre-*Wende* era. The novel is centred around C.'s writer's block, apparently brought on by his arrival in the West: "In dem Land, in dem er sich aufhielt, eignete er sich nicht mehr zum Schriftsteller, dachte er."[29] As we learn toward the end of the book, when he finally reflects on his past in the GDR rather than living in the eternal present of his ceaseless travelling, C. had worked in the industrial sector of the GDR up to the age of forty. He had worked on assembly lines, and then been made a "Heizer" in one of the factories. At that point he had begun writing seriously, and had ultimately become a full-time author. C. does not sentimentalise his past (and he is critical of those who "praise" him for having spent so long in the real world before "becoming" a writer): "Es war der Irrweg eines Vereinzelten durch die brüllende, verschworene, triebhaft arbeitende Masse, zu der er vergeblich Kontakt herzustellen suchte" (*DP*, 274).

Like Struzyk and Jirgl, Hilbig makes use of the fact that the railway line connects the two states. Indeed, as his novel takes place mostly before the *Wende*, he is able to exploit the potential of the "authentic" border experience, noting the difference in the quality between the tracks in West and East, and using this as a metaphor for the smooth running, or otherwise, of the state: "ratternd and schaukelnd" for the GDR, "fast lautlos" for the Federal Republic. The train encapsulates the attitudes of the two states toward one another in this period: the GDR almost coming upon the Federal Republic as if it had not expected it to be there; the Federal Republic resigned to the existence of the GDR, and not expecting anything to change.

Again like Struzyk and Jirgl, Hilbig also uses the train as an emblem of the historical process. Hilbig's central protagonist, the writer C., has collected the traumas of the century (or rather, writings about the traumas of the century) in a number of cardboard boxes in his room. He describes the history of the twentieth century in metaphorical terms which link that process to the rest of the novel:

> Das ganze Jahrhundert sei ein einziger Zug von Lügen gewesen, hatte er zu Hedda gesagt, in Form einer Lüge und beladen mit Lügen sei dieser Zug vorwärtsgefahren, vorübergefahren, mit einer Lokomotive als Führungssymbol. . . . Der Schienenstrang für diesen Zug sei die Fortschrittslüge gewesen. Und der Zug habe die Viehwaggons durch das Land geschleppt, Viehwaggons voller Menschen, kaum noch als Menschen erkennbar, Richtung Auschwitz, Workuta, Majdanek, Magadan, unter einem Himmel, der ein Gespinst aus Lüge war. (*DP*, 255)

For Hilbig's protagonist, the train as the lie of progress is the embodiment of the dialectic of enlightenment, where reason and technological advancement ultimately arrive at barbarism. C.'s relationship to that process is, unsurprisingly, provisional, but "seine erbärmliche provisorische Einstellung" means that he has committed himself ideologically as little as he has made commitments to the various women in his life. Although C. may not have compromised himself, he is at the mercy of these trains and he shows no signs of being able to halt the process. The railway network enables him to travel between East and West, but C. never manages truly to arrive in the West.[30] Unlike the protagonists of Jirgl's and Struzyk's texts, C. cannot establish a space, however provisional, from which to gain a different perspective. When he is not actually on the move, then he is to be found at railway stations, but the railway station, like the train, is symptomatic of C.'s provisional state:

> Seit einer ungewissen Zeit hatte er die Welt nur noch auf den Bahnhöfen wahrgenommen. Er bewegte sich von Bahnhof zu Bahnhof, sie waren ganz zu den Anhaltspunkten seines Bewußtseins geworden. (*DP*, 117)

The opening of this extract is typical for C.'s vague sense of time and unreliable memory (doubtless affected by his phenomenal alcohol consumption), which are further symptoms of his condition. This ensures that, in common with Struzyk's and Jirgl's texts, *Das Provisorium* does not have any clear sense of linear narrative.

The protagonist claims not to know what exactly is the attraction which train stations hold for him, but it is in these places that he becomes unobtrusive "mit seiner Form der Unruhe," "hier mußte er nichts weiter bedeuten als Flucht und Vorbeigang" (*DP*, 121). Railway stations, as Schivelbusch has pointed out, have a dual function: they welcome those arriving in the city and say farewell to those departing.[31] As an "Anhaltspunkt," it allows him to feel located in space, while never fully arriving anywhere. Even though it is a home for some people — the community of the down-and-out, the train station cannot become a home for C. At Nuremberg station: "C. saß auf einer der Treppen und beobachtete [die Obdachlosen] verstohlen; er hatte eine Treppe für sich allein, er gehörte nicht zu ihnen, sie achteten nicht auf ihn."[32]

Train Station / Nation

C.'s dream of the West was never likely to match the reality of the situation as he, coming from the East, would experience it. The distinction between East and West is also drawn out in a comparison between train stations in the East ("viel mehr wirtschaftlichen Belangen untergeordnet als einer reibungslosen Personenbeförderung"), and in the West, which are more and more like "Einkaufszentren . . . die sich von jenen in der Stadt nur dadurch unterschieden, daß hier die Ladenschlußgesetze aufgehoben waren" (*DP*, 122).

Hilbig's novel begins with the protagonist imagining his return to Leipzig railway station, which he recalls as being full of the "werktätigen Massen" (*DP*, 33). The novel ends with the only section set after the *Wende*. It is a description of Leipzig station that begins with the community of the down-and-out also to be found there now, although these homeless people are "abgerissene Osteuropäer." The railway station is an allegory of the GDR in a period of transition. It already displays the influence of the new dispensation: its façade is covered "von jener unüberschaubaren Schriftflut, welche die noch ungewohnte Meinungsfreiheit wieder aufhob, weil sie schnurstracks zum Analphabetismus führte" (*DP*, 315). The texts range from "Wahlplakate" and "Reklame" down to "Partnermassage und Unterweisungen in asiatischer Heil- oder Liebeskunst." The station, "leer wie einer seiner Träume," bears the scars of C.'s experiences in the West. C.'s condition has become that of the state which he grew up in.

> In dem halbrunden Tor weit hinten am anderen Ende des Bahnhofs ging nun ein Licht auf, das halbrunde Tor war von Licht erfüllt wie eine aufgehende Sonne. . . . Und in der aufgehenden Sonne am Ende des Bahnhofs tauchten drei Buchstaben auf, die sich dunkel in der leuchtenden Scheibe abzeichneten, es waren die drei Buchstaben, die für eine große Industriefirma standen, und das siegreiche Zeichen gab der aufgehenden Sonne ihren Namen . . . AEG. (*DP*, 320)

This ironic new dawn with which the novel closes reveals the victorious economic forces cloaked in a spurious magic. The train station already bears the effects of post-unification rationalization, for there are fewer trains and these are much emptier than before. In contrast to the observations made by Walter Benjamin, there are no "masses" travelling on those trains anymore. C. had himself been working in heavy industry; now, as a supposedly full-time writer, he spends all his time as a passenger on that former symbol of heavy industry, the train. As an allegory of the post-*Wende* GDR, the station is a place of provisionality: the state is itself in a state of homelessness. His concluding description of Leipzig station asserts that its appearance has not yet ("noch nicht") changed, implying that the narrator knows the ultimate fate of the station. This was in fact its complete renewal "als Pilotprojekt für die Aufgabenstellung 'Dienstleistungszentrum im Empfangsgebäude'": the train station is a prime site for the service economy.[33] Unlike Struzyk and Jirgl, who both invoke the past in an attempt to reconsider the present, there can be no return for Hilbig. He has moved away from the conception of the nation as a home, even as a lost or ruined home. Instead he presents the dislocation of the subject in a service economy where trains appear to have lost their connection to their origins in heavy industry, but where, in fact, the sign of industrial might (AEG) still reigns.[34]

Trains and/or Literature

All three writers make capital out of the material fact that the railway connects east and west at a time when there would seem to be no real connection between the two Germanies, but this railway network itself is only their starting-point.

In all these texts the train is involved in a complex web of connotations. The train journey is employed to suggest a specific *Lebensabschnitt*, a period of transition for the central protagonist. In all three texts, the individual subject is a passenger, passively experiencing the passage of space and time, at the mercy of the direction laid down by the rail tracks.[35] The only interaction, if there is any, is with the service personnel — in *Abschied von den Feinden*, the brother sits alone in his compartment and talks only to the conductor and the trolley waiter. These train journeys are not, as may have been the case in West German literature in the 1980s, "die Entfaltung individuell erfahrener Zeit in einem poetischen Raum."[36] All the texts examine the search for an individual experience of time, but the space in which these experiences are inscribed is a country in a period of social, economic and political upheaval. The train carries collectives and implies a collective transition. As a result the train also stages the relationship of the central protagonist to the collective moment. The train journey — and it is a journey from east to west — is emblematic of that process of transition, not only because of the material significance of the railways during the period of the Cold War, but also because of their enduring significance as a symbol of impersonal, mechanical, industrial-economic forces. If we look back to Kohl's visionary rhetoric, his "Ver-kehrswege" doubtless signified the traffic of commerce as much, if not more than it did human networks. It may appear in these texts that the train no longer has the clear connections with industrial economic forces that once marked it out and which were still prominent in the GDR. Yet the fact that the train can no longer convincingly symbolise manufacturing industry in fact makes it the perfect vehicle for writers from the former GDR to indicate the hidden truth about a service industry whose economic structure is largely invisible.

The railway setting also implies the absence of a home. There can be no return for these protagonists: the train's direction cannot be reversed, and home, in the case of Hilbig's Leipzig station, is itself undergoing the process of transition. The only way out of that process is to get off the train, but where is this possible? For Struzyk and Jirgl, orientation can only begin with a reexamination of the past. Struzyk's journey ends at her daughter's grave. Jirgl's protagonist steps back into the past, but there is no sense in which this is a nostalgic step backward. In the case of both Jirgl and Struzyk, the ability to step out of the historical process is expressly a literary act. Both books are defences of literature as the opposite of the linear, and apparently inevitable narrative of history which the train and railway line embody. Both are complex constructions that demand time and concentration of the reader, continuing that German literary tradition of creating "the historical and imaginative space for the problematic nation."[37] That space still has to be fought for; it is a case of attempting to bring the train of time to stop, to achieve a "Stillstand." Literary forms of taking stock stand in stark opposition to the rolling stock.

Hilbig's book would appear to be different, in that its protagonist is deeply pessimistic about the potential of, and the market for, literature in contemporary society. The book, published in 2000, combats the self-absorbed failure of its protagonist, however, by becoming a reflection on that process of dislocation and disillusionment, of losing a home and not gaining a new one, of being attracted to and also disappointed by the consumer allure of the West that C. undergoes in the late 1980s, and which his fellow former citizens of the GDR were to experience in the 1990s. In other words, in the tradition of Adrian Leverkühn in Thomas Mann's *Doktor Faustus*, the artist is a seismograph for the changes to come in society as a whole. All three texts affirm literary discourse as a site that, although it cannot offer a secure point of departure or arrival, does combat the apparent inevitability of "Zugzwang."

Notes

[1] *Verhandlungen des Deutschen Bundestages, 11. Wahlperiode, Stenographische Berichte, 177. Sitzung* (28 November 1989), 13510–13514.

[2] G. de Bruyn, *Deutsche Zustände: Über Erinnerungen und Tatsachen, Heimat und Literatur* (Frankfurt am Main: Fischer, 1999), 7.

[3] H. Glaser, *Industriekultur und Alltagsleben: Vom Biedermeier zur Postmoderne* (Frankfurt am Main: Fischer, 1994), 15.

[4] Johann Wolfgang Goethe, *Gedenkausgabe der Werke, Briefe und Gespräche*, ed. Ernst Beutler, vol. 24 (*Gespräche mit Eckermann*) (Zurich: Artemis, 1949), 702.

[5] Karl Beck, "Die Eisenbahn" (1837), quoted in J. Mahr, *Eisenbahnen in der deutschen Dichtung: der Wandel eines literarischen Motivs im 19. und im beginnenden 20. Jahrhundert* (Munich: Fink, 1982), 83.

[6] The phrase "cultural metaphor" is coined by Michael Freeman in his study, *Railways and the Victorian Imagination* (New Haven: Yale, 1999), 18. Freeman's book is one of a few, along with Wolfgang Schivelbusch's pioneering study, *The Railway Journey: The Industrialization of Time and Space in the Nineteenth Century* (Berkeley: U of California P, 1986) and Glaser's study of *Industriekultur und Alltagsleben* (see note 3) to consider the railway in its wider cultural context.

[7] Schivelbusch, *The Railway Journey*, 122.

[8] Schivelbusch, *The Railway Journey*, 29.

[9] Schivelbusch, *The Railway Journey*, 33–44.

[10] This ambivalence of the train as a representative of modernity and technological progress in the literature, and in the particular the poetry, of the nineteenth and twentieth century has been examined in three studies. J. Mahr, *Eisenbahnen* (see note 5); G. Rademacher, *Das Technik-Motiv in der Literatur und seine didaktische Relevanz: Am Beispiel des Eisenbahngedichtes im 19. und 20. Jahrhundert* (Frankfurt am Main: Peter Lang, 1981); A. Heinimann, *Technische Innovation und literarische Aneignung: die Eisenbahn in der deutschen und englischen Literatur des 19. Jahrhunderts* (Bern: Francke, 1992).

[11] Mahr, *Eisenbahnen*, 269.

[12] Mahr, *Eisenbahnen*, 267.

[13] Rademacher, *Das Technik-Motiv*, 85.

[14] Walter Benjamin, *Gesammelte Schriften,* volume 5:2 (Frankfurt am Main: Suhrkamp, 1991), 744.

[15] Hans Werner Richter, "Unterhaltungen am Schienenstrang," *Der Ruf* 4 (1946): 6–7.

[16] The railway as a frequent emblem for transition in literary and journalistic works in the immediate period after 1945 is the focus of Bertram Salzmann's study *Eiserne*

Wege: Die deutsche Nachkriegszeit (1945–1948) im Spiegel des literarischen Eisen-bahnmotivs (Stuttgart: Metzler, 1994).

[17] Geoff Westgate, *Strategies under Surveillance. Reading Irmtraud Morgner as a GDR Writer* (Amsterdam: Rodopi, 2001), 30–33.

[18] I. Morgner, *Das Signal steht auf Fahrt* (Berlin: Aufbau, 1959), 123.

[19] Morgner, *Das Signal steht auf Fahrt*, 9.

[20] W. Schmitz, *Uwe Johnson* (Munich: Beck, 1984), 46.

[21] Something not seen by her boyfriend, the disillusioned Manfred, who is clearly using the train as the metaphor for the GDR economy when he says: "Und unsere ausgediente Lokomotive, dieses Vehikel des vorigen Jahrhunderts, läßt uns wie zum Hohn schon heute im Stich. Welch ein Haufen von unnötiger Mühsal! Die wird kein bißchen leichter durch die glanzvollen Extravaganzen in der Stratosphäre. . ." Wolf, *Der geteilte Himmel*, 146.

[22] Uwe Johnson, *Mutmaßungen über Jakob* (Frankfurt am Main: Suhrkamp, 1992), 246–50.

[23] Most of these are listed by Christine Cosentino in her article on the novel: "'Dieses Deutsche in den Deutschen': Auflösung und Kontinuität in Reinhard Jirgls Alp-traumroman *Abschied von den Feinden*," *Colloquia Germanica* 30 (1997): 307–14.

[24] B. Struzyk, *In vollen Zügen: Rücksichten* (Berlin: Aufbau, 1994), 7. Hereafter cited in the text in brackets after quotations as follows (*IVZ*).

[25] Elsewhere in the book words are carriages drawn along by the GDR locomotive. "Es [Verrat] rangierte auf einer Ebene mit Standpunkt und Parteilichkeit, lauter verplombte Waggons." Struzyk, 76.

[26] R. Jirgl, *Abschied von den Feinden* (Munich: Hanser, 1995), 18. The use of Roman numerals is just of the many eccentricities of Jirgl's stylised orthography. Hereafter cited in the text in brackets after quotations as follows (*AF*).

[27] Cosentino, "Dieses Deutsche," 313.

[28] Jirgl expands on the meaning of these ruins in his interview with Werner Jung in *Neue Deutsche Literatur* 46 (1998): 56–70.

[29] Wolfgang Hilbig, *Das Provisorium* (Frankfurt am Main: Fisher, 2000), 24. Hereafter cited in the text after quotations in brackets as follows (*DP*).

[30] The narrator says of C.'s stay in Munich: "[. . .] im Grunde genommen war seine Reise schon auf dem Bahnhof zu Ende gewesen" (Hilbig, *Das Provisorium*, 23).

[31] Schivelbusch, *The Railway Journey*, 173.

[32] Hilbig, *Das Provisorium*, 306. This is in contrast to the fate of the disillusioned former GDR citizen Heinrich Lobek in Jens Sparschuh's 1995 novel, *Der Zimmer-springbrunnen*, who finds a new community at Berlin's Zoologischer Garten railway station.

[33] G. Kahler, C. Steckeweh, K.-D. Weiß, eds., *Renaissance der Bahnhöfe: Die Stadt im 21. Jahrhundert* (Braunschweig: Vieweg, 1996), 73.

[34] This was also the effect, if not the intention, of *CityExpress*, a television series which ran on ARD in 1999 and which focused on the lives of the service personnel on a train running between Westerland (Sylt), Cologne and Dresden. See: S. Ward, "Train

and Nation: *CityExpress*: The Soap Opera," in *Journal of Popular Culture* 34:3 (2000), 9–25.

[35] There is not space here to discuss the status of these passengers as flâneurs, something that can also be observed in Sten Nadolny's 1981 train novel, *Netzkarte* (1981) and its 1999 post-unification sequel, *Er oder Ich*.

[36] Salzmann, *Eiserne Wege*, 162.

[37] S. Brockmann, *Literature and German Reunification* (Cambridge: Cambridge UP, 1999), 198.

On the Function of the Foreign in the Novels *Andere Umstände* (1998) by Grit Poppe and *Seit die Götter ratlos sind* (1994) by Kerstin Jentzsch

Roswitha Skare

THE IMAGES OF the collapse of the Berlin Wall and the words of the former German Chancellor Willy Brandt: "Jetzt wächst zusammen, was zusammengehört,"[1] still have the power to move us, despite the fact that more than ten years have passed since the events themselves. Amidst the euphoria of 1989/90, indeed, nothing seemed farther from the mark than the SED's claim that the two different states had become different nations and had developed separate identities,[2] in particular, in East Germany, a "Socialist GDR identity." Although the notion that there might exist a separate GDR identity had been raised before 1989, even in the West, what East and West Germany seemed to share nonetheless appeared to be more significant. The continued existence of a German national culture, avowed by many people on both sides of the border, seemed to justify the hope that the two states might be quickly melded, especially considering that the people in East and West were — thus the hyperbole of the time — "brothers and sisters."[3]

As a result of apparently ever worsening "growing pains" after unification in 1990, however, Brandt's image of "growing together" soon became an often-satirized figure of speech. It came to be replaced by other images, such as the metaphor of the "Mauer im Kopf,"[4] coined in the early eighties by Peter Schneider, or by the characterisation of the East German population as "Fremde in ihrem eigenen Land."[5]

There are numerous examples of the alienation felt by east German authors since 1989/90. The younger generation of authors had already been questioning the constraints imposed upon them by the GDR and thus experienced the *Wende* "wohl als einschneidendes Ereignis, meist aber nicht als *Umbruch* ihrer Lebenswelt."[6] Many authors of the "older" and "middle" generation, on the other hand, lost all the truths and certainties that had previously sustained them. They felt that had lost something that had belonged to them, their very property, as Volker Braun's poem "Das Eigentum" illustrates:

> Da bin ich noch: mein Land geht in den Westen.
> Krieg den Hütten Friede den Palästen.
> Ich selber habe ihm den Tritt versetzt.
> Es wirft sich weg und seine magre Zierde.
> Dem Winter folgt der Sommer der Begierde.
> Und ich kann *bleiben wo der Pfeffer wächst.*
> Und unverständlich wird mein ganzer Text.
> Was ich niemals besaß, wird mir entrissen.
> Was ich nicht lebte, werd ich ewig missen.
> Die Hoffnung lag im Weg wie eine Falle.
> Mein Eigentum, jetzt habt ihrs auf der Kralle.
> Wann sag ich wieder *mein* und meine alle.[7]

It is not only previously familiar literary texts that have become incomprehensible since 1990, however. Many life stories now also appear alien and strange. As early as 1991, the east German psychotherapist Hans-Joachim Maaz diagnosed a "DDR-Verlust-Syndrom,"[8] which was held to result from the historical events of 1989/90. Maaz speaks of a "verwirrten Identität" and an "Identitätsbruch,"[9] which, he argues, explain the fact that many east Germans appear unable to muster up any real enthusiasm for their lives in a united Germany. Maaz notes that individuals often said that they felt as if they were living between two worlds without really feeling at home in either. The author Helga Königsdorf, in fact, makes this point with melancholic resignation in the foreword to her protocol, *Adieu DDR*, which appeared in autumn 1990. Here, she speaks of how people from the ex-GDR can now travel abroad yet are unable to change their psychological location:

> Was bleiben wird, sind wir, die Menschen in diesem Territorium . . . Heimat aufgeben kann eine lebenswichtige Operation sein. Doch immer, wenn das Wetter umschlägt, werden wir einander ansehen, lange noch, und diesen Schmerz empfinden, diese Vertrautheit, die keiner sonst versteht.[10]

Ten years after the fall of the Berlin Wall, the mutual preconceptions of "over here" and "over there," of "them" and "us," or even of "*Wessis*" and "*Ossis*," are as present-tense as ever.[11]

In this context, two tendencies in recent east German literature can be discerned:

On the one hand, a significant number of young authors cast back to their youth in the GDR. The desire to remember, as well as the fear of forgetting, leads them to recount a life once lived. The fact that authors who were not even thirty years old when the Wall fell take their childhoods as a literary theme might indicate identity problems in the present: although many of the younger authors view the *Wende* and reunification primarily as a chance for a new beginning, they nonetheless feel compelled to reconfirm their heritage and their lives up until now. In these childhood memories, moreover, the west is completely omitted: it is the realm of the "other."[12]

On the other hand — and these are the kind of texts I will address in this essay — a number of writers set their stories in far-away locations; many heroes and particularly heroines find themselves on trips in the hitherto unknown west.[13] When *Heimat* becomes foreign — the numerous authors who moved from the GDR to the FRG after Wolf Biermann's forced exile in 1976 experienced the "gefährlich nahen Fremde, die die eigene Sprache spricht"[14] (Jürgen Fuchs) — some people thus choose to simply leave it behind. However, within the very concept of foreign[15] resides its opposite. *Heimat*, the non-foreign and familiar, thus also belongs to the foreign.

The foreign can be experienced as something absolutely positive, however, and does not necessarily have to be connected with alienation. In this way, the foreign experience can possess a liberating and identity-building quality.[16] This may generate some objectivity vis-à-vis that which is familiar. Frequently, moreover, it promotes a "Reflexion über Heimat."[17] Understanding the foreign is, therefore, closely connected to experiencing and understanding the self, as foreignness also fulfills, Ortfried Schäffter argues:

> die Funktion eines signifikanten Kontrasts, der als Gegenbild gerade die Identität des Eigenen verstärken kann. Wer noch nicht in der Fremde war, kennt die Heimat nicht — wer keine Fremdsprache erlernt hat, kennt seine Muttersprache nicht.[18]

As Kurt Drawert thus writes in his essayistic novel *Spiegelland* (1992) that a change of location — for Drawert, the change is from west to wast, and since the east is no longer the east, he goes to the Czech Republic — is a prerequisite for being able to find the "distanzierte[n] Blick."[19] Temporal and spatial distance makes the familiar, or that which one thought one knew, unfamiliar. The familiar, uncontroversial and untested perspective previously adopted can no longer be valid, because the narrator has changed during his absence, as has the *Heimat* itself.

I would now like to concentrate on the novels of Grit Poppe and Kerstin Jentzsch. Both take recent history, especially the events of 1989/90, as their theme and thereby respond to the media's desire for *the* "novel of the *Wende.*"[20] However, they employ the genres of popular fiction and crime novel, respectively, but in a manner that extends these genres, satirises them, and opens up a space for social comment.

Both authors were born in 1964, and like Thomas Brussig, Ingo Schramm, Ingo Schulze, Kerstin Hensel or Christoph D. Brumme, they belong to a generation of young East German writers that did not participate in the development of the GDR, but was rather born into it. Nor, unlike older authors, did they feel any socio-pedagogical obligation in their writing. The mix of having been born into the system of the GDR and the lack of constraint that older writers felt as a result of their involvement in the literary apparatus of the GDR — with the exception of Kerstin Hensel, they did not start publishing until after the *Wende* — gives these young authors, as much as their novels differ, the freedom to present their specific experiences in the GDR. Many texts by these young authors were enthusiastically received by the literary media;[21] there was much discussion of a so-called new "Lust am Erzählen,"[22] and of "Unbefangenheit"[23] (Botho Strauss), of a mode of writing that was unburdened by the complex modernist narrative traditions and socio-political moralism that had, it was argued in various quarters, accompanied German literature for half a century.

Kerstin Jentzsch was a teacher until the age of twenty-four, after which she worked as a journalist for the daily newspaper *Der Morgen* and as a managerial assistant in the *Berliner Zeitung* publishing house. Her literary debut was the novel *Seit die Götter ratlos sind* (1994), which was followed two years later by *Ankunft der Pandora.*[24] The story of Lisa Meerbusch, who learns "to live" in the course of this trilogy, ends with Jentzsch's third novel, *Iphigenie in Pankow* (1998).

Grit Poppe studied at the *Literaturinstitut* in Leipzig from 1984 to 1988. During the period of the *Wende*, she became involved in the citizen's movement *Demokratie Jetzt!*. Following the publication of her first piece, *Der Fluch,* in 1990 by the *Mitteldeutscher Verlag,* and various short stories in different anthologies and journals, *Andere Umstände* appeared in 1998[25] as her debut novel. Grit Poppe's first children's book appeared in 1999 with the title *Alabusch oder das Herz des Vulkans.*

Both Jentzsch and Poppe choose as central figures young women who have lived unobtrusive and conformist lives during GDR times and had pretty much slept through the events of the autumn of 1989. While Mila Rosin — the main character in Poppe's novel — is raised by her mother alone, Lisa Meerbusch — Jentzsch's main character — spends her childhood and youth in a parental home dominated by an authoritarian father, a family court judge loyal to the State.[26] Although Mila grows up without a father at home, she still has contact with him and makes his motto her own: "Nutze die Energie deiner Wut." The combination of this motto, her fascination with Jack London's novels, and a pocket knife leads Mila to begin murdering men, randomly at first, but later with design. Mila's ambition is to have a child, yet almost all the men she encounters turn out to be failures, and end up being stabbed, poisoned, or put drunk behind a steering wheel. The astonishing thing about Mila's story is that neither the police nor the secret service manage to pick up her trail, even though there is no lack of conclusive evidence for her crimes. The mentally disturbed mother of her high school boyfriend Fred — the one man who survives his love for Mila — is the only one who pursues Mila and eventually forces her to flee Germany. She travels around San Francisco and the surrounding area with the baby, Alice, and does everything she can to erase their tracks. But even in the New World, she is unable to shake off her memories of the past: memories of Germany and the murdered men allow her no peace. Mila never makes progress: at the end of the novel, her last victim lies in the bathtub of a motel — a dead American whom she actually had wanted to marry in order to get a residency permit, yet Mila simply moves on. Only rarely does she reflect on her losses or on her homesickness: "Heimat, dachte ich. Schachmatt, dachte ich. Ich war eine Verliererin. Ich hatte eine Menge verloren."[27]

In Jentzsch's novel, Lisa Meerbusch's role model is her uncle Willy. At the end of the novel she learns that Willy is her biological father, only to read in the papers a few days later that he had been involved in dubious foreign exchange transactions and had been found murdered in Egypt. While Mila's actions are motivated by her desire for a baby, Lisa wants to find her man for life. Following her lack of success in reunited Germany and her disappointment with both east and west German men, she takes a trip to Crete in the winter of 1990 and plans to settle down there for an indefinite period of time. Lisa is young, pretty and carefree, and her main problem lies in becoming accepted by the villagers and finding a suitable man. In order to achieve this, she adopts their habits without hesitation and even tries to imitate their gestures and facial expressions. Yet it is apparent that she would feel no less foreign in her *Heimat,* the ex-GDR, nor would she be under any less pressure to conform to alien norms there. Thus, she receives post from "home," describing the alienation that inhabitants of the former GDR experience post-unification:

> Die Zeit rast dahin wie ein D-Zug. Auf den Bahnhöfen stehen die Os-
> sis, wie man uns DDR-Bürger jetzt zur besseren Kennzeichnung zu
> nennen pflegt. Der Zug hält nicht, er verlangsamt nicht einmal die
> Fahrt! Niemand kann aufspringen, er fährt zu schnell. Innen im Zug
> glotzen die Wessis mit ihren fremden Gesichtern, fremden Ansichten
> und fremden Geschmäckern. Der Zug rast vorbei, so wie er schon Jahre
> an uns vorbeigerast ist.[28]

As is already clear in this quotation, the novel is full of clichés of east and
west Germans.[29] Accordingly, the east Germans are passive and self-
pitying, or naïve and dumb. West Germans, in contrast, are know-it-alls
who are spiritually empty. The story's narrator, moreover, internalises
such *Ossi/Wessi* stereotypes and describes herself as a "typische Ostmau-
ke, die zu langsam lernt, zu langsam begreift."[30]

Poppe's novel is scarcely free of such clichés, but they are particularly
obvious and numerous in Jentzsch's novel. Along with the constellation
of characters and the plot, this novel reminds even more of popular
fiction, which was how it was usually classified.[31] However, the novel can
also be read as an attempt to reflect upon identity questions: Lisa's search
for a new place to call home represents above all a search for a sense of
belonging and *Heimat*. Because even though Jentzsch follows the conventions of popular literature — schematic building of suspense, black-
and-white character portrayal, unequivocal moral allocations — social
change is a point of reflection in the novel.

It is not surprising that East German authors send their heroes on
trips abroad. After all, the freedom to travel precipitated by the fall of the
Berlin Wall was imagined for years and hotly demanded in the autumn
of 1989. Mila and Lisa had long nursed their longing for foreignness and
the exotic. In the event, travel to an unknown world enables the characters to gain temporal and above all spatial distance from their lives. They
are thus able to reflect upon their past histories and process them. On
the one hand, therefore, the novels of Jentzsch and Poppe stand in the
tradition of the travelogue: a list of the items that were brought along,
the documentation of the route travelled and the progress of the trip
itself are just as much a part of the stories as the description of the region, the composition of the houses, the dress and the food. On the
other hand, the texts are also novels of development, since the two
young women are searching for themselves. The spatial distance presents
to the protagonists the possibility of transgressing their inner borders;
the experience of the foreign triggers the critical distancing from the
familiar. When abroad, Mila and Lisa run into language barriers and

accordingly up against the limits of cultural understanding, but they also encounter other Germans who are only travelling abroad as tourists. Lisa in particular meets east and west German tourists on Crete and reacts differently to them, depending on where they are from. One could say that Lisa was acting out different identities, in that she tries to appear either east German or west German by using the expressions and mannerisms she perceives as typical of one or the other in a given conversation. She had already noticed upon the first encounter that the common language is not able to bridge the differences. Through her learning process, however, Lisa gradually comes to the conclusion that it is necessary to stand by her own heritage and past. Her uncertainty is a result of split identity, the conscious polarization between East and West Germans that needs to be overcome:

> Ich kann kein Westmensch sein, denn ich bin in der DDR aufgewachsen. Das ist meine Heimat. Meine Familie, Silvy, der Müggelsee und das Friedrichshagener Bier. Ich tauge auch gar nicht zum Westmenschen . . . Ich habe andere Dinge gelernt in der Schule, ich bin zu unsicher, als daß ich einem Westmenschen irgend etwas weismachen könnte; beim ersten Westargument falle ich um . . . Aber ein Ostmensch will ich auch nicht mehr sein . . . Ich wünschte, mich könnte dieses Ost-West-Getue genauso kaltlassen wie Stephanos. Ich muß Ost und West aus meinem Kopf verbannen.[32]

Although the foreign location in *Andere Umstände* serves primarily as a background to the narrative — we learn only that in the USA, even the "crazies" are nice[33] — the majority of Jentzsch's plot is set in Crete. Furthermore, Uncle Willy's stories and the novel *Alexis Sorbas* (1946) by Nikos Kazantzakis determine Lisa's image of Crete.

The portrayal of the foreign in the texts discussed here can be read as a projection of a sense of inadequacy of that which is familiar, but also as a wish for change, in which the destinations gain symbolic meaning: Mila travels not only to the land of opportunity, but also to the New World, where she would like to leave the old world behind; Lisa travels to Greece, the "cradle" of democracy and occidental culture, in order to "find herself."

In the novels of Kerstin Jentzsch and Grit Poppe, utopian projections thus penetrate the protagonists' fragmented experiences of the actual foreign culture; their expectations are corrected and expanded by the experience of the "other." Mila and Lisa learn about the foreign but also simultaneously recognize that the familiar can only be comprehended by experiencing the foreign and in so doing differentiating it.

The foreign causes the distance between the familiar and the foreign to appear so large that is impossible to subsume the foreign under the familiar, no more possible than would be a complete assimilation of the foreign or a complete abandonment of the familiar.

As travelling foreigners, the characters in both authors' work are truly — as described by Georg Simmel — the more free ones, viewing "die Verhältnisse vorurteilsloser."[34] Nonetheless, the meaning of the foreign as *Ausland* (abroad) and *Elend* (misery)[35] also applies to the literary figures: they get homesick and lonely and feel like they do not belong anywhere. Accordingly, Lisa must recognise at the end of the novel that she is still a foreigner in the villagers' eyes — in spite of all her attempts to conform:

> Das ganze Dorf geht zur Zeremonie [here, a funeral procession is meant, R.S.]. Ich gehöre nicht dazu, mich will niemand dabeihaben. Lisa Meerbusch ist nur eine von vielen; eine eingemietete Touristin, die zufällig etwas länger bleibt.[36]

While the villagers try to protect their sphere of identity, Lisa senses her position between cultures, yet does not recognize the advantages of a hybrid identity.[37]

Lisa and Mila have indeed willingly set out for a new life, but they have also struck a path back into their past. Lisa and, to a lesser extent, Mila find *Heimat* in the sense of belonging and security not as much in a region or a landscape as they do in a few people who are especially close to them. For Mila, this is her daughter Alice; for Lisa, it is her mother and father. Accordingly, it is her father's death that compels Lisa to return to Germany.

Of particular interest with regard to Jentzsch's and Poppe's novels seems to me to be the tension between *what* is in the narrative and *how* it is conveyed. With Jentzsch and Poppe, the feeling of being uprooted, the connection between that and the reflections on heritage and identity, and the experience of the foreign find an entrée to the genre of *Unterhaltungsliteratur.*[38]

While the crime in Jentzsch's novel — the murder of the biological father and his involvement in the machinations of the state security — become understandable within the context of the familial background and is accommodated by the serialized novel form, Mila's murders do not have any psychological or social causes. Given that Mila commits murder practically without thought or inhibition, yet is pursued only by a deranged old woman, Poppe's novel can be read as a satire[39] of the mystery novel genre, the most distinct characteristic of which being the phenomenon of varying repetition.[40] Mila's exaggerated wish to have a child — a play on the post-*Wende* image of GDR women being primarily focused on the role of mother[41] — as well as her daughter's name — she travels with Alice into the Wonderland USA — are indicative of the fact that this is not the long-awaited novel of the *Wende* offering a realistic narrative of social change. Since all allusions are also "eine Form des kulturellen Wissens" that do not necessary refer to a "vorausgesetzten Text . . . sondern nur die Erinnerung an ihn,"[42] it is relevant to question whether this is not a postmodern popular novel. The postmodern narrative is

> geprägt von Ironie, metasprachlichem Spiel hoch zwei. Es beginnt, historisch gesehen, genau da, wo die (moderne) Vorstellung vom "Ende" und der "Krise der Kunst" umschlägt in den Willen, die traditionellen (und im Sinn der Moderne "verbrauchten") Mittel in reflektierter, ironischer Absicht wieder zu verwenden.[43]

In many cases, the return of the narrative, as well as the new joy of the narrative in the texts of young east German authors can be seen therefore as a "Umbruch von der modernen zur postmodernen Haltung."[44] This might be a way of viewing things that could contribute to a rethinking of the discussion of the modernity of GDR literature[45] by young authors after 1989/90.

Translated by Heather Fleming

Notes

[1] See Gerhart Maier, *Die Wende in der DDR* (Bonn: Bundeszentrale für politische Bildung, 1991), 30.

[2] In the past ten to fifteen years, the term "identity" has appeared with ever increasing frequency: individuals go through identity crises and are looking for their own identity; cities and regions proclaim their identity; minorities insist on their cultural identity and demand the recognition of their rights. See Lutz Niethammer, "Annäherung an ein Plastikwort," in *Kollektive Identität: Heimliche Quellen einer unheimlichen Konjunktur. Rowohlts Enzyklopädie 55594* (Reinbek bei Hamburg: Rowohlt, 2000), 9–70. The concept has been garnering increasing attention as a transdisciplinary term in culture and literature studies as well. Numerous volumes document the range and productivity of the term. See, for example, Aleida Assmann and Heidrun Fries, eds., *Identitäten: Erinnerung, Geschichte, Identität* (Frankfurt am Main: Suhrkamp, 1998); Reinhold Viehoff and Rien T. Segers, eds., *Kultur. Identität. Europa: Über die Schwierigkeiten und Möglichkeiten einer Konstruktion* (Frankfurt am Main: Suhrkamp, 1999).

[3] See Roswitha Skare, "'Real Life within The False One': Manifestations of East German Identity in Post-Reunification Texts," in Laurence McFalls and Lothar Probst,

eds., *After the GDR: New Perspectives on Divided and Reunited Germany* (Amsterdam and Atlanta: Rodopi, 2001), 216–36.

[4] Peter Schneider, *Der Mauerspringer* (Hamburg and Zurich: Luchterhand Literaturverlag, 1991), 102. On this short story, see Ivar Sagmo, "Vom anderen Gesetz im ähnlichen Leben. Fremderfahrungen in und mit Peter Schneiders Erzählung *Der Mauerspringer," Jahrbuch Deutsch als Fremdsprache* 11 (Munich: Max Hueber Verlag, 1985), 191–202.

[5] See, for example, Gerhard Schmidtchen, "Die Ostdeutschen als Fremde in ihrem eigenen Land," *Frankfurter Rundschau* (9 Sept. 1991). See also Ernst-Ullrich Pinkert, "'Fremdlinge im eigenen Haus.' Anmerkungen zu Fremdheitserfahrungen ostdeutscher Schriftsteller nach der Wende," in Alois Wierlacher and Georg Stötzel, eds., *Blickwinkel: Kulturelle Optik und interkulturelle Gegenstandskonstitution. Akten des III. Internationalen Kongresses der Gesellschaft für Interkulturelle Germanistik.* (Munich: iudicium Verlag, 1996), 723–33.

[6] Rainer Zoll, "Einleitung — ein Versuch des Verstehens," in Rainer Zoll and Thomas Rausch, eds., *Ostdeutsche Biographien: Lebenswelt im Umbruch* (Frankfurt am Main: Suhrkamp, 1999), 9–14, 11.

[7] Volker Braun, "Das Eigentum." Reprinted in Karl Otto Conrady, ed., *Von einem Land und vom andern: Gedichte zur deutschen Wende* (Frankfurt am Main: Suhrkamp, 1993), 51. The poem first appeared in *Die Zeit* (10 August 1990) and was included in anthologies later under the title "Nachruf." See also Heiner Müller, "Daily News. Drei Lektionen," *Neue Rundschau* 101 (1990), 2, 101–4.

[8] Hans-Joachim Maaz, *Das gestürzte Volk oder die verunglückte Einheit* (Berlin: Argon, 1991), 10.

[9] Maaz, 10. See on this topic also Ina-Maria Greverus, *Der territoriale Mensch: Ein literaturanthropologischer Versuch zum Heimatphänomen* (Frankfurt am Main: Athenäum Verlag, 1972).

[10] Helga Königsdorf, *Adieu DDR: Protokolle eines Abschieds* (Reinbek bei Hamburg: Rowohlt Taschenbuch Verlag, 1990), 9.

[11] See, for example, Jana Simon, Frank Rothe and Wiete Andrasch, eds., *Das Buch der Unterschiede: Warum die Einheit keine ist* (Berlin: Aufbau-Verlag, 2000).

[12] I am thinking of texts such as: Christoph D. Brumme, *Nichts als das* (Berlin: Verlag Mathias Gatza, 1994); Kerstin Hensel, *Im Schlauch* (Frankfurt am Main: Suhrkamp, 1993); Kerstin Hensel, *Tanz am Kanal* (Frankfurt am Main: Suhrkamp, 1994); Nadja Klinger, *Ich ziehe einen Kreis* (Berlin: Alexander Fest, 1997); Marion Titze, *Unbekannter Verlust* (Berlin: Rowohlt, 1994). See Roswitha Skare, "Auf der Suche nach Heimat? Zur Darstellung von Kindheitsheimaten in Texten jüngerer ostdeutscher Autorinnen und Autoren nach 1990," in Gerhard Fischer and David Roberts, eds., *Schreiben nach der Wende: Ein Jahrzehnt deutscher Literatur, 1989–1999* (Tübingen: Stauffenburg Verlag, 2001), 237–252.

[13] In addition to the texts discussed here by Kerstin Jentzsch and Grit Poppe, see also Helga Königsdorf, *Gleich neben Afrika* (Berlin: Rowohlt, 1992); Angela Krauß, *Die Überfliegerin* (Frankfurt and Main: Suhrkamp, 1995); or Bernd Wagner, *Paradies* (Berlin: Ullstein, 1997). Longing for the foreign is a well-known symptom in art and literature. See, for example, Joanna Jablkowska, "Fremde Heimat — Heimat in der

Fremde?" in Joanna Jablkowska and Erwin Leibfried, eds., *Fremde und Fremdes in der Literatur* (Frankfurt am Main: Peter Lang, 1996), 235–46.

[14] Ian Wallace, "Ein Leben in der Fremde? DDR-Schriftsteller im Westen, 1976–1989," in Elrud Ibsch, Ferdinand van Ingen and Anthonya Visser, eds., *Literatur und politische Aktualität* (Amsterdam and Atlanta: Rodopi, 1993), 179–92, 180. See also Wolf Biermann, "Das Hölderlin-Lied," *Alle Lieder* (Cologne: Kiepenheuer & Witsch, 1991), 198. Following Hölderlin, Biermann refers to "Fremde im eigenen Haus" in this song.

[15] On the various meanings of the foreign, see Ortfried Schäffter: "Modi des Fremderlebens. Deutungsmuster im Umgang mit Fremdheit," in Ortfried Schäffter, ed., *Das Fremde: Erfahrungsmöglichkeiten zwischen Faszination und Bedrohung* (Opladen: Westdeutscher Verlag, 1991), 11–42, esp. 14. See also Erwin Leibfried, "Was ist und heißt fremd? Ein Beitrag zu einer Phänomenologie des Fremden," in Joanna Jablkowska and Erwin Leibfried, eds., *Fremde und Fremdes in der Literatur*, 9–22.

[16] Research on foreignness in German Studies has repeatedly taken as a theme the link between the experience of the foreign and the experience of freedom. See Corinna Albrecht, "Fremdheit und Freiheit oder: Die Schule der Frauen," in Bernd Thum and Gonthier-Louis Fink, eds., *Praxis interkultureller Germanistik: Forschung — Bildung — Politik: Beiträge zum II. Internationalen Kongreß der Gesellschaft für Interkulturelle Germanistik. Straßburg 1991* (Munich: iudicium Verlag, 1993), 775–88.

[17] Greverus 56.

[18] Schäffter 19.

[19] Kurt Drawert, *Spiegelland: Ein deutscher Monolog* (Frankfurt am Main: Suhrkamp, 1992), 149.

[20] The German-speaking media have been waiting for the "*Wende* novel" for years and, at regular intervals, seem to believe they have actually found it. Cases in point: Thomas Brussig's *Helden wie wir* (1997), Bernd Wagner's *Paradies* (1997) or, as recently as 1999, Gert Neumann's *Anschlag*.

[21] Of course, among the "young wild ones" are also young West German authors such as Karen Duve, Michael Kleeberg, Thomas Lehr or the Swiss author Zoë Jenny. For a comparison of the various methods of portrayal and their implications in young East and West German literature, see Cordula Stenger, "Stolz und Vorurteil," in Wolfgang Emmerich, ed., *Junge deutsche Dichter über deutsche Dinge nach der Wende 1989* (Bremen: Universitätsdruckerei Bremen, 1997).

[22] Volker Hage, "Die Enkel kommen," *Der Spiegel* (11 October 1999): 244–54, 245.

[23] Hage 252.

[24] Both novels were published in paperback by the Wilhelm Heyne Verlag in Munich in 1996 and in 1998. They are also on the internet at Kerstin Jentzsch's homepage (www.kerstinjentzsch.desotron.de).

[25] The novel also appeared in 2000 as a Rowohlt Taschenbuch.

[26] The novel can be read as a reconciliation with the previous generation, as can also the novels *Helden wie wir* (1995) by Thomas Brussig or *Fitchers Blau* (1996) by Ingo Schramm.

[27] Grit Poppe, *Andere Umstände* (Berlin: Berlin Verlag, 1998), 235.

[28] Kerstin Jentzsch, *Seit die Götter ratlos sind* (Berlin: Verlag Das Neue Berlin, 1994), 250.

[29] Jentzsch's novel is also full of stereotypes of Southern Europeans (203).

[30] Jentzsch 10.

[31] See, for example Hannes Krauss, "Deutschland, einig Vaterland," Freitag (30 August 1996); Brigitte Zimmermann, "Götter und Leser ratlos," *Neues Deutschland* (8 July 1994); or Hannes Stein, "Lieber selber stricken. Kerstin Jentzsch schreibt über Kapitalisten, Ossis und Ouzo," *Frankfurter Allgemeine Zeitung* (10 October 1994). Volker Wehdeking comes to a similar conclusion in *Die deutsche Einheit und die Schriftsteller: Literarische Verarbeitung der Wende seit 1989* (Stuttgart, Berlin, Cologne: Verlag W. Kohlhammer, 1995), 97–101. See also Stephen Brockmann, *Literature and German Reunification* (Cambridge: Cambridge UP, 1999).

[32] Jentzsch 293.

[33] Poppe 18.

[34] Georg Simmel, "Exkurs über den Fremden," in *Soziologie: Untersuchungen über die Formen der Vergesellschaftung* (Leipzig: Verlag von Duncker & Humblot, 1908), 685–708, 688.

[35] These two words have their etymological roots in the Old High German expression *elli lendi* (outside of the land or country), with the latter being in fact more ancient — suggesting that being away from home was not a pleasant experience at the end of the first millennium.

[36] Jentzsch 394.

[37] Homi K. Bhabha's concept of hybridity appears to provide a suitable way of overcoming dichotomies such as self/other and East/West, as it constitutes an intervention against the hegemonic norms of portrayal without simply antagonistically polarising the opposition or dissipating the intellectual moment of tension. See Homi K. Bhabha, *The Location of Culture* (London: Routledge, 1994). On this concept, see Pnina Werbner and Tariq Modood, eds., *Debating Cultural Hybridity: Multi-Cultural Identities and the Politics of Anti-Racism* (London: Zed Books, 1997).

[38] See Bernd Lenz, "Popular Literature und Cultural Studies. Bilanz und Perspektiven," in Dieter Petzold and Eberhard Späth, eds., *Unterhaltungsliteratur: Ziele und Methoden ihrer Erforschung* (Erlangen: Universitätsbund Erlangen-Nürnberg, 1990), 161–75.

[39] On this term, cf. Michael Schmidt, "Persiflage. Kauserien zu einer 'Ökonomie der Anspielung,'" in: Jürgen Lehmann, Tilman Lang, Fred Lönker and Thorsten Unger, eds., *Konflikt. Grenze. Dialog. Kulturkontrastive und interdisziplinäre Textzugänge. Festschrift für Horst Turk zum 60. Geburtstag* (Frankfurt am Main: Peter Lang, 1997), 55–71, esp. 56.

[40] See Ulrich Suerbaum, "Schwierige Ermittlung: Die Suche nach Gattungsgerechten Programmen zur Untersuchung von Kriminalliteratur," in Dieter Petzold and Eberhard Späth, eds., *Unterhaltungsliteratur: Ziele und Methoden ihrer Erforschung* (Erlangen: Universitätsbund Erlangen-Nürnberg, 1990), 7–17, esp. 13.

[41] In contrast, Lisa Meerbusch has a much more realistic stance on the issue of starting a family. See Jentzsch, 249. On the gender issue in the political discourse of the GDR, see Birgit Dahlke, *Papierboot: Autorinnen aus der DDR — inoffiziell publiziert* (Würzburg: Königshausen und Neumann, 1997).

[42] Karlheinz Stierle, "Werk und Intertextualität," in Karlheinz Stierle and Rainer Warning, *Das Gespräch* (Munich: Fink, 1984), 139–51, 148.

[43] Cf. Hanns-Josef Ortheil, "Texte im Spiegel von Texten. Postmoderne Literaturen," in Rolf Grimminger, Jurij Murasov and Jörn Stückrath, eds., *Literarische Moderne: Europäische Literatur im 19. und 20. Jahrhundert* (Reinbek bei Hamburg: Rowohlt, 1995), 801–23, 813.

[44] Ortheil, "Texte im Spiegel," 801-23, 813.

[45] See, for example, Wolfgang Emmerich, "Gleichzeitigkeit. Vormoderne, Moderne und Postmoderne in der Literatur der DDR," in Heinz Ludwig Arnold, ed., *Bestandsaufnahme Gegenwartsliteratur* (Munich: Verlag edition text + kritik, 1988), 193–211. For critique of this concept, see Horst Domdey, "Die DDR-Literatur als Literatur der Epochenillusion," in Ilse Spittmann and Gisela Helwig, eds., *Die DDR im vierzigsten Jahr. Geschichte, Situation, Perspektiven. Zweiundzwanzigste Tagung zum Stand der DDR-Forschung in der Bundesrepublik Deutschland 16. bis 19. Mai 1989* (Cologne: Edition Deutschland Archiv im Verlag Wissenschaft und Politik Berend von Nottbeck, 1989), 137–48.

Migration Experiences and the Construction of Identity among Turks Living in Germany

Eva Kolinsky

HAVING MIGRATED FROM their native country with the encourage-ment of the German authorities for the purpose of finding work, Turkish residents in the Federal Republic have long been regarded, and are occasionally pitied, as an underclass with lower educational or voca-tional qualifications than Germans of their age group and fewer oppor-tunities for socio-economic participation.[1] In today's "risk society," their place appears to be "ganz unten," that is, at the bottom.[2] Some observers even view Islam, and values or political orientations associated with it, as lacking modernity and believe that Turks would do better to abandon them.[3] Does not present-day Germany offer integration to those who wish to make use of it?[4] Does it not allow, and indeed encourage accul-turation to the practices and practicalities of daily living in Germany, making "otherness" quasi voluntary and ultimately obsolete?[5]

This essay does not share these assumptions about social or cultural boundaries between Turks and Germans and the intrinsically negative meaning of difference. Rather, it starts out from the notion that the only feature common to the population designated as "Turks" in Germany is their country of origin. Even here, region, religion, customs, class, family and social status, to name just a few indicators, determine what being Turkish means to individuals. People of Turkish extraction living in Germany share the fact that somewhere in their biography, or the biog-raphy of their family, the experience of migration and arrival features — no more, and no less.

With reference to Jews who returned to Germany after a period of exile to escape deportation and death in the Holocaust, Borneman and Peck note that biographical narratives of life in present-day Germany are constructed around reiterating the reasons for return and recalling the experience of arrival.[6] Applying these findings to my research on Turks in Germany in 1998/99, I invited respondents to tell me about their migration and arrival as a key stage in their experiences in and with Germany. Going beyond Borneman and Peck, my work has been based on the hypothesis that identity cannot be traced to one event, background or cultural framework such as religion or nationality, but emerges from biography. It is shaped by the individual's experiences with the environment in which he or she is living and may change over time and between generations.[7]

Drawing on interviews I conducted in the late 1990s, this study argues in its first part that migration pushed the members of the first generation to reconstruct their identity with regard to employment, daily living and their place in society. The chapter then goes on to show that identity has become further individualized and diverse as the second generation has translated personal experiences with German and Turkish environments into distinctive interpretations of what they mean by Turkish culture and which elements of it they wish to be incorporated into their own life-style and orientations. The expectation expressed by policymakers that Turkish culture would begin to fade as new generations grow up, attend German schools, become familiar with the German way of doing things and remain settled in the country has not been been fulfilled. Instead, second generation Turks have made Turkish culture more personal and multifaceted as they choose which aspects to build into their perception of identity, and this in accordance with their biographical experiences and individual preferences.

Migration and Identity

The migration of Turks into Germany for the purpose of finding work took place between 1961, when the first inter-governmental agreement was signed, and 1973 when the *Anwerbestopp* (employment stop) put an end to labour recruitment from all foreign countries.[8] Since the right of family reunion continued to apply, and some eight out of ten Turks have tended to marry spouses from Turkey, newcomers have continued to arrive and settle despite the recruitment ban. Moreover, Turkish nationals, and in particular members of the Kurdish minority, have constituted up to one third of asylum seekers in Germany. The majority has ignored repeated financial incentives by German governments in the 1970s and 1980s to those willing to be repatriated.[9] German public policy has always been steeped in contradictions. Successive governments have refused to endorse immigration and have sought to prevent, or even reverse it, while admitting individuals deemed eligible for political asylum. At the same time, however, non-Germans, including former Turkish migrants, have been allowed to ignore the pressure to leave and have settled for good. This second branch of public policy was frequently defined at regional or local level and afforded migrants rights of social citizenship which federal policy could not curtail but would have preferred to restrict.[10]

While there have been constant challenges to the right of settlement in postwar Germany, an important departure from the country's history has nonetheless taken place. Until 1945, social citizenship, that is, rights of settlement and social participation, had been withheld to varying degrees from foreign nationals, culminating in the use of forced labour during the Nazi period.[11] In postwar Germany, the constitutional commitment to human rights was extended to all residents, regardless of nationality. This sea-change in the political culture is the background against which Turkish migration could lead to permanent residency for Turks in Germany.[12]

Even before their arrival in Germany, individuals who undertook migration faced an unfamiliar environment at many different levels.[13] Hussayn K. experienced his recruitment in Istanbul as a kind of selection:

> There were German doctors and German employers. The German doctors examined us and the employers selected us.[14]

For many, employment in Germany meant starting afresh by accepting work which they had not done before, for which they normally received little training and which was often vaguely defined. Abdullah U., who had been an electrician and who thought he had signed on as such in the mining industry, thus found himself working at the coal face without any preparation:

> I had never worked below ground. I thought it would be like a building site, just a couple of metres lower, and I would do the electrical installations there. When I realised what is was, I was vastly disappointed. I had imagined nothing like this. On the very first day, I wanted return home. . . . I did not like it in the mine and handed in my notice as soon as I had found new employment.[15]

Arrival in an often inhospitable environment and the experience of having to cope with the challenges of the unfamiliar work to which they were recruited, forced individuals to reconstruct their lives compared with their experiences in Turkey. Remaining in Germany normally entailed finding new employment or better working conditions after the original contract expired. Migrants who became residents actively shaped their migration biography. It is misleading to construct a picture of Turks in Germany as immobile and stuck at the bottom of the employment hierarchy.

Mehmet Y. and his wife, for instance, arrived together in 1970 to work in a hotel, he as kitchen help, she as chamber maid. After one year, he found better-paid work in the mining industry in the Ruhr region while she took cleaning jobs in private homes. Neither felt that they worked below the level to which they aspired and both perceived their migration biography as a material success. The area in which Mehmet Y. felt he was unfairly treated was with regard to pay: Germans who did the same work belonged to higher wage groups and received higher pay. His protests had no effect, and he lacked the legal and linguistic skills to fight his corner successfully. The perception of being treated unfairly left him feeling betrayed and disheartened:

> I understood far too late what was happening and too late to do anything about it. Now it is too late to change anything.[16]

Many of my interview partners experienced their German environment as potentially hostile and tried to keep their distance in order to avoid conflict. Erkan K. a foreman in a firm of decorators, thus knows that some of his co-workers on building sites do not accept him and act out their prejudice by making things difficult for him at work. Supported by his boss, he has adopted a strategy of cutting direct contact to a minimum. In any case, he feels he has nothing in common with them, since he does not share their interest in football or their obsession with the quality and appearance of their cars. For him, a car is a means of transport, essential but no more and no less than "a donkey on wheels."[17] What, he asks, could he talk about with these people?

When Kahraman E. arrived in 1970 at the age of 26, he thought Germany was wonderful, a welcoming place with clean streets, well-kept houses, net curtains and carefully-tended front gardens. His country of migration seemed to radiate a modernity he had yearned for in Turkey and which, he assumed, would translate into social equality and acceptance for somebody like himself. As soon as he had learned the language and understood what was going on underneath this gleaming exterior, he became more skeptical:

> When I understood very little, my environment did not trouble me. But now I understand what is going on and see things differently. When I first arrived, I thought it was paradise because I could not understand what people were saying and what they thought of me. As soon as I understood what they were talking about and what their views were, I stopped liking it here. These days, when I go into town or have business in the council offices, I cannot help but notice that people who speak little German or who differ in their dress or appear-

ance from Germans are not taken seriously and are not treated with respect. For this reason I cannot feel at home in Germany.[18]

Emine B. speaks the language fluently and does not remember encountering personal problems of orientation or acceptance in her German environment. Central to her easy passage in Germany, however, has been the fact that "people do not see that I am Turkish" since she had blond hair and does not differ in her appearance and personal style from her peers. The close link between appearance and acceptance, however, makes her feel uncomfortable. Although personally shielded, by and large, from negative experiences, she fears things might have been very different for her if her Turkish origin had been visible, or if she had chosen to make it visible by, for instance, wearing a headscarf:

> I personally approve of Turkish women wearing a headscarf if they wish to do so. Sometimes I try to imagine what it would be like if I were to start doing this tomorrow. To be honest, I find the idea terrifying . . . The headscarf would define me . . . This would no longer have anything to do with me, but with what I am supposed to be. I would have to cope with lack of understanding and resistance and would have to explain myself constantly and be pushed into as corner. I could not bear this. I believe that my fears show that other cultures are not readily accepted in Germany and that German society is not multicultural.[19]

Choices of Place and Identity

Migration to Germany had not been intended as a permanent migration but had been undertaken as a temporary measure to improve life-chances and earn enough money to succeed back in Turkey. Arrival, therefore, never meant arrival to stay but rather arrival until departure. For first generation migrants, in particular, living in Germany was intended to improve material circumstances and personal opportunities until a return. Many supported relatives in Turkey financially and continue to do so; many also purchased houses or flats in Turkey in order to prepare for their return which was supposed to occur in a more affluent style than their departure. Germany, therefore, was an interim location, a place to live, not a home. It was a *Wohnort* rather than a *Heimat*.[20]

In the biographies of the migrant generation and their descendants, annual visits to Turkey during the summer months have constituted a normal aspect of living in Germany. Until recently, families would complete the journey by car; since the war in Yugoslavia, they fly.[21] Initially, the purpose of these visits was to visit family in Turkey, remain in touch with friends and former neighbours, and perhaps also to demonstrate the improved life-style and level of affluence that had been achieved and which could serve to justify the initial migration. In recent years, Turkey has also become a holiday destination with visits divided between relations and friends and popular resorts.

Unexpectedly, return has thus become wishful thinking, not reality. As the first generation reaches retirement age and could, therefore, in principle at least, leave their country of employment, the *Arbeitsland Deutschland,* they find that they are more firmly rooted there than they had expected. There are many reasons for finding return impossible. Those friends and family members, for example, who lived in Turkey at the time of migration are often no longer there and new contacts are less firm. Turkey itself has changed and going back would mean moving to an apparently unfamiliar country, and, on a more practical level, social services and medical care in Turkey do not come up to German standards and would leave individuals poorly supported in their old age.

The most important reason for staying on, however, is the fact that their children have no intention of leaving and regard Germany as their *Wohnland,* the place where they wish to live. The *Gastarbeiter* generation may harbour sentimental memories of a lost lifestyle and may be more at ease with Turkish everyday culture and values than with those in Germany, but their children are more familiar with German culture and values and less drawn to living out their Turkish identity in Turkey. The second generation has accepted its Turkish origin, attached its own meaning to Turkish culture, and wishes to live this duality inside Germany, not somewhere else.

The generation change and the confidence of the second generation that their future is located in Germany have confirmed that Turks have become permanent residents of Germany and that they regard themselves as such. The generation change also revealed their parents' narrative of a planned return as not based in reality. The first and second generation must now confront the fact that they will not return one day, that they are living in Germany.

Looking back, Abdullah U. who arrived in 1970, admits that he based his plans for the future on a dream when he bought a nice apartment in Istanbul where the family would live when he retires. Now he knows that two of his three children, including his fourteen-year-old son, have no plans to go and live in Turkey but are planning their own future in Germany. Thus Abdullah U. accepts, somewhat grudgingly, that he also will not leave, despite the fact that he will continue to have to live in a modest rented apartment.[22]

Mehmet Y. has, as his son puts it, never left Turkey. After nearly thirty years in the country, he still compares prices to those in Turkey, keeps himself informed through daily phone calls about what is going on in his home village, and thinks he would like to return. Since neither his wife nor his two children are willing to follow him, he is reduced to daydreaming. Yet, not everything is negative. His is sure that his children stand a better chance of obtaining a good education and qualifications than he or his wife ever had as well as greater opportunities to develop their potential. He also feels confident that equal treatment, which had been denied to him, will be accessible to his son or daughter since they can communicate effectively and defend themselves and their interests, something he and many of the migrant generation never learnt.[23] For the son, returning to Turkey is out of the question.[24] In its resolve to stay, the second generation has ended the uncertainty about how long migration might last and how permanent settlement would be.

This confidence in Germany as a place of residency is paired with the confidence that identity can be defined by the individual and that there are different ways in Germany of articulating one's Turkish origin and culture. Tunja Y., a first-year university student at the time of the interview, stressed that he had grown up in two cultures, an experience he describes as "a super advantage" since he can relate to both and combine them as he wishes.[25]

Yasemin K. found that her mixed-marriage parents expected that she would combine the two cultures equally within herself: 50 percent German and 50 percent Turkish. In her teenage years, she was drawn to the German part of her heritage, chose to be baptised and confirmed and became more "her mother's daughter." At university, she began to discover the Turkish, and in particular Muslim, aspects of her identity, and "converted" to Islam. Previously, when she had subscribed to Christianity, her father had worried that she might not be able to marry a Muslim. Once she had turned towards Islam, her mother felt unsure about her "Turkish daughter."[26] Yasemin K. needed ten years to shrug off parental expectations about how German and Turkish culture should matter to her and to find what she perceived as her personal identity:

> I am a Muslim. This now is me. This is my culture. Some people say that the second generation stands between two cultures. I think this is nonsense. My own life makes it clear that it is never, at no point in time, half-and-half. There were phases when I was 90 per cent German in my orientation, and other phases when I was 90 per cent Turkish.

This is not static or defined for good. I have learned to vary my cultural orientation.[27]

Identity can mean many things: individuals may regard the use of the Turkish language as a particularly important way of expressing what it means to them to be Turkish in an environment where German dominates. The nexus between language and identity can manifest itself in a number of ways: a young mother who speaks fluent German may suddenly switch to Turkish to communicate with her newborn child.[28] A Turk who is happily married to a German may now and again seek the company of fellow Turks to tell jokes and feel emotionally at home.[29] A bilingual couple with German and Turkish friends may choose at times to meet only with Turkish friends in order to use the language which tends to gets displaced in mixed company but which remains important to their sense of self.[30] In each case, the choice of language points to a choice of identity.[31] The search for a means of retaining and articulating Turkish identity in a diaspora setting may involve heritage-like music or poetry, dress and appearance, furnishings or culinary preferences, to name just a few. While there is no one answer as to what constitutes Turkish identity, it always constitutes an attempt to link individual biography to a personal selection from the broad canvas of Turkish history and culture.

Religion is another means of defining Turkish identity in a German environment. Dursun Y. left school without any qualifications and drifted into adulthood, including early marriage and parenthood. After work-experience programmes he found only low-status, unskilled work but was mostly unemployed. Although born into a Muslim family and raised as Muslim, he did not keep to any of the rules, prayers or values of Islam and led what he now regards as a sinful and irreligious life. Given this state of marginality and hopelessness, the discovery of what he called "my religion" gave him a sense of identity and pride.[32] At the time of the interview, he held a one-year appointment in the context of a government funded employment-creation scheme as an administrative and general assistant at a mosque. Although his future seemed far from certain, he appeared to perceive his newly discovered commitment to Islam as a new beginning which had given his life a sense of direction, purpose and security that it had lacked previously.

Melahat M. turned to Islam from a relatively secular and advantaged background. Born and raised in Düsseldorf in a neighbourhood with few Turkish residents, she had attended a grammar school. Although her academic performance has been of high quality, she felt unfairly treated because of her origin and her public protest against being classified as "Turkish" rather than regarded as a human being. Her refusal to accept prejudice meant she had to change schools in order to complete her *Abitur* and proceed to university. There, she found that the lecturing staff once again held Turkish students in low esteem and assumed that their work would be substandard. In similar fashion, German fellow students would regard Turks as a collective entity and groan *"Die Osmanen kommen"* every time they saw two Turkish students together. Melahat M. admits to having been exasperated but avoids open condemnation: "I do not know whether I should take this positively or negatively. I only ask myself: do they have to be like this?"[33]

Biographical and personal experiences of this kind impacted on how Melahat M. perceives her identity today:

> When am I German and when am I Turkish? Am I German when I have a German passport? What use is a German passport if I am excluded from all kinds of places because I do not look German? I can try to convince myself endlessly that I am German, I can try to talk myself into accepting that I am German but this is meaningless as long as others do not accept it. For myself, I would say that I have both sides. I am German as well as Turkish.[34]

Conclusion

The emergence of a democratic constitutional order and civil society in Germany has not entirely shielded Turks (and other minorities) who live there from discrimination and from the fear of persecution or violence. Despite inequalities and obstacles to social participation, however, the reinvented Germany in the West allowed them by and large to develop their own life-styles, individual approaches to their origin and culture and an understanding of their identity. In the East, no such process took place, a legacy of exclusion which remains visible in the demography and attitudes of the former GDR.[35]

Turks experienced a process of identity reconstruction after migration and had to cope with unfamiliar conditions in their employment and in their daily lives. In many cases, this identity construction meant turning migration into a material and personal success story. Until the second generation came of age, most of the former *Gastarbeiter* and their spouses believed that their stay in Germany was only temporary and that they would return to Turkey. Thus many remained on the margins of German society linguistically and culturally and were more interested in Turkish than German political developments and social opportunities.

This has begun to change as residency is being accepted as permanent, although negative experiences with Germans and German society have created their own patterns of distance and distrust.

For the second generation, educational qualifications, fluency in the German language and career opportunities in white-collar employment and the professions have improved greatly. This generation grew up in Germany and expects equal treatment in contrast to their parents who were more helpless and less assertive. Specifically, second generation Turks reject the persistence of inequalities more ardently and attempt to define their identity as Turkish more actively and more personally than their parents had done.

While members of the migration generation were, by and large, Turks living in Germany, members of the second generation have a Turkish and a German background and define their identity by drawing on both cultures. Instead of "integrating" in the manner the German government and the majority of the German population appear to desire, that is, by becoming invisible as Turks, these young Turks insist upon visibility and upon an acceptance of their Turkish identity. Since this is not easily forthcoming, the distance from German society and to Germans remains considerable. Incidents such as the attacks on Turkish families in Moelln or Solingen in 1992 and 1993 have confirmed this distance and the resolve among the second generation to find their own distinctive identity as Turks in German culture and society.[36]

The first generation did not intend to settle in Germany for good, although it also did not plan to leave: the question of leaving or remaining was left unanswered. It was the second generation that answered this question. This does not mean that their experiences with German society have been altogether positive. On the contrary, the second generation has become more sensitive about injustice and discrimination, but also more able to defend itself and stand its ground. Second generation Turks in Germany today expect their German environment to grant them the right to be different. Yet many remain fearful and resentful of being categorised as Turks and denied acceptance as individuals. More than anything, they resent being "made" into Turks and denied the right to be a person and a human being.

Turkish identity means linking German and Turkish components and traditions to create a distinctive and personal orientation. Before Moelln and Solingen, second generation Turks tended to feel safe in Germany and confident that they could improve their position through education, employment success and their own motivation. Since Moelln and Solingen, Germany is perceived as more hostile, and Turkish identity had served more explicitly as a protective shield against negative German agendas.

While the first generation shared the experiences of migration and arrival and constructed their identity as Turks in Germany around these key events in their biography, the second generation has no such shared experiences and no such common core. Instead, their identities have been constructed with reference to personal experiences of growing up in Germany, of encountering Turkish and German culture, and selecting from these cultures those aspects, practices and values that matter most to the individual. For the third generation, parental expectations point to high educational and achievement motivation, a determination to utilise the choices offered within German society, and also an early disillusionment that Turks remain disadvantaged and frequently stereotyped even if they blend into their German environment in terms of appearance or language.

The parents of today's third generation were themselves exposed to negative scenarios of some kind when they grew up. Their response has been, as we have seen, to construct their distinctive identity. They view themselves — emphatically in some cases — as Turkish by origin. They are competent in German everyday culture, they could often pass for Germans, and may hold or intend to apply for German citizenship. However, they also insist on having their Turkish origin recognised and accepted as a key aspect of their existence. In this way, second generation Turks have contributed to rewriting German history by rejecting assimilation and by demanding acceptance of difference. The third generation, the children of today and adults of tomorrow, will be even more skilled at constructing and articulating a distinctive Turkish and German identity. They will also be less inhibited than the older generations to expect social justice and claim rights of equal treatment, including the right to being as Turkish and as German as they wish to be.

Notes

[1] E. Klee, "Gastarbeiter als Subproletariat," in E. Klee, *Gastarbeiter: Analysen und Berichte* (Frankfurt am Main: Suhrkamp, 1975), 25–35; similarly K. Dohse, *Ausländische Arbeiter und bürgerlicher Staat* (Königstein/Taunus: Hain Verlag, 1981); V. McRae, *Die Gastarbeiter: Daten, Fakten, Probleme* (Munich: Beck, 1980) and with a greater emphasis on migration and social justice D. Cohn-Bendit and T. Schmid, *Heimat Babylon: Das Wagnis der multikulturellen Demokratie* (Hamburg: Hofmann & Campe, 1992); C. Koch-Arzberger et al., eds., *Einwanderungsland Hessen? Daten,*

Fakten, Analysen (Opladen: Leske+Budrich, 1993) and Y. Pazarkaya, *Spuren des Brotes: Zur Lage der ausländischen Arbeiter* (Zurich: Unionsverlag, 1983).

[2] For an excellent comparative analysis of poverty among Germans and non-Germans see W. Hanesch et al., eds., *Armut in Deutschland: Der Armutsbericht des DGB* (Reinbek: Rowohlt, 1994); also P. Berger, "Individualisierung der Armut," in M. M. Zwick, ed., *Einmal arm, immer arm? Neue Befunde zur Armut in Deutschland* (Frankfurt am Main: Campus 1994), 21–22; also the quasi-autobiographical documentary by G. Wallraff, *Ganz unten* (Cologne: Kiepenheuer & Witsch, 1985).

[3] For a general discussion of modernity see U. Beck, *Risikogesellschaft: Auf dem Weg in eine andere Moderne* (Frankfurt am Main: Suhrkamp, 1986). German and Turkish views of religion are the theme of *Religion — ein deutsch-türkisches Tabu?* (Hamburg: Körber Foundation, 1997) while W. Heitmeyer, J. Müller and H. Schröder, *Verlokkender Fundamentalismus: Türkische Jugendliche in Deutschland* (Frankfurt am Main: Suhrkamp, 1997) equates Islam with anti-modernism.

[4] P. H. Schuck and R. Münz, eds., *Paths to Inclusion: The Integration of Migrants in the United States and Germany* (New York/Oxford: Berghahn, 1998) use socioeconomic indicators and citizenship rights as a yardstick of migration success; similarly K. Bade, *Vom Auswanderungsland zum Einwanderungsland? Deutschland 1880–1980* (Berlin: Colloquium, 1983); W. Benz, ed., *Integration ist machbar: Ausländer in Deutschland* (Munich: Beck, 1993).

[5] F. Heckmann, *Die Bundesrepublik: Ein Einwanderungsland? Zur Soziologie der Gastarbeiterbevölkerung als Einwandererminorität* (Stuttgart: Klett-Cotta, 1981) identifies "acculturation," i.e. the adjustment of migrants to the "majority" society, as a precondition for migration success while American researchers speak of "the other" to underline the legitimacy of ethnic and cultural distinctiveness, e.g. L. Adelson, "Migrants' Literature or German Literature?" in *German Quarterly* 63:3–4 (1990): 382–89; A. Tereoka, "'Gastarbeiterliteratur': The Other Speaks" *Cultural Critique 7* (1987), 77–101; K. J. Milich and J. Peck, eds., *Multiculturalism in Transit: A German-American Exchange* (Oxford: Berghahn, 1998), esp. the chapters by Hayek (111–12) and Kvistad (238–39).

[6] J. Borneman and J. M. Peck, *Soujourners: The Return of German Jews and the Question of Identity* (Lincoln and London: U of Nebraska P, 1995).

[7] For a detailed discussion see the introduction to E. Kolinsky, *Deutsch und türkisch leben: Bild und Selbstbild der türkischen Minderheit in Deutschland* (Bern/ Berlin/ New York: Peter Lang, 2000).

[8] F. Sen and A. Goldberg, *Türken in Deutschland: Leben zwischen zwei Kulturen* (Munich: Beck 1994). See also E. Kolinsky, "Non-German Minorities in Contemporary German Society" and E. Kürsat-Ahlers, "The Turkish Minority in German Society," in D. Horrocks and E. Kolinsky, eds., *Turkish Culture in German Society Today* (Oxford: Berghahn, 1996), 71–112 and 113–36. See also the excellent collection of articles, testimony and documents in A. Erylmaz and M. Jamin, eds., *Fremde Heimat: Eine Geschichte der Einwanderung aus der Türkei* (Essen: Klartext, 1998).

[9] C. Joppke, *Immigration and the Nation State: The United States, Germany and Great Britain* (Oxford: Oxford UP, 1999), 78–81.

[10] F. Franz, "Die Rechtsstellung der ausländischen Arbeitnehmer in der Bundesrepublik Deutschland" (in Klee, *Gastarbeiter,* 36–57) stresses that regional differences in applying the legislation facilitated settlement; on regional differences, Joppke, *Immigration and the Nation State* (65–75) shows the path-breaking role of the courts.

[11] E. Kolinsky, "Non-German Minorities, Women and the Emergence of Civil Ssociety," in E. Kolinsky and W. van der Will, eds., *The Cambridge Companion to Modern German Culture* (Cambridge: Cambridge UP, 1998), 110–31.

[12] C. Joppke, *Immigration and the Nation State*, 69–75; for an analysis of citizenship rights see R. Brubacker, *Citizenship and Nationhood in France and Germany* (Cambridge: Harvard UP 1992) while A. Goldberg and R. Sen, eds., *Deutsche Türken — türkische Deutsche* (Münster: Lit Verlag, 1999) presents responses by Turks in Germany to the citizenship debate.

[13] The biographical examples are taken from a study, funded by the Nuffield Foundation, of Migration and Identity Constructions of Turks in Germany. Interviews were conducted mainly in Essen between December 1998 and May 1999; details on the design of the study and key findings are published in E. Kolinsky, *Deutsch und türkisch leben* (Bern/Berlin/ New York: Peter Lang, 2000).

[14] Interview with Hussayn K., 5 May 1999. Recordings and transcriptions of the interviews (in German) are accessible through the author at the Oral History Resources Collection, University of Wolverhampton.

[15] Interview with Abdullah U., 5 May 1999.

[16] Interview with Mehmet Y., 16 December 1998.

[17] Interview with Erkan K., 17 December 1999.

[18] Interview with Kahraman E., 2 May 1999.

[19] Interview with Emine B., 7 May 1999

[20] See Erylmaz and Jamin, *Fremde Heimat*. Similarly with regard to the Jewish minority in Germany, see E. Kolinsky, "Wohnort Deutschland. Ansätze jüdischer Identität nach dem Holocaust," in W. Menninghaus and K. R. Scherpe, eds., *Literaturwissenschaft und politische Kultur* (Stuttgart: Metzler, 1999), 281–89.

[21] L. Yalcin-Heckmann, "Zum kollektiven Gedächtnis türksicher Migranten," in H.-P. Waldhoff, D. Tan and E. Kürsat-Ahlers, eds., *Brücken zwischen Zivilisationen: Zur Zivilisierung ethnisch-kultureller Differenzen und machtungleichheiten: Das türkisch-deutsche Beispiel* (Frankfurt am Main: Iko Verlag, 1997), 191–93 views the annual visit to Turkey as a key "ritual" in the construction of migrant identity.

[22] Intgerview with Abdullah U.

[23] Interwiew with Mehmet Y.

[24] Interview with Tunja Y, 16 December 1998.

[25] Tunja Y., 16 December 1998.

[26] Interview with Yasemin K., 10 December 1999.

[27] Yasemin K., 10 December 1998.

[28] Interview with Hasan O., Keele University, November 1998.

[29] Interview with Mehmet B., 10 December 1998.

[30] Interview with Hayrettin A., 18 December 1998.

[31] For a fuller account see chapter eight "Erfahrungen mit Kommunikation," in E. Kolinsky, *Deutsch und türkisch leben*.

[32] Interview with Dursun Y., 16 Dezember 1998.

[33] Interview with Melahat M., 14 December 1998.

[34] Melahat M., 14 December 1998.

[35] E. Kolinsky, "Multiculturalism in the Making? Non-Germans and Civil Society in the New Länder," in C. Flockton and E. Kolinsky, *Recasting East Germany: Social Transformation after the GDR* (London: Cass, 1999), 192–214.

[36] Xenophobic attacks in Solingen (1992) and Moelln (1993) on the private homes of Turkish residents resulted in several deaths among the occupants. Although the attacks of Moelln in particular generated protests among Germans against xenophobia (*Lichterketten* — candle-light chains), Turks came to regard these events as a reminder that despite their long-term residency in Germany and their plans to stay, their German environment remained potentially hostile. Among the second generation, "Solingen" and "Moelln" became something of a wake-up call against too much confidence in their German environment. See also my interviews with Meral R., 18 December 1998, Faruk S., 4 May 1999, Yasemin K., 10 December 1998 and Suleiman A., 5 May 1999.

Diasporic Identity in
Emine Sevgi Özdamar's *Mutterzunge*

Margaret Littler

A S THE UNITED GERMANY enters the twenty-first century and officially declares itself a country of immigration, it is acknowledging a
state of affairs which has existed *de facto f*or at least fifty years. The
country which is now contemplating a new wave of young, skilled workers from abroad has yet to come to terms with the legacy of the recruitment of foreign workers in the postwar economic boom. The fact that
the *Anwerbestopp* in 1973 resulted in the transformation of migrant
labour into minority populations is well-documented, as is the predomi-
nance of the Turkish minority. In 1973 Turks constituted a quarter of
the non-German workforce, rising to a third by 1990, by which time the
Turkish population numbered nearly two million.[1] This chapter will
explore emerging identity-formations in the Turkish-German diaspora
as exemplified in the literary work of Emine Sevgi Özdamar. Özdamar
came to Berlin in 1965 as a *Gastarbeiterin*, working in factories and
housed in a hostel with other workers. She also started to learn German,
became involved in the theatre, and became politicised in the student
protests which were reaching a peak in 1967. She then trained as an
actress in Istanbul, but returned to Germany in 1976, where she continues to act, direct and write for the theatre. To date she has published two
novels and two volumes of short prose.[2]

   She is undoubtedly the most prominent and successful example of
the minority writing, or *MigrantInnenliteratur,* which is becoming an
increasingly popular focus of German Studies in Great Britain and North
America, but remains very marginal in German *Germanistik*, with the
exception of those institutes specialising in *Deutsch als Fremdsprache* and
the associated discipline *Interkulturelle Germanistik*. It is far from being
accorded a place within mainstream German Literature, as demonstrated
by the debate surrounding the award of the prestigious *Ingeborg-
Bachmann-Preis* to Özdamar in 1991.[3] Since the first wave of *Gastarbeiterliteratur* appeared in the 1980s, no consensus has developed as to

how to approach minority writing in German, even among its strongest advocates. While the practitioners of *Interkulturelle Germanistik* seek inter-cultural dialogue from within the tradition of German hermeneutics, cultural studies approaches draw on insights from poststructuralist and postcolonial theory to interrogate the ontological assumptions on which this tradition is based.[4] There are those who caution against the application of inappropriate western theoretical frameworks to interpret the products of emphatically non-western cultures,[5] and those who object to the ghettoisation of minority writing which can result from such scruples.[6]

This paper will argue for a cultural studies approach to writers of the Turkish-German diaspora, on the basis that Turkish authors emerge from a background already so infused with western influence that they are perhaps uniquely placed to articulate the interpenetration of a traditional culture and western modernity. Emine Sevgi Özdamar is a good example because, as most commentators agree, her representation of Turkey in the novels *Das Leben ist eine Karawanserei* (1992) and *Die Brücke vom Goldenen Horn* (1998) is shot through with internal contradictions; she depicts a hybrid world of western secularism juxtaposed with Islamic tradition. Yet the fascination of her work lies in her unsettling of these very polarities, religious/secular, traditional/modern, and in her playful, but politically engaged representation of Turkish identity from the German diaspora.

Having spent much of her adult life in East and West Germany, it is arguably as important to understand Özdamar's western intellectual heritage as it is to contextualise her writing in a Turkish tradition. With her training in the theatre, Özdamar presents identity as an embodied and performative category, inviting comparison with western postmodern feminist theories.[7] At the same time her wilfully unorthodox manipulation of the German language communicates to the German-speaking reader the incommensurability of cultural difference, rather than offering the assurance of a comfortable common ground. The literal translation of Turkish idioms into German is part of this strategy, producing a defamiliarisation effect for the non-Turkish-speaking reader, who is often deprived of an authoritative reading position in her own language. As Soheila Ghaussy has put it, Özdamar confronts us with "a gap in signification in which meaning cannot be simply transported from one cultural system into another."[8] Indeed, it is significant that a writer who makes so few concessions to her western readership is one whose work lends itself to postcolonial analysis.

Özdamar herself (provocatively) argues that the Turkish experience of migrant labour in Germany represented a kind of "inner" colonialism,[9] and she calls for an increased *Überfremdung* rather than assimilation or cosmopolitanism.[10] Hence she writes in a German which sounds very "un-German," but bears comparison with the English of Salman Rushdie, in whose work Homi K. Bhabha has said that the "'foreignness of language' becomes the inescapable cultural condition for the enunciation of the mother tongue."[11] The very title of Özdamar's collection constitutes a faintly estranging neologism in German, but allows its (Turkish) meaning to be understood. Attractive as such comparisons are, they inevitably beg questions as to the difference between Rushdie's evocation of postcolonial India and Özdamar's writing in the Turkish-German diaspora. The similarities might be said to efface the very important political and historical differences.[12] Nonetheless, I would contend that neither Rushdie nor Özdamar write "about" India or Turkey in any simply empirical way. Rather, they are both concerned with the patterns of individual and collective identity construction resulting from relations of political and cultural hegemony and requiring new forms of representation. I would therefore argue with Stuart Hall for a "properly universalising" use of the term "colonisation," understood as "part of an essentially trans-national and trans-cultural 'global' process," one which "produces a decentred, diasporic or 'global' rewriting of earlier, nation-centred Imperial grand narratives."[13]

I would further argue that the provocation involved in reading the cultural products of the Turkish-German diaspora through the critical lens of postcolonial theory is *not* due to the fact that Germany cannot be said strictly speaking to have "colonised" Turkey.[14] It is rather due to the way in which postcolonial theory forces us to challenge notions of homogeneous cultural identity which still prevail in Germany. To quote Hall again: "It obliges us to re-read the binaries as forces of transculturation, of cultural translation, destined to trouble the here/there cultural binaries for ever."[15] My interest in Özdamar's writing is precisely in its articulation of cultural difference in Homi Bhabha's sense; as an emerging cultural form which resists contextualisation within any determinate or fixed origin, and one which works against the homogenisation of experience and culture, be it Turkish or German.

What I intend to do is show how a postcolonial perspective can offer some historically specific insights into the construction of Turkish minority identity in Özdamar's work, and to suggest that her presence on the German literary scene opens up a space for minority discourse which poses a potential challenge to the supposed homogeneity of German culture. Thus I do not share Azade Seyhan's view that her work is an expression of "diasporic pathos,"[16] primarily concerned with the restoration of collective memory as a foundation for identity. Such a reading could all too easily depoliticise the writing in relation to its contemporary German context. It also fails to acknowledge internal tensions in Özdamar's work. In my analysis of the 1990 texts "Mutterzunge" and "Großvaterzunge," I will firstly consider the protagonist's problematic relationship to the Turkish and Arabic languages in terms of a broadly acknowledged critique of Kemalism. I will then show how the texts complicate and render this critique ambiguous, and how they represent identity as embodied and performative — as a form of mimicry which undermines any idea of an authentic self. This is difficult to reconcile with the texts' ostensible theme; the nostalgia for lost origins. I will finally propose the notion of "palimpsest" to describe the outcome of the protagonist's search for cultural continuity. I shall argue that the quest for the lost mother tongue in *Mutterzunge* is in one important respect doomed to failure, if we accept Stuart Hall's proposition that: "cultural identity . . . is not a fixed origin to which we can make some final and absolute Return."[17] This is most strikingly evident in the way in which "Großvaterzunge" reinforces the Kemalist narrative of nationhood which it sets out to criticise. None of this is calculated to deny a significance to the history which Özdamar's text uncovers, but it is to suggest a view of Turkish identity as a process, simultaneously in dialogue with its Ottoman heritage, and in dispute with the Arabic Islamic culture through which this is mediated. What emerges is an acceptance of alienation within identity which disturbs the very oppositions that structure the texts: Arabic and Turkish, religious and secular, old and new. To this extent they articulate a notion of difference reminiscent of what Homi K. Bhabha (with reference to Frantz Fanon) has called "the otherness of the Self inscribed in the perverse palimpsest of colonial identity."[18] The implied closure and restoration of continuity in the text is simultaneously undermined, casting doubt on all notions of "origins" and on the possibility of absolute inter-cultural communication.

"Großvaterzunge" and The "Foreignness of Language"[19]

The first two texts in *Mutterzunge* are concerned with the female Turkish protagonist's loss of her mother tongue, after many years spent in Germany. In order to recreate a sense of cultural continuity, she tries to learn the Arabic script which was outlawed in 1928 as part of Atatürk's west-ernising reforms. Thus implicitly her sense of dislocation is attributed not to her own migration to Germany, but to Atatürk's attempt to obliterate from the Turkish language all traces of the imperial Ottoman past. Azade Seyhan has seen in the protagonist's fascination with Ottoman Turkish a reappropriation of authority: "Özdamar excavates the lost accents of a language evocative of a long bygone era of power."[20] By highlighting the status of the language of the Ottoman court, Seyhan argues that Özdamar's text is concerned implicitly with the relationship of German to Turkish, as its disavowed, but increasingly widespread "other." At the same time, the protagonist's attempt to retrieve Arabic words which survive in modern Turkish is undoubtedly also a reaction against *öz Türkçe,* the "authentic" Turkish free from Arabic or Persian influence used by Turkish intellectuals.[21] It is also a way of overcoming the cultural dislocation symbolised in the text by the fact that the protagonist and her grandfather could not read the same script.

Nevertheless, I take issue with Seyhan's suggestion that what is at stake in *Mutterzunge* is the rediscovery of an authentic but repressed cultural identity. In relation to the colonial experience, Stuart Hall ques-tions the adequacy of such a gesture: "Is it only a matter of unearthing that which the colonial experience buried and overlaid, bringing to light the hidden continuities it suppressed? Or is a quite different practice en-tailed — not the rediscovery but the *production* of identity. Not an identity grounded in the archaeology, but in the *re-telling* of the past?"[22] This is in my view a more appropriate description of Özdamar's textual strategy in "Großvaterzunge" which sets out to excavate the past but also raises questions as to the viability of this project.

Indeed, the critique of Kemalism is relativised in Özdamar's text, which articulates an irrevocably westernised consciousness. This becomes clear in the love story in "Großvaterzunge" where a problematic relation-ship to the Arabic legacy of Ottoman Turkish comes to light. As the love between the protagonist and her Arabic teacher, Ibni Abdullah, grows, so does the conflict between sexual desire and spiritual devotion, be-tween modernity and tradition, although, as we will see, the treatment of Islam confounds such easy dichotomies. For the western feminist reader it is clear that the Koranic texts from which she learns represent the Law of Islam, a patriarchal symbolic system which permits no expres-sion to the protagonist's desire: "ich habe kein Wörterbuch gefunden für die Sprache meiner Liebe" (30).

To this westernised, emancipated woman the Arabic texts speak only of discipline, denial and retribution, but at the same time they distract her with their picture-language of hearts, arrows, and women's eyes:

> Es kamen aus meinem Mund die Buchstaben raus. Manche sahen aus wie ein Vogel, manche wie ein Herz, auf dem ein Pfeil steckt, manche wie eine Karawane, manche wie schlafende Kamele, manche wie ein Fluß, manche wie im Wind auseinanderfliegende Bäume, manche wie laufende Schlangen, manche wie unter Regen und Wind frierende Granatapfelbäume, manche wie böse geschreckte Augenbrauen, manche wie ein in einem türkischen Bad auf einem heißen Stein sitzender dicker Frauenarsch, manche wie nicht schlafen könnende Augen (16).

By foregrounding the visual impact of Arabic calligraphy instead of the symbolic content of the script, Özdamar unsettles the authority of the latter. She estranges Arabic in a way reminiscent of Bhabha's notion of cultural translation. Drawing on Walter Benjamin's view of the task of the translator, Bhabha describes the act of translation between cultures as follows:

> The "foreignness" of language is the nucleus of the untranslatable that goes beyond the transferral of subject matter between cultural texts or practices. The transfer of meaning can never be total between systems of meaning, or within them, for "the language of translation envelops its content like a royal robe with ample folds . . . [it] signifies a more exalted language than its own and thus remains unsuited to its content, overpowering and alien". . . . The ill-fitting robe of language alienates content in the sense that it deprives it of an immediate access to a stable ? or holistic reference "outside" itself.[23]

By liberating the signifiers from their signifieds and allowing them to tell different stories from that of their symbolic reference, Özdamar engages in a quite radical way with "the sign as anterior to any *site* of meaning," and thereby overpowers the reality-effect of content, thus making the Arabic language "foreign to [it]sel[f]."[24]

This textual strategy contributes to the impression of a fundamental discrepancy between the narrative of initiation into the sacred texts of Islam, and the desire articulated in the poetic images and rhythms of the text. Although the scripts are described as Ibni Abdullah's "guards," left in charge of his wayward pupil, it is the letters which finally undermine her resolve to suppress her sexual desire and devote herself to the Arabic script:

> Seine Wächter, seine Wörter standen im Zimmer, manche saßen fest über ihren Beinen. . . . Weil ich vor seinen Wörtern, die im Zimmer sa-

ßen, erstmal Angst hatte, sagte ich, ich werde ihn heilig lieben. Ich
werde die Schrift weiterlernen. Ich machte ein Blatt auf. In der Schrift:
Ein Pfeil ging aus einem Bogen raus. Da steht ein Herz, der Pfeil ging,
blieb stehen im Herz, ein Frauenauge schlug mit den Wimpern. (42)

Just as the letters take on stylised human form, so also human faces take
on the shapes of Arabic letters, as when Ibni Abdullah's face is said to
resemble "ein zorniger Buchstabe" (17), expressing the conflict between
his sexual desire and his intellectual discipline. The letters both inscribe
the Law, and liberate themselves from it, becoming materialised as shapes
which are no longer bound within the Islamic signifying chain: "Ich ging
mit Kamelen und weinenden Frauenaugen wieder zum anderen Berlin"
(16). Words are used both literally and metaphorically, introducing another element of undecidability into the reading of the text. For example,
the "divan" on which she sits to learn her Arabic is both an item of fur-
niture and a text which disciplines her: "Der Diwan, auf dem ich saß,
machte mich artig. Ich sah dort auf mich wartende Buchstaben" (16).
This further unsettles the stability of meaning and representation, leaving
open possibilities which would normally be foreclosed. Thus the treatment of language in "Großvaterzunge" is unsettling on more than one
level. Stylistically, it defamiliarises the German language, evoking an oral
poetic tradition with its roots in the Ottoman past. But the recovery of
this cultural legacy via the Arabic script proves problematic, as the disjuncture of content and signifier disrupts any direct reference to an un-
broken cultural identity.

Embodiment and Performance

Soheila Ghaussy has noted in Özdamar's writing the production of "a
text which acknowledges its own production through the body, as well
as the concrete materiality of words."[25] We have seen this in the embodiment of words in *Mutterzunge* as well as in the sensuousness of the
prose. But the body is also thematically significant from the first time the
protagonist enters Ibni Abdullah's mosque-like room, when she is overwhelmed by the silk hangings and the scent of roses.[26] Eating and drinking play an important part in their meetings, and when she falls in love
with him it is described in terms of his having entered her body (19,
29).[27] The poetic imagery often suggests the inseparability of the spiritual
and the corporeal, with Ibni Abdullah embodying both divine and secular love. When he is overwhelmed by her passion and pleads for a purely
spiritual love, she opposes to this her emphatically embodied subjectivity:

"Wenn die Körper sich vergessen, vergessen die Seelen sich nicht?" (41).[28]

Özdamar has spoken of the performative aspect of language, and the significance of her work in the theatre, as factors in her adoption of German as her literary medium.[29] Her writing does seem to suggest a performative aspect of *all* identity, explicitly so in the recent collection *Der Hof im Spiegel*, in which she observes the over-determined performance of German-ness by Turkish youth in Germany: "Dort kann man an manchen Gesichtern der 18–19–jährigen Türken das Deutsche finden. Diese Gesichter identifizieren sich mit der Gestik der Deutschen und spiegeln manchmal die Deutschen mehr als ein Deutscher."[30] In a similar way, in "Großvaterzunge" the repetitive exchanges of greetings and sayings appear almost to be a performance of a shared Middle Eastern identity, in order to establish common ground. Thus, although they are in Germany for very different political reasons (he as a pacifist Arab in the Arab-Israeli wars; she as a communist dissident in Turkey), their iterative assurances of the proximity of death provide a cultural bond which differentiates them from their western European environment. He interpellates her as an "Orientalin" when they first meet, lamenting the fact that their only common language is German. Her Arabic tuition begins with a parodic enactment of Muhammed's revelation,[31] and "shame" is personified in an ironic gesture to her female virtue: "Er, ich und die Scham sitzen in dem Schriftzimmer" (21).

The protagonist's identification with Ibni Abdullah sensitises her to her own "aping" of German culture, prompting her to ask passers-by: "Spielt in meinem Gesicht ein Affe?" (19).[32] She becomes acutely aware of her own difference and imagines acting out an orthodox Islamic identity with Arab women in Berlin: "Ich ging den arabischen Frauen mit Kopftüchern hinterher, ihre schwangeren Töchter neben ihnen, ich will unter ihre Röcke gehen, ganz klein sein, ich will ihre Tochter sein in Neukölln" (19–20). This improbably naïve identification with the Muslim women is immediately undermined by a potentially sacrilegious fantasy scene, which disrupts the Islamic laws governing female dress and gender segregation:[33] she sees herself wearing half woman's half man's clothing, and making love with Ibni Abdullah in a mosque. This suggests a conflict between her appropriation of an Islamic cultural identity and her own (inappropriate) sexuality, which can be attributed both to her westernised identity and, as we shall see later, to a more ancient mystical tradition emerging in the text.

In marked contrast to an Islamic worldview, there are frequent suggestions that gender identity is negotiable, as when Ibni Abdullah is repeatedly likened to a "mother." He appears at times as both man and woman simultaneously: "Ibni Abdullah schlief da mit Ruhe, er war Mann und Frau, er lag da wieder wie eine Mutter, die ihr Kind gut zugedeckt hatte, sein Penis atmete wie ein Herz" (34). Their accounts of their first sexual experiences reverse the conventional gender-norms, as she actively sought to lose her virginity, while he was the passive object of an older woman's desire. On one level this reproduces the stereotype of the sexually predatory oriental woman, but it also draws attention to its constructedness, and its function as a justification of social control.

They play ironically on their respective degrees of assimilation to German culture, each accusing the other at different times of being "sehr deutsch," by which she means cold and formal (38), and he means sexually promiscuous (40). Again, the self-conscious use of stereotypes serves only to undermine them, as we are left in no doubt as to their very different attitudes to West German capitalist society. While both of them have suffered at the hands of military governments, he retains a pan-Islamic idealism and is blind to the flaws of capitalism. She is sceptical about his faith in western democracy, asking him: "Und wieviele Mal sind Sie in diesen neun Jahren in den Park gegangen und haben Ihre Meinung laut gesagt, das Geld hat keine Angst hier, es hat Zähne" (14). The influence of Brecht and her work at the Berliner Ensemble suggest a critical awareness in the protagonist of the material and political realities of migration.[34] This knowledge tempers the play with oriental stereotypes and recalls the relations of economic dependency governing countries like Turkey's relations with the West.

Identity as Palimpsest

As an Arab pacifist, Ibni Abdullah is tormented by the memory of the death of an Israeli soldier, who was about to kill him. This prompts the protagonist to reflect on the death and suffering caused by the Arab-Israeli conflict over Palestine, which can be construed as an indirect comment on her own experience of diaspora. This is not just the collective response to traumatic loss, but rather a dynamic creativity born of displacement. Stuart Hall uses the negative example of Palestine to represent "the old, the imperialising, the hegemonising form of 'ethnicity,'" in contrast to his positive notion of diaspora, which is defined by "the recognition of a necessary heterogeneity and diversity; by a conception of 'identity' which lives with and through, not despite, difference; by *hybridity*. Diaspora identities are those which are constantly producing and reproducing themselves anew, through transformation and difference."[35] What I have been concerned to illustrate is precisely this hybridity in the female protagonist, for whom the search for "roots" in Turkey's Ottoman cultural heritage results in the discovery that this, too, has a repressed pre-history, which was never entirely erased by the Ottoman Empire.

As she collects Arabic words which survive in Turkish, the protagonist realises that they are pronounced differently in Turkish, due to its phonological system.[36] The Turkish language has eight vowels, whereas Arabic has only three, hence the difference in pronunciation of the word for patience, that all-important female virtue, which is *sabr* in Arabic, but *sabír* in Turkish. This linguistic slippage between the languages is indicative also of a different interpretation of Islam in Arabic and Ottoman cultures. Azade Seyhan has identified one of Özdamar's achievements as the portrayal of "Islam with a Turkish accent."[37] Orthodox Sunni Islam was incompletely imposed on the nomadic Turkic tribes of Anatolia, and popularised as a "folk religion" in the Ottoman Empire, retaining elements of mystical Sufism and shamanism, some of which survive in contemporary Alevi belief. This emerges twice in the juxtaposition of passages from the Koran and from Turkish folksongs; where the Koran speaks of Allah's judgemental wrath, the protagonist's inner voice speaks of his creative goodness (23–24);[38] where the Koran speaks of the endless damnation of sinners, the Turkish folksong in her head sings of endless desire (31). In each case, the sub-text disrupts the authority of Sunni Islam with the heterodox beliefs which date from pre-Ottoman Anatolia.[39]

Ibni Abdullah, whose very name associates him directly with the prophet Mohammed, is himself a somewhat unorthodox Muslim. He drinks rakí and wine, is both ascetic and sensual, using sex (and its withdrawal) as an incentive to diligence. The ritual eating and drinking in the text suggests sacred overtones, the food and wine (or rakí) taking on mystical significance closely bound up with human love. This, like the symbolic forty days which the protagonist spends in his room, recalling the number of Ali's followers, is redolent also of Alevi ritual surviving in Turkey today.[40] Nevertheless, Ibni Abdullah makes his living teaching Arabic through the medium of the Koran in West Berlin, and the passionate affair with his pupil begins to threaten his livelihood; physical arousal detracts from his intellectual discipline. While the protagonist's love poetry celebrates the loss of reason, he feels threatened by the "madness" induced by her presence within him. The total identification with the beloved implied by his "entering her body" could be construed as an echo of the Sufi desire to overcome the painful separation from God, obliterating the sense of self to experience oneness with Allah. In several places Ibni Abdullah is represented in sacred terms, and much of the poetry in the text conflates sacred and carnal love. The hellfire of the Koran is transformed into consuming desire in the love poetry of the protagonist, as she conducts her dialogue not with the man himself, but with the Ibni Abdullah "within" her. In order to banish him from her body again, she has to subject herself to extreme physical privation; the end of the story sees her spending an uncomfortable night in a railway mission hostel.

What the text reveals is not a return to an originary identity by means of the Arabic script, and opposed to Atatürk's westernisation, but a "postcolonial" trajectory extending in two directions, back from the secular republic into the Ottoman past, with its imposition of a mono-lithic religion onto the shamanistic beliefs of the Turkic tribes, and forwards to the Americanisation of Turkey, and to the economic imperialism of the trade in migrant labour. The Turkish past to which the protagonist returns is no longer accessible in any pure form; it has been subsumed within the narrative of the modern nation state of which she is a product.[41] The very oppositions which the text sets up, between secular republic and Islamic imperial past, are rendered infinitely more complex by the fact that the mystical pre-Islamic traditions evoked survive in aspects of the Alevi faith, which is in many respects the branch of Islam most compatible with the republican state. Indeed, the state ideology of "Turkishness" incorporated precisely such a harking back to the pre-Islamic past, along with its populist privileging of Turkish over the Arabic and Persian languages.[42] Thus the very Kemalist ideology which is the target of Özdamar's attack is reinstated in her text, in the form of the folkloric mysticism which she opposes to Sunni orthodoxy. The text sets out to show that the Arabic Islamic tradition was both imperfectly imposed on the nomadic Turkic culture it sought to contain, and cannot assert its control over a westernised female sexuality. But it also articulates an identity irrevocably shaped by the secular republic, not just by the experience of radical politics and Marxist theatre in Berlin.

Özdamar's text, then, constructs a subject whose hybridity is not only the result of her migration to Germany, but is characteristic of the national narrative of Turkey and its accommodation of Islam. Nonetheless, it has important implications for her relationship to her German environment. Hybridity, for Bhabha, also implies the acceptance of irreducible cultural difference, and thus only ever an approximation to cross-cultural communication. Thus "Großvaterzunge" ends with a tenuous cross-cultural proximity on the basis of the "false friends" "ruh"

(Turkish *soul*) and "Ruh" (German *peace*). In the protagonist's encounter with a young woman mourning her lover's suicide, some critics have seen the evidence of cultural continuity restored, and cultural difference overcome.[43] This, in my view, is to detract from the complexity of Özdamar's text. If "Mutterzunge" begins with an expression of loss, the outcome of "Großvaterzunge" is, I would argue, not a restoration of plenitude, but an acceptance of ambivalent and provisional identifications which simultaneously displace and reinscribe the "national narrative" of Turkey. Moreover, her re-writing of Turkish identity confounds attempts to fix it in simple dichotomous relationship *either* to the West, *or* to the Ottoman imperial past, and the implications of this for contemporary *German* identity need urgently to be addressed.

Notes

[1] Eva Kolinsky, "Non-German minorities in contemporary German society," in David Horrocks and Eva Kolinsky, eds., *Turkish Culture in German Society Today* (Oxford: Berghahn, 1997), 71–111, 83. The Turkish population of Germany stabilised during the 1990s, shrinking from 2,107,400 in 1997 to 2,053,564 in 1999 according to the Statistisches Bundesamt Deutschland (www.statistik-bund.de/d_home.htm).

[2] *Mutterzunge* (Berlin: Rotbuch, 1990). Subsequent references will be to this edition and page numbers given in parenthesis in the text; *Das Leben ist eine Karawanserei — hat zwei Türen — aus einer kam ich rein — aus der anderen ging ich raus* (Cologne: Kiepenheuer and Witsch, 1992); *Die Brücke vom Goldenen Horn* (Cologne: Kiepenheuer and Witsch, 1998); *Der Hof im Spiegel* (Cologne: Kiepenheuer and Witsch, 2001).

[3] See Karen Jankowsky, "'German' Literature Contested: The 1991 Ingeborg-Bachmann-Prize Debate, 'Cultural Diversity,' and Emine Sevgi Özdamar," *German Quarterly* 70:3 (1997): 261–76. Deniz Göktürk also points to the orientalising tone of the jury's positive responses to Özdamar's text, and the outrage of opponents at the award of the prize for a "hilfloser Text einer deutschschreibenden Türkin," Deniz Göktürk, "Multikültürelle Zungenbrecher: Literatürken aus Deutschlands Nischen," *Sirene* 12/13 (1994): 77–92.

[4] *Interkulturelle Germanistik* relies heavily on the hermeneutics of Hans-Georg Gadamer for its model of intercultural communication. Azade Seyhan has pointed to the weaknesses of this position: "Although Gadamer maintains that the desire for understanding originates in the self's experience of its otherness . . . and understanding is always the interpretation of the other, the realization of historical understanding takes place in the fusion of familiarity and foreignness. And this fusion comes very close to consuming the foreign. The ontological ground of understanding in language, the fusion of horizons in interpretation, cannot explain other, vastly different cultures that do not share our histories," Azade Seyhan, *Writing Outside the Nation* (Princeton and Oxford: Princeton UP, 2001), 6. See also the debate between

Leslie Adelson and Ülker Gökberk on Sten Nadolny's novel *Selim oder die Gabe der Rede*: Leslie Adelson, "Opposing Oppositions: Turkish-German Questions in Contemporary German Studies," *German Studies Review* 70:2 (1994): 305–30; Ülker Gökberk, "*Culture Studies* und die Türken: Sten Nadolnys *Selim oder die Gabe der Rede* im Lichte einer Methodendiskussion," *The German Quarterly* 70:2 (1997): 97–122.

[5] Elizabeth Boa, "Sprachenverkehr. Hybrides Schreiben in Werken von Özdamar, Özakin und Demirkan," in Mary Howard, ed., *Interkulturelle Kommunikationen: Zur deutschsprachigen Prosaliteratur von Autoren nichtdeutscher Herkunft* (Munich: iudicium, 1997), 115–37. Boa argues that to apply Lacanian feminist theory to the representation of Islam in Özdamar's *Mutterzunge* would amount to epistemological violence, as it would disregard the importance of cultural and linguistic continuity in the diasporic experience.

[6] Deniz Göktürk, "Schwarzes Buch in weißer Festung. Entschwindende Erzähler auf postmodernen Pfaden in der türkischen Literatur," *Der Deutschunterricht* 45:5 (1993): 32–45. Göktürk calls for Turkish writers in Germany to be taken more seriously by the literary establishment by highlighting the cosmopolitanism and postmodernism of contemporary Turkish literature.

[7] Soheila Ghaussy has demonstrated the productive application of postmodern and psychoanalytical feminist theories to Özdamar's writing in her essay "'Das Vaterland verlassen': Nomadic Language and 'Feminine Writing' in Emine Sevgi Özdamar's *Das Leben ist eine Karawanserei*," *The German Quarterly* 72:1 (1999): 1–16.

[8] Ghaussy 7.

[9] In the interview "Living and Writing in Germany. Emine Sevgi Özdamar in Conversation with David Horrocks and Eva Kolinsky," Özdamar states: "It is true that the older colonial powers have managed the business of immigration much more successfully. The Germans came by their colonies relatively late in the day, and they have ended up creating new colonies on their home territory." In Horrocks and Kolinsky 45–54, 52–53.

[10] Interview with Özdamar in Annette Wierschke, *Schreiben als Selbstbehauptung: Kulturkonflikt und Identität in den Werken von Aysel Özakin, Alev Tekinay und Emine Sevgi Özdamar* (Frankfurt am Main: Verlag für Interkulturelle Kommunikation, 1996), 263.

[11] Homi K. Bhabha, *The Location of Culture* (London: Routledge, 1994), 166. I shall return to Bhabha's notion of the "foreignness of language" later.

[12] Critics of postcolonial theory such as Ella Shohat and Anne McClintock object to its depoliticising implications and universalising tendency to collapse different histories and racial formations into one category: the "postcolonial." See Ella Shohat, "Notes on the Post-Colonial," *Social Text* 31/32 (1992): 99–113; Anne McClintock, "The Myth of Progress: Pitfalls of the Term 'Post-Colonialism,'" *Social Text* 31/32 (1992): 84–98.

[13] Stuart Hall, "When Was 'the Post-Colonial'? Thinking at the Limit," in Iain Chambers and Lidia Curti, eds., *The Post-Colonial Question: Common Skies, Divided Horizons* (London: Routledge, 1996), 242–60, 247.

[14] Abdul JanMohammed differentiates usefully between the "dominant" phase of colonisation, characterised by direct bureaucratic and military control, and the "hegemonic" phase, when the coloniser's modes of production and cultural norms have been internalised by the colonised. In a certain sense Turkey's relationship to Western modernity could be said to come close to the latter. See Abdul JanMo-hammed, "The Economy of Manichean Allegory: the Function of Racial Difference in Colonialist Literature," *Critical Inquiry* 12:1 (1985): 59–87.

[15] Hall, "When Was 'the Post-Colonial'?" 247.

[16] Azade Seyhan, *Writing Outside the Nation*, 13.

[17] Hall, "Cultural Identity and Diaspora," in Patrick Williams and Laura Chrisman, eds., *Colonial Discourse and Postcolonial Theory* (London: Harvester Wheatsheaf, 1993), 392–403, 395.

[18] Bhabha 44.

[19] Homi Bhabha takes this expression from Walter Benjamin's essay, "The Task of the Translator" in *Illuminations*, trans. H. Zohn (London: Cape, 1970) in his own essay "DissemiNation," Bhabha 139–70.

[20] Azade Seyhan, "Geographies of Memory. Protocols of Writing in the Border-lands," in Klaus J. Milich and Jeffrey M. Peck, eds., *Multiculturalism in Transit: A German-American Exchange* (New York/Oxford: Berghahn, 1998), 193–212, 205.

[21] As Seyhan acknowledges, Özdamar's protagonist's desire to study the Arabic language could be construed as politically reactionary in the context of modern Turkish secularism. Azade Seyhan, "Geographies of Memory: Protocols of Writing in the Borderlands," 210.

[22] Hall, "Cultural Identity and Diaspora," 393.

[23] Bhabha 163–64.

[24] Bhabha 164.

[25] Ghaussy 5.

[26] Roses evoke both the romantic connotations of the Western poetic tradition and the rather more sinister Turkish association: "die Hand der schlagenden Meister stammt aus dem Paradies, wo Sie schlagen, werden dort die Rosen blühen" (13).

[27] The potentially mystical significance of this complete identification with the be-loved will be discussed in more detail later.

[28] The implied critique of the mind-body dichotomy has resonances with the work of Western postmodern feminist philosophers such as Adriana Cavarero and Christine Battersby. It is somewhat surprising in relation to Islam, however, which does not share Christianity's revulsion for sex and the body.

[29] Horrocks and Kolinsky 47.

[30] Emine Sevgi Özdamar, *Der Hof im Spiegel* (Cologne: Kiepenheuer and Witsch, 2001), 83.

[31] When he was commanded by the Angel Gabriel to read the words of Allah in a dream, Muhammed protested that he was illiterate, as does the protagonist here. A miracle occurred and on the third attempt he read the 96th Sura of the Koran. Like Gabriel, Ibni Abdullah commands: "Lese, Gott hat es uns gschickt," Özdamar, *Mutterzunge*, 16.

For more detail on this passage in the Koran, see Tahire Kockturk, *A Matter of Honour. Experiences of Turkish Women Immigrants* (London/New Jersey: Zed, 1992), 35.

[32] Claudia Breger analyses Özdamar's use of mimicry in her essay: "'Meine Herren, spielt in meinem Gesicht ein Affe?' Strategien der Mimikry in Texten von Emine Sevgi Özdamar," in Cathy S. Gelbin, Kader Konuk and Peggy Piesche, eds., *Aufbrüche: Kulturelle Produktionen von Migrantinnen, Schwarzen und jüdischen Frauen in Deutschland* (Königstein/Taunus: Ulrike Helmer Verlag, 1999), 30–59.

[33] The Arabic word *fitna* denotes both "beautiful woman" and "chaos," and is crucial to the imperative to control female sexuality, which occupies an important place in the social project of Islam. See Nilüfer Göle, "Islamism, Feminism and Post-Modernism: Women's Movements in Islamic Countries," *New Perspectives on Turkey* 19 (1998), 53–70.

[34] A dream sequence in the text *Mutterzunge* shows the paranoid fear of arrest if recognised as a Turkish worker (10).

[35] Stuart Hall, "Cultural Identity and Diaspora," 402.

[36] She tells Ibni Abdullah: "Bis diese Wörter aus deinem Land aufgestanden und zu meinem Land gelaufen sind, haben sie sich unterwegs etwas geändert" (27). Many of the words listed in the text have a modern Turkish equivalent, such as Arabic *sine* (breast) which coexists with Turkish *göğüs*, and *mazi* (past) which is also *geçmiş* in modern Turkish.

[37] Azade Seyhan, "Lost in Translation: Re-Membering the Mother Tongue in Emine Sevgi Özdamar's *Das Leben ist eine Karawanserei*," *The German Quarterly* 69 (1996): 414–26, 422.

[38] In this passage, the story of creation is juxtaposed with that of the judgement of sinners, eternally separated from Allah. One of the main Koran texts which the protagonist is required to study is the 82nd Sura, "The Splitting," which depicts the last judgement and is quoted in full on 17 and 21–22.

[39] The contrast between the fear of a punishing, transcendent God and an emphasis on God's creative power and love is suggestive of that between Sunni and Alevi faith, the latter bearing traces of pre-Ottoman mysticism. See David Shankland, *Islam and Society in Turkey Today* (Huntingdon: Eothen Press, 1999), 132–177.

[40] Alevis follow the nephew of Mohammed, Ali, whose martyrdom is commemorated in "The Dance of the Forty" (*kırklar sema*) which is at the heart of Alevi ritual. See Shankland 140.

[41] Similarly, Stuart Hall says that the Africa of black Carribbean identity is "always-already fused, syncretised, with other cultural elements." Stuart Hall, "Cultural Identity and Diaspora," 399.

[42] See Shankland 22.

[43] Wierschke interprets this exchange as signalling "die Ganzheit eines in sich ruhenden Selbst als einer heilen integren Identität," 180. Isolde Neubert also offers a conciliatory reading which suggests that "the Turkish and German women share the fate of lost love and find a common language," Isolde Neubert, "Searching for Intercultural Communication. Emine Sevgi Özdamar — a Turkish woman writer in Germany," in Chris Weedon, ed., *Post-War Women's Writing in German* (Oxford:

Berghahn, 1997), 153–68, 162. While it seems likely that the author intended such a conciliatory reading, I find it unsupported by the text itself.

Difficult Stories: Generation, Genealogy, Gender in Zafer Şenocak's *Gefährliche Verwandtschaft* and Monika Maron's *Pawels Briefe*

Katharina Gerstenberger

MORE THAN TEN YEARS after the fall of the Wall *Vergangenheitsbewäl-tigung* is out of favor with most Germans. The unified country, it seems, requires a self-definition in which the Holocaust no longer plays a central role. Fundamental to these efforts is the desire to establish Germany's normalcy as one democratic nation among others. Leading politicians such as Secretary of State Joschka Fischer envision a Germany that is mindful of its past yet at the same time a self-confident member of the new Europe. Coming to terms with the past was a West German project of the 1970s and 1980s, to a significant degree propelled by the antagonism between members of different generations and proponents of different political convictions. The GDR, by contrast, claimed an anti-fascist tradition and rejected responsibility for the crimes of the Third Reich altogether. Yet Germany's Nazi history continues to impel writers to represent this past in literature and in essays. Since the early 1990s a number of authors have commented on this topic from a post-unification perspective. Among them are Günter Grass, who insists that writing in Germany will continue to be writing after Auschwitz.[1] Martin Walser, one of his opponents in this argument, believes that Germans have the right not to be incessantly confronted with Auschwitz.[2] Yet others, such as Peter Schneider, take the German past as their point of reference as they explore post-unification Germany from the perspective of East and West Germans as well as the many foreigners who live on both sides of the former Wall.[3] For many, however, the mastery of the present is enough of a challenge, as can be seen in the trials and tribulations of Ingo Schulze's heroes in *Simple Storys* (1998), whose protagonists from the former GDR barely cope with the realities of united Germany.[4] During the last ten years, writers from the former West Germany have shown more interest in the Nazi past than their eastern German counterparts, many of whom have thematized the loss of GDR society.[5] This essay focuses on recent texts by two writers — neither of them a west German in the traditional sense — of different generation, background, and gender in which the protagonists find themselves confronted with their families' past. Their difficult stories suggest ways in which united Germany might view its past.

Set in the 1990s, Zafer Şenocak's novel *Gefährliche Verwandtschaft* (1998) and Monika Maron's *Pawels Briefe* (1999) revolve around letters and diaries of a grandparent which surface unexpectedly in the protagonists' lives.[6] Letters and diaries create a particular relationship to the past. They are personal documents which chronicle their writers' present, they are often preserved and passed on within the writer's family, and, with time, they become witnesses of the past. In most cases, they are not historical documents yet they document history. The intimate authenticity of the messages from grandparents to grandchildren in Şenocak's and Maron's stories possesses a disruptive quality, forcing the unsuspecting recipients to revise the stories of their own lives. Skipping over the generation of the parents, the letters serve to reconfigure the relationship between generations in ways that move beyond the accusations of guilt or indifference characteristic of the *Väterliteratur* of the 1970s and 1980s. As "stranded objects," these documents set in motion a process in which history, memory, and identity form new narrative alliances.

In father literature, sons, and in a few instances daughters, confront their ex-Nazi fathers (and mothers) with their refusal to accept responsibility for Nazi crimes.[7] Often, the guilt of the fathers is the guilt of forgetting. What the sons remember, by contrast, is to a large extent the story of their own victimization by their fathers. These texts chronicle what Michael Schneider in a 1984 article has described as the "damaged relationship between two generations."[8] The authors of father literature vent their anger against the domestic brutalities they experienced at the hands of their fathers and the damage they sustained in the process. The fathers stand for the German Nazi past, and the generation of the sons are its latest victims. In the end, Schneider argues, the second generation remains closer to the psychic and behavioral patters of their parents than they realize. Father literature locked sons and fathers into an oedipal drama in which the son played the role of yet another victim of his father.

In the 1990s new modes and models of literary writing about the Nazi past emerge that experiment with psychological constellations beyond the generational confrontation between son and father. There is Martin Walser's semi-autobiographical attempt to separate German culture from Nazi barbarism as he traces his alter ego's love for the German language to his father.[9] The elegiac yet humorous reminiscences of a childhood in the 1950s in Hans Ulrich Treichel's *Der Verlorene* (1998) recount the trauma of the postwar generation with irony rather than antagonism.[10] Marcel Beyer's *Flughunde* (1995), a novel about the last months of the Goebbels family interspersed with the story of a Nazi sound technician, recreates the Nazi past through fiction. Even though Beyer's protagonists have historical models, it is the use of fiction that gives the writer the necessary creative space.[11] Finally, there are the novels and short stories of writers in their early thirties such as Tanja Dückers or Judith Hermann, whose protagonists explicitly refuse to participate in their 1968-parents' pursuit of *Vergangenheitsbewältigung*.[12] In the 1990s themes such as memory and history, memory and forgetting, cultural memory and trauma, memory and narrative, memory and mourning, have taken the place of the more politically oriented project of coming to terms with the past.[13] The theoretical preoccupation with memory and its connection to national culture has yielded new ways of conceptualizing the transference of memory from one generation to the next.[14] In addition, the "inability to mourn" has regained importance as an analytical tool and a number of literary texts explore states of mourning rather than confrontation.[15] Importantly, many of these impulses stem from writers and scholars who focus on the victims of the Holocaust and their children rather than the perpetrators and their off-spring. Nevertheless, German literature of the 1990s reflects these developments in thinking about the past by introducing plots beyond *Väterliteratur* and its calcified psychological patterns.

Gefährliche Verwandtschaft and *Pawels Briefe* focus on the family as the institution through which the protagonists experience the connection between present and past. Zafer Şenocak was born in 1961 in Ankara; Monika Maron, born in Berlin, is twenty years his senior. Şenocak grew up in Istanbul and Munich; Maron lived in East Berlin until she left the GDR in 1988. Maron's autobiographical narrative intertwines the writer's story with that of her Jewish grandfather and her communist mother. Şenocak's essayistic novel explores the protagonist's German-Jewish-Turkish affinities from the vantage point of post-unification Berlin. The communication between generations of Germans is also the engagement with ancestors of different ethnic and national background. Both writers and their texts contribute to the "heterogeneity that *already* exists within Germany," as Gerd Gemünden phrased it in a recent essay.[16] Maron and Şenocak challenge the division between Germany and its "Others" by revealing the unstable nature of these divisions not only today but also in the past. In doing so, they rewrite the project of *Vergangenheitsbewältigung* itself. The connections between generations they create and the mixed genealogies they design exceed the parameters of the perpetrator-victim scheme. With their stories across generations, cultures, and gender divisions, Şenocak and Maron break the spell of the fathers and their hold on the past and replace the male literary tradition of patricide and the solidified narrative patterns it spawned. Changed definitions of gender roles and relations play an important role here as well. The sexual oppression so prevalent in *Väterliteratur* no longer serves to document the son's victim status. The grandchildren achieve a "mobility of . . . script" that was not available to most writers of the 1970s and 1980s.[17] The grandparents' letters and diaries are messages from the past that engender new narratives in and for the present. Instead of closure, we get more — difficult — stories.

Şenocak's *Gefährliche Verwandtschaft* resonates with the title of another German novel that appeared 190 years earlier. Like Goethe's *Wahlverwandtschaften,* Şenocak's book is about genealogies, family relationships, sexual desire, and broken marriages. Unlike Goethe's "affinities," Şenocak's *Verwandtschaft* is singular rather than plural and its members, moreover, are not elective. Dangerous they are in both cases but Şenocak is much more open about this fact. In Goethe's novel, the pivotal transgression, Charlotte's and Eduard's adultery, takes place in the imagination only. In *Gefährliche Verwandtschaft,* imagination supersedes factual reality as the narrator claims his right to invent his family's story without being restricted by historical facts. Both Goethe and Şenocak are interested in the formation of genealogies and the sexuality without which there is no kinship.

The plot of Şenocak's novel is easily recounted. After his parents' death Sascha Muhteschem, a Berlin-based writer in his mid-thirties and the book's first-person narrator, inherits — in addition to a significant amount of money — a silver box which contains his Turkish grandfather's diaries from the years 1916–1936. What follows is no oriental fairy tale but a novel interspersed with essayistic passages and interviews. The open form of the novel is as much a renunciation of generic conventions as an expression of the narrator's (as well as the writer's) need to make use of a variety of forms to tell his story. Şenocak's silver box turns out to be unlocked and no magic word or key is needed to gain physical access to its content. The ensuing quest is for a key of a different kind. The diaries motivate the narrator to explore his German-Jewish-Turkish family history and to assess this complicated heritage as he reflects on his own position as a writer and journalist, whose first novel had flopped. The protagonist's voice as a writer here does not depend upon his psychological separation from his family but rather on his creative appropriation of his family's history.

It is upon his return to Berlin that the narrator inherits the silver box and resolves to write about his paternal grandfather. He makes several attempts to find a suitable translator for the diaries which he cannot read, for they are written in Cyrillic and Arabic script. The undertaking is made even more difficult by the discovery that his grandfather used Cyrillic letters to write in Russian as well as in Turkish. In present-day Berlin, the doubly encoded documents are at the margins of the translatable. Trained to think in Freudian terms, we might expect the transmission of narratives between generations and across cultures to be hindered by psychological barriers. Şenocak's post-Freudian scenario is about different cultures and the possibility of cross-cultural story-telling rather than oedipal dramas. The protagonist's parents are no enemies that stand in the way of their son's emotional or professional development, and there is no need to kill an overbearing father. "Meinem Vater mußte ich nicht einmal ausweichen. Er verschwand von sich aus" (24). The traditional father-son plot plays no role in this narrative about generations. Gender, moreover, does not function to divide Şenocak's characters into victims and victimizers. On his mother's side Sascha descends from German Jews who survived the Nazi time in Turkish exile. His maternal grandfather had served in the German army on the Turkish battlefields of World War I and emigrated to Istanbul in 1934, where he and his immediate family survived in exile while their relatives perished in German concentration camps. Several years after the war the family returned to Munich, where the narrator was born in 1954 (54). How this mixed heritage in terms of bloodlines and culture has shaped him and which influences he sees at work he does not spell out. His languages are German and English, and he rather quickly abandons an attempt to learn Turkish, a language that was rarely spoken at home. His emotional loyalties are with certain German cities rather than with Germany. Most important to his sense of being at home are his apartments, which he tends to sublet from friends and change quite frequently. He does not apply the term Turk or Jew or German to himself but he does not reject any of them either. He reads widely on world religions but he does not identify with any one. Şenocak's narrator, whose name is used only once or twice throughout the entire novel, is a postmodern subject who is well aware of his family history but refuses to let the past delimit his psychological and narrative options.

Sascha Muhteschem's German-Jewish-Turkish *Verwandtschaft* includes Holocaust victims on his mother's side and perpetrators of the

Armenian genocide on his father's side. His Turkish grandfather, he knows, helped compile lists of Armenian deportees. He thus inherits links to "both" genocides of twentieth-century European history. Şenocak does not compare the magnitude of atrocities committed by the Turks and the Germans, nor does he juxtapose guilt versus innocence, victim and perpetrator. His protagonist does not identify with one side of the family over the other, and he does not view himself as either damaged or redeemed by his ancestors. His *Verwandtschaft* is singular in the sense that he refuses to make choices among the plurality of bloodlines and, more importantly, the moral implications of these different histories. "Ich bin ein Enkel von Opfern und Tätern. Ich glaube nicht, daß Schuld übertragbar ist" (40), he writes, not contemplating the possibility of inheriting innocence. Instead, he engages in a philosophical quest how to tell his grandfather's story.

Gefährliche Verwandtschaft is interspersed with essayistic passages, reflections on language, identity, united Berlin, and several biographical sketches of Turks in Germany, including one titled "Zafer. Schriftsteller. Wie ich unter die Fremden kam" (102). What ties these fragments together is the interest in narrative and Sascha's insistence on telling the story his way. While Sascha is plotting his story about his grandfather, his girlfriend Marie is working on a documentary film about Talat Pascha, a leader of the Young Turks, one-time foreign minister, and primary instigator of the Armenian genocide, who was assassinated in Berlin in 1921 by a young Armenian. Through the center of the novel runs the juxtaposition of Marie's quest for historical accuracy as she is reconstructing the life of Talat Pascha, and Sascha's resolve to put his grandfather's life into words. The filmmaker Marie engages in extensive library research and travels to Turkey, trying to determine with as much precision as possible what exactly happened in order to document the events in pictures. The narrator, by contrast, is less interested in historical facts. "Marie sammelt Fakten für ihren Film. Alte Dokumente, Fotos, Zeugenaussagen. Für mich wertlose Dinge. Ich für meinen Teil habe beschlossen zu schreiben" (39–40). Marie and Sascha work on related topics — both Talat Pascha and Sascha's grandfather witnessed the decline of the Ottoman Empire, fought in World War I, were involved in the persecution of Armenians, and admired Kemal Atatürk. More important is the transformation of this topic into narrative. While the film documentary is "limited" by facts, Sascha's resolve to write translates into Şenocak's loosely structured novel.

In the end, Sascha finds a suitable translator for his grandfather's diaries but does not wait for him to complete his work. "Ich hatte längst beschlossen, das Leben meines Großvaters nicht zu rekonstruieren, sondern zu erfinden" (38). Fictions of the past supersede historical truth:

> Geschichte hat immer eine verbrauchte und eine unverbrauchte Seite. An der verbrauchten Seite sind die Historiker am Werk. Sie versuchen zu rekonstruieren. An der unverbrauchten Seite wollte ich tätig sein. Ich verknüpfte die Fäden in meinem Kopf zu einem Roman, dessen zentrale Figur mein Großvater sein sollte. Meine Aufgabe war es zu konstruieren, was nicht zu rekonstruieren war. (51)

His narrative is born out of the difference between reconstructing and constructing. "Sollte ich seine Tagebücher vernichten, um mein Gedächtnis gänzlich frei zu machen?" (38), he asks himself at some point. The novel closes with Sascha's rendition of the events that led to his grandfather's suicide at the age of forty. His grandfather, the narrator surmises, received a letter from the woman he had loved twenty years earlier, informing him that they have a daughter, that she was raped during the war, and reminding him of his promise to end his life should they ever get separated. The love relationship dates back to 1916, the year in which he started to keep a diary. The letter has neither name nor return address. Upon its receipt, Sascha writes, his grandfather took his own life. Sascha solves the mystery of his grandfather's — belated — suicide without relying on his diaries as a source. The grandfather's story also attests to the precarious nature of genealogies. Had his grandfather kept his promise earlier, the narrator would have never been born. In telling his grandfather's story, Sascha gives himself a second chance as a writer, whose new novel will hopefully not share the fate of his first.

Şenocak's novel opens with two epigraphs about memory and narrative. The epigraphs, a "Sumerischer Spruch," and a "Weisheit aus der Levante" originate in regions once part of the Ottoman empire. They can neither be attributed to an individual author nor can they be dated with any precision, yet they do betray the author's affinities with Mediterranean and middle Eastern literature and culture. Şenocak's fragmented novel, in which the restlessness of narrator and narrative complement each other, refuses closure and conclusions. Sascha thinks about his origins (47) but does not formulate results; he and Marie go separate ways without officially ending their relationship. Sascha occupies himself with his Turkish grandfather but reads in the archives about the 1930s in Germany. The quest for the translation of the diaries, which connects the disparate parts of the novel, turns out to be insignificant in the end. Writing as such is privileged in this novel about the writing of a novel. In the end, this self-referential structure points to the subjects involved in the act of writing and reading. "Die entscheidende Frage beim Erzählen ist, ob Schreiber, Figuren und Leser im Bann des Erzählten sich selbst finden können" (41). What kind of a self writer, protagonists and reader will find, is left open.

Gefährliche Verwandtschaft creates genealogies and subject positions that do not lock the individual into specific plots or identities. The past is a resource for stories for the writer to choose from. In one way, however, Şenocak's postmodern and post-national narrator does remind us of the heroes who have been staffing the novel since the eighteenth century: the young men who want to be writers.

Monika Maron gave *Pawels Briefe* the subtitle *Eine Familiengeschichte*. While she did not call it "meine Familiengeschichte," the autobiographical quality of the narrative is apparent. Readers of Maron's work will recognize references to her other publications, the members of her family appear under their own names, dates of events can be confirmed through external sources. *Pawels Briefe*, however, is not the story of Maron's life but an account of her attempts to link together pieces of her family's history. Like Şenocak's, Maron's text begins with the discovery of a box full of letters from a grandparent, whose unexpected appearance needs to be integrated into existing family narratives. Unlike Şenocak's protagonist, Maron is perfectly capable of reading the recovered documents and, moreover, she has been familiar with her grandfather's story all along. In fact, she has told the story before. The opening chapter of *Flugasche* (1981), Maron's first book, is based on the lives of her grandparents.[18] She told the story again in 1989, less than a month after the opening of the Wall, in an article published in *Die Zeit* about her family's history.[19] The intent of these different versions varies, however. In *Flugasche*, the first-person narrator creates an identity for herself in response to what she has been told about her grandfather, whose "unruhig, jähzornig, verträumt" personality, she insists, she inherited.[20] His genetic heritage absolves her from what she does not want to be during her adolescence: a German. In the 1989 version, the focus shifts from personality and selective affinities to postwar history and the division of Germany, which also split Maron's family along ideological and geographical lines. Family history, these different versions show, can serve different purposes, ranging from adolescent protest to understanding national history. In *Pawels Briefe*, Maron reflects on memory as an unreliable yet indispensable transmitter between four generations of twentieth-century Germans living under four different political systems.

Pawels Briefe, then, is not so much about her maternal grandfather Pawel Iglarz but about his letters — discovered by Maron in 1994 in her mother's attic — and about their effect more than fifty years after they were written. It is a mother-daughter story about fundamental political and personal differences between Maron's communist mother Hella and her non-communist daughter Monika. For Maron's literary alter ego the discovery of the letters sets in motion a process of trying to understand her mother as she is getting to know her as her father's daughter. Through conversations and reflections she reconstructs a genealogy no longer driven by the adolescent rebellion of *Flugasche* but by the desire to comprehend how the generations of her family connect to one another and the political contexts within which these relations took shape. Central to Maron's narrative are the mechanisms of memory and its often less appreciated opposite — forgetting. "Wir können uns erklären, warum wir uns an etwas erinnern, aber nicht, warum wir vergessen, weil wir nicht wissen können, was wir vergessen haben, eben weil wir vergessen haben, was uns zugestoßen ist" (18). The story of Pawel's letters is accompanied by a meta-discourse about memory not merely as an individual capacity but also as a connective medium between generations.

The particulars of Pawel Iglarz's Polish-German-Jewish-Baptist biography, which is as multicultural as Şenocak's dangerous relations, emerge as Maron quotes from his letters, relates how she, together with her mother and her son, visit the Polish villages where her grandparents lived, as she narrates the story of her own life, and, time and again, through conversations with her mother about her life as Pawel's daughter. The process of assembling the story of his life is as important as the biography itself. Pawel Iglarz was born a Polish Jew in 1879. At the age of 19 or 20, he left his home town and his family, became a Baptist in 1900, and shortly thereafter met his future wife, Josefa, a Polish Catholic who had likewise converted to Baptism. The two moved to Berlin-Neukölln in 1905, where Pawel found work as a tailor for Peek & Cloppenburg. They had four children; the youngest of them, Hella, became Monika Maron's mother. In 1938, the Nazis expelled Pawel and his wife from Germany because they had remained Polish citizens. After several month of living in a tent at the German-Polish border, they moved to Josefa's hometown of Kurow, a village fifty kilometres from Lòdz. They lived there until the spring of 1942 (132), Josefa's health steadily declining, when Pawel, the born Jew, was forced to move to the near-by Belchatow ghetto. Josefa remained behind and died shortly thereafter, presumably of cancer (112). The circumstances of Pawel's death are unclear, his last letter dating from August 8, 1942. Maron assumes that he was killed at the Kulmhof concentration camp in August 1942 (89).

Maron's mother Hella found Pawel's letters in a box in the attic after a Dutch film team had asked to interview both mother and daughter for a documentary about post-unification Germans. The foreign film team's interest in contemporary Germany, which itself is inspired by Germany's history, confronts Hella and her daughter with their own treatment of their family's past. Pawel Iglarz had written the letters, which now resurfaced unexpectedly, between 1938 and 1942 from his forced exile in Poland to his adult children who had remained in Berlin. The box also includes some of his children's responses. Hella, who prides herself in having a good memory, cannot recall having received or written any of these letters. Her own handwriting on her letters to her father looks uncannily familiar yet completely foreign to her. In a case of reverse *déjà vu* Hella reprimands herself that she should remember these letters when she simply does not recall their existence. In fact, Hella forgot the letters twice. Once, that she ever received or wrote them; and a second time, when she obtained the box after her sister's death in the mid-eighties, stored it without having gone through its contents and — forgot about it (10). The box full of documents proves to be an irritating presence because the letters "in meiner Mutter nicht nur die vergrabene Trauer weckten, sondern sie in anhaltende Verwirrung stürzten" (10). Maron leaves open whether her mother's grief is for her father and his fate, or for herself and the loss of certainty. Not only her mother's forgetting becomes a topic of intense occupation for both of them but also the question how they each remember. "Hella erinnert sich anders, Hella erinnert sich an Glück" (70), writes Maron, where her own memory is blank. More important than facts, memory is about the emotions it conjures up.

If history versus memory is the central issue in Şenocak's novel, remembering and forgetting is what propels Maron's book. Pawel's letters are moving testimonials to events that have been documented by historians many times. They do not provide new insights into the history of the Holocaust but as "stranded objects" they set in motion reflections on the emotional impact of remembering and forgetting. Maron's narrative, in fact, begins with her thoughts on the politics of remembering and forgetting in a society heavily preoccupied with questions of public memory and collective commemoration. "Acts of memory are performed by individuals in a cultural framework that encourages these acts," writes literary critic Mieke Bal.[21] Forgetting in such a context can be interpreted as a personal failure or, worse, an act of willed denial. "Als meine Mutter sich an einen Briefwechsel, in dem es um ihr Leben ging, nicht erinnern konnte, war das Vergessen in der öffentlichen Meinung gerade zu einem

Synonym für Verdrängung und Lüge geschrumpft" (11). *Pawels Briefe,* however, is no example of father-literature, and the mother's forgetting is not interpreted as an act of denial or aggression against the daughter. Yet here, too, the family genealogy can be accessed only once the parents no longer presents a psychological obstacle. Maron writes: "Ich mußte aufgehört haben, meine Eltern zu bekämpfen, um mich über das Maß der eigenen Legitimation hinaus für meine Großeltern und ihre Geschichte wirklich zu interessieren" (13). Despite this common generational conflict, her mother's memories are indispensable to telling her grandfather's story. Maron thus sees herself confronted with the double dilemma posed by the fact of forgetting on the one hand, and the unreliability of that which is remembered on the other.

A trip to Poland, which Maron undertakes in 1995 together with her mother and her son, does not shed light on her grandparents' life story. After a visit to Pawel's hometown she concludes: "Über Pawel hatten wir nur erfahren, daß er aus einem armseligen Städtchen kam" (109). More gravely, the trip to Poland does not bring back memories. "Ich hatte gehofft, die Sprache und der Ort, auch wenn Hella ihn nie zuvor betreten hatte, würden andere Erinnerungen in ihr wecken, einen Satz, vielleicht nur einen halben Satz ihres Vaters, ein zufällig gehörtes und sorglos vergessenes Wort" (108). Hella, however, try as she might, does not remember. Maron here alludes to Freud's model of the human psyche as comparable to the layers of a buried city whose remnants can be accessed with skill or by force of luck. Memory, she suggests, is a living yet dormant entity inside us that we may or may not be able to arouse with the help of external stimulants. In this case the experiment does not yield the desired results. Şenocak's narrator insisted on the freedom of the blank page against documentary evidence. On their trip to Poland Maron's travelers come to learn that even physical evidence does not always inspire the imagination enough to tell the story they have set out to find. The Polish villages with their houses, graveyards, local archives, and even relatives offer only tenuous connections to Pawel and Josefa: " . . . sogar als wir vor ihrem Grab standen, fragte ich mich, ob mich all diese Bilder nicht eher störten, ob die Festlegungen mir meinen Weg der Annäherung nicht verstellten" (94).

The forgotten letters, then, are the medium that contains evidence of the lived relationship between Pawel and his children, and they turn out to reveal disturbing insights into Hella's personality. After her mother's death, Hella in a letter encouraged her father, who at that time was already interned in the Belchatow ghetto, to try to get over his wife's death: "Elf Tage nach Josefas Tod schrieb Pawel an seinen Sohn Paul: 'Hella schrieb mir ich soll versuchen (darüber) hinwegzukommen, ich kann es aber nicht'" (129). The line is repeated in a letter to Hella herself: "Und du, liebe Hella schreibst mir, ich soll versuchen, darüber hinwegzukommen. Kann man das?" (138). Hella is deeply distraught at the rediscovery of this sentence which Pawel had quoted back to her almost fifty years before. Her despair over the letter, Maron notes in the same paragraph (129), is matched only by the desperation Hella felt on the day when the Wall came down. The story of Pawel and his letters is tied to the rise and fall of the GDR and the conflict between mother and daughter over political beliefs.

Among the letters is one by Josefa, Maron's illiterate grandmother who spoke little German — in German and typed. Hella cannot explain the origin of this document. From a letter by Pawel to his son, Paul, Maron learns that Pawel had sent this letter, the last one he received from his wife before her death, to his children with the direction to have the letter translated and typed. "Schließt ihn in irgendein Fach ein, daß er nicht verloren geht, und wenn Monika groß ist zeigt ihr den Brief und erzählt ihr, wie tief unglücklich ihre Großeltern gerade in den alten Tagen geworden sind, vielleicht weint sie dann auch eine Träne" (113). Hella and her siblings did as they had been asked and forgot the letter. "Vor diesem Vergessen stehe ich ratlos, so ratlos wie Hella selbst" (113). In addition, several of Pawel's letters contain greetings to his grandchild Monika whom he never had the chance to see. "Wenn ich mir vorstelle, daß der Mann, der diese Briefe schrieb, an mich dachte, auf mich hoffte, verliert das Wort Vergangenheit für Minuten seinen Sinn. Dann werden die Jahre durchlässig und der 26. Juli oder der 8. August 1942 gehören zu den Tagen meines erinnerbaren Lebens" (141). Pawel's letters, then, juxtapose her mother Hella's forgetting with the daughter Monika's remembering. Maron, moreover, does offer an explanation for her mother's forgetting. 1945, she notes, was a "Wiedergeburt" for the communist Hella (113) and the GDR took the place of her parents. Using the example of her mother, Maron shows that German political history repeatedly interrupted her family's physical and emotional genealogy. Nazis killed her grandfather but communism almost obliterated Pawel's legacy for his granddaughter. As the anticommunist Maron incorporates her grandfather's life into her own memory she assumes the privileged position of the one who puts together again these severed ends.

In 1995 *Spiegel* journalists discovered that Monika Maron had had contact with the State Security in the mid-1970s. Eager to confront Maron with Germany's "other" past, a TV-reporter claimed to be in possession of a report Maron supposedly wrote about one of her closest friends. The accusation triggered severe doubt in her own capacity to remember. "Es gab eine Stunde, in der ich bereit war, alles für möglich zu halten" (200). It is her mother who assured her: "Du hast so einen Bericht nicht geschrieben, und jetzt beruhige dich" (200). The finality of this maternal pronouncement is underscored by the three stars that signal the end of the section. In the end, the daughter learns to accept that her mother does not remember what seems impossible to forget and that she herself was almost willing to remember what never happened. Through the center of Maron's mother-daughter story runs a political and personal conflict without the psychological damage so fundamental to father-literature. While the story of Pawel and his letters illustrates what separates mother and daughter in terms of politics and personality, they understand the imperative to work together if they want to remember Pawel and his contribution to the family genealogy. Germany's *Vergangenheiten* do not release either of them from that uneasy realm of remembering and forgetting.

Both Şenocak and Maron privilege personal memory over factual history. Since both are writers rather than historians this does not come as a surprise yet they are writers who know their history exceedingly well. The resulting narratives are personal, the answers they offer are tentative and do not claim to possess general validity. Individual memory can be "crowded out by cultural memory," Mieke Bal cautions us.[22] Şenocak and Maron let the memories of their protagonists chart their individual courses to tell stories that are ultimately political. Importantly, both Şenocak and Maron tell German stories from the margins of the German center. Based on their own biographies, the stories they chose to tell are not those of Nazi perpetrators and their children or grandchildren. Yet the past they put into words pertains to the German present of the protagonists. Writing is Şenocak and Maron's answer to the enigma of memory, both of whom have created protagonists who define themselves as writers. In their texts they identify memory as a source for stories. Forgetting can become an integral element of a narrative about remembering and the refusal to let facts interfere with memory does not mean that the story contains no truth. Şenocak's concept of memory is a post-Freudian one. There are no buried, displaced or repressed memories that resurface unexpectedly or refuse to emerge on demand. For him, memory is a blank page, whose emptiness is the necessary precondition of narrative. Maron remains committed to a Freudian model of memory in that she works with the idea that memories can be lost and, perchance, retrieved. For her, memory itself becomes a topic of intense interest, which, in the end, however, evades our final understanding. Where Freud sought to provide answers why and how we forget and remember, Maron accepts forgetting and not remembering as a reality that can be narrated but not always explained. Gender no longer has a rigid hold over the protagonists who are also writers. Neither Maron nor Şenocak feature the tyrannical fathers of *Väterliteratur* in their narratives and neither of them feels the need to commit literary patricide. Both of them explore new ways of writing gender and generation as well as nation. In doing so, they also find new narrative means of writing the difficult stories of Germany's past.

Notes

[1] Günter Grass, *Schreiben nach Auschwitz: Frankfurter Poetik-Vorlesung* (Frankfurt am Main: Luchterhand, 1990).

[2] Martin Walser, "Erfahrungen beim Verfassen einer Sonntagsrede," in *Die Walser-Bubis-Debatte: Eine Dokumentation*, ed. F. Schirrmacher (Frankfurt am Main: Suhrkamp, 1999), 7–17. See also Walser's autobiographical novel *Ein springender Brunnen* (Frankfurt am Main: Suhrkamp, 1998).

[3] Peter Schneider, *Extreme Mittellage: Eine Reise durch das deutsche Nationalgefühl* (Reinbek bei Hamburg: Rowohlt, 1990).

[4] Ingo Schulze, *Simple Storys: Ein Roman aus der ostdeutschen Provinz* (Berlin: Berlin Verlag, 1998).

[5] Examples are Klaus Schlesinger, *Trug* (Berlin: Aufbau, 2000); Thomas Brussig, *Das kürzere Ende der Sonnenallee* (Berlin: Verlag Volk und Welt, 1999), and Jens Sparschuh, *Der Zimmerspringbrunnen* (Munich: Kiepenheuer und Witsch, 1995).

[6] Zafer Şenocak, *Gefährliche Verwandtschaft* (Munich: Babel, 1998). Monika Maron, *Pawels Briefe: Eine Familiengeschichte* (Frankfurt am Main: Fischer, 1999). Subsequent references appear in the text.

[7] Examples of father literature include Bernward Vesper's *Die Reise* (1977), Ruth Rehmann's *Der Mann auf der Kanzel* (1979), Peter Härtling's *Nachgetragene Liebe* (1980), Christoph Meckel's *Suchbild* (1980), and Peter Schneider's *Vati* (1987).

[8] Michael Schneider, "Fathers and Sons, Retrospectively: The Damaged Relationship Between Two Generations," *New German Critique* 59 (1984): 3–51.

[9] Martin Walser, *Ein springender Brunnen* (Frankfurt am Main: Suhrkamp, 1998). See Stuart Taberner, "A Manifesto for Germany's 'New Right'?: Martin Walser, The Past, Transcendence, and *Ein springender Brunnen*," *German Life and Letters* 53:1 (2000): 126–39.

[10] Hans-Ulrich Treichel, *Der Verlorene* (Frankfurt am Main: Suhrkamp, 1998). See Stuart Taberner, "Hans-Ulrich Treichel's *Der Verlorene* and the Problem of German Wartime Suffering," *The Modern Language Review* 97:1 (2002): 123–34.

[11] Marcel Beyer, *Flughunde* (Frankfurt am Main: Suhrkamp, 1995). An Austrian example of powerful fiction about the Nazi past is Christoph Ransmayr's *Morbus Kitahara* (Frankfurt am Main: Fischer, 1995).

[12] Tanja Dückers, *Spielzone* (Berlin: Aufbau, 1999); Judith Hermann, *Sommerhaus, später* (Frankfurt am Main: Fischer, 1998).

[13] See Eric Santner, *Stranded Objects: Mourning, Memory, and Film in Postwar Germany* (Ithaca, NY: Cornell UP, 1990). Santner's analysis of contemporary German film takes its point of departure from *The Inability to Mourn*. See also Andreas Huyssen, *Twilight Memories: Marking Time in a Culture of Amnesia* (New York: Routledge, 1995); Marianne Hirsch, *Family Frames: Photography, Narrative, and Postmemory* (Cambridge, MA: Harvard UP, 1997), and Mieke Bal et al., eds., *Acts of Memory: Cultural Recall in the Present* (Hanover, NH and London: UP of New England, 1999).

[14] Marianne Hirsch introduced the term postmemory for the "memories" of children of Holocaust survivors in her *Family Frames*. Similarly, cultural memory refers to the transference of memory from one generation to the next.

[15] See Santner, *Stranded Objects*.

[16] Gerd Gemünden, "Nostalgia for the Nation"; Bal, *Acts of Memory*, 120–33, 131.

[17] Sidonie Smith, "The Other Woman and the Racial Politics of Gender: Isak Dinesen and Beryl Markham in Kenya," in Sidonie Smith, ed., *De/Colonizing the Subject: the Politics of Gender in Women's Autobiography* (Minneapolis: U of Minnesota P, 1992), 410–35, 413.

[18] Monika Maron, *Flugasche* (Frankfurt am Main: Fischer, 1981). Maron refers to *Flugasche* in the opening paragraphs of *Pawels Briefe* as she reflects as to why she chose to write this book now.

[19] Monika Maron, "Ich war ein antifaschistisches Kind," in *Nach Maßgabe meiner Begreifungskraft: Artikel und Essays* (Frankfurt am Main: Fischer, 1993), 9–28. The article first appeared in 1989 in *Die Zeit*. Some passages from this article made it into *Pawels Briefe* without changes.

[20] Maron, *Flugasche*, 9.

[21] Bal, *Acts of Memory*, xiii.

[22] Bal, *Acts of Memory*, xii.

Drowning or Waving:
German Literature Today

Stuart Parkes

CONCERN ABOUT THE HEALTH of German literature is nothing new. Firstly, in comparison with Britain or the USA, literature and literary life in Germany have been more frequently linked with questions of national status and prestige. How far back this kind of concern reaches can be seen from the references to efforts to create a national theatre as a kind of compensation for the lack of political unity in Goethe's *Wilhelm Meisters theatralische Sendung*. Almost two centuries later, in the postwar period, such concern was particularly visible in the case in the GDR for which the acknowledgement of literary achievement was part of the overall search for legitimacy and recognition, the policy pursued in so many areas ranging from diplomacy to sport. Moreover, it has been a feature of German literary life that writers and intellectuals themselves have been concerned to analyse the condition of literature at a particular time. On many occasions, the diagnosis has been far from positive. Most famously in recent decades, at the same time as the student movement was at its height, literature was apparently pronounced dead, and there was a widespread public perception that this was indeed the case. As early as 1965 Peter Schneider had wondered whether it was a time for writing political manifestos rather than traditional works of literature.[1] It was, however, two essays that were published in the journal *Kursbuch* in 1968 that sparked off the most intense debate. Both appeared to question the value of literature at a time of supposed revolutionary change. Accordingly, in his essay "Ein Kranz für die Literatur," Karl Markus Michel bemoaned literature's distance "zur gesellschaftlichen Praxis,"[2] while, most famously, Hans Magnus Enzensberger in his "Gemeinplätze, die Neueste Literatur betreffend" claimed: "Für literarische Kunstwerke läßt sich eine wesentliche gesellschaftliche Funktion in unserer Lage nicht erkennen."[3] In reality, neither of these statements amounts to a pronouncement of literature having died. Both are statements about the position of literature in society, which imply that socio-political concerns take precedence over a literature that has nothing to offer at a time of social upheaval.

Unsurprisingly, given the mood of the time, few appreciated the nuances of the argument with the inevitable result that the idea of the "death of literature" dominated public consciousness. Moreover, this mood had an impact not just on potential consumers of literature, but also on writers themselves. Martin Walser, for instance, having accepted the futility of the Proustian project of re-creating the past through literature in his 1966 novel *Das Einhorn*, largely restricted himself for a number of years to editing the autobiographies of underprivileged members of society and to stream of consciousness passages that abandoned traditional concepts of narration.[4] The sixties were also the age when literature sought authenticity through the use of documents. Documentary drama became a major genre with the appearance of such works as Heinar Kipphardt's *In der Sache J. Robert Oppenheimer* (1964), which deals with the question of possible disloyalty among American nuclear scientists, and Peter Weiss's *Die Ermittlung* (1965), which re-creates the trial of Auschwitz guards that took place in Frankfurt in the first part of the decade. However, it must be stressed that this search for authenticity did not amount to the death of literature. Rather than being dead, literature, or at least parts of, it had developed a new paradigm in keeping with the mood of a particularly political decade. In that many works were no longer traditional *Kunstwerke* dominated by the primacy of aesthetic considerations but sought to convey political messages, it was coming close to fulfilling the kind of role Michel and Enzensberger had, at least by implication, envisaged for it.[5]

By the mid-1970s the "death of literature" metaphor was no longer dominant. Instead of the "objective document," it was the personal and subjective, as stressed by the term "New Subjectivity," that was seen as dominant. The critic Volker Hage entitled his collection of essays about the literature of the 1970s *Die Wiederkehr des Erzählers*, which would appear to signify the return of some kind of literary normality.[6] Nevertheless, concerns about the health of German literature have never been far below the surface. It was, as in the 1960s, political developments that brought them to the fore again, namely the massive changes of 1989 and 1990. The events of that time have undoubtedly led to a re-thinking in all kinds of areas: in politics and economics to concern about the sustainability of the "German model" in the age of globalisation, and, in history, to new debates about the German past, particularly the era of National Socialism. Literature has been no exception. At the time of unification, particularly in 1990, the merits (or otherwise) of GDR literature came under scrutiny in what became known as the *deutsch-*

deutscher Literaturstreit, with particular attention being paid to the question of whether most GDR writers had shown excessive loyalty to a repressive state. At the same time, West German literature was criticised for paying too much attention to political issues at the expense of aesthetics. Subsequently, attention has centred on the overall quality of writing in Germany with there again being no shortage of negative diagnoses. The remainder of this essay will therefore focus on the various arguments that have been advanced in the many debates about the current health of German literature that have been a feature of the last decade.

One of the main factors perceived as having a negative impact on literature is the social conditions under which writers have to practise their profession. The novelist Sten Nadolny, for instance, in his 1992 essay "Roman oder Leben —?," puts the position as he sees it particularly directly. Although he defensively concedes that German literature is the subject of frequent criticism over the lack of outstanding individuals, he claims that there are good reasons for any shortcomings, specifically the constraints imposed upon writers by the literary market place. This state of affairs leads him to conclude: "Die deutsche Literatur könnte gar nicht besser sein, selbst wenn die ersehnten Genies vollzählig wären."[7] The critic Frank Schirrmacher had advanced similar arguments three years earlier. He spoke of writers being unable to devote sufficient time to researching their work with the result that they could only offer fragmentary detail: "sie beschreiben die Details in der Hoffnung, man werde sich das Ganze schon zurechtreimen."[8]

Concentrated efforts by writers to improve their position in society go back at least three decades, by no coincidence to the time of the student movement. Heinrich Böll famously demanded an end to modesty,[9] while Martin Walser played a leading role in the establishment of the writers' union, the *Verband deutscher Schriftsteller,* which is now, in keeping with Walser's wishes of the time, incorporated into the mainstream trade union movement as part of the media workers trade union (*IG Medien*). How successful these efforts to improve the social security of writers have been cannot be discussed in any detail here. More relevant in this context is the market situation, as referred to by Nadolny, and the effect it has on German literature. The bare facts are depressing. In pure market terms, both at home and in other countries, German literature enjoys only a modest level of success. A glance at the bestseller lists — fifteen titles in all — in any copy of the weekly news magazine *Der Spiegel* will invariably confirm this. In the 20 March 2000 edition, for example, it contained only two German names, Bernhard Schlink with his collection of stories *Liebesfluchten* and Doris Dörrie, who first made her name as a film director and because of this enjoyed some kind of bonus, with her novel *Was machen wir jetzt?* Three months later in the 19 June edition the same two names remained. As for the impact of German literature in other countries, the 1980s and 1990s arguably only saw two major international successes: Schlink's earlier novel *Der Vorleser* (1995) and Patrick Süskind's *Das Parfum* (1985). This is not to say that literature should be judged solely or even at all in market terms. Nevertheless the bare facts of the market can, as Nadolny's comment shows, be linked with a general sense of unease felt by writers about their circumstances within the wider world of literature that comprises the market, the media and the critics. To use the metaphor of the title of this essay: is German literature drowning in the stormy seas whipped up by these increasingly hostile forces?

There is no shortage of suggestions that this might indeed be the case, and not only from writers of literature themselves. In the second of the essays contained in the volume *On Television and Journalism,* the sociologist Pierre Bourdieu berates the role of the press within the sphere of cultural production. He claims that "journalist-intellectuals," by which he undoubtedly means critics, "reinforce the impact of audience ratings or the best-seller lists on the reception of cultural products and ultimately if indirectly, on cultural production itself."[10] Throughout this essay, Bourdieu is concerned about the intrusion of the market into the cultural sphere, a development that can undoubtedly be related to the area of German literature. The world of publishing provides a particularly clear example. Increasingly, as in other countries, it is dominated by large corporations such as the Axel Springer or Holtzbrinck group, which seek as their first priority a good return on their investments. When this does not occur, the result is inevitably swingeing cuts of the kind imposed on the S. Fischer imprint, one of the best-known names of German publishing, by the parent Holtzbrinck group in mid-2000.[11] An article by Rainer Traub that appeared in *Der Spiegel* in March of that year points to the key paradox of this situation — the conflict between the world of the book and that of the modern market economy: "Um zu wirken braucht das Medium Buch Zeit — aber eben davon gönnen ihm die konkurrierenden Konzerne und Buchhandelsketten immer weniger."[12] Nevertheless, Traub is not entirely pessimistic. The scramble by the large concerns for potentially best-selling foreign authors leaves space for smaller publishers for whom literary as well as financial concerns play a role and who remain willing to support German-language writers. That such policies can be rewarded is illustrated by the example of Patrick Süskind's above-mentioned novel *Das Parfum*. After being turned down by several publishers, it was accepted by the relatively small Zurich-based Diogenes Verlag, which by its decision stole a major march on its rivals. Yet it is too simple to see a kind of benign dichotomy between German and foreign authors. When, in the autumn of 1999, *Der Spiegel* gave over its cover story to new German authors, who were allegedly at the forefront of a rebirth of German literature, one reader suggested that it was not just a question of literary quality. Equally relevant was the fact that publishers were only increasingly marketing German authors, because the advances needed to secure famous foreign titles were beyond their purses.[13] Whatever the truth of this claim — and the privately owned Frankfurt-based Eichborn Verlag makes a virtue of such a policy — there can be no doubt that German literature is increasingly caught up in a globalised publishing industry in which a high rate of profit is progressively more important and likely to remain so in the age of "shareholder value." It is, of course, always easy to glamorise a past era, in which publishers gave their authors financial support over long unproductive periods (the examples of Wolfgang Koeppen and Uwe Johnson, who were sustained by the Suhrkamp Verlag, are well-known). Nevertheless, the present market situation hardly seems propitious when it comes to the question of literary quality.

Within the kind of area Bourdieu is addressing, what in German is frequently denoted as *Literaturbetrieb,* writers' ire has been directed in recent years at the role of the media. It goes without saying that writers' interest in the media is anything but new, nor is it a phenomenon restricted to German literature. It is only necessary to recall Enzensberger's famous coinage *Bewußtseinsindustrie* (a play on Adorno and Horkheimer's *Kulturindustrie*),[14] and, in the case of English literature, Evelyn Waugh's satire *Scoop* (1943) or more recently Ian McEwan's *Amsterdam* (1998). What seems different, however, in Germany over the last decade is the intensity of the concern with the media as a negative force that stands in almost total opposition to the values of literature. In addition there is the view, not restricted to writers, that the media now play a pivotal role in society. This perceived development is reflected in the increased use of the term *Mediengesellschaft* to characterise the Federal Republic. In fact, it seems to have replaced or at least gained the same status as earlier definitions such as *Wohlstandsgesellschaft* or *Zwei-Drittel-Gesellschaft*.

The remark by Traub quoted above about books needing time lies at the core of the problem. The media are invariably seen as dealing in the ephemeral whereas literature is traditionally connected with the longer term. It is only necessary to recall the clichés about yesterday's newspaper being of no interest today and the quality of a given work of literature only being determined a century or longer later to illustrate the point. Bodo Kirchhoff has spoken of the media having been able to force "ihre kurzlebige Zeitvorstellung" onto society and the need for literature to resist this development.[15] By contrast, Kirchhoff claims, literature has always created its own time. The problem also seems to be encapsulated in Nadolny's title *Die Entdeckung der Langsamkeit* (1983). Whereas it would be too simple to see this novel as a simple endorsement of not rushing headlong into decisions or actions, it seems clear that the author is generally sympathetic to his hero John Franklin's principle of slowness, even though it finally brings about his death. Indeed, Günter Grass, in his May 1999 speech "Der lernende Lehrer," speaks of introducing a new course "Erlernung der Langsamkeit"[16] into the school curriculum, an idea he says he owes to Nadolny. What such a course would provide, in Grass's view, is a "Gegengift zur allgemein vorherrschenden Beschleunigung" (22). The motifs of slowness and the need to counteract the rapid passing of time are not new in Grass's work. In his much earlier work *Aus dem Tagebuch einer Schnecke* (1972) he speaks of the joys of the measured approach, be it in story-telling or making love, while the writer is characterised as someone whose work is directed against "die verstreichende Zeit."[17] What is particularly meant in this particular context is the passage of time that covers over the Nazi past, a state of affairs that favours those who have something to hide. What this can mean in a German context is immediately obvious. Maintaining the memory of the past has, in fact, been arguably the major concern of postwar German literature in a society that has frequently sought to erase its troubled history. That, however, is a topic that goes far beyond the scope of this essay.

In the case of the media, writers' concern has not been restricted to the question of their ephemeral nature. There is also the problem of triviality: the belief that the media increasingly concern themselves with the superficial or, to use the current phrase, have "dumbed down." In his essay on television, Bourdieu devotes six of approximately sixty pages to the talk show, the phenomenon that seems to arouse the most ire in Germany. Indeed, it is hard to find a piece of cultural criticism that does not direct its shafts at this phenomenon, which has multiplied with the increasing commercialisation of television. Bourdieu's main point is the ultimately pseudo-democratic nature of what may appear to be open discussion of serious issues; in Germany concern seems to relate as much to the daytime shows, in which "ordinary people" appear, as to more heavyweight discussions. The ills German intellectuals see in the talk show are summed up in an essay by Nikolaus von Fürstenberg, who complains about "so viel Gequatsche, so viel lärmende Eitelkeit, so viel Gedankenverhinderung."[18] The ultimately ridiculous lengths to which those who condemn the talk show are prepared to go can be illustrated by reference to an article by Reinhard Mohr in *Der Spiegel* in early 2000 that regretted the way that the far-right Austrian politician Jörg Haider was invariably able to wipe the floor with interviewers. The blame was put on "Vertalkshowierung der Kultur," which renders difficult, if not impossible, any "Selbsterkundung der Gesellschaft." Mohr goes on to talk of the "rasante Dauergeschwätz über alles und jedes" which leads to a fictionalisation of reality.[19] The reason for this vitriolic dislike of the talk show can therefore be seen to be rooted, as the comments by Fürstenberg and Mohr suggest, in the question of language. If the writer's main concern is quality of language, then the talk show lives off unreflected language, or, to use a more direct term, verbal diarrhoea.

Writers' suspicion of the mass media is not limited to their use of language. The domination of the visual image is also often seen as problematic. This concern is at the heart of Peter Handke's long essay on developments in the former Yugoslavia that created such a furore in 1996 because of the sympathy shown to the Serbian cause. Handke asks: "Was weiß der, der statt der Sache einzig deren Bild zu Gesicht bekommt, oder, wie in den Fernsehnachrichten, ein Kürzel von einem Bild . . . ?"[20] One does not have to share Handke's views on Serbia to accept the validity of the question. The danger of the "picture" or "image" in all its senses surely cannot be ignored by anybody with a basic knowledge of the works of Max Frisch. It will be recalled that the Biblical injunction not to make graven images is the key idea behind his play *Andorra,* in which the main character Andri is destroyed, because all see him simply as a Jew with inevitable "Jewish" characteristics. Among them is the priest who only after the tragic turn of events recalls Biblical teaching and admits that he too failed to follow God's teaching: "Auch ich habe mir ein Bildnis gemacht von ihm, auch ich habe ihn gefesselt, auch ich habe ihn an den Pfahl gebracht."[21]

References above to Grass and Handke show that worry about phenomena in the media is the preserve of neither those associated with the political Left nor the political Right. The criticism of the media found in the writings of the Frankfurt School, and especially in the work of Theodor W. Adorno, appear all-pervasive. This can be seen in Botho Strauß claim in his controversial 1993 essay "Anschwellender Bocksgesang." This attack on contemporary society, which was seen by some as a kind of manifesto for the New Right in the wake of unification, contains the categorical statement: "Das Regime der telekratischen Öffentlichkeit ist die unblutigste Gewaltherrschaft und zugleich der umfassendste Totalitarismus der Geschichte."[22] What remains problematical about such comments, however justified specific criticisms of the media may be, is their blanket nature. It is still possible to discern differences between the various outpourings of the media, something which many writers seem increasingly unwilling to consider.

Nevertheless, given the relevance of many of their concerns, it would be too harsh to say that writers are making the media a scapegoat for their own failings. At the same time, any consideration of the present state of German literature cannot ignore the criticisms to which it has been subjected over recent years. In his essay "Roman oder Leben —?," Sten Nadolny speaks of the novel as being an unsuitable vehicle for the "Verbreitung lobenswerter Meinungen."[23] This comment contains one of the major accusations levelled at postwar German literature: that it has concentrated excessively on the political to the detriment of the aesthetic. A similar disparagement of *Meinung* can be found in Martin Walser's highly controversial 1998 speech when he was awarded the *Friedenspreis des deutschen Buchhandels* (Peace Prize of the German Book Trade) in which he coins such terms as "Meinungsdienst" with its echoes of "Staatssicherheitsdienst" and "Meinungssoldaten" to denounce those who do not share his attitude toward the discussion of the German past.[24] Both Walser and Nadolny are picking up on the quarrels at the time of unification when the term "Gesinnungsästhetik," as used by Ulrich Greiner to describe literature in which the author's political standpoint took precedence over all other considerations, entered public consciousness.[25]

The question that has to be asked is whether these criticisms are aimed at writing with any kind of political dimension or at writing that appears to address political issues from a particular standpoint. In this context, it is useful to refer to one of the major literary debates of 1998 that followed the claim by Max Sebald that representations of the bombing raids on German cities during the Second World War were lacking in postwar German literature. Although this statement is not entirely accurate — one can think, for example, of Giordano's *Die Bertinis* (1988), in which the RAF's major raid on Hamburg features, or Walser's *Die Verteidigung der Kindheit* (1991) with its descriptions of the attack on Dresden[26] — it certainly struck a chord. Frank Schirrmacher, for instance, claimed that there were further omissions to be regretted: namely the expulsion of ethnic Germans from their traditional homes in the aftermath of war and the early occupation of the east by the Red Army.[27] Here, too, one can speak of exaggeration.

These events do feature, for example, in the works of Grass and Christa Wolf, as well as the autobiographical writing of Gudrun Pausewang.[28] The occupation of Danzig by the Red Army is described in Günter Grass's *Die Blechtrommel* (1959), while Christa Wolf's novel *Kindheitsmuster* (1976) describes the flight westwards in the face of advancing Soviet troops of the Jordan family, within which the daughter Nelly bears a close resemblance to Wolf herself. The fear of rape by Red Army soldiers is a motif in Gudrun Pausewang's autobiographical work, specifically *Fern von der Rosinkawiese: Geschichte einer Flucht* (1989). It should also be remembered that the topos of the marauding and raping Soviet soldier, allegedly spurred on by Ilya Ehrenburg's contention that German women were fair game, was part of the anti-communist ideology of the first years of the Federal Republic. There is, however, the danger that the treatment of these themes could lead to a one-sided presentation of the Germans as victims. Clearly, as such they cannot be taboo; nevertheless, any neglect of the historical context of these in themselves clearly horrendous occurrences would run the risk of being a distortion of historical truth.

Whether any postwar German literature had told the truth about the Nazi era and the war was a question raised by Maxim Biller in the course of the debate over Sebald's remarks. His essay "Unschuld mit Grünspan" is an attack on those postwar writers such as Heinrich Böll who are generally regarded as having brought issues relating to the German past to public attention. He speaks of "das Versteckspiel mit der unverstellten Realität, das Heinrich Böll und seine 'Gruppe 47' Kameraden einst spielten,"[29] claiming that the characters in the relevant works are invariably outsider figures, who, for example, as soldiers are never shown killing. Biller's use of the word "Kameraden" is particularly barbed. It underlines the fact that many members of the Group, like Böll himself and not least the Group's convener Hans Werner Richter, had been soldiers in the *Wehrmacht* during the Second World War, although, in the case of Böll there can be little doubt that he performed this role most reluctantly.

This kind of debate shows clearly that the issue is not politics as such. In some cases, for example Walser, it may well be a dislike of writing that reflects one particular political standpoint. At the time of the 1990 *Literaturstreit,* which was in many ways more about politics than literature, writers were castigated primarily for having shown too conciliatory an attitude toward communism and having failed to join in the celebration of unification. It is as well to remember George Orwell's comment that "no book is entirely free of political bias" and that to demand the exclusion of politics from literature "is itself a political attitude."[30] The real question has to do with the nature of the representation of the chosen themes. Here, too, caution is appropriate. Does the castigation of *Meinung* include such famous literary openings as: "All happy families are alike but an unhappy family is unhappy after its own fashion" and: "It is a truth universally acknowledged, that a single man in possession of a good fortune, must be in want of a wife," which can be seen as expressions of authorial opinion?[31] What is the status of the essay as a genre or the plays of Bernard Shaw, which seem to consist of opinionated outpourings and are invariably supplemented by prefaces stating the author's opinions? The real issue is, of course, the way in which authorial opinion is expressed with one obvious danger, especially in the drama, being the author's putting his or her views into the mouth of a character who cannot credibly express such views on the basis of the way (s)he is presented in the rest of the work.

The question of the political content of literature leads to a second major area of concern about recent German writing: its inability to engage and divert the reader. That this complaint is clearly linked to the question of politics can be seen by Biller's comment immediately following his castigation of Böll and the writers of the Gruppe 47. He sees their work as "das ästhetische Vorspiel zu dem romantischen Haken-schlagen" of the next generation of authors such as Handke and Strauß whose work, it is claimed, is characterised by "bedeutungsleeren Wort-neuschöpfungen, alles kaschierenden Akademismen und schwammigen Pauschalgefühlen."[32] For Biller, this is a kind of writing that will never be attractive to a majority of readers.

Biller, not surprisingly, was also at the centre of a debate that erupted earlier in the decade about the overall quality of contemporary German literature. His essay "soviel Sinnlichkeit wie der Stadtplan von Kiel" begins with the categorical statement: "Es gibt keine deutsche Literatur mehr."[33] He suggests that the books that appear in small print runs are read solely by those professionally involved with literature and "einigen letzten, versprengten Bildungsbürgern" (281). His cure for this situation lies in a return to realism which is uncompromisingly described as "die absolute Grundvoraussssetzung der Literatur" (288) and therefore the only kind of writing which can appeal to sensitive people with an interest in the condition of the world. Biller's arguments, which were first published in 1991, were taken up a year later in *Der Spiegel* by another writer, Matthias Altenburg. His essay is entitled "Kampf den Flaneuren," and has the subtitle "Über Deutschlands junge, lahme Dichter." Since the text shows that, as the title suggests, one of Altenburg's major targets is Peter Handke, the term "junge Dichter" appears somewhat problematical. The same is true in the case of Sten Nadolny, whose espousal of slowness is ridiculed. Altenburg mocks writers who rush from one poetics seminar to the next by Intercity-Express but write as if they were travelling on the back of a mule. He demands a literature where "die Sätze Tempo kriegen und die Geschichten Drive."[34] Even if one allows for the genre of the polemic with its penchant for exaggeration, the use of such terminology is perhaps questionable in that it conjures up a superficial world of instant stimulations that run counter to normal conceptions of literature, as referred to above.

According to Martin Hielscher, this kind of attack on German literature can be seen as a manifestation of German self-hatred. In an essay published in 2000, he cites other instances of negative criticism which can only contribute to a decline of esteem for German literature and increasing difficulties for authors seeking to establish or enhance their reputations.[35] Although one can understand the frustrations felt by Hielscher, given his work as a publisher, it would be wrong to see all the debate about the quality of German literature as undifferentiated. Particularly important in this context is Uwe Wittstock, who has been arguably the key figure in the debates about the quality of German literature over the past decade. In addition to editing publications about the state of contemporary German literature he produced in 1995 the long essay *Leselust,* the title of which, especially together with the sub-title *"Wie unterhaltsam ist die deutsche Literatur?"* shows something of his views. The use of the term "unterhaltsam" is significant in itself, if it is recalled that many German critics distinguish, or at least used to, between true literature and the greatly inferior "Unterhaltungsliteratur."

Wittstock shares the doubts expressed by others about the political role of the author and points to some of the false doctrines ("ideologische Torheiten") that have been embraced by writers.[36] Another major concern is the tendency of German writers to set themselves at a distance from their readers (157),[37] which may be understandable historically (in a period in which writers had little faith in the democratic convictions of their readers), but is no longer relevant as the Federal Republic increasingly becomes a democratic state like any other. Coupled with this, Wittstock perceives among critics and scholars a belief in literary progress that damns writing that makes use of literary traditions and sees works that use more traditional narrative techniques as outdated "Museumsstücke" (26). For Wittstock traditional techniques are there to be adapted to modern conditions. Moreover, there is in his view nothing wrong with adapting the narrative practices of popular authors. He refers to the use of such techniques by celebrated authors such as Kafka. Having quoted the opening sentence of "Die Verwandlung," Wittstock suggests that Kafka had "einen gut entwickelten Sinn für *special effects*" (23). The nub of his argument is that the use of these techniques will not necessarily lead to trivial writing.

In the last section of *Leselust* Wittstock refers to the debates provoked by his previous comments on the need for literature to be entertaining. These give some idea of the controversial nature of his claim that it is possible to write high-quality literature that will appeal to readers by making appropriate use of traditional narrative techniques. In general, however, it seems that his arguments have had some effect, that there is a new belief in narrative and in the ability of German writers to tell stories. The title article in *Der Spiegel* in autumn 1999, referred to above, which spoke of the grand-children of Grass and Co., is a sign of this, albeit at a journalistic level. A recent critical work by Nikolaus Förster on the literature of the 1980s and 1990s is entitled *Die Wiederkehr des Erzählens*. Förster is making a clear distinction between his title and that of Hage, *Die Wiederkehr des Erzählers,* referred to above. Whereas the 1970s were the decade of New Subjectivity, which Förster sees as another example of the search for authenticity found in the previous decade, the 1980s and 1990s, according to Förster, have been characterised by narrative that clearly reveals its "Konstruktcharakter."[38] In the light of this comment, it is small wonder that Förster concentrates on such writers as Patrick Süskind, Christoph Ransmayr and Robert Schneider.

Martin Hielscher in the essay mentioned above also refers to writers whose original talents belie the claim that German literature is in any way inferior. In fact, there would appear to be a new mood of self-confidence in the world of German literature. This is visible in a comment made by Thomas Brussig, himself one of a new generation of east German writers seen as being at the forefront of a literary revival in that part of Germany. Writing about a first novel *Liegen lernen* by the west German Frank Goosen, he claims that the work destroys three current myths: "Dass West-deutsche nichts zu erzählen hätten, dass deutsche Autoren nicht zu rühren verstünden — und dass man nach dem letzten Hornby nur schicksalserge-ben auf den nächsten Hornby warten müsse, da niemand sonst so schreibe wie er."[39] Besides self-confidence, this comment also suggests that the literary paradigm advanced by Biller and Wittstock has gained widespread currency, as reflected in the new slogan about contemporary writing "Neue Lesbarkeit." What is more, it can be pointed out that German literature has become much more varied and international, not least through its wider choice of settings. In addition to Nadolny's historical novel about the "slow" English sea captain, John Franklin, there are, for example, the novels *Infanta* (1990) and *Der Sandmann* (1992) by Bodo Kirchhoff set in the Philippines and North Africa respectively, while Urs Widmer's *Liebes-*

brief für Mary (1993) consists in part of a letter written in English, although the native speaker will note a few linguistic infelicities.

On the basis of the choice of themes and the aesthetic characteristics of much recent German writing, it is perfectly possible to argue that German literature has come out of the national ghetto and moved much closer to other western literatures. In many cases, such as the works discussed by Förster, the term post-modernism inevitably springs to mind. It is of course not surprising that, as this essay has shown, there are different views about individual works and the overall direction literature in the German-speaking countries has taken. However, what such intense debate suggests, at the very least, is — pace Biller — that there remains life in the subject under discussion. Accordingly, it does seem possible to say, using a slight variation of Mark Twain's celebrated comment about his wrongly announced demise, reports of the death of German literature have been and remain much exaggerated.

Notes

[1] P. Schneider, "Politische Dichtung. Ihre Grenzen und Möglichkeiten," in Stein, ed., *Theorie der politischen Dichtung* (Munich: Nymphenburger, 1973), 154.

[2] K. M. Michel, "Ein Kranz für die Literatur," *Kursbuch* 15 (1968): 169–186, 177.

[3] H. M. Enzensberger, "Gemeinplätze, die Neueste Literatur betreffend," *Kursbuch* 15 (1968): 187–97, 195.

[4] Walser was responsible for the publication of two pieces of social reportage: U. Trauberg, *Vorleben* (Frankfurt am Main: Suhrkamp, 1968) and W. Werner, *Vom Waisenhaus ins Zuchthaus* (Frankfurt am Main: Suhrkamp, 1969). His longest "stream of consciousness" text is M. Walser, *Fiction* (Frankfurt am Main: Suhrkamp, 1970).

[5] For a more detailed analysis of writing and politics in the 1960s and since, see my *Writers and Politics in West Germany* (London: Croom Helm, 1986).

[6] V. Hage, *Die Wiederkehr des Erzählers* (Frankfurt am Main, Berlin, Vienna. Ullstein, 1982).

[7] S. Nadolny, "Roman oder Leben —?" in U. Wittstock, ed., *Roman oder Leben: Postmoderne in der deutschen Literatur* (Leipzig: Reclam, 1994), 219–37, 236.

[8] F. Schirrmacher, "Idyllen in der Wüste oder Versagen vor der Metropole," in A. Köhler and R. Moritz, eds., *Maulhelden und Königskinder* (Leipzig: Reclam, 1998), 15–27, 19. Schirrmacher's criticism appears to contradict the widely-held view that great literature is characterised by attention to detail.

[9] H. Böll, "Ende der Bescheidenheit," in H. B. *Ende der Bescheidenheit: Schriften und Reden 1969–72* (Munich: dtv, 1985), 54–67.

[10] P. Bourdieu, *On Television and Journalism*, trans. Parkhurst (London: Pluto, 1998), 74–75.

[11] See R. Traub, "Bedrohter Kafka," *Der Spiegel* 22 (29 May 2000), 86.

[12] R. Traub, "Die Luftnummern der Lizenzstrategen," *Der Spiegel* 10 (6 March 2000), 244–50, 246.

[13] The original essay is: V. Hage "Die Enkel kommen," *Der Spiegel* 41 (11 Oct. 1999), 244–54. The title refers to a new generation that might be regarded as the grandchildren of Grass, Walser, Lenz etc., in the same way as the current generation of SPD politicians has been seen as the grandchildren of Willy Brandt. The comment about commercial considerations in a letter by the reader Svea Reiners is to be found in *Der Spiegel* 43 (25 Oct. 1999), 10.

[14] This is the subtitle of the first volume of Enzensberger's *Einzelheiten*: H. M. Enzensberger, *Einzelheiten I* (Frankfurt am Main: Suhrkamp, 1964).

[15] B. Kirchhoff, "Der Autor hat nur eine Chance: Er muß den Kritiker überleben. Bodo Kirchhoff im Gespräch mit Uwe Wittstock über die Brauchbarkeit der Literatur und über Kopfjägerei sowie das katastrophale deutsche Unterhaltungsverständnis," *Neue Rundschau* 104 (1993): 3, 69–81, 78.

[16] G. Grass, "Der lernende Lehrer," in G. G. *Für und Widerworte* (Göttingen: Steidl, 1999), 7–35, 23.

[17] G. Grass, *Aus dem Tagebuch einer Schnecke* (Reinbek: Rowohlt, 1974), 98.

[18] N. von Fürstenberg, "Talk und Teufel," *Der Spiegel* 13 (25 March 1996), 236–38, 236.

[19] R. Mohr, "Die Aura des Teflon-Jörgl," *Der Spiegel* 7 (14 February 2000), 116–17, 117. More recent intelligence from the talk show front, however, suggests that the phenomenon is in decline: see O. Geres, "'Schweigen ist Gold,'" *Der Spiegel* 21 (22 May 2000): 114–18.

[20] P. Handke, *Eine winterliche Reise zu den Flüssen Donau, Save, Morawa und Drina oder Gerechtigkeit für Serbien* (Frankfurt am Main: Suhrkamp), 30.

[21] M. Frisch, *Gesammelte Werke in zeitlicher Folge: Jubiläumsausgabe in sieben Bänden,* ed. Hans Mayer (Frankfurt am Main: Suhrkamp, 1986), vol. 4, 509.

[22] B. Strauß, "Anschwellender Bocksgesang," in B. Strauß, *Der Aufstand gegen die sekundäre Welt* (Munich: Hanser, 1999), 57–78, 68.

[23] Nadolny, "Roman oder Leben —?" 234.

[24] M. Walser, *Erfahrungen beim Verfassen einer Sonntagsrede* (Frankfurt am Main: Suhrkamp, 1998), 25. See my "Auschwitz und kein Ende: The Recent Controversies Surrounding Martin Walser," in Christopher Hall, David Rock, eds., *German Studies towards the Millenium*, (Bern: Peter Lang, 2000), 91–106.

[25] See, for example, U. Greiner, "Die deutsche Gesinnungsästhetik," in T. Anz, ed., "*Es geht nicht um Christa Wolf*": *Der Literaturstreit im vereinten Deutschland* (Munich: Edition Spangenberg, 1991), 208–16.

[26] See my "Looking Forward to the Past: Identity and Identification in Martin Walser's *Die Verteidigung der Kindheit*," in Arthur Williams, Stuart Parkes, eds., *The Individual, Identity and Innovation: Signals from Contemporary Literature and the New Germany* (Bern: Peter Lang, 1994, 54–74).

[27] F. Schirrmacher, "Luftkrieg. Beginnt morgen die deutsche Nachkriegsliteratur," in V. Hage, R. Moritz, H. Winkels, eds., *Deutsche Literatur 1998* (Stuttgart: Reclam, 1999), 62–267, esp. 65. This volume contains an overview of the debate between pages 249–90.

[28] The renewed topicality of these themes can be seen by the reprinting of the almost forgotten work from 1956 *Vergeltung* (Frankfurt am Main: Suhrkamp) which deals with bombing raids and the success of Hans-Ulrich Treichel's *Der Verlorene* (Frankfurt am Main: Suhrkamp, 1998) which concentrates on the fate of a family expelled from Germany's former eastern territories. See Stuart Taberner, "Hans-Ulrich Treichel's *Der Verlorene* and the Problem of German Wartime Suffering," *The Modern Language Review* 97:1 (2002): 123–34. The theme of German suffering, in this case the sinking in 1945 with major loss of life of the *Wilhelm Gustloff,* a ship laden with German refugees, is also at the centre of Günter Grass's *In Krebsgang* (Gottingen: Seidl, 2002). Given Grass's status as a Nobel Laureate, this seems a particularly significant development. The work itself immediately shot to the top of the bestseller lists.

[29] M. Biller, "Unschuld mit Grünspan," in Hage et al., *Deutsche Literatur 1998*, 278–81, 281.

[30] G. Orwell, *Collected Essays* (London: Secker & Warburg, 1961), 438.

[31] These are the opening sentences of Tolstoy's *Anna Karenina* and Jane Austen's *Pride and Prejudice* respectively.

[32] M. Biller, "Unschuld mit Grünspan," 281.

[33] M. Biller, "soviel Sinnlichkeit wie der Stadtplan von Kiel," in F. J. Görtz, V. Hage, U. Wittstock, eds., *Deutsche Literatur 1992* (Stuttgart: Reclam, 1993), 281–89, 281.

[34] M. Altenburg, "Kampf den Flaneuren," in Görtz et al., *Deutsche Literatur 1992* (Stuttgart: Reclam, 1993), 290–95, 291.

[35] See M. Hielscher, "The Return to Narrative and to History: Some Thoughts on Contemporary German-language Literature," in A. Williams, S. Parkes, J. Preece, eds., *Literature, Markets and Media in Germany and Austria Today* (Bern: Peter Lang, 2000), 295–309.

[36] U. Wittstock, *Leselust* (Munich: Luchterhand, 1995), 31.

[37] There are of course dangers in pandering too closely to readers' wishes. Where this can lead in a German context becomes apparent in a recent interview with Chancellor Schröder's first minister of state for culture, Michael Naumann. Although the interview was concerned with film, the dangers of the "it might frighten the horses" ideology espoused by Naumann apply to all art forms. His comments are concerned with the effects on some potential filmgoers of films which deal with the Nazi past. Having asked for films that relate moving love stories and mentioned *Gloomy Sunday*, he bemoans "diesen kleinen deutschen Touch: Immer wirkt die SS mit." He suggests "es könnte doch möglich sein, Filme jenseits der deutschen Geschichte zu machen." ("Man wird bescheiden," *Der Spiegel* 24 [18 June 2000], 202–5, 204.)

[38] N. Förster, *Die Wiederkehr des Erzählens: Deutschsprachige Prosa der 80er und 90er Jahre* (Darmstadt: Wissenschaftliche Buchgesellschaft, 1999), 25. More recently, a collection of essays has appeared that reflects both sides of the argument. It is the

volume *Maulhelden und Königskinder* (Leipzig: Reclam 1998) referred to variously above. One of the contributors to take issue with those demanding realist literature is Heinrich Vormweg in the piece "Literaturzerstörung" (110–26). The accusation in the title is directed at, among others, Wittstock.

[39] Th. Brussig, "Liebe zur Zeit der Kohl-Ära," *Der Spiegel* 5 (19 January 2001): 168–70, 170.

Contributors

FRANK BRUNSSEN is a Lecturer in German at the University of Liverpool. He has published a book on Günter Grass and numerous articles on contemporary German history. His second book, *The Making of the Berlin Republic: Rethinking Contemporary German History,* will be published in 2002 by Liverpool University Press as part of the series on Studies in Social and Political Thought. He is currently writing an article on "The Project of *Inner Unity* in the Berlin Republic."

INGO CORNILS is a Senior Lecturer in German at the University of Leeds. He has published widely on the German Student Movement and German Science Fiction. He is currently working on the representation of the German Student Movement in German literature.

FRANK FINLAY is Professor of German Literature at the University of Leeds. His publications include books and articles on literature, culture and aesthetics in contemporary Germany and Austria. He is editor of the new 27-volume Cologne Edition of Heinrich Böll's works and is currently collaborating with Stuart Taberner on a project devoted to emerging German writers.

KATHARINA GERSTENBERGER is Associate Professor of German at the University of Cincinnati. She is the author of *Truth to Tell: German Women's Autobiographies and Turn-of-the-Century Culture* (2000). She has also published a large number of pieces on twentieth-century literature.

EVA KOLINSKY is Emeritus Professor of Modern German Studies at Keele University and Professorial Research Fellow in German History at the University of Wolverhampton. Relevant publications include *Deutsch und türkisch leben* (2000); *Turkish Culture in German Society Today* (co-ed., 1996); "Multiculturalism in the Making? Non-Germans and Civil Society in the New Länder" in *Recasting East Germany* (co-ed., 1999); "Unexpected Newcomers: Asylum Seekers and other non-Germans in the New Länder" in *The New Germany in the East* (co-ed., 2000) and "Meanings of Migration in East Germany" in *United and Divided: Germany since 1990* (co-ed., in press).

Sabine Lang is Assistant Professor of Political Science at the Freie Universität in Berlin. She has published widely on gender in western democracies as well as on media and political communication, including a book on *The Public Sphere in the Modern State* (2001). She is co-editor (with Birgit Sauer and Eva Kreisky) of *The Gender of the State — Transformations of the State in Europe* (2001).

Karen Leeder is Lecturer and Fellow in German at New College, Oxford. She has written on modern German poetry, including a book on GDR poetry: *Breaking Boundaries: A New Generation of Poets in the GDR* (1996), and recent articles on Brecht, Raoul Schrott, and post-1945 women's poetry. She is currently working on a book on contemporary German poetry and a book about angels. An edited volume, *Empedocles' Shoe: Re-Reading Brecht's Poetry*, will appear with Methuen in 2002.

Margaret Littler is a Senior Lecturer in German at the University of Manchester. She has published widely on postwar women's writing in German, and is editor of *Gendering German Studies: New Perspectives on German Literature and Culture* (1997). She is completing a co-authored book on postwar women's writing and developing a specialism in Turkish-German literature.

Stuart Parkes is Emeritus Professor of German at the University of Sunderland. He has authored a large number of pieces on contemporary German literature and society. In 1997 he published *Understanding Contemporary Germany* and has also co-edited seven volumes on contemporary German literature. He is currently working on a revision of his previous volume on writers and politics in Germany.

Kathrin Schödel is a Ph.D. student in German literature at the University of Erlangen-Nürnberg. Her thesis is on Martin Walser's *Friedenspreis* speech, the Walser debate, Walser's novel *Ein springender Brunnen*, and other depictions of the National Socialist period in German literature of the 1990s.

Roswitha Skare is Assistant Professor in the Department of Documentation Studies, University of Tromsø, Norway. Her research interests include the East German public sphere; German Unification and the Literature of the 1990s. Her publications include: *Wendezeichen? Neue Sichtweisen auf die Literatur in der DDR* and articles on Christa Wolf, Christoph Hein and Thomas Brussig.

JANET STEWART is Lecturer in German at the University of Aberdeen and Co-Director of the Centre for Austrian Studies at the Universities of Aberdeen and Edinburgh. She has published on Austrian literature and cultural history, including *Fashioning Vienna: Adolf Loos's Cultural Criticism* (Routledge, 2000). She is currently working on a cultural history of communication in fin-de-siècle Vienna.

CHRIS SZEJNMANN is a Reader in Modern European History at the University of Leicester. He has written on modern Germany including *Nazism in Central Germany: The Brownshirts in "Red" Saxony* (1999) and *Vom Traum zum Alptraum: Sachsen während der Weimarer Republik* (2000). He is currently working on a comparative regional history of Nazism for Berghahn Books, and a biography of a man from Leipzig before and after the revolution in 1989.

STUART TABERNER is Lecturer in German at the University of Leeds. He has published widely on postwar German authors, including Martin Walser, Günter Grass, Uwe Johnson, Stefan Heym, Monika Maron, Arnold Stadler and Hans-Ulrich Treichel. He is particularly interested in the connection between writing and politics and is working on a book on German fiction in the "age of normalisation." He is currently collaborating with Frank Finlay on a project devoted to emerging German writers.

PETER THOMPSON is a Lecturer in German at the University of Sheffield. His publications include articles on German and Austrian politics and he is one of the editors of *Debatte: A Review of Contemporary German Affairs*. He is currently working on a book on the PDS and forthcoming studies on the British Left and the GDR under Honecker as well as Nietzsche in contemporary film.

SIMON WARD is a Lecturer in German at the University of Aberdeen. He has published on "inner emigration" and postwar German literature, including a book on Wolfgang Koeppen, as well as articles dealing with aspects of travel in literature and popular culture.

ULRIKE ZITZLSPERGER is a Lecturer in German at the School of Modern Languages at Exeter University. She has published both on sixteenth-century literature and topics concerned with Berlin in the 1990s. She is currently working on the perception of the Metropolis during the 1920s.

Index